"Light Horse Harry" Lee
in the War for Independence

"Light Horse Harry" Lee

In

The War for Independence

By

JIM PIECUCH and JOHN H. BEAKES, JR.

The Nautical and Aviation Publishing Co. of America
Charleston, South Carolina

Library of Congress Catalog Card Number: 2013935920

ISBN: 978-1-877853-73-9

Printed in the United States of America

First Printing May, 2013

Picture and map credits:
Map and jacket design by William Allport, Studio Nudge, Charleston, S.C. Map six is based on a map of Ninety-Six from "The Pictorial Field-Book of the Revolution, Volume 2" by Benson J. Lossing published in New York by Harper Brothers in 1852.
Front cover portrait courtesy of Stratford Hall, Va.
Back cover art by Pamela Patrick White

The portraits in this book are reproduced courtesy of the Independence National Historic Park unless specifically noted otherwise.

CONTENTS

PREFACE

When George Washington took command of the Continental Army near Boston, Massachusetts in July, 1775, it was a ragged, undisciplined force that was accurately described by one British general as a "rabble in arms." Six years later, in October, 1781, at Yorktown, Virginia, the victorious American Army had been transformed into a well-led fighting force that could stand toe-to-toe with the best combat troops in the world. During these long and difficult years, Washington was able to find and develop many young men into superb leaders. They formed the officer corps of the tough, disciplined army that achieved victory over one of the mightiest empires on earth—Great Britain. Washington had a gift for spotting these talented young men and helping them develop into officers of great merit. One need only recall the names Nathanael Greene, Henry Knox, and Alexander Hamilton to find the truth in this assertion. This book, the second in our series on Washington's officers, adds a young cavalryman, Henry Lee of Virginia (later to be called by the sobriquet "Light Horse Harry") to the company of Washington's chosen leaders.

Our first book in this series ("Cool Deliberate Courage") tells of the wartime career of the quintessential infantry commander, John Eager Howard of Maryland. It is the story of a taciturn, dependable, unflappable infantryman, who could sense the critical moment amidst the massive confusion of the battlefield, remain calm while engulfed in the horror and carnage of eighteenth century combat, and direct his men to the exact spot where their hard-hitting assault would break the enemy line. When he joined the Army in 1776, Howard was the twenty-four-year-old son of a wealthy Maryland farmer, with only the scantest military education. His development into an exceptional leader of infantry does great credit to this young Marylander, but it is also the work of a Commander-in-Chief who knew how to find such men and assign them to the positions for which they were most fitted, and inspire them to lead their soldiers to victory.

This book on Henry Lee is the wartime story of a cavalry leader whose personal and professional attributes were quite different from those of John Eager Howard in almost every particular. Only twenty when he joined the army in 1776, Henry Lee was a member of one of the most powerful families in Virginia, and one that had close connections to Washington, a relationship that was unique among the other young men upon whom the Commander-in-Chief came to rely. A graduate of the College of New Jersey (later Princeton University) at age seventeen, Lee was well educated, an eloquent speaker and writer, an animated conversationalist, and an ardent believer in American independence, Washington's ideals, and his own ideas. Though young in years, he corresponded directly with Commander-in-Chief Washington while he served in the North, and with the Commander of the Southern Army, Nathanael Greene, after he transferred to the South in 1781, a liberty which Howard would never have considered, unless asked.

Lee's personal traits and Virginia roots were not the reasons that Washington came to rely upon the dashing young horseman. The Commander-in-Chief's stern and uncompromising standard was for leadership, for the proper care of the men under one's command, and for performance under fire. Henry Lee won the trust and confidence of George Washington and of his protégé Nathanael Greene because he performed up to their demanding standards in camp, on the march, and on the battlefield. Lee was in the saddle and in the presence of the enemy almost every day for the six long years between 1776 and 1782.

It is astonishing to think of the demands of such service—there was no rotation home after a year in combat as with the modern military, nor was there any understanding of such debilitating issues as post-traumatic-stress-syndrome, although trauma, stress, and exhaustion must have been a very real part of the life of our Revolutionary War forebears. Those soldiers were certainly very, very tough men who were accustomed to surviving in a world of adversity, but they were also human. Washington himself set the standard by being in uniform and away from home almost every day for over eight years from June 15th, 1775 to December 23rd, 1783, an amazing testament to his commitment to the Revolution.

The stories of John Eager Howard and Henry Lee tell of the feats of two young soldiers who learned the military arts in the Army of George Washington. He did not force men into a pre-determined template, but instead found the role that enabled each man to excel. Thus, Howard would stand firm at his assigned post, no matter how strong the onslaught, while Lee would use his mobility to dash to the point where he perceived the greatest need. Lee's Legion was sent forward to reconnoiter, to thrust and parry with the enemy army, to gather intelligence, and to carry out the special daring raids that he loved to plan and lead. During much of the time when Lee was moving rapidly about the countryside, Howard was with his men in the infantry camp or column, insuring that this valuable unit was ready to strike the decisive blow where and when it was needed.

In writing this book on Henry Lee, the authors have made every effort to use original sources to resurrect the true story of Lee's service during the Revolutionary War. His later life had travails, challenges, and political disputes that seem to have tinged many writers' appreciation for his many contributions to the success of the war effort. The early records show clearly that Washington and Greene relied on this young warrior far beyond what any current-day commander would ask of a cavalryman in his early twenties. Years later, when President Washington was seeking a commander for the American Army during his first administration, he cemented his long record of respect for Lee's military accomplishments by assuring him that he was eminently qualified for the post.

A son named Robert E. Lee was born to Henry Lee and his second wife in 1807, just a few days short of the old soldier's fifty-first birthday and long after the guns of the Revolution had gone silent. The child would grow up to become an exceptional soldier and military commander, with his own long story of accomplishments in the Mexican and Civil Wars. In that son's final years, he produced a new version of Henry's memoirs, using his military experience and judgment to describe his father's wartime accomplishments and ignoring the critics that had searched deeply for flaws in his fighting record.

Our purpose here has been to tell the story of the outstanding war service of the same brave, indefatigable cavalryman of the Revolution that his son wrote about, and that George Washington and Nathanael Greene had relied upon so heavily in the war that won our nation's independence.

INTRODUCTION

Despair gripped George Washington's beleaguered Continental Army as his cold and hungry soldiers huddled in the log huts that they had built at Valley Forge, Pennsylvania. Washington and the remnants of his army had retreated to this camp just before the Christmas of 1777. Here they endured the brutal winter of 1777-1778, after having been defeated by the British at the battles of Brandywine and Germantown the preceding autumn. The victorious British army occupied the American capital, Philadelphia, twenty-five miles southeast of Valley Forge, and the king's troops nestled in the comparative comfort of the homes and public buildings of America's largest city, while the American army suffered every imaginable privation in the countryside.

Washington described his army's desperate situation in a letter to John Bannister, one of Virginia's delegates to the Continental Congress:

> *"Men without Cloathes to cover their nakedness, without Blankets to lay on without Shoes, by which their Marches might be traced by the Blood from their feet, and almost as often without Provisions as with; Marching through frost and Snow, and at Christmas taking up their Winter Quarters within a day's March of the enemy, without a House or Hutt to cover them till they could be built."[1]*

In the midst of all the gloom of this difficult winter, Washington's General Orders of January 20th, 1778, announced a remarkable engagement fought earlier that day by one of his cavalry officers, twenty-one-year-old Captain Henry Lee:

> *"The Commander in Chief returns his warmest thanks to Captn. Lee and Officers and men of his Troop for the Victory which by their superior Bravery and Address they gain'd over a party of the Enemys dragoons, who trusting in their numbers and concealing their march by a circuitous road attempted to surprise them in their quarters; He has the Satisfaction of informing the Army that Captn. Lee's Vigilance baffled the Enemy's designs by judiciously posting his men in his quarters, although he had not a Sufficient number to allow one for each window, he obliged the party consisting of two hundred, disgracefully to retire after repeated fruitless attempts to force their way into the house."[2]*

The battle that Washington described was a dawn attack by British cavalry on Captain Henry "Light-Horse Harry" Lee and a handful of his men at Spread Eagle Tavern, an abandoned inn outside Philadelphia. By resolutely defending the building and boldly shouting that reinforcements were at hand, Lee fought and bluffed his way out of what appeared to be an inescapable trap. Not content with his public praise of Lee, General Washington also sent the young captain a personal letter of appreciation.

> *"My dear Lee: Altho I have given you my thanks in the general orders of this day, for the late instance of your gallant behaviour I cannot resist the Inclination I feel to repeat them again in this manner. I needed no fresh proof of your merit, to bear you in remembrance, I waited only for the proper time and season to shew it. … Offer my sincere thanks to the whole of your gallant party and assure them that no one felt pleasure more sensibly, or rejoiced more sincerely for yours and their escape."[3]*

Washington's praise for Lee's performance demonstrated the great appreciation that the commander-in-chief felt for a victory that helped to revitalize the army's morale during the ordeal at Valley Forge. Furthermore, the salutation "My dear Lee" showed the personal attachment that Washington felt for his young cavalryman. The general's profession of support for Lee's advancement indicated that Washington would work hard to find as many opportunities as he could to help his promising subordinate satisfy his ambition to win glory in the fight against the British. The military partnership between these two Virginians, who had been neighbors and friends before the war, was off to a promising start.

Henry Lee's performance at Spread Eagle Tavern marked the beginning of an outstanding career as an officer in the Revolutionary War. Lee's service earned him the complete trust of his two demanding commanders, George Washington and Nathanael Greene. He also held the confidence of his men, and impressed many with his martial appearance and equestrian skills. Private Moses Hall of the North Carolina militia, who became acquainted with Lee during the southern campaign in 1781, described him as "one of the finest looking men & best riders on horseback." Lee made certain that his soldiers equaled his own standards of military appearance and ability. "Col Lee's troop of horse was the best troops I ever saw," noted William Clenney, a Continental soldier from North Carolina. As Lee continued to achieve success on the battlefield, the American people came to share this admiration for his accomplishments.[4]

Despite earning renown among his contemporaries for his military exploits,

Henry Lee's services during the Revolution have been nearly forgotten by historians. Few biographies of Lee have been written, and those often devote little attention to Lee's military career, instead emphasizing his long postwar political career and the financial misfortunes that plagued him later in life.[5]

This volume seeks to rectify the omissions of earlier Lee biographies by focusing on Lee's military services during the American Revolution. As one of the most effective cavalry commanders of the war, Henry Lee's leadership and campaigns certainly merit a deeper examination than they have received thus far.

Fortunately for historians, Lee left a great deal of material documenting his life and military service. His habit of corresponding directly with his superiors resulted in the preservation of many of his letters in the papers of George Washington and Major General Nathanael Greene. Additional letters and documents can be found in other collections, and in archives such as the Virginian Historical Society and the Library of Virginia. These materials, supplemented by others including Lee's own memoirs and relevant British documents, provided the basis for this biography.

The intention of this volume is to chronicle Lee's career as a Revolutionary officer for general readers of American history, for those with a personal or professional interest in military history, and for readers interested more specifically in Virginia history and the history of the American Revolution. It is the story of an officer commissioned at the young age of twenty, who served under Washington in the North and Greene in the South and earned the respect and trust of both men. Self-confident, brilliant, sometimes arrogant, Lee distinguished himself at the head of an elite corps of cavalry and light infantry that bore his name, Lee's Legion. He was the only American soldier below the rank of general to be awarded a gold medal by Congress during the Revolution.

Lee's experiences after the Revolution will be covered only briefly, with emphasis upon his return to military service during the Whiskey Rebellion of 1794, and during the War of 1812. Other biographers have examined Lee's post-Revolutionary political and personal life in great detail, making it unnecessary to do so once again.[6]

In presenting an account of Lee's military service, this volume seeks neither to glorify Lee, nor to dwell on his character flaws and the sad financial difficulties that plagued his postwar life. Rather, the goal is to tell the story of Lee's role in the American Revolution, and his many contributions to winning the struggle for independence.

---

1   George Washington to John Bannister, April 21, 1778, Papers of George Washington (hereafter

Washington Papers), Library of Congress, Washington, DC (hereafter LOC).

2 George Washington, General Orders, Jan. 20, 1778, Washington Papers, LOC.

3 Washington to Henry Lee, Jan. 20, 1778, Washington Papers, LOC.

4 Moses Hall, Pension Application W10105, Nov. 7, 1835, National Archives, Washington, DC (hereafter NA); William Clenney, Pension Application S32182, Nov. 16, 1839, NA.

5 Biographies of Lee include Thomas Boyd's *Light-horse Harry Lee* (New York: Charles Scribner's Sons, 1931), Cecil B. Hartley, *Life of Major General Henry Lee* (New York: Derby & Jackson, 1859), and Noel B. Gerson, *Light-Horse Harry: A Biography of Washington's Great Cavalryman, Henry Lee* (Garden City, NY: Doubleday, 1966). Of the three, another Lee biographer, Charles Royster, remarks that the last two "have little to recommend them." Royster's own biography of Lee, *Light-Horse Harry Lee and the Legacy of the American Revolution* (Baton Rouge: Louisiana State University Press, 1981), devotes only one of its seven chapters to Lee's military service in the Revolution. For Royster's assessment of earlier biographies, see p. 285. A more recent biography of Lee, *The American Partisan: Henry Lee and the Struggle for Independence, 1776-1780* (Shippensburg, PA: Burd Street Press, c. 2000), by John W. Hartmann, does not cover Lee's military service in the South. Michael Cecere's *Wedded to My Sword: The Revolutionary War Service of Light Horse Harry Lee* (Westminster, MD: Heritage Books, 2012), is more comprehensive in scope.

6 As previously noted, Royster's *Light-Horse Harry Lee* devotes six of its seven chapters to Lee's postwar activities.

CHAPTER ONE

THE MAKING OF A SOLDIER

The threat of war loomed over the American colonies in the Spring of 1775. After more than a decade of increasing tension between the colonists and the British government, events were approaching the breaking point. Colonial opposition to a series of taxes imposed by Parliament had culminated in the Boston Tea Party of December 16th, 1773, prompting British officials to retaliate with a series of punitive laws called the Coercive Acts. In response, leaders from twelve of the thirteen colonies had gathered in Philadelphia, Pennsylvania, in 1774 to devise a coordinated policy to defend their rights against the harsh policies of King George III and Parliament. Military experience was a rare commodity among the delegates who had been chosen to represent their colonies at the Congress, but it would become increasingly important as open conflict began to seem inevitable.[1]

The best known former soldier to attend the Congress was George Washington, a Virginian who had earned a reputation for bravery and combat leadership during the French and Indian War of 1754-1763. He had commanded Virginia's militia during the war, but laid down his sword afterward to take up the life of a wealthy planter. As he prepared to attend the Second Continental Congress in the spring of 1775, Washington reached out to some of the most experienced former soldiers in the colonies to discuss strategy and military affairs. One of the most knowledgeable was Charles Lee, an acerbic, opinionated, eccentric and supremely self-confident former British army officer who had moved from England to Virginia. Washington invited Lee to dine with him at Mount Vernon on April 16th, 1775, where the two men were joined at dinner by Washington's nineteen-year-old neighbor, Henry Lee III. Although they shared the same surname, Charles Lee and Henry Lee were not related.[2]

Washington had known Henry Lee III since he was born on January 29th, 1756 nearby at the Leesylvania plantation to Henry Lee, Jr., and Lucy Grymes Lee. At that time, Lee's father commanded the Prince William County militia and worked closely with Washington to defend the colony from attacks by Indian nations allied with the French. Henry Lee III grew up to become a superb horseman in a society that prized equestrian skills, and he had also developed a deep interest in military history during his time at college. He was fascinated by Charles Lee and the military knowledge that the loquacious former British officer was happy to share with any who would listen. Charles Lee was equally impressed by Washington's young dinner guest, later declaring that Henry Lee seemed to "have come from his mother's womb a soldier."

The mutual regard that the two Lees had for one another would continue until Charles Lee's death in 1782. As the three men enjoyed their dinner and discussions in the luxury of the Mount Vernon mansion, they could not have known that only three days later, war would break out with Britain at Lexington and Concord in faraway Massachusetts.[3]

Only a month before his meeting with the two Lees, Washington had attended the Second Virginia Convention, which had convened at Henrico Parish Church. There, in response to Patrick Henry's stirring appeal to "give me liberty or give me death," the delegates resolved to begin preparations for possible war with Great Britain. Virginia's royal governor, Lord Dunmore, had already dissolved the colony's elected legislature, and the Convention members, acting in the legislature's place, appointed Washington to a committee charged with raising troops. The Convention also elected him to represent Virginia as a delegate to the upcoming Second Continental Congress. Washington had been both a prominent political figure in Virginia and an active opponent of British policy since the beginning of the colonists' dispute with Great Britain. In both capacities he again worked with his friend Henry Lee, Jr.; the two were elected to Virginia's colonial legislature, the House of Burgesses, and worked together on several important committees during the crucial years of 1770-1772 while the American colonies moved slowly and cautiously down the path toward rebellion. Lee and Washington signed the Association Agreement of June 22nd, 1770, an early statement to Virginia's royal governor of the principles that eventually led to the Revolution.[4]

That same summer, Henry Lee III, now fourteen years old, and his twelve-year-old brother Charles, left Leesylvania to continue their studies at the College of New Jersey (now Princeton University). As was customary among Virginia's planter aristocracy, the two boys had been educated at home by private tutors, and had reached the age when students of that era went to college. Henry Lee III had done so well under his tutors that William Lee, a relative living in England, urged Henry Lee, Jr., to send his son to be educated in the mother country.

> *"Your son Harry is a boy of fine parts," William Lee wrote from London in 1770. "Therefore it surely is incumbent to you to spare no pains or cost to give him a compleat education. This you know cannot be done in Virginia, therefore I wou'd advise his being sent over here immediately for that purpose."*

Henry Lee, Jr. chose instead to send his sons to the College of New Jersey, where the Lees had another family connection. Their cousin Alice, the sister of Richard Henry Lee, was married to Doctor William Shippen of Philadelphia, a noted physician and professor of medicine who was a founder and supporter of the New Jersey school.[5]

Henry Lee III excelled in his studies. He was particularly attracted to the classic writers of the ancient world such as Homer and Demosthenes, as well as the great military commanders of the past, including Alexander the Great, Hannibal, and Julius Caesar. Lee's ability as a scholar so impressed his guardian, Doctor Shippen, that he informed his brother-in-law, Richard Henry Lee, that "your young cousin Henry Lee is in college, and will be one of the first fellows in this country. He is more than strict in his morality, has a fine genius, and is diligent."[6]

In addition to his studies, Henry Lee III remained well aware of the political dispute between Great Britain and the American colonies. The college's president, the Reverend Doctor John Witherspoon, was a fervent supporter of colonial rights in addition to being a highly respected scholar. Witherspoon readily shared his political opinions with his students and imbued the whole college with his deep belief in the importance of liberty. When John Adams met Witherspoon in 1774, he declared the college president to be "as high a Son of Liberty as any Man in America." Witherspoon served in the Continental Congress, signed the Declaration of Independence, and produced a generation of leaders for the soon-to-be independent United States.[7]

With their father in attendance, both Henry Lee III and Charles Lee delivered their "final orations" on September 30th, 1773, and were awarded their degrees. Shortly afterward, they returned to Leesylvania. Henry Lee III intended to study law at London's famed Middle Temple, but this plan came to naught when tensions between Great Britain and the colonies flared higher than ever with the passage of the Coercive Acts in 1774. Given the commitment of Henry Lee III, his father, and his cousins Richard Henry Lee and Francis Lightfoot Lee to the colonial cause, Lee and his family decided to postpone his studies in London to await further developments in the British-colonial dispute.[8]

The conflict between the colonies and parent country escalated over the subsequent months, leading to the dinnertime discussion of the military situation between Washington, Charles Lee, and Henry Lee III on that April evening in 1775. Henry Lee's early interaction with some of America's leading military thinkers added to his interest in the science of warfare. Further, the experience of associating with such high ranking officers later encouraged Lee, despite his youth, to express his views openly to his superiors on matters that were normally decided at the highest levels of command.

Amid the uproar that ensued as news of the fighting in Massachusetts spread throughout the colonies, Washington prepared to leave for Philadelphia, where the Continental Congress was scheduled to meet. Before he departed, he was visited by another retired British army officer, Horatio Gates. Like Charles Lee, Gates had embraced the colonial cause and taken up residence in Virginia. Gates was widely considered an expert in military matters, and he and Washington met on May 2nd and 3rd to discuss the nascent conflict.[9]

Washington and Gates, along with Charles Lee, soon found themselves assigned key roles in the struggle. After the delegates accepted a request from Massachusetts's leaders that the Continental Congress assume control of the colonial forces gathered outside Boston, the representatives in Philadelphia unanimously chose Washington to be commander-in-chief of the new Continental Army on June 15th. Two days later, Congress appointed Charles Lee major general and second-in-command, while Gates was named adjutant general of the army (the equivalent of chief of staff) with the rank of brigadier general.[10]

Washington left Philadelphia immediately to take command of the forces at Boston. The colonial troops who had gathered from across New England and as far away as Virginia, had besieged British General Thomas Gage's army in the city. Washington, Charles Lee, and Gates trained and organized the troops while searching for a way to drive out the British. The Americans finally succeeded by placing artillery, hauled by sled from New York's Fort Ticonderoga, on Dorchester Heights overlooking Boston. This forced the British to evacuate the city on March 17th, 1776.[11]

As Washington led his army toward New York to defend that city against a British move to occupy it, Henry Lee III began his own military career at home in Virginia. Lee had made his first attempt to obtain an appointment in the army on July 5th, 1775, when he wrote to Charles Lee requesting an appointment to the general's staff. "The familiarity with which you treated me in Virginia," Henry Lee wrote, referring to the dinner at Mount Vernon, "has induced me to ask to enlist under your command in order to acquaint myself with the art of war." If Charles Lee replied to the letter, no record of his response has been found. Perhaps he recognized that an active and ambitious young man like Henry Lee would find staff work too mundane. Henry Lee would reach the same conclusion later in the war. Although Henry Lee must have been greatly disappointed with the lack of a response or a rejection of his offer, he made a second effort in March 1776. When he learned that Charles Lee had been ordered to take command of the Continental Army in the Southern Department, and would be passing through Virginia en route to Charleston, South Carolina. Henry Lee sent another note to the general, pledging "that I shall be particularly attentive to the discharge of any office you may think proper to honour me with." Once again, no records exist to show that Charles Lee answered his youthful admirer.[12]

Charles Lee did provide Henry Lee an opportunity for military service indirectly. While in Virginia, he urged the colony's leaders to organize troops of light dragoons. In European military theory, dragoons were mounted soldiers trained to fight as both cavalry and infantry, but in practice during the Revolutionary War dragoons served almost exclusively as cavalry. The Virginia Convention endorsed Charles Lee's proposal, and on May 20th, 1776, passed legislation authorizing "that four Troops of Horse be raised for the better Security and Defence of this Colony." Officers and enlisted men were required to provide their own horses, weapons, and equipment. On June 13th, the Convention ordered the formation of two additional troops of cavalry.[13]

The dragoons were raised quickly and gathered at Williamsburg, where they were organized into a regiment commanded by Colonel Theodorick Bland. Henry Lee was elected to command the 5th Troop (the cavalry equivalent of an infantry company), and on June 18th, 1776, Virginia governor Patrick Henry commissioned Lee a captain in the Virginia Light Horse. Most of the recruits in Lee's company came from northern Virginia. Lee's election may have been helped by his family connections. His commanding officer, Bland, was Lee's cousin.[14]

Service in the cavalry was a logical choice for Lee, as he had developed an unerring eye for good horses, a thorough knowledge of their proper care, and a commitment to their well-being. These attributes were typical among members of Virginia's planter aristocracy, and Lee shared them with Washington, who also "had been virtually raised in the saddle, and ... came from a class that prided itself on the knowledge of good horseflesh. Horse breeding and racing constituted a virtual mania among the Virginia gentry." Virtually every large plantation boasted its own stable and "a respectable line of thoroughbreds."[15]

Lee promptly put his expertise with horses to good use, ensuring that the troopers under his command had the best mounts available; he knew that cavalry's effectiveness depended upon the quality of its horses. "It was well understood that ... Lee would always have the best horse the country afforded," one of his contemporaries later observed, and a historian noted that the horses of Lee's cavalry, "under the inspection of the Virginian commander, were superior in bone and figure" to their counterparts in other mounted units. Lee's emphasis on procuring superior mounts for his men continued throughout the Revolution, and later in the war he was chastised for impressing prime stallions of considerable value over the objections of their owners.[16]

In addition to his expertise with horses, Lee possessed a soldierly appearance that belied his youth and lack of military experience. He was physically well suited for cavalry service, being "of a height not exceeding the middle stature, with a form light and agile, a quick and penetrating glance." This gave Lee an air of authority that, along with the advantages of wealth and family status so important to Virginians, assured him the respect and obedience of his troops.[17]

*****

The Role of American Cavalry Early in the War

Unfortunately, Lee's leadership abilities and his efforts to outfit his unit properly did not initially help the American cause, because at the beginning of the war neither George Washington, other senior officers of the Continental Army, nor members of the Continental Congress believed that the Americans had any need for cavalry. In addition to being costly to equip and maintain in the field, cavalry units did not seem particularly well suited to operations in New England and lower New York state, where rough terrain, dense patches of forest, and the innumerable stone walls that bordered farm fields were all impediments to the employment of mounted troops.[18]

It was not until late June of 1776, in response to a proposal from some of the citizens of New York City, that Washington began to consider that cavalry might prove useful. Forwarding the proposal to Congress "in behalf of a body of men who are desirous of being employed in the Continental Service, as a Troop of Horse," the general remarked that "such a Corps may be extremely useful in many respects. In a march they may be of the utmost service, in reconnoitering the Enemy and gaining Intelligence, and have it in their power to render many other important benefits."[19]

Washington's initial impression regarding the advantages of cavalry soon faded when the state of Connecticut sent between four and five hundred militia cavalrymen to aid in defending New York City against an expected British attack. Already fretting over a shortage of forage for the horses needed to haul the army's artillery and supply wagons, Washington did not believe enough food was available for the militia's mounts. He asked the troops to remain but to send their horses home, which they refused to do. The general's dissatisfaction at this disregard for his instructions was partly mollified by the militiamen's pledge to pay for the care of their horses from their personal funds. However, the Connecticut soldiers' neglect of duty soon completely alienated Washington. In a July 16th letter to the militia cavalry's commander, Thomas Seymour, Washington's famous temper flared: "Your men think themselves exempt from the common Duties of a Soldier, will not mount Guard, do Garrison Duty, or the Service separate from their Horse," the general asserted. Therefore, "they can be no longer of Use here, where Horse cannot be brought to Action, and I do not care how soon they are dismissed." Angered by this rebuke, Seymour and his troops ended their service with the Continental Army that same day.[20]

In the months following the debacle with the Connecticut militia cavalry, the Continental Army lacked a cavalry force throughout the campaign that cost the Americans control of New York City and the surrounding area. Washington did not consider the two regiments of British cavalry with General Sir William Howe's army to be of much value, either. In his General Orders of October 27th, the American commander-in-chief chided his soldiers for allowing themselves to be intimidated by the British dragoons:

> "*The General observing that the Army seems unacquainted with the Enemy's Horse; and that when any parties meet with them, they do not oppose them with the same Alacrity which they shew in other cases; thinks it necessary to inform the officers and soldiers, that, in such a broken Country ... there is no Enemy more to be despised, as they cannot leave the road; So that any party attacking them may be always sure of doing it to advantage, by taking post in the Woods by the Roads, or along the stone-walls, where they will not venture to follow them.*"[21]

These orders marked the final time that Washington dismissed cavalry as ineffective. The very next day, at the Battle of White Plains north of New York City, Lt. Col. Samuel Birch's British cavalry regiment, the 17th Light Dragoons, played a key role in driving the Continental Army from its position. British mounted troops also harassed the Americans as they retreated across New Jersey, and on December 13th scored a major coup when troopers of the 16th Light Dragoons captured Major General Charles Lee at Basking Ridge, New Jersey.[22]

Washington had to reconsider his estimate of the value of mounted troops, and indeed reversed himself just two days before Charles Lee's capture. "From the Experience I have had in this Campaign of the Utility of Horse," Washington advised the Continental Congress on December 11th, "I am Convinced there is no carrying on the War without them, and I would therefore recommend the Establishment of one or more Corps ... in Addition to those already raised in Virginia."[23]

*****

Henry Lee Joins Washington's Army

Congress responded to Washington's recommendation by approving the creation of a cavalry force numbering three thousand men. Washington decided to organize the new mounted units into four regiments. After a debate among Virginia officials as to whether the state's cavalry regiments, which had been raised for local defense, could be sent on service outside Virginia, state leaders relented in view of the crisis the American army faced in the north. Three troops of Colonel Bland's dragoon regiment, including the one commanded by Captain Henry Lee, were dispatched to join Washington and arrived in Pennsylvania in early 1777. On January 14 Congress formally accepted the Virginians into Continental service as the 1st Regiment of Light Dragoons, with Bland retaining his position as colonel and commander of the regiment. The congressional resolution made the unit's Continental status retroactive to November 25th, 1776. Three additional regiments of Continental Light Dragoons were also created.[24]

Little is known of the details of Lee's service during his first years of duty in the north. This was largely the result of the manner in which Washington employed his mounted troops. Rather than keeping the regiments together, the commander-in-chief decided to "split them up among the Divisions of his Main Army to serve as messengers and escorts for himself and his major subordinates, and as scouts and pickets for the infantry." Bland's regiment was also frequently assigned to collect wagons, horses, and cattle for the army. Such duties, while considered routine, were often of great importance, particularly scouting and intelligence gathering in the no-man's-land between the American and British lines. Skirmishes between detachments of the opposing armies often resulted from these operations. By April 1777, Washington noted that the strength of Bland's regiment was "greatly reduced by their constant service since they joined me."[25]

Washington had a gift for recognizing the potential of his officers. He was able to look past the inexperience of these officers to grasp their enormous potential, lead them to exceptional performance, and help them to build the character and leadership skills that would enable them to excel in command. In the case of Henry Lee, Washington was already well acquainted with his young neighbor from Virginia and sought to provide him with opportunities that would help him to develop as a leader while benefiting the American cause.[26]

Lee's close relationship with the commander-in-chief, unusual because of their great difference in age and rank, and Lee's own penchant for seizing opportunities without awaiting permission from his superiors rankled many of his fellow officers. Lee was hardly unique in becoming embroiled in feuds with other Continental officers; jealousy and squabbling plagued the entire Continental Army. As a member of Congress, John Adams had to deal with such issues, and lamented that

> *"I am wearied to Death with the Wrangles between military officers, high and low. They Quarrel like Cats and Dogs. They worry one another*

like Mastiffs. Scrambling for Rank and Pay like Apes for Nuts."[27]

In late August 1777, during the campaigning south of Philadelphia, Lee first became entangled in this web of infighting. He was formally charged with disobedience of orders and tried by court martial on the 23rd. Lieutenant Colonel Anthony Walton White presided over the court, whose members declared themselves "unanimously of opinion, that Capt. Henry Lee is not guilty of the charge exhibited against him, and do acquit him with honor. And they are also unanimously of opinion, that the charge against Capt. Lee is *groundless* and *vexatious*, and that Capt. Lee … acted merely for the good of his troop." Washington announced his concurrence with the court's decision in general orders on August 25th.[28]

Lee did not let the affair affect his activities. On August 29th, in the skirmishing between the two armies, Lee and his troop captured twenty-four British soldiers. Washington heartily approved of this action "by Captn. Lee of the Light Horse" and continued to entrust his young friend with demanding assignments. In mid-September, after the Americans lost the Battle of Brandywine, Washington dispatched his aide, Lieutenant Colonel Alexander Hamilton, and Lee with a "small party" of Lee's dragoons to destroy several grist mills and their stores of flour to prevent them from falling into British hands. While the troops were engaged in that task, two of Lee's scouts rushed up to report that British cavalry were racing toward the Americans. Lee and the two scouts created a diversion by galloping across the bridge over the millstream, drawing the British in pursuit and allowing Hamilton and the rest of the men to escape in a flatboat. Miraculously, Lee and his two dragoons emerged unscathed "although the enemy's front section emptied their carbines and pistols at the distance of ten or twelve paces."[29]

A few days later, the British occupied Philadelphia, and on October 4 defeated the Americans at the Battle of Germantown. General Howe then turned his attention to opening a secure supply line to Philadelphia via the Delaware River. The Americans still occupied two posts: Fort Mifflin on Mud Island in the Delaware, and Fort Mercer at Red Bank on the New Jersey side of the river. These forts protected obstructions that the Americans had sunk in the river to prevent the British fleet from reaching Philadelphia. Howe was forced to unload provisions south of the city and bring them northward by land, a slow process that could be disrupted by American raids. Lee, having scouted the area south of the Schuylkill River, described Howe's supply line to Washington in a letter written on October 31st:

"*They have a body of men, (not five hundred in number) on Carpenters island; the possession of this post secures a constant & ready sup-*

ply of provision. It is brought up by water, from the fleet off Chester, reposited under cover of the ships against the chevaux de frise [sunken obstacles], & then conducted thro' Carpenters island to the new lower ferry; & so on to Philada. If this communication is not interrupted, supplies of provision will be as abundant, as if the fleet lay off the wharfs of the city. There is a beef trade carried on between the inhabitants, & the enemy at a place called Grubs landing, about six miles below Chester. This illicit correspondence came to my knowledge but yesterday. I have detached a party of dragoons to disturb them; & make no doubt my endeavours to interrupt this connexion, will be effectual."[30]

Washington instantly realized the importance of Lee's information and assigned him to assist Brigadier General James Potter in gathering any available flour and then disabling the grist mills at Chester, Pennsylvania, Wilmington, Delaware, and elsewhere in the area to make it difficult for the British troops to obtain food supplies. While carrying out these duties, Lee continued his effort to impede the flow of supplies to Philadelphia. On November 2nd, in an attempt to disrupt trade between local residents and the British, Lee rode with twelve of his dragoons to Robinson's Mill on Namur Creek, where he surprised a British foraging party. "The enemy ran without giving one fire," Lee noted. He pursued them, capturing a captain, seven soldiers and sailors, and a merchant from Baltimore County, Maryland, who was trading with the British. Lee's interrogation of the prisoners revealed that the British were preparing to attack Fort Mifflin. He suggested that Washington drive the enemy from Carpenter's Island and fortify that place to thwart the anticipated assault on Fort Mifflin. Lee added that he had also learned of a "brisk trade carried on at New-castle," Delaware, between the inhabitants and the enemy, and had dispatched some of his dragoons to warn the people of the consequences of such behavior.[31]

Washington did not follow Lee's advice to capture and fortify Carpenter's Island, and the British used their position there and on nearby Province Island to bombard Fort Mifflin. Initially the fire of the light British field pieces had little effect, but on November 9th two heavy guns positioned on Province Island joined the bombardment, and the next day warships of the Royal Navy added their firepower to the effort. The fort's defenses, Lee observed, "were soon battered down," and the American garrison evacuated the post during the night of November 15th, crossing the river to Fort Mercer. Hoping to save that post, Washington dispatched reinforcements, including Lee and his dragoons. However, Major General Nathanael Greene, commander of the relief force, did not find the additional troops he had been expecting in

New Jersey and concluded that his detachment was too weak to oppose the large British force Howe had sent to take Fort Mercer. The American garrison abandoned the fort on November 18th, and most of the army returned to Pennsylvania. Greene ordered Lee's dragoons and a corps of riflemen to remain near Haddonfield in New Jersey "to encourage the Militia and awe the enemy, to prevent their coming out in small parties."[32]

With winter approaching and his Delaware River supply line secure, General Howe cantoned his troops in and around Philadelphia, where they generally enjoyed warm quarters and adequate supplies of provisions. The American commander selected Valley Forge, twenty-five miles northwest of Philadelphia, as the site of the Continental Army's winter camp. While the infantry sheltered in log huts and endured food shortages and bitter cold, Washington kept his cavalry units dispersed across the area between the two armies, where they could provide early warning of any British sortie from Philadelphia, and procure supplies for themselves and the rest of the army. Lee and his men were withdrawn from New Jersey to assist in this extremely difficult duty, which required constant vigilance and rapid movement. Skirmishes with enemy cavalry occurred frequently. Major Benjamin Tallmadge of the 2nd Continental Light Dragoons, who was engaged in the same activities as Lee at that time, recalled that "my duties were very arduous, not being able to tarry long in a place, by reason of the British Light Horse, which continually patrolled this intermediate ground. Indeed it was unsafe to permit the dragoons to unsaddle their horses for an hour, and very rarely did I tarry in the same place throughout the night."[33]

It was during these operations that Lee began to distinguish himself. Washington, observing Lee's effectiveness, urged his immediate superior, Colonel Bland, to make every effort to maintain Lee's troop at full strength. "You will be pleased to send all Captn. Lee's troop that remain behind with the Regiment, to join the detachment now with him," Washington instructed Bland in December. "You will also return immediately to him, whatever men he may send with prisoners, or on any other errand. He is so enterprising and useful an Officer that I should wish him not to be Straitened for the want of Men." Lee needed all the dragoons he could muster given the quality of the British mounted force opposing him. On December 23rd, Lee urged Washington to take note of "the superiority of the enemy cavalry in the excellence of their horses & discipline."[34]

The commander-in-chief was not the only American to recognize Lee's ability to succeed against tough British opposition. Over the course of the winter of 1777-1778, Lee proved himself to be "a champion raider." His success in "raiding British supply convoys ... made him nothing less than a living legend to the half-starved Continentals at Valley Forge." By mid-

January 1778, Lee had captured more than one hundred British and Hessian soldiers in addition to large quantities of supplies destined for General Howe's army. An American newspaper, the *New Jersey Gazette*, reported on January 14th, 1778, that Lee's troop, although "seldom having more than 25 men and horses fit for duty," had taken nearly 130 prisoners since August 1st, 1777, "with the loss of only one horse." The writer praised the conduct of "this Gallant Corps ... under the command of Captain Lee," and expressed the hope that the "merit and services" of Lee and his soldiers "will not be passed unnoticed or unrewarded."[35]

Lee also made great efforts in gathering intelligence. In January 1778, an informant told him that an officer in an Anspach regiment, one of the many German units hired by the British government to bolster the strength of their army, was willing to desert with three hundred of his men. Lee informed Washington, who authorized him to handle the matter but to proceed cautiously. The German officer allegedly offered to allow his troops to join the American army provided he be given command of them. It is doubtful that three hundred soldiers, no matter how determined, could have left their quarters in Philadelphia and marched into the American lines without interference from British forces, and perhaps this was the reason that nothing came of the matter.[36]

*****

Spread Eagle Tavern

While Lee pursued, through intermediaries, his unsuccessful effort to secure the defection of the Anspach troops, he continued his operations between the lines. On the night of January 19th, Lee established his headquarters at an abandoned inn, Spread Eagle Tavern, outside Philadelphia while his cavalrymen scouted the surrounding countryside for British detachments and supply trains. The British had secretly learned of his location, probably from local Loyalists who acted as spies. British officers were eager to capture or kill Lee, since they had identified him as the cause of so many of their difficulties. Hessian Captain Johann Ewald observed that Lee's dragoons "constantly alarmed our outposts," and upon receiving news of Lee's location, General Sir Thomas Erskine ordered a force assembled to attack Lee at the tavern.[37]

Major Richard Crewe of the 17th Light Dragoons commanded the detachment, which consisted of some of his own mounted troops plus additional cavalry from the Queen's Rangers, a Loyalist unit commanded by Lt. Col. John Graves Simcoe. Captain Banastre Tarleton, an officer of the King's Dragoon Guards, who had been serving as a volunteer in America since the beginning of the war while his regiment remained in England, accompanied the British and Loyalist cavalry. Estimates of the strength of Crewe's and Simcoe's force vary widely, from as few as forty to as many as two hundred men.[38]

The British left Philadelphia after dark on the nineteenth and, "concealing their march by a circuitous road," successfully avoided Lee's pickets. They did encounter a patrol consisting of five of Lee's dragoons and captured them after a brief fight. The sounds of the skirmish did not reach the tavern, where Lee, two officers, a quartermaster sergeant, and four dragoons of his own troop, and a visiting officer, fellow Virginian Major John Jameson of the 2nd Continental Light Dragoons, remained unaware of the enemy's approach.[39]

One of Lee's dragoons, looking out a tavern window as the sun was rising, saw the approaching British cavalry and shouted a warning. The quartermaster sergeant, seeing how badly outnumbered the Americans were, took to his heels, leaving Lee and the other seven men to face the enemy. Lee, however, did not panic. He recalled afterward that "we manned the doors and windows" of the stone building. "The contest was very warm; the British dragoons trusting to their vast superiority in numbers, attempted to force their way into the house."[40]

Crewe led his men in two mounted charges on the tavern, but as George Washington noted, "Lee's Vigilance baffled the Enemy's designs by judiciously posting his men ... although he had not a Sufficient number to allow one for each window." Both charges were repulsed by the defenders' fire. During one of the attacks, Tarleton spotted a high window that appeared to be unguarded. Reining his horse to a halt below the window, Tarleton attempted to climb in, only to be met by one of Lee's dragoons, Ferdinand O'Neal. From only a few feet away, O'Neal aimed his carbine at Tarleton's head, but the weapon misfired. Unruffled, Tarleton quipped: "You have missed it my lad for this time," and rode off. Some of Lee's men directed their fire at him and wounded his horse; however, he escaped unscathed except for some bullet holes in his uniform coat.[41]

Frustrated by the failure of his assaults, Crewe shifted his efforts to the outbuildings in an attempt to capture the stable where Lee's horses were sheltered. Heavy fire from the tavern repulsed the British, whose numbers had dwindled because many of the cavalrymen had abandoned the fight in favor of looting the tavern's outbuildings. Recognizing the futility of further attacks, Crewe ordered a withdrawal. The British left two dead troopers and four others wounded on the field, and some less seriously wounded men may have been able to ride away. The sole American casualty was a lieutenant of Lee's troop, "slightly wounded" in the hand.[42]

Although the engagement at Spread Eagle Tavern was small and had no effect on the larger course of operations, it provided a great boost to American morale and further enhanced Lee's reputation. Coming amid the grim winter struggle to survive at Valley Forge, Lee's repulse of a large British detachment with only a handful of determined troopers provided a much needed ray of hope to the Continental Army and the American people. Washington made much of the event, issuing a general order giving his "warmest thanks to Captn. Lee and Officers and men of his Troop for the Victory which by their superior Bravery and Address they gain'd over a party of the Enemy's dragoons."

Lee's gallant stand at Spread Eagle Tavern validated the high opinion that Washington had long held of his friend and subordinate. The general keenly sought new opportunities for Lee, whose abilities were clearly of great value in the struggle against Great Britain. Washington's support would advance Lee's military career, but it would also arouse jealousies and accusations among the army's officers, like those that had led to Lee's earlier court martial.

---

1 Jeremy Black, *War for America: The Fight for Independence, 1775-1783* (Gloucestershire, UK: Wrens Park Publishing, 1998), 8-9, 11.
2 George Washington, Diary, April 16, 1775, in Donald Jackson and Dorothy Twohig, editors, *The Diaries of George Washington*, Vol. 3 (Charlottesville: University Press of Virginia, 1978), 339; Ron Chernow, *Washington: A Life* (New York: Penguin Press, 2010), 58-59; John W. Shy, "Charles Lee: The Soldier as Radical," in George Athan Billias, editor, *George Washington's Generals and Opponents: Their Exploits and Leadership*, Vol. 1 (New York: Da Capo Press, 1994), 22-26.
3 Henry Lee, *Memoirs of the War in the Southern Department of the United States*, ed. Robert E. Lee, reprint edition (New York: Da Capo Press, 1998), 15; for examples of the cooperation between George Washington and Henry Lee, Jr., during the French and Indian War, see "Minutes of a Meeting of the Virginia Regiment War Council," May 14, 1756, Henry Lee, Jr., to Washington, May 16, 1758, Washington Papers, LOC, and Cecere, 2-3; Royster, *Light-Horse Harry Lee*, 14 (quotation).
4 Chernow, 176; George Washington, *Diary*, Sept. 24, 1768, Oct. 19, 1768, Jackson and Twohig, eds., Vol. 2 (1976), 113, 208; John Kennedy Pendleton, ed., *Journals of the House of Burgesses of Virginia, 1770-1772*, Vol. 12 (Richmond: Virginia State Library, 1906), 1-2, 79, 113-114, 125, 143-144, 204, 292.
5 Cazenove Gardner Lee, Jr., *Lee Chronicle: Studies of the Early Generations of the Lees of Virginia*, ed. Dorothy Mills Parker (New York: New York University Press, 1957), 86-87 (quotation); Paul C. Nagel, *The Lees of Virginia: Seven Generations of an American Family* (New York: Oxford University Press, 1990), 3; Ethel Armes, *Stratford Hall: The Great House of the Lees* (Richmond, VA: Garrett and Massie, 1936), 229; Alexander Leitch, *A Princeton Companion* (Princeton, NJ: Princeton University Press, 1975), 283.
6 Armes, 230-231 (quotation); Royster, *Light-Horse Harry Lee*, 119; Leitch, 283, 329-330; William Shippen to Richard Henry Lee, Aug. 25, 1770, in Henry Lee, *Memoirs*, 16 (quotation).
7 Leitch, 110, 283, 523, 525, 527.
8 Cazenove Lee, 86-87; Cecere, 12; Nagel, 161; Armes, 232.
9 Washington, *Diary*, May 2 and 3, 1775, in Jackson and Twohig, eds., 3:343.
10 Worthington Chauncey Ford, editor, *Journals of the Continental Congress* (hereafter *JCC*), Vol. 2 (Washington, DC: US Government Printing Office, 1905), 91, 97.
11 Edward G. Lengel, *General George Washington: A Military Life* (New York: Random House, 2005), 107-109, 111, 122-124, 126.
12 Cecere, 22 (quotation), 24 (quotation).
13 Jim Piecuch, ed., *Cavalry of the American Revolution* (Yardley, PA: Westholme Publishing, 2012), xv; Cecere, 24-25.
14 Francis Bernard Heitman, *Historical Register of Officers of the Continental Army during the War of the Revolution, April, 1775, to December, 1783* (Washington, DC: W. H. Lowdermilk, 1893), 260; Nagel, 161; Cecere, 25; Robert K. Wright, Jr., *The Continental Army* (Washington, DC: US Army Center of Military History, 2000), 348.
15 Gregory J. W. Urwin, *The United States Cavalry: An Illustrated History, 1776-1944* (Norman: University of Oklahoma Press, 1983), 9.

16 Eli Caruthers, *Interesting Revolutionary Incidents and Sketches of Character, Chiefly in the "Old North State," Second Series* (Philadelphia, PA: Hayes & Zell, 1856), 154 (quotation); George Washington Parke Custis, *Recollections and Private Memoirs of Washington, by his Adopted Son, George Washington Parke Custis. With Illustrations and Explanatory Notes by Benson J. Lossing* (Philadelphia, PA: J. W. Bradley, 1861), 358 (quotation); Nathanael Greene to Henry Lee, Feb. 17, 1781, in Richard K. Showman and Dennis M. Conrad, editors, *The Papers of General Nathanael Greene* (hereafter *Greene Papers*), Vol. 7 (Chapel Hill: University of North Carolina Press, 1994), 299-300.

17 Custis, 356.

18 Urwin, *United States Cavalry*, 9-29.

19 Washington to the Continental Congress, June 21, 1776, Washington Papers, LOC.

20 Gregory J. W. Urwin, "The Continental Light Dragoons, 1776-83: 'There Is No Carrying on the War Without Them'" in Piecuch, ed., *Cavalry of the Revolution*, 2-3; George Washington to Thomas Seymour, July 16, 1776, Washington Papers, LOC (quotation).

21 Washington, General Orders, Oct. 27, 1776, Washington Papers, LOC.

22 Urwin, "Continental Light Dragoons," in Piecuch, ed., *Cavalry of the Revolution*, 3.

23 Washington to the Continental Congress, Dec. 11, 1776, Washington Papers, LOC.

24 Urwin, "Continental Light Dragoons," in Piecuch, ed., *Cavalry of the Revolution*, 4; Washington to Theodorick Bland, Dec. 30, 1776, Washington Papers, LOC; Heitman, 260; Wright, 348; Cecere, 27, 30, 34; Ford, ed. *JCC*, 7:34.

25 Urwin, *United States Cavalry*, 17 (quotation); Cecere, 31, 34 (quotation); Lee, *Memoirs*, 16 (quotation).

26 Nagel, 161.

27 John Adams to Abigail Adams, May 22, 1777, in C. James Taylor, editor, *Founding Families: Digital Editions of the Winthrops and the Adamses* (Boston: Massachusetts Historical Society, 2007).

28 George Washington, General Orders, Aug. 25, 1777, Washington Papers, LOC.

29 Washington to the President of Congress, Aug. 30, 1777 (quotation), Washington Papers, LOC; Lee, *Memoirs*, 90-91 (quotations). The reference to "Captn. Lee of the Light Horse" in Washington's August 30 letter is very similar in phrasing to Henry Lee's later sobriquet, "Light Horse Harry." However, it is not clear exactly when the name "Light Horse Harry" was first applied to Lee. It does not appear in the papers of George Washington or Nathanael Greene, Lee's commanding officers, nor was it used by early historians of the Revolution. Robert E. Lee did not use the term in his biographical sketch of his father in the 1869 edition of Henry Lee's *Memoirs*. The only nickname given Lee in the first half of the nineteenth century was "Dragoon Harry," used by Charles Campbell, editor of *The Bland Papers: Being a Selection from the Manuscripts of Colonel Theodorick Bland, Jr. of Prince George County, Virginia*, Vol. 1 (Petersburg, VA: Edmund & Julian C. Ruffin, 1840), xxv.

30 Lee, *Memoirs*, 97; Lee to Washington, Oct. 31, 1777, Washington Papers, LOC (quotation).

31 Washington to James Potter, Oct. 31, 1777, Washington Papers, LOC; Lee to Washington, Nov. 3, 1777, Washington Papers, University of Virginia, Charlottesville (quotation).

32 Lee, *Memoirs*, 100, 102 (quotation), 103-105; Cecere, 60-61.

33 Quoted in Urwin, *United States Cavalry*, 18.

34 Washington to Theodorick Bland, undated letter of December 1777 (quotation), Washington Papers, LOC; Lee to Washington, Dec. 23, 1777, Washington Papers, University of Virginia (quotation).

35 Urwin, *United States Cavalry*, 18 (quotation); John Milton Hutchins, *Light Horse Harry Lee Versus Bloody Ban at the Action at Spread Eagle Tavern, January 20, 1778* (Lakewood, CO: Avrooman-Apfelwald Press, 2007), 2; Cecere, 68 (quotation).

36 Notes to George Washington's letter to Samuel Ellis, Jan. 18, 1778, Washington Papers, University of Virginia.

37 Hutchins, 2.

38 Hutchins, 2-3; Ewald put the strength of the British party at eighty men, while another German officer estimated it as only forty, Cecere, 68. Washington gave the figure of two hundred in his General Orders of Jan. 20, 1778.

39 Hutchins, 3; George Washington, General Orders, Jan. 20, 1778 (quotation), Washington Papers, LOC.

40 Hutchins, 3-4.

41 Washington, General Orders, Jan. 20, 1778 (quotation), Washington Papers, LOC; Hutchins, 4; Caldwell Woodruff, "Capt. Ferdinand O'Neal of Lee's Legion," *William & Mary Quarterly*, Second Series, Vol. 23, No. 3 (July 1943), 328 (quotation).

42 Hutchins, 4-5; Washington, General Orders, Jan. 20, 1778 (quotation), Washington Papers, LOC.

CHAPTER TWO

INDEPENDENT COMMAND

Lee's exploit at Spread Eagle Tavern did not afford him any rest from his regular duties. Instead, in February 1778, Washington ordered him to march southward and operate with a force of Maryland Continentals at Wilmington, Delaware, to procure supplies for the troops at Valley Forge. Washington told Lee to take his cavalry troop to the vicinity of Dover, Delaware, and the Head of Elk in Maryland, and "there, exert your utmost endeavours, to hasten to this Army all ... provisions deposited in the Magazines, at those places." The commander-in-chief authorized Lee to impress as many wagons as were needed to haul the supplies to Pennsylvania. Once that task was accomplished, Lee and the commander of the Maryland soldiers, Major General William Smallwood, were to discuss "the propriety and expediency of collecting Cattle and Forage about the Country to which you are sent, and if any resources can be derived thence towards the relief of our distresses it will be infinitely desirable." Washington informed Smallwood of Lee's mission and urged the Marylander to do all in his power to assist "the zealous activity of Capt. Lee." The supply situation at Valley Forge was critical, Washington noted, therefore "every aid you can possibly afford [Lee] is demanded by the exigency of the occasion."[1]

After Lee outlined his intentions to the commander-in-chief, Washington expressed his approval of Lee's plans, describing the preliminary measures Lee had taken as "extremely judicious," and adding that he had "no doubt that by your activity and prudent management, you will avail yourself of all the resources of the Country, without giving unnecessary umbrage to the inhabitants." Washington seconded Lee's efforts by writing to state officials to procure their cooperation, both with Lee's gathering of supplies and with another task, the capture of deserters from the Continental Army. Upon receiving a report from Lee that Loyalists in Delaware were providing refuge to an estimated three hundred American deserters, Washington asked the Vice President of Delaware, George Reed, to induce the state legislature to pass a law establishing criminal penalties for those who harbored deserters.[2]

Upon completing his mission in Maryland and Delaware, Lee rejoined Washington's army in Pennsylvania. The general was pleased with his subordinate's performance, writing to Congress on April 3rd that "Captain Lee of the light Dragoons and the Officers under his command ... uniformly distinguished themselves by a conduct of exemplary zeal, prudence and bravery."

The letter demonstrated that Washington harbored no ill feelings toward Lee, who only two days before had declined a great honor that the general had offered him. Having sought an appropriate way to reward Lee's services since the clash at Spread Eagle Tavern, Washington decided at the end of March to offer Lee a position on his staff. He made the offer through his aide-de-camp, Lt. Col. Alexander Hamilton. Although this was one of the highest honors the general could bestow, Lee declined the appointment, preferring to serve on the battlefield rather than at headquarters. Lee explained his decision in a letter he wrote to Washington on March 31st:

> *"I must here take the liberty of laying before your Excellency, the reasons which have influence on my judgement, respecting the proposal you was pleased to make me thro' Col. Hamilton. Permit me to premise that I am wedded to my sword, and that my secondary object in the present war, is military reputation. To have possessed a post about your Excellency's person is certainly the first recommendation I can bear to posterity, affords a field for military instruction, would lead me into an intimate acquaintance with the politics of the States, and might present more immediate opportunitys of manifesting my high respect and warm attachment to your Excellencys character and person. I know, it would also afford true and unexpected joy to my parents and friends. On the contrary, I possess a most affectionate friendship for my soldiers, a fraternal love for the two officers who have served with me, a zeal for the honor of the Cavalry, and opinion, that I should render m[ore] real service to your Excellency's arms."*[3]

Washington accepted Lee's refusal graciously, telling the dragoon captain that "the undisguised manner in which you express yourself cannot but strengthen my good opinion of you." Washington explained that his offer of the staff position "was purely the result of a high sense of your merit, and as I would by no means divert you from a Career in which you promised yourself greater happiness, from its affording more frequent opportunities of acquiring Military fame, I entreat you to pursue your own inclinations, as if nothing had passed on this Subject." The general was sincere in his remarks, and decided to wait for some other opportunity to advance his fellow Virginian.[4]

The American cavalry was proving its value during the winter operations of 1777-1778, and Washington desired to increase the size of his mounted force. On January 29th, 1778, he described the importance of the Continental Light Dragoons to Congress:

> *"The benefits arising from a superiority in horse, are obvious to those who have experienced them. Independent of such as you may derive from it in the field of action, it enables you, very materially, to control*

the inferior and subordinate motions of an enemy, and to impede their knowledge of what you are doing, while it gives you every advantage of superior intelligence and, consequently, both facilitates your enterprises against them and obstructs theirs against you. In a defensive war as in our case it is peculiarly desirable; because it affords greater protection to the country, and is a barrier to those inroads and depredations upon the inhabitants, which are inevitable when the superiority lies on the side of the invaders. The enemy fully sensible of the advantages, are taking all the pains in their power, to acquire an ascendancy in this respect."

Congress, however, faced enough difficulty simply trying to maintain the strength of the Continental Army's existing units, and did not approve the creation of new cavalry units.[5]

If Washington could not convince Congress to authorize additional mounted regiments, he decided that he could still augment his cavalry by a smaller amount and create a new opportunity for Henry Lee by organizing a partisan corps under Lee's command. The general sent his proposal to Congress on April 3rd. Washington reminded Congress that he had given Lee his personal assurance that the young captain and his men would be recognized for their services, and that he believed Congress shared his desire "to give every encouragement to merit" and would seize this opportunity to do so. Having consulted with the members of a congressional committee on the matter, Washington had reached agreement with them "that the giving Capt. Lee the command of two troops of Horse … with the Rank of Major, to act as an independent partisan Corps, would be a mode of rewarding him, very advantageous to the Service. Capt. Lee's genius particularly adapts him to a command of this nature, and it will be most agreeable to him." Washington concluded with a reminder that "the Campaign is fast approaching, and there will probably be very little time, to raise and prepare the Corps for it."[6]

Congress concurred with the commander-in-chief's recommendation. The fact that two influential members of the Virginia delegation, Richard Henry Lee and Francis Lightfoot Lee, were Henry Lee's relatives, could only have helped obtain speedy approval of the measure four days later. In addition to approving the creation of a partisan corps and Henry Lee's promotion to major, Congress lavished him with official praise, declaring that "his conduct during the last campaign, has proved himself a brave and prudent officer, rendered essential service to his country, and acquired to himself, and the corps he commanded, distinguished honour." Lee, at the age of twenty-two, had achieved a goal that most of his older and higher ranking fellow officers could only dream of—an independent command.[7]

Washington and Lee promptly began to collaborate on organizing the new partisan corps, working with a committee of army officers and congressmen headed by Major General Horatio Gates called the Board of War that was charged by Congress with oversight of the Continental war effort. The commander-in-chief met with Lee to select officers "and devise ways and means of procuring the additional Men, Horses, Arms and accoutrements." Meanwhile, the Board decided on April 27th to send Lee's unit to "the Peninsula formed by the Delaware and Chesapeake Bays," because the members expected that in the coming campaign the British would take advantage of the large numbers of Loyalists there to "draw very considerable Supplies of Horses therefrom." To forestall the anticipated British action, the Board authorized Lee "to seize and take so many Horses as are necessary to mount his Corps, from the Inhabitants of the said Peninsula." Lee was to avoid taking horses from people who supported the Revolution, focusing instead on the animals owned by Loyalists. He would pay the owners "a reasonable Price," and should anyone refuse to sell their horses, Lee could impress them and pay the owners the animals' value as determined by "two or more indifferent and honest Men." The Board provided Lee $50,000 in Continental currency to purchase the mounts. A month later, Congress decided to increase the size of Lee's corps by adding a third cavalry troop. The delegates instructed Washington to appoint the additional officers.[8]

Although Congress and General Washington were pleased with Lee's elevation to command of a partisan corps, the young Virginian's promotion to major left some of his fellow officers disgruntled. Perhaps they believed that Lee's elevation was based more on the favoritism of his relatives in Congress and the commander-in-chief than on merit; one of them, a Captain Jones of Bland's regiment, made a formal protest. Washington dismissed the complaint, declaring it wholly unjustified.[9]

*****

The Battle of Monmouth and the Court Martial of Major General Charles Lee

When the British opened the 1778 campaign, events did not unfold as the Board of War had anticipated. Instead of pushing to expand its control of southeastern Pennsylvania, Delaware, and eastern Maryland, the British army evacuated Philadelphia. The withdrawal was the result of General Gates's capture of an entire British army at Saratoga, New York, the previous October. That decisive American victory convinced the French government to enter the war as an ally of the United States. Uncertain when or where the French would strike in North America, British officials decided to consolidate their forces at New York. General Howe came under heavy criticism for contributing to the disaster at Saratoga by delaying his operations against Philadelphia for several months the previous summer, thus allowing Washington to reinforce Gates. Howe resigned his command and was replaced by Lt. Gen. Sir Henry Clinton, who began the overland march from Philadelphia to New York on June 18th.[10]

Seeing an opportunity to strike the British as they retreated, Washington led the Continental Army in pursuit across New Jersey. Burdened by its supply trains and suffering from unusually intense heat, the British army marched slowly. The Americans caught up with Clinton's column on the night of June 27th near Monmouth Court House, and Washington ordered an attack to be made the next morning. Major General Charles Lee, having been freed in a prisoner exchange, led the Continental Army's vanguard of 5,400 men. His advance was slowed by unexpectedly difficult terrain—his troops had to cross three ravines to reach the British rear guard, and when they did, they found that General Clinton had expected an attack and was waiting with 6,000 troops. Lee probed the British position and found it too strong to assault with his force. Believing that Washington and the main army were too far away to support him, and that the numerically superior British detachment might counterattack and trap his Continentals against one of the ravines, Lee ordered a withdrawal.[11]

Washington rode up, saw Lee's troops retreating, and exploded in rage. The two officers exchanged harsh words before Washington assumed direct command of the troops. After forming the Continentals in line of battle, Washington held his ground against several British attacks while launching occasional counterattacks. The battle ended at nightfall. Clinton regarded the engagement as a minor, and successful, rear guard action, while the Americans took pride in having held their position against the British regulars who had defeated them so often in the past. The Continental troops had clearly benefited from the rigorous training they received at Valley Forge from the Prussian officer, Baron Friedrich von Steuben, whom Congress had appointed a major general and inspector general of the Continental Army on May 8th, 1778.[12]

Furious because he believed that Charles Lee had squandered a golden opportunity to defeat part of the British army, Washington formally charged Lee on three counts: "disobedience of orders," "misbehavior before the enemy … by making an unnecessary, disorderly, and shameful retreat," and "disrespect to the Commander-in-Chief" for the contents of two letters that Lee had written to Washington on June 28th and July 1st. The subsequent court martial found Lee guilty on all three counts, and ordered him suspended from the army for one year. Lee tried to persuade Congress to reverse the decision, but failed despite the support of Richard Henry Lee. He furiously—

and publicly—denounced Washington, Alexander Hamilton, and eventually added Congress to his list of enemies. That body responded by dismissing Lee from the army, and he remained at his Virginia home, embittered, until his death in 1782.[13]

Richard Henry Lee was not the only member of the Lee family to believe that Charles Lee had been unjustly treated. His cousin, Major Henry Lee, shared that opinion, although Lee and his partisan corps did not fight at Monmouth. Washington had sent Lee to Maryland and Virginia to procure saddles and other badly needed equipment for his troops. Lee's command had made a favorable impression wherever it appeared; the *Virginia Gazette* printed a letter describing the ...

> *"large body of cavalry, under the command of the celebrated Major Lee, who has so frequently distinguished himself as a partisan. This corps consists of chosen men, whose courage and activity the Major has tried; and being completely uniformed and extremely well mounted, they made an elegant and martial appearance."*

Lee, however, sorely wished that he and his corps had been on hand to participate in the Battle of Monmouth. He wrote his friend, Brigadier General Anthony Wayne, that "I have been almost melancholy by my absence from the army. The name of Monmouth reproaches me to my very soul."[14]

Lee wisely withheld his views regarding the Monmouth controversy, not wanting to damage his relationship with George Washington, and ruin his own military career in the process, by openly defending Charles Lee. When he wrote his memoirs, however, he expounded at length on what he perceived as the injustice of Charles Lee's treatment, asserting "that the veteran soldier who had relinquished his native country" (Great Britain), to fight for American independence, "a cause dear to his heart," was no longer able to employ his military abilities on behalf of the United States, and instead the remainder of Charles Lee's life was consumed by "envy and hate." Such an outcome, Henry Lee insisted, could not be supported by the facts of the case. He wrote:

> *"The records of the court-martial manifest on their face the error of the sentence; and it is wonderful [amazing] how men of honor and of sense could thus commit themselves to the censures of the independent and impartial. If General Lee had been guilty of all the charges as affirmed by their decision, his life was forfeited; and its sacrifice only could have atoned for his criminality. He ought to have been cashiered and shot; instead of which the mild sentence of suspension, for a short*

time, was the punishment inflicted. The truth is, the unfortunate general was only guilty of neglect in not making timely communication of his departure from orders, subject to his discretion, to the commander in chief, which constituted no part of the charges against him. This was certainly a very culpable omission; to which was afterwards added personal disrespect, where the utmost respect was not only due, but enjoined by martial law, and enforced by the state of things: two armies upon the very brink of battle, himself intrusted with the direction of an important portion of one of them, for the very purpose of leading into action, to withhold the necessary explanations from his chief, and to set the example of insubordination by his mode of reply to an interrogatory, indispensably though warmly, put to him, merited punishment. But this offence was different, far different from 'disobedience to orders,' or 'a shameful retreat,' neither of which charges were supported by testimony; and both of which were contradicted by fact."[15]

Four years later, when Henry Lee was unhappy with his own treatment by his commander at the time, Major General Nathanael Greene, Lee would complain that "no [other] officer was treated so badly ... except General Lee."[16]

Nevertheless, Henry Lee never criticized George Washington for the outcome of the court martial. Even in his memoirs, written after Washington's death, Henry Lee continued to insist that Charles Lee's insubordination toward Washington was both wrong and worthy of punishment. Henry Lee retained his steadfast loyalty to the commander-in-chief, and Washington likewise continued to support and maintain his friendship with the young major. Normally rigid in adhering to the army's chain of command, Washington made repeated exceptions in regard to Lee. It was unusual for the commanding general to begin a letter to a twenty-two-year-old major with the salutation "Dear Lee," discuss the matter of horses, and then ask: "Will you come and dine with me today?" However, such intimacy was an integral part of Washington's and Lee's relationship. Lee's performance as a soldier earned him a place in Washington's inner circle, where their longstanding personal ties enhanced their military relationship. Yet such a relationship was not without its drawbacks, as Lee's rivals in the army's officer corps seized on such instances as evidence of favoritism on the part of Washington.[17]

*****

With the British army ensconced in New York City and its environs after the Battle of Monmouth, the two armies resumed sparring between the lines. As he had done in the area around Philadelphia, Lee participated actively in these operations. His partisan corps conducted raids, skirmished with British patrols and outposts, and screened the movements of the American infantry. For example, in the autumn of 1778 Lee's corps formed part of a larger party that surprised about one hundred Hessian jaegers near Tarrytown, New York, killing ten and taking nineteen prisoners.[18]

Lee carried out these operations as part of a larger screening force commanded by another Virginian, Brigadier General Charles Scott. To reduce their vulnerability to Lee's attacks, the British sharply curtailed the number of detachments they sent into the countryside. Frustrated by this change of tactics, Lee complained that

> *"I have been indefatigable in my exertions to strike a blow on some part of The enemy; I find myself baffled by the new system of conduct they have introduced. Neither officer nor soldier is permitted to advance on any occasion beyond their picquets ... and the out-posts are drawn in. ... No decoy can take effect, they will not pursue. [Hessian] Gen. [Wilhelm] Kniphausen has ordered the advanced corps to act totally on the defensive."*[19]

In late November, Washington scaled back the Continental Army's operations and prepared to take up winter quarters at Middlebrook, New Jersey. Both armies remained largely inactive during the winter, but in May 1779 General Clinton dispatched an expedition from New York to raid along the shores of Chesapeake Bay. Virginia's congressional delegation immediately pressed Washington to send Lee's corps to its home state to check the enemy incursion; however, Washington refused. He did not believe that the British expedition included a significant force of cavalry, and he asserted that the state government could organize a unit of mounted militia to deal with any British horsemen. Furthermore, he noted that his Continental cavalry regiments were in a "broken and shattered condition" after several encounters with British cavalry that had recently launched raids from their lines around New York. Under those circumstances, Washington declared, "Major Lee's corps of Horse ... is what I have principally to depend on in this line, and without it we might experience at least, great inconvenience."[20]

Washington needed Lee to maintain pressure on the British. On June 6th, 1779, just two weeks after he had rejected the Virginia congressmen's request to transfer Lee's corps to their home state, the general ordered Lee to harass the enemy and gather intelligence along the Hudson River north of New York City. Washington ordered Bavarian-born Major General Baron Johann De Kalb, a very experienced officer who had distinguished himself while serving in the French army, to detach and reinforce Lee with two companies of light infantry. With these troops acting under Lee's command, the major was to support the local militia, "plague the enemy and cover the country from the depredations of their light parties, as much as possible." In addition, Lee received instructions to monitor the activities of a British force at King's Ferry and to verify reports that General Clinton was fortifying a position at Stony Point on the west bank of the Hudson just south of Peekskill. As usual, the commander-in-chief allowed Lee great latitude in conducting his operations, telling Lee that

> *"I leave you at perfect liberty to dispose of yourself as you think most proper for answering the purposes I have mentioned consistent with the security of your corps .... you will be entirely detached and unsupported."*

Lee learned on June 9th that he was to be further reinforced by Captain Allen McLane's company of Delaware Continentals. In the three days since beginning his mission, Lee had already discovered and removed a cache of supplies to keep them out of British hands, and was preparing to move livestock from the area for the same reason.[21]

The next month, while Lee was still operating in the Hudson Valley, he exceeded the latitude Washington had granted him, resulting in a gruesome incident that earned a rebuke from the commanding general. Lee had always been irritated by desertion, and believed that deserters and those who aided them should be severely punished, as he had indicated during operations south of Philadelphia the previous year. Despite the best efforts of Washington and his officers, desertion continued to weaken the Continental Army. In early July, Lee sent Washington a proposal that all deserters captured by the army should be immediately executed, beheaded, and their severed heads displayed. Washington replied on July 9 that the measure

> *"would probably tend to discourage the practice. But it ought to be executed with caution .... I think that that part of your proposal which respects cutting off their heads ... had better be omitted. Examples however severe ought not to be attended with an appearance of inhumanity otherwise they give disgust, and may excite resentment rather than terror."*[22]

Before Washington's advice reached Lee, the major took it upon himself to put his plan into practice. During the night of July 8th, some of Lee's troops patrolling the outpost line captured three deserters. Captain Philip Reed, commander of the detachment and apparently acting on Lee's orders, told the prisoners that he would make an example of them "by cutting off their heads, and sending them to be exposed to the whole army." Reed then relented a bit, suggesting that the men determine which of the three would suffer execution. They refused, whereupon Reed ordered one, a corporal, shot without benefit of trial by court martial. Reed then made the "appalling decision to decapitate the corpse." Whether or not Lee knew of Reed's actions before the execution or only learned of them afterward, he approved and then ordered the head exhibited "among his troops to encourage their obedience." The bloody relic sat atop the gallows on July 10th when another deserter was hanged. When Lee reported what had transpired, Washington lamented that he wished that Lee had received his letter of the ninth "before the transaction you mention had taken place. I fear it will have a bad effect both in the army and in the country." Washington forbade any such actions in the future and ordered Lee to bury the deserter's body; the general feared that the corpse might "fall into the enemy's hands" and be used as propaganda against the Americans.[23]

Members of Lee's family worried that impulsive actions such as these would damage Henry's reputation. His brother Charles shared his concerns with their father, who "agreed that some of [Henry's] recent activities 'cast a shadow' over the son's earlier achievements." However, the elder Henry Lee believed that his son and namesake would surmount his difficulties. "I flatter myself it will not be in the power of his enemies to pluck from him those laurels they cannot acquire," he reassured Charles.[24]

In fact the incident involving the deserter did not harm Henry Lee's career. If Washington questioned Lee's judgment in matters of discipline and martial law, he continued to trust the major's abilities as an officer in the field. Thus the commander-in-chief supported the plan to increase the strength of Lee's corps, which had been put forward at the end of June, to proceed. Lee had cooperated well with De Kalb's light infantry companies during the brief period they served under him, and continued to work effectively with Captain McLane's company. Lee found that the addition of an infantry unit to his cavalry greatly increased the effectiveness of his partisan corps. Therefore, on June 27th, Lee wrote Washington requesting that McLane's company be permanently incorporated into his command. Washington agreed that "the measure is desirable" and that he was well aware "of the advantage to be derived from Horse and foot acting together." But, he noted, only Congress had the power to alter the status of Lee's corps. The general promised that "no time shall be lost" in referring the measure to that body. Then, reminding Lee of the value of his mounted troops to the army, Washington added that Lee should not dismount his dragoons to create a force of infantry.[25]

Congress acted on July 19th, adding McLane's infantry company to Lee's three troops of cavalry. Lee's partisan corps thereby became a legion, the term used to designate a mixed force of cavalry and infantry. A few days later, Lee wrote to his friend, president of the Pennsylvania Executive Council Joseph Reed, declaring that he had "long wished my Corps was legionary." Lee's desire was now fulfilled, and what had formerly been known as the partisan corps would soon become famous as "Lee's Legion."[26]

*****

Stony Point /779

While Lee awaited Congress's decision on converting his corps into a legion, he continued his intelligence gathering, communicating directly with the commander-in-chief. The task was complex, since it involved keeping a close watch on British activities in both the Hudson Valley and northeastern New Jersey. On July 5th Washington instructed Lee "to pay the strictest attention to the movements of the enemy below, lest they may undertake an excursion into" New Jersey "by the way of Tappan ... should it take place, I must request the earliest information." Washington urged Lee to hire local people, who were less likely to be noticed than his troops, to monitor British activities and keep him informed. By July 12th, Washington had shifted his concern to British forces maneuvering east of the Hudson. The general feared that his adversary's actions might be a feint "to divert part of our force that way; then to make a rapid movement back[,] embark and proceed up to the forts" the Americans held higher up the Hudson River.[27]

Lee handled these tasks, although at Washington's insistence he focused most of his efforts on gaining information about the post the British had established in early June at Stony Point. In a letter to the president of Congress, Washington explained the reason for his concern: "from its peninsula and commanding form" the position at Stony Point "is naturally strong; and which from the narrowness of the neck which connects it to the Main[land], may be insulated and maintained without any very great difficulty." From Stony Point, General Sir Henry Clinton could advance farther north into the Hudson Highlands, threatening the key American fortress at West Point and interfering with the communications between New England and the states to the west and south.[28]

Through his aide Robert Hanson Harrison, Washington instructed Lee on June 15th to

> *"use your best endeavours to obtain satisfactory accounts ... of the situation movements and designs of the Enemy; and in a particular manner, to ascertain what Corps they have at Stoney point, and their strength, the number of Cannon and Mortars, "*

1779

and if any British ships were moored near the post, their size and identity. Hanson added that if Lee found it necessary to bribe local inhabitants for the information, Washington would provide the funds. Lee supplied the intelligence Washington requested, leading the commander-in-chief to suggest that Lee "employ some person, in whom you can confide, and at the same time that is intelligent, to go into the works at stony-point." If getting someone inside the British fort proved impossible, Washington urged Lee to at least "obtain the best knowledge" possible, including "the particular kind of works, the precise spots on which they stand and the strength of the garrison." The general advised Lee not to rely solely on the testimony of others for this information. "You will take the best view you can, that you may the better know whether the report you get … is to be relied on," Washington ordered.[29]

Washington was seeking as much information as possible about Stony Point because he had decided to attack the post, and he had selected Brigadier General Anthony Wayne to lead a surprise nighttime assault with 1,350 light infantrymen. Wayne and Washington discussed the operation in detail, after which the commander-in-chief permitted Wayne "to choose between the different plans on which we have conversed." Washington also reminded Wayne that "it is important to have every information we can procure," and therefore advised him to meet with Lee. The major, Washington stated, "has been so long near the spot and has taken so much pains to inform himself critically concerning the post, that I imagine he may be able to make you acquainted with some further details."[30]

On the morning of July 15th, Wayne ordered Lee "to join the Light Infantry with my Corps." When Lee arrived, Wayne described his plan of attack and, Lee wrote, "as my station was the post of intelligence, he also consulted with me on the lines of approach." During the march that night, Lee's dragoons rode ahead of Wayne's two storming columns, simultaneously securing the route of march and preventing anyone from warning Stony Point's defenders. It was a difficult trek. Lee noted that the right column had to cross a "morass up to their knees in mud & water," while the troops on the left moved "thro' the marsh over the relicts of the bridge altho' the passage was very difficult." Lee's infantry under Captain McLane "followed on in the rear of the two columns, as a reserve."[31]

Wayne achieved complete surprise. He had ordered his troops not to load their muskets and instead rely on their bayonets, and shortly after midnight the assault overran the shocked defenders. Sixty-three British soldiers were killed and five hundred captured, along with fifteen pieces of artillery and a large quantity of supplies. The Americans lost fifteen killed and eighty-five wounded, including Wayne, whose skull had been grazed by a musket ball.[32]

Wayne, along with his officers and men, received lavish praise for their victory. Washington extolled their efforts, as did the members of Congress, who awarded Wayne a gold medal. Henry Lee likewise expressed admiration for Wayne's achievement, writing later that the battle was a "shining exploit," where Wayne "received a wound in the head, and exhibited a love of glory far stronger than love of life." The gold medal Wayne received from Congress, Lee declared, was "an honor equal to a Roman triumph."[33]

Amid all the celebration, Lee's name was conspicuously absent when accolades were dispensed. Despite his intelligence gathering that had made the successful attack possible, and his screening of the assaulting columns, his name did not appear in any of the general orders, congressional resolutions, or other reports crediting those who had a hand in Wayne's victory. Some of Wayne's own officers had not been mentioned either, including Lt. Col. Isaac Sherman, who complained of this neglect and earned a sharp rebuff from Wayne. Lee, given his ambition for military success and personal glory, must have been equally disturbed at the slight. However, he remained silent as he had done regarding Charles Lee's treatment after the Battle of Monmouth. He returned to his duties gathering intelligence in New York and New Jersey while contemplating a plan for an operation of his own, one that would eclipse the affair at Stony Point and bring him the glory that he pursued so zealously.[34]

1 Washington to Henry Lee, Feb. 16, 1778 (quotation); Washington to William Smallwood, Feb. 16, 1778 (quotation), Washington Papers, LOC.
2 Washington to Henry Lee, Feb. 21. 1778 (quotation); Washington to Lee, Feb. 25, 1778; Washington to George Reed, Feb. 21, 1778, Washington Papers, LOC.
3 Washington to the Continental Congress, April 3, 1778 (quotation), Washington Papers, LOC; Lee to Washington, March 31, 1778, Washington Papers, University of Virginia (quotation); Cecere, 77.
4 Washington to Lee, April 1, 1778 (quotation), Washington Papers, LOC.
5 Washington to the Conference Committee of the Continental Congress, Jan. 29, 1778, Washington Papers, LOC.
6 Washington to the Continental Congress, April 3, 1778, Washington Papers, LOC.
7 Ford, ed., JCC, April 7, 1778, 10:314-315; Nagel, 161.
8 Washington to Henry Lee, April 12, 1778 (quotation), Washington Papers, LOC; Proceedings of the Board of War, April 27, 1778, in Ford, ed., JCC, 10:401-402 (quotations); JCC, May 28, 1778, 11:545 .
9 Washington to Theodorick Bland, July 3, 1778, Washington Papers, LOC.
10 Don Higginbotham, The War of American Independence: Military Attitudes, Policies, and Practice, 1763-1789 (Boston, MA: Northeastern University Press, 1983), 197, 231-232, 248.
11 Higginbotham, 246.
12 Higginbotham, 247; Washington, General Orders, May 9, 1778, Washington Papers, LOC.
13 Proceedings of a General Court Martial, held at Brunswick, in the State of New Jersey, By the Order of His Excellency Gen. Washington, Commander-in-Chief of the Army of the United States of America, for the Trial of Major-General Lee (New York: J. M. Bradstreet & Sons, 1864), 1 (quotations); Shy, "Charles Lee," in Billias, ed., Washington's Generals and Opponents, 1:45-46.
14 Benjamin Temple to Theodorick Bland, June 29, 1778, in Bland Manuscripts, 1:88; Cecere, 81-82, 84 (quotations).
15 Lee, Memoirs, 115-116.
16 Henry Lee to Nathanael Greene, Feb. 18, 1782, in Dennis M. Conrad, editor, Greene Papers, Vol. 10 (Chapel Hill: University of North Carolina Press, 1998), 378.

17 Washington to Henry Lee, Dec. 14, 1778, Washington Papers, LOC.
18 Washington to Charles Scott, Sept. 15, 1778; Washington to the President of Congress, Oct. 3, 1778, Washington Papers, LOC.
19 Cecere, 91.
20 Chernow, 351; Washington to the Virginia Delegates to the Continental Congress, May 25, 1779, Washington Papers, LOC.
21 Washington to Henry Lee, June 6, 1779 (quotation), and June 9, 1779, Washington Papers, LOC.
22 Washington to Henry Lee, July 9, 1779, Washington Papers, LOC.
23 Nagel, 162 (quotation); Washington to Lee, July 10, 1779 (quotation), Washington Papers, LOC; Charles Royster, *A Revolutionary People at War: The Continental Army and American Character, 1775-1783* (Chapel Hill: University of North Carolina Press, 1979), 81.
24 Nagel, 162-163.
25 Washington to Henry Lee, June 30, 1779, Washington Papers, LOC.
26 Ford, ed., *JCC*, July 13, 1779, 14:822-823; Henry Lee to Joseph Reed, July 18, 1779, in "Letters of General Henry Lee," *Virginia Magazine of History and Biography*, Vol. 6, No. 2 (Oct. 1898), 156 (quotation).
27 Washington to Henry Lee, July 5, 1779 (quotation); Washington to Henry Lee, July 12. 1779 (quotation), Washington Papers, LOC.
28 Washington to the President of Congress, June 6, 1779 (quotation), Washington Papers, LOC; Hugh F. Rankin, "Anthony Wayne: Military Romanticist," in Billias, ed., *Washington's Generals and Opponents*, 1:273.
29 Robert Hanson Harrison to Henry Lee, June 15, 1779 (quotation); Washington to Henry Lee, June 28, 1779 (quotation), Washington Papers, LOC.
30 Chernow, 362; Washington to Anthony Wayne, July 14, 1779 (quotations), Washington Papers, LOC.
31 Henry Lee to Joseph Reed, July 18, 1779, "Letters of Lee," 155.
32 Chernow, 362; Rankin, "Anthony Wayne," in Billias, ed., *Washington's Generals and Opponents*, 1:273-274.
33 Washington to the President of Congress, July 21, 1779, Washington Papers, LOC; Henry Lee, *Memoirs*, 595 (quotation).
34 Rankin, "Anthony Wayne," in Billias, ed., *Washington's Generals and Opponents*, 1:274-275. For Lee's role in intelligence gathering after the Battle of Stony Point, see Washington to Henry Lee, July 25, 26, 29, and Aug. 2, 1779, Washington Papers, LOC.

CHAPTER THREE

THE PAULUS HOOK AFFAIR   *1779*

In 1779 Paulus Hook was a 65-acre expanse of sand hills jutting southeastward from the New Jersey shoreline into the Hudson River opposite Manhattan Island. Surrounded by the river on three sides, Paulus Hook was virtually an island. It was separated from the mainland by a salt marsh and a creek that were completely flooded at high tide. A roadway to the mainland was built atop a causeway, with a wooden bridge spanning the creek below. The causeway connected with the road to Bergen, New Jersey, which in turn was part of the road between New York and Philadelphia. A ferry that had been operating since 1764 linked Paulus Hook with Manhattan, just two thousand yards to the east. The British had occupied Paulus Hook without resistance on September 23rd, 1776, after capturing New York City, and by the summer of 1777 Paulus Hook was the westernmost anchor of a chain of British defenses that extended for over one hundred miles in an arc around Manhattan to Long Island. The approaches to the post were protected by two miles of salt marsh with a flooded ditch and two rows of abatis in front of the fortifications, which consisted of an outer wall, three blockhouses, a small circular redoubt, and a large redoubt that contained the artillery. The garrison troops were quartered in a barracks building and tents, and storage buildings contained supplies and ammunition. The post was manned by a corps of invalids commanded by British Major William Sutherland. It also served as the base for a Loyalist force under the command of Lt. Col. Abraham Van Buskirk of Saddle River, New Jersey. Van Buskirk and his troops launched frequent raids from Paulus Hook into the New Jersey countryside, utilizing their knowledge of the area to avoid detection as they struck American detachments and supply depots. It was this post that Major Henry Lee targeted for attack. The destruction of the British works at Paulus Hook would not only improve the American military situation, but would also bring Lee the laurels he believed he had been unfairly denied for his role at Stony Point.[1]

Lee began planning the attack on Paulus Hook almost immediately after Anthony Wayne's successful attack on Stony Point. Lee's independent command gave him the privilege of communicating directly with General Washington and his staff, and he conferred frequently in person with the commander-in-chief, as he had done during the preparations for the attack on Stony Point. This personal contact helped to protect the secrecy of the planning by minimizing the need for written documents that might fall into the hands of the enemy. Upon receiving Lee's July 28th request to discuss the Paulus Hook operation with the general, Washington's aide Richard Kidder

Aug 17, 1779

Schraalenburgh

Old Bridge

Totowa

Paramus

Departure 4 PM, Aug, 18 NewBridge **Return 1 PM, Aug, 19**

Saddle River

Teaneck   Liberty Pole

Hackensack

Acquackanonk

Old Hackensack

English Neighborhood

Leydecker's Farm Landing

Fort Lee

Fort Washington

Hudson River

Harlem River

Hackensack River

Bourdetts Landing

Second River

New Barbadoes Neck

Secaucus

Bergen Woods

Three Pidgeons

Hudson River

Passaic River

Weehawken

Hoboken

East River

Doww's Ferry

Hoboken Ferry

NEW YORK CITY

Brown's Ferry

Bergen

Prior's Mill

Attack at 4 AM, Aug, 19   Paulus Hook Ferry

NEWARK

n   5 mi   10 mi

The Paulus Hook Raid

Meade summoned Lee to the army's headquarters at West Point to present details of "the scheme you propose."[2]

After considering Lee's idea, Washington authorized him to formulate a specific plan to seize Paulus Hook. Lee worked closely with the commander of his Legion's infantry, Captain Allen McLane, to gather intelligence about the British post and its approaches. During his meeting with Lee, Washington had made several suggestions regarding which routes should be scouted, and Lee relayed that information to McLane. The Delaware captain diligently examined the areas Lee mentioned on August 8th and 9th, and sent Lee a disappointing report. "Find the passes leading through the Mountains from Fort Lee to Bergen to be difficult for foot and impassable for horse," McLane wrote. "The road by way of Van Horn's Mills, likewise difficult for foot and impassable for horse; the marsh near the Mill being miry."[3]

Shrugging off these obstacles, Lee went ahead and presented a plan to Washington. After careful study, the general rejected this initial plan on August 10, telling Lee that

"in the present position of the enemy's army, I should deem the attempt too hazardous and not warranted by the magnitude of the object. We should lose more in case of failure than we could gain in case of success; and a single deserter or disaffected inhabitant may disclose the design and involve the party in ruin."

Nevertheless, Washington remained open to an attack on Paulus Hook, providing that Lee found a better means of carrying it out. The commander-in-chief suggested that Lee consider alternative routes of approach, including by water, and submit a revised plan. However, Washington declared that he would allot no more than three hundred troops to attack Paulus Hook. A larger force would be "too many to expose to any material danger."[4]

Lee quickly devised a new plan for the capture of Paulus Hook that won Washington's approval. The assault force would assemble near New Bridge, march twenty miles to Paulus Hook, attack the post, and escape with their prisoners to Douw's Ferry, where boats would be waiting to transport them across the Hackensack River. Wanting to insure that preparations would not be delayed, Washington informed Major General William Alexander of the operation. Alexander, a New Yorker who insisted that he was heir to a Scottish noble family and therefore styled himself "Lord Stirling," an eccentric affectation for an officer fighting for American independence, commanded the Continental troops in the vicinity of Paulus Hook. On August 12th, Lee personally delivered a letter from Washington to Alexander. "I have had in contemplation an attempt to surprise the enemys Post at Powlus Hook and have employed Major Lee to make the necessary previous inquiries," Washington explained to his subordinate, implying as he did in a September 1st letter to Lee that the idea to strike Paulus Hook may have originated with him rather than Lee. The commander-in-chief told Alexander that Lee had initially proposed to undertake the assault with six hundred men, but that on August 11th Lee had suggested making the attack with four hundred, of which three hundred would "be employed in the attack," the number that Washington had indicated was acceptable to him. "Success must depend on surprise," Washington asserted, and "the troops must be principally furnished from your division" since Lee's Legion lacked sufficient infantry. The commanding general left the final determination regarding the assault to Alexander, instructing him to "consult Major Lee fully and if, upon the whole you deem the undertaking eligible you have my consent to carry it into execution." Washington attached two conditions to his approval: first, that no more than three hundred men make the attack, and second, that "a retreat by Secocus Island be made practicable." Alexander could take any other measures he thought necessary to assist Lee, but absolute secrecy had to be maintained because "the least alarm would probably occasion disappointment and ruin the [assaulting] party."[5]

Despite giving Lee permission to make the attack, Washington harbored concerns that Lee's troops might encounter difficulties. After the operation, when Lee asked the general for a written version of the verbal orders that Washington had originally issued to him, the commander-in-chief provided his recollections of his views at the time:

> *"My principal fear, from the moment I conceived a design against the post, was on account of the difficulty of the retreat, founded on the relative situation of the post to that of the Enemy on York [Manhattan] Island. This circumstance induced me to add, that in case the enterprise should be found eligible ... no time should be lost in case it succeeded, in attempting to bring off Cannon, Stores or any other article, as a few minutes delay might expose the party, at least to imminent risk. ... I likewise said that no time should be spent ... in collecting Stragglers of the Garrison, who might skulk and hide themselves, lest it should prove fatal; also, that if the post could not be carried in an instant by surprise, the attempt must be relinquished. My objects were to surprise it, to bring off the Garrison immediately, and to effect a secure retreat."[6]*

Speed was therefore the essential element in the operation, and since rapid movement had long been a hallmark of Lee and his troops, the young Virginian did not doubt that he could carry out his commander's orders. Lee sent Captain McLane and his infantry ahead on August 17th to scout the projected approach route, gather intelligence, and keep the roads clear for the assault force. McLane was not entirely successful, for on that same day the British intercepted two letters addressed to Lee that contained crucial information regarding the attack. One, written by a militia officer who was then at Newark, reported that he had obtained fifty additional men at Eliza-beth Town and "they will be in readiness & you may rely that if Capt. Pey-ton arrives with the boats in time, they shall be at Douw's ferry at the time appointed." The officer added that American riflemen had captured some of "the Enemy" who "had intelligence that a party of your Dragoons" were in Bergen the previous day. The second letter, from Captain Henry Peyton, assured Lee that "you may rely on the Boats being at the given Point at the wished for Hour," and that he would find sailors to man them. Fortunately for Lee, the letters did not alert the British to his plan, either because they did not reach General Clinton's headquarters in New York in time for the British to decipher their meaning, or they did reach headquarters but British officers failed to realize their significance.[7]

*****

The Attack

On the morning of August 18th, Lee ordered McLane to obtain the lat-est intelligence regarding the British post and secure the approaches. "Take down fifteen good Men including the Riflemen, to proceed by the most secret Route to the Vicinity of Bergen," Lee instructed his Legion's infantry com-mander. McLane was then to contact an American agent named Van Riper, and "engage him to go into the Hook" to learn any news from New York and the position of the British fleet. After dark, McLane was to leave his fif-teen-man patrol "close to the communication leading from Bergen to Prior's Mills," and accompany Van Riper to meet Lee and make a report.[8]

That afternoon, Lee made the final preparations for the attack. His own Legion would not participate in the actual assault. McLane's infantry company would continue to protect the routes used by the storming columns, while the Legion cavalry would act as rear guard because the terrain was unsuitable for the use of mounted troops. The three hundred Virginia and Maryland Continentals who comprised the assault force had been drawn from Colonel Nathaniel Gist's regiment on the orders of General Alexander, and placed under Lee's command. Gist, like Lee, was a Virginian and a longtime associ-ate of George Washington. To conceal the detachment's aggressive intentions, Alexander had also assigned some wagons to it, so that Loyalist spies or Brit-ish patrols that spotted the force might be deceived into believing that it was a foraging party. All of the units rendezvoused at New Bridge, twenty miles from Paulus Hook, where Lee issued his orders.[9]

Lee divided his force into three parts that would commence their march as a single column and then separate as they neared Paulus Hook. The portion on the left had orders to oppose any British force advancing in that vicinity and to cover the withdrawal of the center and right divisions after the operation was completed. The center division was assigned to "guard the passage at Prior's Mill," where there was a bridge. Lee would personally command the right division "to prosecute the object of the expedition." The Legion cavalry, meanwhile, would "assume an intermediate position on the plains of Bergen, from whence they may with ease cooperate as occasion may require." The fields between the town and the mill, in Lee's opinion, rendered any movement by his mounted troops "very convenient." When the right division withdrew after the raid, the unit would fall back to Bergen, with the cavalry and center division moving into position as a rear guard. When the right and center divisions reached safety, the left division would fall back "& in conjunction with the cavalry take measures to secure the retreat of the whole to the road leading to Bulls ferry," where they would link up with a detachment of light infantry that Alexander had posted to meet them. Declaring that he had so much faith in "the gallantry of the officers & men under his command, that he feels exhortation useless," Lee concluded his orders with a reminder that surprise was essential, and a warning that death would be "the immediate fate of any soldier who may violate in the least degree the silence [Lee] has ordered to be observed."[10]

The Americans left New Bridge late in the afternoon on August 18th with Captain Levin Handy's two companies of Maryland Continentals in the lead, following the Bergen road, while patrols of the Legion cavalry were detached to watch the routes leading to the Hudson River. Unknown to Lee, the garrison of Paulus Hook was weaker than usual. Lt. Col. Van Buskirk had set out earlier that day on another foray into New Jersey with 130 of his Loyalist troops "to intercept some parties of rebels who made a practice of interrupting the usual supplies of provision from the country." A detachment of forty Hessian soldiers of the regiment "Prince Hereditaire" under the command of Captain Friedrich von Schellern was sent from New York to replace Van Buskirk's men, but that reinforcement still left Major Sutherland with ninety less men than were normally stationed at Paulus Hook. Altogether, some three hundred British, Hessian, and Loyalist soldiers constituted the garrison that night.[11]

Things began to go wrong almost immediately, and Lee's column experienced delays from the outset. "To render the march as easy as possible," Lee altered his original plan and decided "to pursue the Bergen road lower than intended." When his troops reached the hilly area southeast of Bergen, Lee became lost despite his extensive scouting of the area. He blamed the confusion on "the timidity or treachery of the principal guide." The troops were forced to struggle "through deep mountainous woods, to regain our route," resulting in the anticipated "short march" being extended to a length of three hours. In addition, some of the troops became separated from the main column in the woods which, Lee noted, "not only diminished the number of men destined for the assault, but deprived me of the aid of several officers of distinguished merit."[12]

The delay led to further difficulties. Lee had originally intended to send "eight or ten soldiers disguised as countrymen carrying provisions for sale" to deceive the British sentries into opening the gate of the fort—allowing the attackers to dash through. However, the lateness of the hour made that plan unworkable, since no sentry would believe that farmers would bring goods to the fort in the middle of the night. Furthermore, the tide was rising, necessitating a quick crossing of the rapidly flooding marsh. As Lee assessed the situation, Lieutenant Michael Rudulph of the Legion arrived with some good news. Having been sent ahead to scout the fortifications and the ditch that protected them, Rudulph "reported that all was silenced within the works, that he had fathomed the canal and found the passage on the centre route still admissible." Lee ordered the van of his column to begin crossing the marsh. As the first troops sloshed into the grass-choked water, another officer arrived and informed Lee "that near one half of my countrymen left me." Many of the Virginia officers and enlisted men, already chafing at having been detached from their own units to serve under Lee's command, and further angered by the delay occasioned by the confused march, refused to participate in the operation. This further reduced the strength of Lee's force.[13]

"Not a moment being to spare," as Lee later wrote, the major wasted no time on recriminations or in attempting to adhere to his original plan, which circumstances had rendered "impracticable." Instead, he simply ordered the troops forward from where they were standing in the marching column. Lee later remarked that the Maryland Continentals "stood by me faithfully," and Captain Handy and his troops demonstrated their reliability in the advance through the marsh. "We had a morass to pass of upwards of two miles ... and several canals to ford up to our breast in water," Handy stated. "We advanced with bayonets, pans open, cocks fallen, to prevent any fire from our side" that might alert the British sentries. Lee's efforts enabled his men to make up some of the time lost during the march, although the attack began two hours later than Lee had planned.[14]

At Paulus Hook, Major Sutherland had taken precautions to secure his post against a surprise attack. British commander-in-chief Sir Henry Clinton had long been concerned about the possibility of an attack there; in August

1777, when "a considerable body of rebels" appeared nearby at New Bridge, Clinton had gathered boats and readied two battalions of infantry with artillery to reinforce the garrison. Although the American maneuvers at that time proved to be a feint, Clinton kept a watchful eye on Paulus Hook and Sutherland was equally alert. The garrison had removed the planks from the bridge that formed part of the causeway, and the blockhouse guarding the bridge contained a British officer and eighteen men, with five sentries on watch outside. A second blockhouse to the right (northeast) held a Hessian sergeant and fifteen soldiers, also with five sentries stationed in front. The leftmost Hessian sentry was posted so that he could communicate with the rightmost British sentry. The third blockhouse, to the left (southwest) of the bridge, was manned by a British sergeant and fifteen men, with another five sentries in advanced positions outside. Sutherland had ordered the commanders of the blockhouses to dispatch patrols throughout the night; however, while the Hessians conducted at least one such patrol, no one in the garrison recalled the British troops making any patrols that night. Behind the blockhouses, a British noncommissioned officer and five men occupied a small redoubt, supported by Captain von Schellern and twenty Hessians on a hill to the rear. In case of an attack, von Schellern had instructions to occupy the small redoubt with his troops. The large redoubt, where the artillery was located, was empty save for a single sentry and possibly a few sleeping soldiers. Three of the guns were loaded to be fired if an alarm were sounded. The rest of the garrison lay asleep in the barracks and a few tents, with orders to hasten to the large redoubt if the post came under attack.[15]

The American attacking force was spearheaded by two specially designated assault teams, commanded by lieutenants Archibald McAllister of the Maryland Line and Michael Rudulph of Lee's Legion. These units were designated "forlorn hopes," in the military parlance of the era, because of the high risk they faced. Shortly after 2:30 in the morning on August 19th, they approached the defenses of Paulus Hook.[16]

McAllister's and Rudulph's men moved forward "with trailed arms, in most profound silence," Lee reported. He believed "that the first notice to the [British] garrison was the forlorns plunging into the canal." The defenders, however, learned of the attack in different ways, depending on their position in the line. Private Bahnus Hielholtz, a Hessian advance sentry on guard near the abatis, had been relieved at 11 p.m. and returned to his post at 2:30 a.m. Hielholtz declared that the first warning he had of the American attack "was seeing them approach on my left," when the assaulting troops were already inside the abatis. He neither saw nor heard the British sentry posted to his left. From the blockhouse on the right, Captain von Schellern heard a sentry issue a challenge. No reply came, so the sentry called out a second time for the men in the darkness ahead to identify themselves. He was again met with silence, and fired. Inside the center blockhouse, Private John Rinn of the 5th Garrison Company and his comrades heard the sentry's shot, whereupon "we all run out of the Blockhouse."[17]

The storming parties found their task made easier by what Lt. John Cockburn of the Royal Artillery described as "several openings in the Abbatis, there was a Very Particular large one, upon the Right of the Center Blockhouse," and he believed that was the spot where Lee's troops first entered the post. Alerted by the sentry's warning shot, some of the defenders hastened to their assigned positions. "A firing immediately commenced from the blockhouses and along the line of the abatis, but did not in the least check the advance of the troops," Lee observed. The two assault units, along with other troops commanded by Major Jonathan Clarke who had been on their right, "broke through all opposition, and found an entrance into the main work." The Americans benefited even more from the ill-advised decision of the British troops in the center blockhouse to leave their fortified position. British Private Rinn realized the unidentified troops in front of him were American when he heard one of them reply "Stony Point" in response to another of Lee's troops asking for the countersign. Rinn fled, but the rest of his comrades were killed or captured, leaving the blockhouse undefended.[18]

With the center blockhouse in American hands, Sutherland's defensive plan was entirely disarranged. Lee's troops captured the large redoubt and its artillery before Cockburn's artillerists could fire the signal guns. Loyalist James Addo, a quartermaster sergeant in the 4th Battalion of the New Jersey Volunteers, was sleeping in a tent when he heard the firing. In accordance with Sutherland's orders, he "Repaired to the Grand Redoubt, which I found occupied by Rebels." Rather than risk death or capture, Addo "Ran down along the [river] bank, where I lay concealed till morning." Having planned to occupy the large redoubt with most of his men and fight "to the last extremity" in the event of an attack, Major Sutherland found Lee's troops in possession of his most important fortification, and he had also lost about fifty men who had been bayoneted by the attackers. In addition to the parties under McAllister, Rudulph, and Clarke, other American units under captains Robert Forsyth, Levin Handy, and Lieutenant John Armstrong had entered the fortifications and were attacking the blockhouses and barracks.[19]

The Americans quickly overran most of the post without firing a single musket shot, Lee remarking that "we were completely victorious in the space of a few moments." Lee's officers made certain that none of the troops lost time plundering the abundant quantity of supplies, and instead focused their efforts on rounding up the stunned defenders. Seven officers and 151 enlisted men were taken prisoner. Lee "intended to have burned the barracks, but on finding a number of sick soldiers and women with young children in them, humanity forbade the execution of my intention." Several attempts were made to break into the magazine and destroy the arms and gunpowder it contained, but the American troops were unable either to find a key or to smash through the solid door. Lee ordered the effort abandoned, and after consulting another officer, decided that "it was completely impracticable to bring off any pieces of artillery," or to spike the cannon in the large redoubt.[20]

While Lee's men gathered prisoners and unsuccessfully tried to force the magazine, Major Sutherland and some of the British soldiers who had been in the barracks managed to evade capture and make their way to the small redoubt, where Captain von Schellern had taken his twenty Hessians in accordance with Sutherland's orders. They opened fire on the Americans as Lee prepared to withdraw his troops. Von Schellern estimated that the British and Hessians in the redoubt fired about two hundred shots, although Quartermaster Sergeant Addo believed it was half that number. The defenders' fusillades had little effect on the Americans. "After most of the troops had retired from the works, and were passed and passing the canal, a fire of musketry commenced from a few stragglers, who had collected in an old work, on the right of the main fort," Lee reported. "Their fire being ineffectual, and the object trifling, I determined not to break in upon the order of the retreat" to deal with them. Hoping to sow confusion among the attackers that might give his soldiers an advantage, Sutherland emerged from the redoubt and shouted: "Come my boys we will give them a flogging, the Boats are Coming!" Sutherland's ploy, however, proved ineffective. Lee's men, if they heard him, ignored the cry, and the British and Hessians failed to draw inspiration from Sutherland's words, since they were fully aware that no boats loaded with reinforcements were en route from New York.[21]

*****

The Retreat

Lee knew that if the British in New York learned of the attack, General Clinton might send reinforcements, and if they arrived quickly, they could pose a threat to his force. Lee also had other, more immediate concerns. "The appearance of daylight, my apprehension lest some accident might have befallen the boats, the numerous difficulties of the retreat, the harassed state of the troops, and the destruction of all our ammunition by passing the canal, conspired in influencing me to retire in the moment of victory," he explained. Lee ordered Captain Forsyth to go ahead of the troops to Prior's Mill, "collect such men from the different columns as were most fit for action," and occupy the high ground at Bergen "to cover the retreat." Major Jonathan Clarke led the exodus from Paulus Hook with his column and the majority of the prisoners, followed by Captain Handy's Marylanders with the rest of the captives and then a rear guard under two lieutenants.[22]

The Americans headed for Douw's Ferry, where Captain Henry Peyton was supposed to be waiting for them with the boats. When Lee reached Prior's Mill, however, he learned from an officer he had sent there to coordinate the embarkation with Peyton that a messenger sent to confirm that the boats were in position "had not arrived, nor had [the officer] heard from Captain Peyton." Lee "rode forward to the front," and found Major Clarke with his troops "very near the point of embarkation, and no boats to receive them." Because Lee had arrived much later than planned, Peyton assumed that the attack on Paulus Hook had been postponed and moved the boats away from the ferry. This circumstance forced Lee to alter his plan. "In this very critical situation," he observed, "I lost no time in my decision, but ordered the troops to regain Bergen road and shove on to the New Bridge." After dispatching a courier to General Alexander to inform him of the change of route, Lee returned to his rear guard at Prior's Mill.[23]

The march further strained the stamina of Lee's already exhausted soldiers. He described the difficulties that he and his men faced as they struggled forward in the darkness:

> "Oppressed by every possible misfortune, at the head of troops worn down by a rapid march of thirty miles, through mountains, swamps, and deep morasses, without the least refreshment during the whole march, ammunition destroyed, incumbered with prisoners, and a retreat of fourteen miles to make good, on a route admissible of interception at several points ... under all these distressing circumstances, my sole dependence was in the persevering gallantry of the officers and obstinate courage of the troops. In this I was fully satisfied."[24]

In addition to the difficulties of fatigue and distance, Lee had to remain alert to the possibility of a British or Loyalist attack on his retreating column. Lee was keenly aware that the garrison's survivors might pursue his troops and attack them from the rear, and the British officers captured at Paulus Hook told him that it was likely that the Americans might encounter another enemy force "well advanced on our right." Perhaps the prisoners were referring to Van Buskirk's raiding party, or they may simply have been trying to impede Lee's march by sowing confusion. Not wanting to face a surprise attack when his men could not defend themselves because of their sodden ammunition, Lee divided his column near Weehawken. He sent Captain Handy's Marylanders and their prisoners along the road through the hills, Major Clarke's command on the Bergen road, and a third unit northward along the bank of the Hudson. Just as the troops had set out, Captain Thomas Catlett of the Second Virginia Continental regiment arrived with fifty men whose ammunition was sound. Lee sent part of Catlett's unit to follow the soldiers moving on the riverside route, while Lee and Catlett followed Clarke's center column. Satisfied that his force was now secure from sudden attack, Lee pushed toward the Fort Lee road, and soon encountered more reinforcements commanded by Colonel Henry Ball, who had been "pushed forward" by Alexander to help cover Lee's retreat.[25]

A short time after Lee and Ball joined forces, "a body of the enemy made their appearance, issuing out of the woods on our right, and moving through the fields directly to the road." The attackers consisted of some of Van Buskirk's Loyalists and a few British regulars. "As soon as the noise of the firing reached New York, some troops were thrown into boats as quickly as possible and passed across the river," Clinton noted. After reaching the west bank of the Hudson, these reinforcements set off in pursuit of Lee. They met some of Van Buskirk's men along the way, and caught up with the rear of one of Lee's columns near Liberty Pole Tavern. The British and Loyalists opened fire on the Americans. In response an American officer led several of his men "into a stone house which commanded the road." When the assailants saw Lee's troops take that position, "they immediately retired by the same route they had approached, and gained the woods," having succeeded in capturing three of Lee's men.[26]

At about one o'clock on the afternoon of August 19th, Lee and his troops arrived at New Bridge, along with Catlett's and Ball's parties. The prisoners were sent under guard to Philadelphia while the soldiers finally enjoyed a brief period of rest. Lee's men exulted in their victory. In a span of less than twenty-four hours they had marched over forty miles through difficult terrain, surprised an important British post, and killed or captured more than two-thirds of its garrison. Captain Levin Handy remarked that the feat "is thought to be the greatest enterprise in America." Lee originally estimated American casualties at no more than twenty killed, wounded, and missing. As the last stragglers rejoined their commander, a more accurate count revealed that only two Americans had been killed in the operation, another three wounded, and three captured. Given the success of his attack, Lee considered his losses "very trifling."[27]

Lee effusively praised his officers and men for their efforts. "The whole of the officers behaved with the greatest propriety," he informed General Washington, taking care to mention each officer by name, so that none would be overlooked as he and others felt had been done in the official reports of the assault on Stony Point. "My endeavours were fully seconded by every officer in his station. ... The troops vied with each other in patience under their many sufferings, and conducted themselves in every vicissitude of fortune with a resolution which reflects the highest honour on them."[28]

Lee had achieved his own equivalent of Anthony Wayne's triumph at Stony Point. As the commander of the operation against Paulus Hook, Lee felt certain that most of the victory laurels would be awarded to him.

*****

The British Response

Still angry over the American victory at Stony Point, General Clinton was stung by the news of Lee's raid on Paulus Hook. "I own I was not very well pleased at this affront, happening so recently after the one at Stony Point," Clinton confessed. He immediately ordered a court of inquiry to convene at Paulus Hook, as he suspected that Lee's successful surprise attack "had arisen from some relaxation of discipline" in the garrison. On August 20th the court, consisting of two brigadier generals and three lieutenant colonels, made a preliminary investigation and concluded

> *"that the Causes proceed from a general misconduct in the Commandant, a totall neglect of Duty in the Garrison, And the particular shameful misbehaviour of the Artillery in the Fort, and the Guards in the Blockhouses appointed for the defence of the works that night; The Officers & Hessians excepted, that threw themselves into, and defended the circular Redoubt."*

The officers recommended that Sutherland be tried by court martial.[29]

The initial inquiry may have blamed Major Sutherland and the Paulus Hook garrison for the disaster, but as the army's commanding general, "Clinton bore the brunt of criticism." Lieutenant Colonel Charles Stuart, one of Clinton's confidants, noted that "this affair treading upon the heels of the former contretemps [Stony Point], served to inspirit the rebels and gave a degree of venom to the General's enemies. I pitied and felt for him, and indeed he was tremendously depressed; and I am afraid his temper from these two unlucky blows of fortune became much soured."[30]

While awaiting Sutherland's trial by court martial, the British attempted to downplay the effects of Lee's raid. An unidentified Loyalist published an account of the attack in the *New York Gazette and Mercury* on August 23rd that portrayed the Americans as bunglers. Admitting that Lee's troops succeeded in capturing most of the defensive works because "the block house guards … in place of defending their post, ran out to see what was the matter," the Loyalist writer went on to describe the attackers as "so confused and alarmed, [that] they neither spiked the cannon nor damaged the barracks. …

The panic amongst them was occasioned by an incessant fire kept on them from a small redoubt into which Major Sutherland threw himself with a captain subaltern and 25 gallant Hessians." The account also exaggerated Lee's strength, stating that the attackers numbered four hundred, and minimized British losses, giving a figure of "about 100 prisoners."[31]

Clinton similarly tried to minimize the importance of the raid on Paulus Hook in his report to his superiors in London. The Americans, Clinton explained, "found the Garrison so scandalously absorbed in confidence of their Security," that Lee's men occupied most of the post "with scarcely any difficulty." Clinton asserted that the defenders' fire "forced the Enemy to quit the Post without either damaging any of the Cannon, or setting fire to the Barracks. In short their retreat was as disgraceful as their attempt was well conducted." Clinton admitted to the loss of only "near Forty Invalids prisoners." However, he remarked that "I cannot as yet decide upon this affair," and added that he had ordered Sutherland "to be tried on a charge of general misconduct."[32]

Sutherland's trial began on August 25th and concluded on the twenty-seventh. Lieutenant Colonel Andrew Bruce of the 54th Regiment of Foot presided over a board of twelve officers that tried Sutherland. Detailed testimony was provided by Captain von Schellern, Major Sutherland, and several other officers and enlisted men. The witnesses agreed that if the guards assigned to the center blockhouse had remained inside and resisted the Americans, instead of emerging where they were easily killed or captured, the garrison would have had adequate time to put Sutherland's defensive plan into effect, and the post would have been held. Therefore the court found Sutherland not guilty of the charge of misconduct, and acquitted him with honor. Clinton professed himself satisfied with the decision. In early September, one soldier of the Paulus Hook garrison was also tried by court martial. Sergeant John Taswell of the 4th Battalion of the New Jersey Volunteers was found guilty of "quitting his post at the Left Hand Block House at Paulus Hook in a shameful and scandalous manner." The court sentenced Taswell to be hanged, but Clinton pardoned him "in Consideration of his former Good Character" and discharged him from the British army. The execution of Taswell would only have called further attention to the Paulus Hook affair and Clinton was eager to put the matter behind him.[33]

*****

The American Reaction

Lee, recovering from the arduous raid, did not immediately report the results to George Washington, but he did relate the details of the operation to General Alexander, who in turn informed Washington on August 19th. The commander-in-chief welcomed the news "of Major Lee's having succeeded against Powles Hook." Washington congratulated Lee for his efforts and thanked Alexander for the assistance that he had provided. He asked Alexander to express his gratitude to "the officers and troops concerned in the capture of Powles Hook for their good conduct and gallant behaviour." Washington declared that Lee's victory would increase the morale of the Continental Army, but at the same time warned Alexander to be wary of a British counterstroke. "As the enemy must feel disgraced … he may endeavour to lessen it by a retaliation in kind," Washington observed, unaware that General Clinton was so angry over the surprise attack that his focus was on fixing blame rather than striking back.[34]

On August 22, Washington announced the victory to his troops in general orders: *The General has the pleasure to inform the army that on the night of the 18th instant, Major Lee at the head of a party composed of his own Corps and detachments from the Virg'nia and Maryland lines, surprized the Garrison of Powles Hook and brought off a considerable number of Prisoners with very little loss on our side. The Enterprise was executed with a distinguished degree of Address, Activity and Bravery and does great honor to Major Lee and to all the officers and men under his command, who are requested to accept the General's warmest thanks.*[35]

The next day, Washington forwarded Lee's report to Congress, along with a letter of his own praising his subordinate. "The Major displayed a remarkable degree of prudence address enterprise and bravery upon this occasion, which does the highest honor to himself and to all the officers and men under his command," Washington told the delegates. "The situation of the Post rendered the attempt critical and the success brilliant." Washington also sent Congress the garrison's flag, which Lee's troops had captured during the attack. North Carolina congressman William Sharpe reported the arrival of the British flag in Philadelphia, and told fellow North Carolinian Thomas Burke of his pleasure in learning of "the success of Major Lee against Powles hook. The very difficult approaches, and the very dangerous retreat, makes it if possible a more brilliant affair than that of Stoney point."[36]

In his private correspondence, Washington expressed similar happiness at the results of the raid.

"We have given the enemy another little Stroke in the Surprise of Powles-hook (within Cannon shot of N: York) and bringing off 7

Officers and 151 Non-Commd. Officers and privates," Washington
wrote to John Parke Custis. *"This was a brilliant transaction and
performed by a detacht. of Virginians and Marylanders under the
Comd. of Majr. Lee of the light Horse with the loss of not more than
ten or a dozen men."*[37]

*****

If George Washington, General Alexander, members of Congress, and the
Continental Army's rank-and-file celebrated Lee's success at Paulus Hook,
some of the officers were far less jubilant. The thirst for personal glory, desire
for promotion, and accompanying jealousy that had long plagued the officer
corps, and to which Lee had already been subjected, began increasing from
their usual simmer to a boil even before Washington issued his congratulatory
general orders on August 22nd. Brigadier General Anthony Wayne, aware
of the envious anger aroused by his triumph at Stony Point, warned Lee on
August 24th to be wary of the resentment of other officers. "Be well guarded
my friend," Wayne advised, "there are not a few, who would not feel much
pain on a small Disaster happening to either you or me."[38]

Resentment surfaced as soon as Lee and his troops returned from Paulus
Hook. Colonel Nathaniel Gist protested to Alexander about having troops
detached from his command and placed under Lee for the operation. Upset
by what he considered an unjustified complaint, Alexander told the Virginian on August 20th, the day after the raid, that he had "felt the greatest pain
and distress of the Virginia Line within these two days at my having put a
detachment of troops of that Line under the command of Major Lee for the
reduction of the garrison at Powles Hook." Alexander asked Gist and his
officers "candidly dispassionately & explicitly to point out in writing to me
what is the injury you conceive I have done you." Then, Alexander pledged,
he would "be able to render you with the satisfaction in my power."[39]

Gist shared Alexander's letter with the other officers, and on August 21st
they submitted a lengthy reply that specified five points that had caused their
dissatisfaction. The first "injury," as they termed it, was the two Virginia brigadier generals were not included in planning or executing the raid on Paulus
Hook. The second grievance was Alexander's detaching four hundred men
for the operation, of which three hundred under Major Clarke were then sent
"with a view and for the express purpose of putting them under the command
of Major Lee" while higher ranking officers were left with only the remaining
hundred men; that is, an officer junior in rank had charge of a larger force
than that of his superiors. Next, the officers complained that Alexander had
not remedied this problem when they had informed him of it before the
troops began their march to Paulus Hook. The fourth point was related and

specifically raised the issue of Lee's rank as well as his qualifications. Alexander had acted with impropriety "in ordering Major Clark under the command of Major Lee, who was a junior officer, no way connected and truly unacquainted with the discipline of infantry by which every military principle was subverted, by establishing as a precedent that a senior officer may at the pleasure of a Commander in Chief be placed under his junior." Finally, the officers accused Lee of lying to Clarke, alleging that Clarke asked Lee "for the date of his commission" as major, and that Lee had replied 1777, making him appear senior to Clark when in fact Lee had been promoted to major in 1778 and therefore should have been subordinate to Clarke. In a long concluding paragraph, the Virginians criticized Lee further, pointing out again that since he was not an infantry officer, Lee should not have commanded foot soldiers. That Lee was "an officer of dragoons ... renders the injury more pointed and strikes deep at the reputation of every officer of infantry," they asserted.[40]

Alexander's reply attempted to assuage the feelings of the officers while justifying the actions he had taken. "The Enterprise against Powles Hook was not originally planned here," he reminded them. "It was communicated to me from Head Quarters with an injunction of absolute secrecy and the number of troops to be employed in the attack pointed out." Alexander admitted that he had revised the plan in order to give the assault force "the appearance of a large foraging party." Any offense to the brigadier generals, he declared, arose from the orders for secrecy and did not reflect a lack of confidence in them. Regarding the second and third complaints, Alexander explained the necessity of providing the required number of troops for the operation. As to the fourth complaint regarding Major Clarke's seniority over Lee, Alexander stated that when he ordered Clarke to serve under Lee, "I understood the former was junior to the latter," and did not learn that Lee was the junior officer until after the operation, whereupon "I took the earliest opportunity ... to apologize to Major Clark." The last point in the list of grievances was irrelevant, Alexander wrote, since it "contains matters that must have happened out of my knowledge and therefore [I] cannot be answerable for this." Alexander concluded by justifying Lee's selection as commander of the assault force:

> *"Major Lee had this enterprise in contemplation for some time before it was communicated to me he had gained perfect knowledge of the country, of all the paths leading to the works, of the situation & shape of all the different forts, redoubts & block houses. ... These things he communicated to his Excy. General Washington and the enterprise was recommended to me in such a manner that I could not avoid leaving the conduct of the attack to Major Lee."*[41]

Because Washington had issued the orders for the attack on Paulus Hook, Alexander dutifully forwarded copies of the Virginia officers' letter of complaint and his reply to the commander-in-chief. Washington was taken aback, telling Alexander that the officers' protests "are to me as painful as they were unexpected." He assured Alexander that his reply had been appropriate and defended his choice of Lee to command the operation. "The only point I shall take notice of is the giving the command to Major Lee," Washington wrote. "This could be exceptionable but on three principles, his being a horse officer, his being unconnected with the division from which the greatest part of the detachment was drawn, or the number of men employed, being too large for his rank." The first, Washington declared, had no foundation, since infantry and cavalry operated upon the same general principles. Besides, "the nature of Major Lee's corps being of the Legionary and partisan kind and consisting both of horse and infantry gave him an additional right to a command of this sort." The second objection "can have no weight," Washington continued, as "circumstances alone must determine" who would command a particular force in a specific operation, and "in this instance [circumstances] were in favour of Major Lee." Washington also dismissed the third possible basis for the officers' complaint, noting that it was not unusual, in either the American or British armies, for a major to command a force of five hundred men. Lee "executed the trust with great address intelligence and industry." Lee was thoroughly acquainted with the defenses at Paulus Hook, and "after having taken so much pains personally" to prepare for the attack, "it would have been a piece of hardship, if not injustice to him to have given the honor of the execution to another." Washington expressed his confidence that "the Gentlemen who have complained on more cool reflection will be satisfied that they have not been injured ... and that the giving the command to Major Lee was agreeable to the strictest military propriety." The general intended this final admonition to reach the protesting officers, as he instructed Alexander that the letter was "to be communicated to the Gentlemen of your division."[42]

Learning of the complaints being made against him, Lee seethed with rage. Instead of applauding him for his success, envious fellow officers sought to tear the hard-won laurels from his head. Lee refused to tolerate such carping. "I never conceived myself so important, in the army, as I find I am," Lee informed his friend Joseph Reed of Pennsylvania in a tone dripping with sarcasm.

> *"Captains & Lets. [lieutenants] used to pick me, Generals & Colo.s are now barking at me with open mouths. Colonel Gist of Virginia ... has formed a cabal. I mean to make the matter very serious; because a full explanation will recoil on my foes & give new lustre to the enter-*

prize." Lee noted that "*brave & generous officers*" *such as generals Anthony Wayne and Nathanael Greene had congratulated him and "support me warmly.*" Lee added that in his public letter he had generously praised everyone who had served under him in the Paulus Hook operation, but that in fact "*near one half of my countrymen left me.*" He implied that he would reveal this information if necessary to discredit his critics. "*I am determined to push Col. Gist & [his] party,*" Lee declared.[43]

*****

Court Martial

Gist and his supporters acted before Lee did. Washington's and Alexander's explanations failed to mollify them, so they filed formal charges against Lee and had him arrested pending his trial by court martial. The first count with which Lee was charged was "for withholding a letter" addressed to Gist that Lee had received from Alexander on August 16th, "by that means keeping [Gist] ignorant of a matter which required his immediate information." The second charge was that Lee had lied about the date of his commission as major to Major Clarke, "thereby assuming command" of Clarke and his three hundred men when Clarke, as the ranking officer, should have commanded the attacking force. Next, the officers accused Lee of mismanagement while in command during the march to Paulus Hook, resulting in "so much disorder and confusion as to cause almost the whole of the 1st battalion under his immediate command to be lost." Fourth, Lee was charged with placing one of Gist's captains under the command of a Legion captain who was junior in rank. Fifth, Lee had allegedly rejected the request of some officers that the selection of a commander for one of the "forlorn hopes" be done by vote, and instead Lee had made his own choice of commander. The sixth charge was that Lee had withdrawn from Paulus Hook "before a party of the enemy in a redoubt had been made prisoners, which might easily have been effected and was solicited by many of the officers," and also "suffering the Stores, Block Houses and Works to remain entire when they might easily have been destroyed." This accusation was similar to the claims of the British and Loyalists who had tried to mitigate the importance of Lee's raid. Echoing the third charge, and ignoring the fact that Lee did successfully fend off an enemy force during his retreat, the seventh count accused Lee of "bringing off the party in such a confused, irregular and unmilitary manner that they might have fallen an easy prey to a very inconsiderable number of the enemy, had they attempted to have intercepted them." The final charge against Lee was "for behaving in a manner unbecoming an officer and a Gentleman."[44]

Lee, shocked and infuriated at the hostility of his fellow officers, prepared to defend himself vigorously. He solicited information from both Alexander and Washington that would help him refute the charges. "The vindictive nature of a few obliges me in my own defence to request your Lordship will be pleased to state the nature of the two ltrs received from your Lordship at Paramus on the 18th," Lee explained to Alexander. Lee asked Washington to provide him with a written version of the verbal orders that the commander-in-chief had given him for the Paulus Hook operation, which Washington provided on September 1st. While awaiting this material from his superiors, Lee composed the testimony he would give in his own defense.[45]

The court convened on September 2nd to hear testimony from Lee's accusers and from Lee himself. After the charges had been presented with supporting statements, Lee testified eloquently in his own behalf, his words ringing with the indignation he felt at what he believed was a great injustice:

> *"It is something new and unheard of till this day for an American officer to be arraigned for a successful enterprise. What are or may be the motives that produced the arrest I will not undertake to explain. … The Gentleman who heads the prosecution has conducted himself during the trial with candour and civility—I lament from my heart that an aged and meritorious officer should have committed himself so hastily into an act of so much consequence. He has I am persuaded done it from the best of principles—he has done it because he conceived it his duty. … How these gentlemen who caused and urged the prosecution can reconcile their conduct to the principles of virtue, justice and soldiership. Men who possess neither candor nor courage sufficient to act for themselves, but who have basely pushed forward a friend under the perversion of justice to injure character disgustful to them only from its fairness. I view such groveling beings with sovereign contempt."*[46]

Lee then introduced the evidence he had gathered, consisting of letters, orders, and reports concerning the attack on Paulus Hook. He ended his statement by declaring to the court that "my reputation is dearer to me than life. … If any part of my accusation is supported by truth, punish me with severity—If on the other hand the charges should appear malicious, groundless, and vexatious, I make no doubt but you will tell the world so, and that you will give full reparation to an injured character." Lee expressed his hope that his exoneration would "deter the envious from sporting with the reputation of their superiors." Given that many of his accusers were of higher rank, Lee clearly implied that his superiority was of a moral nature, rather than a matter of military rank.[47]

Despite the confidence he professed in his statement, Lee was filled with apprehension as he awaited the court's verdict. As he had told Joseph Reed on August 27th, he was convinced a web of conspirators surrounded him, lusting for his downfall. He had also informed Reed that he hoped "Congress will do me the justice to publish" the report on Paulus Hook that he had sent to Washington, and which the commander-in-chief had forwarded to Congress. Now Lee began to believe that if Congress published his report, it might lead to his public vindication regardless of the court's decision. Lee also worried that unknown enemies in Congress could be deliberately delaying the publication of his report. He therefore asked Washington for permission to write to Congress and request that the delegates publish the document. Washington rejected the request and counseled patience. It was not proper for the general to tell Congress how to proceed, Washington replied, and in any case, "I am firmly persuaded the event will shew you they cannot possibly intend you injustice. I should be sorry you would suffer your sensibility to betray you into an error which on reflexion you would condemn."[48]

When a week had passed without a verdict, Lee grew increasingly jittery over the outcome of his trial. He wrote to his friend on Washington's staff, Lt. Col. Alexander Hamilton, and asked Hamilton to send him additional documents related to the Paulus Hook raid. "The emmissarys from the Virginia party have been industrious to injure my military character," he told Hamilton in explaining his request.[49]

On September 11th the court finally reached a verdict and reported its decision to General Washington, who announced it in general orders the same day. The verdict completely exonerated Lee. The first charge was dismissed as "groundless." Regarding the second count, the court found that Lee's having given Major Clarke "a wrong date of his commission" was the result of "inattention" on Lee's part, but the matter was irrelevant because Washington had given Lee command of the expedition. The court conceded that "there were some disorders in the line of march to Powles Hook" that caused some of the troops to become separated from the main force as charged in the third count; however, the court attributed these to darkness and the terrain and concluded that Lee was not to blame. The fourth and fifth accusations regarding Lee's assignment of officers were dismissed as consequences of the circumstances that Lee faced at the time, while the sixth charge was also without foundation since Lee had "acted in perfect conformity to the orders of His Excellency the Commander in Chief," and the threat of being intercepted during the retreat further justified the rapid withdrawal. Lee was likewise acquitted of the seventh charge, the court finding that "perfect military order was preserved in the retreat ... where Major Lee commanded," and that Lee had successfully thwarted the British effort to intercept his troops. The eighth count of conduct unbecoming an officer was declared unfounded, the court determining that "Major Lee's conduct was uniform and regular, supporting his military character with magnanimity and judgment." Washington confirmed the court's decision of acquittal with honor on all charges, and ordered that Lee be released from arrest.[50]

Lee exulted in the court's decision, as his friend Hamilton knew that he would. "If I did not think your vanity would be intolerable at the manner of your acquittal, I should congratulate you upon it," Hamilton wryly told Lee on September 13. Two days earlier, in a letter to another of Washington's staff officers, John Laurens, Hamilton had privately shared his high opinion of Lee along with his concern that the Legion commander's inflated ego might undermine his effectiveness. "The Philadelphia papers will tell you of a handsome stroke by Lee on Powles Hook," Hamilton wrote. "Some folks in the Virginia line jealous of his glory had the folly to get him arrested. He has been tried and acquitted with the highest honor. Lee unfolds himself more and more to be an officer of great capacity, and if he had not a little spice of the Julius Caesar or Cromwell in him, he would be a very clever fellow."[51]

With Lee cleared of the charges against him, Congress added its official opinion of Lee's conduct during the Paulus Hook operation in a series of resolutions passed on September 24th. After thanking Washington and General Alexander for their contributions to the effort, the delegates voted that "the thanks of Congress be given to Major Lee, for the remarkable prudence, address and bravery displayed by him on the occasion." Congress commended the officers and men who participated in the attack, awarded a payment of $15,000, along with an additional bounty for each British prisoner taken, with instructions that Lee distribute the money among the troops according to Washington's directions, gave Lee a brevet (honorary) promotion to the rank of lieutenant colonel, and finally, "Resolved, That a medal of gold, emblematic of this affair, be struck ... and presented to Major Lee."[52]

Lee at last had the "Roman triumph" he had sought, although the effects of his victory were limited. The British retained control of Paulus Hook and would do so until the end of the war. Washington, in an August 21st letter to Joseph Reed, characterized Lee's raid as having "given the enemy another little touch," hardly the description of a decisive battle. As Washington explained to General Alexander, the operation derived its importance primarily from the boost it provided to American morale and its corresponding dampening of British spirits. Lee's gold medal was the only one that the Continental Congress awarded to an individual who was not a general, and the Paulus Hook raid, while daring, hardly seemed worthy of such an honor. Perhaps factors such as Lee's friendship with Washington, the presence of two members of the Lee family in Congress, and a burst of public enthusiasm over the victories at Stony Point and Paulus Hook contributed to this unusual act by Congress. Wayne's and Lee's achievements stood in stark contrast to what had otherwise been a year of stalemate in the northern theater and to several recent American defeats in the South. American leaders were understandably seeking news that would sustain morale and support for their cause.[53]

Perhaps Lee realized that the honors he had received were not entirely justified by his accomplishments. Historian Paul C. Nagel noted that despite his exoneration by the court martial, Lee's "pride and confidence never recovered" from the traumatic experience of his arrest and trial. "Thereafter," Nagel observed, "his rage fed on the realization that others doubted his judgment, accomplishment, and character." Nevertheless, Lee retained the confidence of the commander-in-chief and other high-ranking officers. The Marquis de Lafayette assured Lee that "the more I have considered the situation of Paulus Hook, the more I have admired your enterprising spirit and all your conduct in that business." Lee's gold medal was proof that he also had the trust of Congress. Yet neither his acquittal, nor the trust of his superiors, nor the glittering medal, put an end to the envy and resentment of Lee's fellow officers. Until the end of the war Lee remained alert to every slight, actual or perceived, ever ready to find offense even where none was intended.[54]

---

1   Craig L. Symonds, *A Battlefield Atlas of the American Revolution* (Baltimore, MD: Nautical & Aviation Publishing, 1986), 69; Henry Clinton, *The American Rebellion: Sir Henry Clinton's Narrative of His Campaigns, 1775-1782, with an Appendix of Original Documents*, William B. Willcox, editor (New Haven, CT: Yale University Press, 1954), 47, 63, 189; George H. Farrier, *Memorial of the Celebration of the Battle of Paulus Hook, August 19th 1779* (Jersey City, NJ: M. Mullone, 1879), 16, 21, 24; Lee, *Memoirs*, 22. An abatis was an entanglement of felled trees, with their branches pointed toward the enemy to delay or obstruct an attacking force. Sometimes the branches were sharpened to make the obstacle more effective. Paulus Hook is now the site of Jersey City.
2   Richard Kidder Meade to Henry Lee, July 28, 1779, Washington Papers, LOC.
3   Farrier, 25, 27.
4   Washington to Henry Lee, Aug. 10, 1779, Washington Papers, LOC.
5   Washington to Henry Lee, Aug. 12, 1779; Washington to William Alexander, Aug. 12, 1779 (quotations), Washington Papers, LOC. The name "Paulus" Hook was spelled in a variety of ways at the time, including "Powlus,", "Powls," "Powell's" and others.
6   Washington to Henry Lee, Sept. 1, 1779, Washington Papers, LOC.
7   Allen McLane, Journal, Aug. 17, 1779, in Henry Steele Commager and Richard B. Morris, editors, *The Spirit of Seventy-Six: The Story of the American Revolution as Told by Its Participants* (New York: Harper & Row, 1967), 726; J. Burnet to Henry Lee, Aug. 17, 1779 (quotation), and Henry Peyton to Henry Lee, Aug. 17, 1779 (quotation), intercepted letters in the Henry Clinton Papers, Vol. 66, William L. Clements Library, Ann Arbor, MI.
8   Farrier, 27.
9   Wright, 100-101, 321; William Alexander to the Officers of the Virginia Line, Aug. 1779, William Alexander (Lord Stirling) Papers, New-York Historical Society, New York City.
10 Lee, Paulus Hook Attack Order, copy dated Oct. 6, 1780, Lee Family Papers, Virginia Historical Society, Richmond (hereafter VHS).
11 Levin Handy to George Handy, Aug. 22, 1779, in Commager and Morris, 726-727; Farrier, 24-25; Clinton, *American Rebellion*, 139 (quotation); Henry Lee to George Washington, Aug. 22, 1779, http://

secondvirginia.wordpress.com/2010/08/19/battle-of-paulus-hook/, accessed Jan. 16, 2012. Handy stated that the Americans began their march at 5 p.m., while Lee reported that it began an hour earlier.
12 Lee to Washington, Aug. 22, 1779.
13 Henry Lee, *Memoirs*, 23 (quotation); Lee to Washington, Aug. 22, 1779 (quotation); Lee to Joseph Reed, Aug. 27, 1779, Lee Family Papers, VHS (quotation).
14 Lee to Washington, Aug. 22, 1779 (quotations); Lee to Reed, Aug. 27, 1779 (quotation), Lee Family Papers, VHS; Levin Handy to George Handy, Aug. 22, 1779, in Commager and Morris, 726-727 (quotation).
15 Clinton, *American Rebellion*, 67-68 (quotation); "Proceedings of a General Court Martial held at New York in the Province of New York, the 25th August and Continued by Adjournments to the 27th August 1779, by Virtue of a Warrant from His Excellency Sir Henry Clinton, K.B. Commander in Chief," Sir Henry Clinton Papers, Vol. 66, William L. Clements Library, Ann Arbor, MI (hereafter WCL).
16 Lee to Washington, Aug. 22, 1779; "Proceedings of a General Court Martial," Clinton Papers, WCL.
17 Lee to Washington, Aug. 22, 1779 (quotations); "Proceedings of a General Court Martial," Clinton Papers, WCL (quotations).
18 Lee to Washington, Aug. 22, 1779 (quotations); "Proceedings of a General Court Martial," Clinton Papers, WCL.
19 Lee to Washington, Aug. 22, 1779; "Proceedings of a General Court Martial," Clinton Papers, WCL (quotations); Levin Handy to George Handy, Aug. 22, 1779, in Commager and Morris, 726-727.
20 Lee to Washington, Aug. 22, 1779 (quotations); Levin Handy to George Handy, Aug. 22, 1779, in Commager and Morris, 726-727; Washington to John Parke Custis, Aug. 24, 1779, Washington Papers, LOC.
21 Lee to Washington, Aug. 22, 1779 (quotation); "Proceedings of a General Court Martial," Clinton Papers, WCL (quotation); Farrier, 32.
22 Lee to Washington, Aug. 22, 1779.
23 Lee to Washington, Aug. 22, 1779.
24 Lee to Washington, Aug. 22, 1779.
25 Lee to Washington, Aug. 22, 1779.
26 Lee to Washington, Aug. 22, 1779 (quotation); Clinton, *American Rebellion*, 139 (quotation).
27 Farrier, 35-36; Levin Handy to George Handy, Aug. 22, 1779, in Commager and Morris, 726-727 (quotation); Lee to Washington, Aug. 22, 1779 (quotation).
28 Lee to Washington, Aug. 22, 1779.
29 Clinton, *American Rebellion*, 139 (quotations); "Proceedings of a Court of Inquiry held at Paulus Hook 20th. August 1779 by order of the Commander in Chief to inquire into the Causes of the affront suffered from the Enemy on the Morning of the 19th instant," Clinton Papers, Vol. 66, WCL (quotation).
30 William B. Willcox, *Portrait of a General: Sir Henry Clinton in the War of Independence* (New York: Alfred A. Knopf, 1964), 279.
31 *New York Gazette and Mercury*, Aug. 23, 1779, in Commager and Morris, 727.
32 Farrier, 35-36.
33 "Proceedings of a General Court Martial," Clinton Papers, Vol. 66, WCL; Clinton, *American Rebellion*, 139; Farrier, 57-58 (quotations).
34 Washington to William Alexander, Aug. 21, 1779, Washington Papers, LOC.
35 George Washington, General Orders, Aug. 22, 1779, Washington Papers, LOC.
36 Washington to the Continental Congress, Aug. 23, 1779, Washington Papers, LOC (quotation); William Sharpe to Thomas Burke, Aug. 30, 1779, Thomas Burke Papers, North Carolina State Archives, Raleigh (quotation).
37 Washington to John Parke Custis, Aug. 24, 1779, Washington Papers, LOC.
38 Royster, *Light-Horse Harry Lee*, 40.
39 William Alexander to Nathaniel Gist, Aug. 20, 1779, Stirling Papers, NYHS.
40 William Woodford and ten other officers of the Virginia Line to William Alexander, Aug. 21, 1779, Stirling Papers, NYHS.
41 William Alexander to the Gentlemen of the Virginia Line, Aug. 24, 1779, Stirling Papers, NYHS.
42 Washington to William Alexander, Aug. 28, 1779, Washington Papers, LOC.
43 Henry Lee to Joseph Reed, Aug. 27, 1779, Lee Family Papers, VHS.
44 Washington, General Orders, Sept. 11, 1779, Washington Papers, LOC.
45 Henry Lee to William Alexander, Aug. 1779, Stirling Papers, NYHS (quotation); Washington to Lee, Sept. 1, 1779, Washington Papers, LOC; "Major Lee's Defense," Aug. 1779, Stirling Papers, NYHS.
46 "Lee's Defense," Aug. 1779, Stirling Papers, NYHS.
47 "Major Lee's Defense," Aug. 1779, Stirling Papers, NYHS.

48 Lee to Joseph Reed, Aug. 27, 1779, Lee Family Papers, VHS (quotation); Washington to Lee, Sept. 3, 1779, Washington Papers, LOC (quotation).
49 Lee to Alexander Hamilton, Sept. 10, 1779, in Harold C. Syrett, editor, *The Papers of Alexander Hamilton*, Vol. 2 (New York: Columbia University Press, 1961), 164.
50 Washington, General Orders, Sept. 11, 1779, Washington Papers, LOC.
51 Hamilton to Lee, Sept. 13, 1779, in Syrett, ed., *Papers of Hamilton*, 2:117 (quotation); Hamilton to John Laurens, Sept. 11, 1779, in ibid., 2:168 (quotation).
52 Journals of the Continental Congress, Sept. 24, 1779, LOC.
53 Washington to Joseph Reed, Aug. 22, 1779 (quotation); Washington to Alexander, Aug. 21, 1779, Washington Papers, LOC.
54 Nagel, 162 (quotation); Royster, *Light-Horse Harry Lee*, 27 (quotation).

George Washington's remarkable leadership was again evident when devising a winning strategy for the Southern campaign. His insightful choice of officers for the mission and his unwavering support for their efforts led to an improbable victory in a little more than a year.

Courtesy of Independence National Historical Park.

Nathanael Greene was Washington's choice to succeed Gates. His adroit application of Washington's instructions led to the ultimate defeat of General Cornwallis at Yorktown.

Courtesy of the National Park Service.

Thomas Sumter, a general and skillful leader of South Carolina Militia, was nicknamed the "Carolina Gamecock". He was an aggressive but fiercely autonomous leader, who was often unwilling to cooperate with continental commanders such as generals Daniel Morgan and Nathanael Greene.

Painting by Rembrandt Peale. Courtesy of the U.S. Army.

Francis Marion was both a Colonel in the Continental Army and also a General in the South Carolina Militia. Nationally renowned for his guerilla tactics, he attacked the British army's supply lines during the Revolutionary War when few other leaders were still active in the field. He was widely known as the "Swamp Fox".

Painting by John Blake White of South Carolina

Andrew Pickens, a South Carolina Militia General, was known to the Cherokee tribes in western South Carolina as the "Wizard Owl" for his military prowess. He served the Patriots' cause in the Carolinas earning the praise and admiration of General Greene. He operated effectively throughout the war, teaming up with Daniel Morgan at the Battle of Cowpens, Francis Marion, Thomas Sumter, Henry Lee, and other leaders as the need arose.

Courtesy of Fort Hill in Clemson, South Carolina.

Colonel Otho Holland Williams was "Ligh Horse Harry" Lee's commander during th Race to the Dan (River) and commander c the 6th Maryland Regiment. He participate in most of the major battles in the Carolina Williams was a valued and successful leade often given independent commands und Greene.

Courtesy of the National Park Service.

This is a depiction of the Battle of Guilford Courthouse.
Courtesy of the U.S. Army Center for Military History. Painting by H. Charles McBarron.

enry Lee II, "Light Horse Harry" Lee's
ther, was a prominent and capable
ndowner in Virginia who took his many
sponsibilities seriously, especially his
iildren's education. His decision to send two
f his sons to a college in New Jersey (now
rinceton University) instead of to England
as typically considered with great care. This
d to Henry III's staunch support for the
evolution when it came.

Lt. Colonel "Light Horse" Henry Lee
successfully abetted General Greene's efforts
either by fighting as part of his force or by
cooperating with partisan leaders, such as
Francis Marion, to harass loyalist or regular
British units.

Courtesy of the National Park Service.

t. Colonel William Washington was a
ireless cavalry leader who fought throughout
he Southern Campaign. He made a pivotal
ttack on Tarleton's right flank at Cowpens.
n the end he was wounded and captured at
iutaw Springs in September, 1781. He was
George Washington's cousin.

Courtesy of the National Park Service.

This is a painting of British Lt. Colonel
Banastre Tarleton, one of Cornwallis' most
aggressive and able officers, who earned the
nickname "Bloody Tarleton" and was accused
of the massacre of Colonel Buford's
Continental troops after they surrendered at
the Waxhaws in South Carolina.

Courtesy of the National Park Service.

A portrait of General Henry Lee, father of Robert E. Lee, made after the Whiskey Rebellion.

Painting by Gilbert Stuart. Courtesy of the National Portrait Gallery.

Robert E. Lee at age 31 as a young Lieutenant of Engineers.

Painting by William Edward West. Courtesy of the U.S. Army.

Original gravesite of "Light Horse Harry" Lee, located at Nathanael Greene's plantation on Cumberland Island, Georgia.

This photo shows Robert E. Lee and his father "Light Horse Harry" Lee buried next to each other at the Washington & Lee University Chapel.

CHAPTER FOUR

LEE'S LAST OPERATIONS IN THE NORTH
AND THE PLOT TO CAPTURE BENEDICT ARNOLD

Two days after Lee's acquittal, George Washington dispatched the major and his Legion on a new assignment. France had recognized American independence and entered the war as an ally of the United States in March 1778. Eager for French troops and warships that might enable him to strike the British army in New York, Washington met with the French minister to America, the Chevalier de la Luzerne, in the army's headquarters at Fishkill, New York, on September 12th, 1779. Luzerne informed him that a French fleet with several thousand troops commanded by the Comte D'Estaing was en route to North America. Washington believed that D'Estaing would most likely sail to the New York area to form a junction with the main Continental Army. "It is of the utmost consequence that Count D'Estaing … should as soon as possible receive some necessary information from me," Washington informed Lee. The general ordered Lee to "immediately move with the remainder of your Corps to the County of Monmouth and take a position as near the coast as you can." Lee would watch for the arrival of the French fleet, and upon sighting it, "proceed yourself with the inclosed letter and deliver it to the Admiral Count D'Estaing."

While awaiting the French, Lee would also gather intelligence regarding British naval strength at New York. Washington instructed Lee to keep his mission "a profound secret even from your own Officers" by pretending that the move to New Jersey was to obtain better forage for the Legion's horses. Lee's lookouts along the coast should be told only that they were guarding against a British surprise attack. The mission was important, but Washington undoubtedly also wanted to put some distance between Lee and the officers responsible for his court martial, in the hope that their mutual animosities might have time to subside.[1]

Washington demonstrated that the repercussions of the Paulus Hook operation had not caused him to lose confidence in Lee. Besides entrusting the major with a crucial assignment, Washington relied on Lee to maintain secrecy, even when dealing with officers of higher rank. After Lee forwarded his first reports from Monmouth County through his immediate superior, Major General Alexander, leaving them open to be read in accordance with standard policy, Washington ordered Lee to refrain from that practice. "I would wish you in future, to send your dispatches to me sealed, and communicate any thing, necessary for [Alexander] to know, to him separately," the commander-in-chief wrote. "When an enterprise of any kind is in agitation

61

the fewer to whom it is intrusted the better, and as to the particular business, upon which you are sent, I wish it to remain a secret." Washington noted that these instruction were not the result of a lack of trust in Alexander; however, he counseled, "secrecy 'till the moment of execution is the life of enterprise."[2]

In late September, Washington shared a disquieting report with Lee. News had reached the general that D'Estaing had taken his fleet and army to Savannah, Georgia to attack the British garrison there. Nevertheless, Washington continued to hope that even if the reports were true, D'Estaing would quickly conclude operations in Georgia and sail northward. He thus composed a letter to D'Estaing in early October and forwarded it to Lee, who in turn would present it to the Comte on the latter's arrival off the New Jersey coast. Washington also planned to provide D'Estaing with harbor pilots, and several pilots who were familiar with the waters around New York City were stationed with Lee so they could be put aboard D'Estaing's ships as soon as the French fleet arrived.[3]

Unfortunately for the revolutionaries, D'Estaing had encountered serious trouble at Savannah. The French admiral had landed his three thousand troops outside the city on September 13th, 1779. Joined shortly afterward by several thousand American troops under Major General Benjamin Lincoln, the commander of the Continental Army in the South, the allies besieged Savannah. The British commander, Major General Augustine Prevost, had been surprised by the arrival of the French forces, but he distracted his opponents by engaging in lengthy and insincere surrender negotiations while strengthening Savannah's feeble fortifications. When two weeks of bombardment failed to produce a British capitulation, D'Estaing decided to assault the city. French and American troops stormed the British lines on October 9th and were repulsed with over eight hundred casualties. The allies blamed each other for the defeat. D'Estaing boarded his troops and sailed to the French West Indies. Lincoln marched his American army back to South Carolina.[4]

Because communications were slow, Washington remained unaware of D'Estaing's situation until mid-November. Lee maintained his vigilance, supplementing the observations of his scouts and lookouts by hiring spies to go behind British lines in search of information. Washington approved of Lee's methods, although he cautioned the major on October 7th that while he would make good all of Lee's promises to pay spies in gold or silver, "we have so little of this to spare for even the most pressing and important purposes within the enemy's lines – you will be careful to effect as much as possible with such other means as we have in our power." Despite all of Lee's various efforts, the American high command remained completely in the dark regarding D'Estaing's whereabouts or plans.. By mid-November, Washington could not contain his frustration. "I am precisely in the predicament you are, with respect to the Count, his intentions or Ultimate operations," he complained to French brigadier general Louis Le Beque DuPortail and Lt. Col. Alexander Hamilton. "I have not heard a single syllable about either" except the report in late September that D'Estaing was at Savannah. "From this circumstance and the lateness of the season, I do not expect myself that he will arrive in this quarter, or if he should, that the Enterprise which was proposed, could now be prosecuted. It is too late to begin it." Washington's plans for an autumn campaign had depended upon the ships and troops of D'Estaing, but the French officer's decision to strike Savannah instead of sailing to New York had derailed the northern campaign while producing disaster in the South.[5]

*****

With the campaigning season at an end, Washington sent his army into winter quarters at Morristown, New Jersey, a secure position close enough to New York to monitor British activities. Lee's Legion would remain in a separate post at Burlington, with some of his dragoons detached to Monmouth to support a force of light infantry in an effort to prevent the British from obtaining information about the Continental Army's strength and position from New Jersey's inhabitants.[6]

Washington explained another problem that he wanted to eliminate in a letter of December 20th. "The practice of trading [with the enemy] under the cover of procuring intelligence has grown to such a height that there is an absolute necessity of putting a stop to it," the commander-in-chief told Lee. The matter had to be handled carefully, "to avoid giving any umbrage to the Government of the State." Washington advised Lee to stop sending spies into New York City and limit his intelligence gathering to observing any movements of the British fleet. That would reduce the number of civilians receiving approval to pass into British lines, and the patrols of light infantry and Legion dragoons would make it more difficult for those who wished to make the trip surreptitiously. To make it easier for Lee to carry out his responsibilities, Washington indicated that he preferred that the Legion remain in Monmouth County, although if proper quarters could not be found there he granted Lee the latitude to move his camp to Burlington as originally ordered.[7]

A few days later, Washington reinforced Lee with Armand's Legion, a unit composed primarily of foreign volunteers commanded by Colonel Charles Armand Tuffin, Marquis de la Rouerie, a former French army officer. Washington ordered Armand to "proceed with your corps to Monmouth County and take such station as will best … enable you to communicate with Major Lee, for the purposes of mutual security, covering the country and preventing all intercourse between the inhabitants and the enemy." On December 28th, Lee received instructions from Washington regarding the joint operations the two legions were to conduct. Washington urged that if possible, both corps should remain in Monmouth County. If forage in that area was insufficient for the horses, the general suggested that the cavalry move to Burlington and the infantry of both commands be posted close to the shore, "to be able to send patroles towards those places at which the enemy most commonly land and to which the Country people usually carry their produce."[8]

Washington learned on December 23rd that a large number of Royal Navy warships and transports were assembling off Sandy Hook, New Jersey, a six-mile long spit of land separating New York Bay from the Atlantic Ocean. The commander-in-chief ordered Lee to watch the vessels and report their movements directly to Congress. General Clinton had begun preparing for another attack on Charleston, South Carolina, as soon as he received word on November 19th that the British had repulsed the Franco-American attack on Savannah. The first of 8,700 troops began boarding the transports on December 16th, and the fleet sailed ten days later. Lee knew that South Carolina was vulnerable; three weeks before the British ships left New York, he had informed his friend William Carr of Williamsburg, Virginia, that "at Charles Town they are in a Pitious shaking for fear of being over-run by the Enemy this Winter." State officials had asked for reinforcements, but, Lee noted, "I fear it will be out of our power to comply."[9]

Clinton's departure weakened the British garrison in New York, but the Continental Army could not take advantage of the situation because extremely cold weather and supply shortages forced the troops to endure an ordeal even worse than the one they had suffered at Valley Forge the previous winter. Once again, Washington turned to Lee for assistance in securing provisions for the army. In a circular letter to all the commanders of detached forces, Washington remarked upon the "present distresses of the Army" and outlined the steps he had taken for procuring supplies. Lee and other officers would seek cooperation from local officials, to whom they would deliver an address from Washington, "enforcing it with a more particular detail of the sufferings of the Troops the better to convince them of the necessity of their exertions." The appeal would be accompanied by a threat, to be expressed "delicately," that if sufficient supplies were not provided the officers were authorized "to impress the Articles called for." The officers and civilian officials would designate a date and place for the collection of the requested goods, and "the Owners will bring their Grain and Cattle to this place," where local authorities would determine the value and an army commissary officer would make the payments.[10]

To insure the cooperation of New Jersey's civilian officials, Washington

1780

sent a similar letter to the magistrates of the towns and counties where the
army officers would be gathering supplies. "I have intire confidence that you
will do everything in your power to give efficiency to this requisition," the
commander-in-chief wrote. Nonetheless, Washington added a veiled threat
that if his officers' efforts were obstructed, they had his approval to impress
supplies by force. "I think it my duty to inform you," he remarked, "that
should we be disappointed in our hopes, the extremity of the case will compel
us to have recourse to a different mode, which will be disagreeable to me ...
and less convenient to the inhabitants than the one now recommended."[11]

Lee's endeavors met with rapid success. On January 13th, 1780, he
reported that he had procured a quantity of supplies, leading Washington
to urge him to expand his efforts to Salem, Cumberland, and Cape May
counties. Lee continued to collect provisions with little difficulty and on
January 21st Washington told him that "I am happy to find such a disposi-
tion in the good people to relieve us, and for their ready and zealous com-
pliance with my requisition." The general urged Lee to take advantage of a
break in the weather and forward the corn and salted meat he had gathered
to Morristown.[12]

While working to collect supplies, Lee continued his attempts to disrupt
the shipment of goods to the British in New York, and occasionally skirmished with British forces that landed along the New Jersey coast. In early
January, Lee's troops captured a British officer "and his Associates," perhaps
loyalists who were providing intelligence. A detachment of the Legion under
Captain Henry Peyton burned three British vessels at Sandy Hook and took
twelve prisoners on January 17th. The troops also mortally wounded a man,
apparently a civilian, and seized a quantity of counterfeit Continental currency that he had in his possession. Washington welcomed the news that
Lee had ordered the forged bills to be burned. In early December, the general had learned of "the indefatigable indeavours of the enemy to increase
the depreciation of our currency, by increasing its quantity in Counterfeits,"
and that the British had somehow managed to procure "several Reams of the
paper," manufactured especially for a new issue of Continental currency, from
Philadelphia. He suspected that the British intended "the entire ruin of our
Money," resulting in Congress's inability to purchase supplies for the army.
The Legion's success had thwarted part of that plan, although Lee regretted
that the man found with the counterfeit money had died of his wound before
the Americans could learn where he had obtained the currency.[13]

In late January, when Lee and many of his men had completed their foraging duties and were permitted to return briefly to Virginia on furlough, Lee
urged Washington to promote the Legion's infantry commander, Captain Allen
McLane. Washington demurred, however. His strict sense of fairness would

not allow him to promote McLane when so many other captains in the army were equally deserving of advancement. Therefore Washington denied Lee's request, although he declared that his opinion of McLane's "military merits would induce me to do every thing in his favor consistent with propriety."[14]

Lee stubbornly refused to accept Washington's decision, and several months later tried to bypass the commanding general by appealing directly to the Board of War. Lee justified his request for McLane's promotion on the grounds that in February, at the request of Major General Friedrich von Steuben, a Prussian officer who served as the Continental Army's inspector general, Congress had authorized that the Legion's infantry contingent be increased by seventy men. Lee argued that because McLane now commanded a larger force, he deserved to be promoted to major. Rather than act on the matter, the Board informed Washington, who again refused to promote McLane. The commander-in-chief explained to the Board that there were numerous captains senior to McLane, and that since Lee already held the rank of major, there was no reason why the Legion needed a second major. Frustrated at his inability to obtain a promotion, McLane resigned from the army in late summer. Lee complained to Washington of the loss of such a valuable officer, prompting the general to restate the reasons for his refusal to promote McLane. "I see no injustice done Captn. McLean," Washington insisted, whereupon Lee dropped the matter. Apparently Lee recognized the validity of the commanding general's arguments, while Washington understood that Lee had been motivated solely by a desire to reward a capable officer; the disagreement did not damage their friendship.[15]

Washington may have been irked by minor squabbles over promotion, because much of his attention was focused on more vital issues, such as affairs in the South. In November 1779, anticipating the planned British attack on Charleston, South Carolina, he had detached all of the North Carolina and Virginia Continental infantry from his army, along with the 3rd Regiment of Continental Light Dragoons, to reinforce General Lincoln in the South. Earlier, in July 1779, he had ordered the 1st Continental Light Dragoons to South Carolina, so that only two Continental cavalry regiments and the mounted troops of Lee's and Armand's legions now remained in the North. In January 1780, Lee heard rumors that his Legion might be ordered to the southern theater as well, but Washington assured him that "there is not the least foundation, that I know of, for the report of your corps going to the Southward."[16]

By late March, Washington had changed his mind. The British fleet had entered Charleston harbor and cut off all access to the city by sea, and General Clinton's British troops pushed steadily forward on land. Lincoln had decided not to oppose the British army's advance, electing instead to retire into Charleston's fortifications and prepare for a siege. Under these circumstances, Washington decided to send Lincoln additional reinforcements. "Upon receiving information that the enemy are preparing to send a reinforcement to the southward, I have determined to detach Major Lee's Corps, both Horse and Foot to that quarter," Washington informed the Board of War on March 30th, 1780. He asked the Board to provide the Legion with the supplies necessary for its journey. The same day, Washington ordered Lee, "upon the receipt of this, to take the most expeditious measures for putting the whole Corps ... in readiness to march. If you move, your destination will be South Carolina." The cavalry would travel by land, while the infantry moved by water via Chesapeake Bay to reunite with the dragoons at Petersburg, Virginia. "As soon as you have given the necessary orders ... you had best repair to Philadelphia, and apply to the Board of War ... for the Articles wanting to equip the Corps for so long a march."[17]

Lee rode from his headquarters at Burlington, New Jersey, to Philadelphia, where he began making arrangements for the march. Washington pressed him to hurry. "I have to request you not to lose a moment in commencing your march to South Carolina after your Corps is ready," the general wrote on April 9th. However, supply shortages and other problems delayed Lee's departure. "I am sorry to find that the repairs of your accoutrements and the general indisposition of your Horses, will prevent your moving so soon as could have been wished," Washington noted four days later, "but I have confidence in your making no greater delay than is absolutely necessary."[18]

While in Philadelphia, Lee met with Anthony Wayne and several lower ranking officers to discuss the poor condition of the army and their opinion of its cause: a lack of public support. The group composed a document expressing their desire for a more energetic government that shared the Continental officers' commitment to the Revolution. They demanded an end to "the spirit of insolence and audacity" shown by loyalists and lukewarm patriots alike, and which they blamed on "the lenity of Governments" whose excessive commitment to liberty undermined their ability to support the war effort. Finally, they announced that they would not associate with anyone who did not share their commitment to the American cause, and regard any officers who disagreed with them "as a proper subject of contempt." The declaration had no practical effect beyond allowing the signers to voice their dissatisfaction with the Continental Congress, the state governments, and the public.[19]

Lee's own frustration grew as he encountered one delay after another. It was not until May 17th, more than six weeks after he had been ordered to the South, that he was able to set a date for the Legion's march. "The period is at length arrived when I must move for the southern army," he informed Joseph Reed. "Want of cash detains us for a day—tomorrow we are to reviewe; the day following we march." Other reinforcements that Washington had dispatched southward, seven regiments of Maryland Continentals and an eighth regiment from Delaware, had already departed on April 14th under the command of Major General Johann De Kalb. Although they had set out long before Lee's Legion was prepared to march, De Kalb's infantry did not arrive in time to assist in the defense of Charleston. On May 12th, 1780, General Lincoln surrendered the city, its 3,500 Continental defenders, and more than 2,000 militia to General Clinton's British army. Only the two Continental light dragoon regiments of lieutenant colonels William Washington and Anthony Walton White escaped capture, but they had suffered such heavy losses at the hands of the British cavalry that they required several months of recruiting and recuperation before the units could return to action. Meanwhile, De Kalb marched his Delaware and Maryland troops to Hillsborough, North Carolina, thereby keeping a small Continental force of some 1,400 rank and file infantrymen in the Carolinas to maintain a presence and await developments. This tiny group of disciplined, well-trained soldiers would form the core of the Southern Army in the coming campaigns.[20]

By May 20th, Washington had not yet learned of Charleston's surrender, but he knew the American situation in the South appeared bleak and he therefore decided to halt Lee's march. The commanding general told Lee to await further orders, keeping the Legion's horses in a location where there was adequate forage. "A very few days will probably determine whether you are to proceed further just now," Washington wrote. Lee did not reply, leaving Washington to wonder where the Legion might be. "If Major Lee's Corps is still at Philadelphia or within its vicinity, or has not advanced more than three or four days march towards the Southward, I request that you will order it to join this Army as soon as it can be done," Washington wrote to the Board of War on June 8th. "His Horse in particular is infinitely wanted. ... The Enemy are out in force in Jersey and lie just below Springfield. They have a considerable body of Horse which we want Horse to counteract, and we want them as well for the purpose of reconnoitering."[21]

Fortunately for the commander-in-chief, Lee was still in the Philadelphia area, having halted his march southward when he received Washington's letter of May 20th. Thus Lee was able to respond immediately to Washington's June 8th instructions, and the Legion cavalry rejoined the main army on June 11th after a rapid three-day march that fatigued their horses. The unit still made a fine appearance, however. James Thacher, a Continental Army surgeon, noted that Lee...

> *"...arrived in camp with a beautiful corps of light-horse, the men in complete uniform, and the horses very elegant and finely disciplined.*

Major Lee is said to be a man of great spirit and enterprise, and much important service is expected from him."[22]

Washington appreciated Lee's haste and was happy to have the Legion available if it were needed to counteract a British attack. Hessian General Wilhelm Knyphausen, who was in command of the British army in New York while Clinton was in Charleston, had launched an offensive into New Jersey on June 7th with six thousand men, hoping to drive Washington's army from its camp at Morristown. Washington expressed his appreciation for Lee's rapid return, writing that "The spirit which has been exhibited by your corps on the present occasion gives me pleasure, and be assured meets with my Thanks and Approbation." He suggested that Lee post his troops in or near Chatham, where the horses could rest and enjoy an adequate supply of forage.[23]

Lee and his mounted troops resumed their observations on the coast, and spotted the British fleet on its return voyage from Charleston. Lee's report indicated that at least four thousand British troops had returned to New York with General Clinton. Washington immediately redeployed his forces to meet any potential threat now that his adversary had been reinforced. "The arrival of Sir Henry Clinton from Charleston has urged us to motion," Lee informed Joseph Reed on June 20th. Washington led the "main body of the Army" toward the Hudson River, while a smaller force under Major General Nathanael Greene remained behind. Lee's dragoons were assigned to Greene. As soon as he joined Greene's force at Springfield, "I was immediately ordered to the front, and honored with the command on the lines," Lee wrote.[24]

Despite his anger at Knyphausen for undertaking an offensive without permission, Clinton decided to support the Hessian general's operation in hopes of defeating the Continental Army. Washington shifted most of his troops northward, expecting the British and Hessians to move in that direction. Greene held his position at Springfield with about one thousand Continental troops and some local militia, while Lee's dragoons monitored the British and Hessians. From his advanced post, Lee became thoroughly familiar with "the springs of action in both armys," as he termed it, and shared his impressions of the British army with Reed:

> *"Be assured that the enemy conduct themselves with much wisdom. Not only their movements are material & military, but their positions are circumspect, & their discipline rigid. A very different chief Mr. Clinton from Sr Will. Howe. They have made two fruitless excursions on my post; we have made prisoners one Lt. & his party—every day we kill, & are killed."*[25]

Lee suggested to Greene on June 20th that the Legion cavalry be reinforced from other units to a strength of three hundred men, and be permitted
to attack and capture the pickets on Knyphausen's right flank. Such a move,
Lee believed, would "oblige Mr. Kinsihausen either to extend his picquets
or to contract his lines." Lee did not expect Greene to approve the proposal
because "it might produce the loss of 20 or 30 lives in the operation of the
plan," and his prediction proved correct as Greene declined to authorize the
foray.[26]

On the morning of June 23rd, some of Lee's scouts learned that
Knyphausen was advancing from his camp at Elizabethtown in two columns.
They informed Lee, who forwarded the intelligence to Greene. Upon receiving Lee's report, Greene deployed his troops to block Knyphausen's march at
the Rahway River bridges.[27]

At the bridge on the road leading directly to Springfield, Greene and
most of his force held their position against British and Hessian assaults for
approximately forty minutes before the Americans were forced to retreat. On
Greene's left the second bridge, defended by Lee's Legion and a regiment of
New Jersey Continentals, also came under heavy attack. Lee's soldiers bore
the brunt of the defense, and the major had posted them "on the heights
overlooking the bridge in such a way as to concentrate their fire on the bridge
and road." From this vantage point Lee and his men prevented their opponents from crossing the bridge until Lt. Col. John Graves Simcoe discovered
a gully that would conceal an attacking force while bypassing Lee's position.
Simcoe, who commanded a loyalist legion similar to Lee's that was called the
Queen's Rangers, led his troops along that route, outflanked Lee, and forced
the Americans to retreat. Greene's force abandoned Springfield and reunited
in a strong position beyond the town. Knyphausen then burned Springfield
and withdrew. Greene assigned Lee and his dragoons to monitor the British withdrawal, but Lee found no opportunity to strike Knyphausen's rear
guard.[28]

The infantry of the Legion had been left in the Philadelphia area when
Lee's cavalry rejoined Washington's army and therefore did not participate in
the action at Springfield. Having decided that these foot soldiers were "too
inconsiderable in number to make any difference in the scale of Southern
affairs," on June 21st Washington ordered them to return northward. With
his Legion reunited, Lee resumed the now familiar routines of outpost duty:
reconnaissance, intelligence gathering, and checking similar efforts by the
enemy, with occasional forays to procure supplies. Despite being assigned to
Greene's command, Lee frequently received orders directly from Washington. For example, on June 27th, the commander-in-chief instructed Lee "to
reconnoitre the country well" between Totawa and Pompton, New Jersey,

"and report to me the kind of roads, passes, and quantity of green forage, with other circumstances that come under a military view." Washington asked Lee to pay particular attention to the geography near Preakness, where the general was eager to learn of any passes through the mountainous terrain and if it were possible to secure an army's flank there.[29]

In July, Washington ordered Lee to move the Legion to Monmouth, where he could communicate with militia officers keeping watch for the appearance of a French fleet. If a fleet arrived, Lee was to dispatch one dragoon to army headquarters and another to the French minister in Philadelphia, then board the flagship and deliver dispatches from Washington to the French commander. Lee would also provide pilots that Washington had ready nearby. Once those tasks were accomplished, Lee was to "instantly impress every kind of refreshment the Country affords ... for the use of our allies."[30]

To Washington's chagrin, British naval reinforcements arrived before the French did. Lee sent no report of the British ships to Washington, prompting a rebuke from the general. "We have received advice from New York of the arrival of ... six sail of the line" on July 13th, Washington notified Lee three days after the Royal Navy appeared offshore. "We think it very extraordinary if the fleet has arrived that we should have heard nothing of it from you." Lee replied the same day, in a defensive tone. He attributed the failure to report the British naval movements to Brigadier General David Forman of the New Jersey militia, whose men were actually watching the coast. Lee wrote that he presumed Forman had notified Washington of the ships' arrival, and that his responsibility was merely "to expedite [Forman's] dispatches, to collect provision for the [French] fleet and to protect the guides." Four days later, Lee again justified his silence on the grounds that "I conceived it a matter of delicacy in communicating with H. quarters, unless advised to do so by Gen. Forman to whom the business had been committed."[31]

The commander-in-chief crisply explained what he expected of Lee in a letter of July 19th. "You mistook the point of giving me intelligence as by recurring to your instructions you will find," Washington wrote, rejecting Lee's explanations. "I now depend on you for information of every occurrence. ... For the future you will make a report every two days ... in which the more detail the better." Stung by the rebuke, Lee overcompensated by submitting intelligence prematurely. His next report stated that the entire British fleet had arrived off New York, but he had to retract it after confirming that in fact only three frigates had reached port.[32]

Soon afterward, Washington gave Lee another assignment: gathering supplies. On July 24th, Washington ordered Lee to Monmouth County after learning from General Forman that a "great number of horses" belonging to loyalists were there, and thus "within the enemy's power" to obtain. Lee's instructions were to round up all horses fit for cavalry use or drawing wagons and deliver them to the army's quartermaster general. When that task was completed, Lee was to move to Easton, Pennsylvania, "for an impress of teams" of horses to haul supplies.[33]

Lee did not welcome the Legion's new tasks. He informed Washington that he would leave for Easton as soon as he completed his work in Monmouth County. "I wish to expedite the business," Lee noted, "not only as it tends to the good of the army but as it will releive me from a tour of duty which is foreign to the employment I would wish to be engaged in." The aggressive major had clearly tired of intelligence gathering and procuring livestock and supplies, and his comment politely hinted that the Legion might better serve in an area where some combat might be expected.[34]

Despite his avowed dissatisfaction with his assignment, Lee went about his task with characteristic energy. By August 6th, working with local officials, he had arranged for "the furnishing of one hundred four-horse wagons" from Easton and the surrounding area to transport "the ordnance, military stores, and provisions" he and his troops had assembled. Lee planned to impress a further hundred wagons and teams from Berks County, and the same from Bucks County. Washington was pleased with Lee's success. He informed Joseph Reed that of all the army's cavalry units, "Major Lees Corps is the only one upon which we can place dependance either for military operations, to collect supplies ... or to impress teams for the transportation of provision and stores."[35]

In late August, Lee and the Legion returned to New Jersey, where they continued their efforts to provision the army. Washington directed Lee to various areas where supplies might be found, and provided a list of badly needed articles: oats and hay for the horses, wheat, cattle, hogs and sheep to feed the troops.[36]

During the foraging operation, three of Lee's officers became involved in a controversy with some of the local inhabitants. The people's complaints appeared so serious that New Jersey's chief justice, David Brearley, thought it necessary to bring the matter directly to General Washington's attention. Washington relayed the judge's grievances to Lee in a letter dated September 3rd:

> "Several days ago I received a Letter from the Honble Mr Brearly, Chief Justice of Jersey in which he mentions that 'Complaint has been made to me by a Member of the Legislature of Somerset County, together with other respectable inhabitants, that a detachment of Major Lee's light Dragoons have quartered themselves upon the Inhabitants of the county near Rockey Hill, without any order of Law, are impressing

*forage by their own authority, and committing other great outrages
on the Inhabitants. The persons particularly complained against, are
Captain Rudulph, Doctor Irvin and One Stephen Lewis, supposed to
be a Commissioned Officer.' I would willingly hope that this Complaint has been exaggerated and profered in much stronger terms than
facts would warrant. There is nothing I wish for more than harmony
and a good understanding to prevail between the Country and the
Army; it [is] essential to our success and whenever circumstances compel to any measures out of the common line and which may bear hard
upon the Inhabitants, they ought not to be carried farther than necessity may absolutely require."*[37]

The accused individuals—Captain Michael Rudulph, Surgeon Matthew
Irvine, and Cornet Stephen Lewis, who was the dragoons' quartermaster—
were three of Lee's most valuable officers, and he quickly made inquiries
and came to their defense. Lee admitted that many of his soldiers had been
quartered in the homes of local residents, but that the inhabitants knew the
troops well and gave them a "hearty welcome." Several people did not want
to be paid for housing the soldiers; those who did, and those who provided
forage for the Legion's horses, received warrants from a local official so that
they would be paid for their assistance. Lee "visited the quarters of the 2nd
& 3rd troops," and observed that "I never saw people more pleased or more
affectionate. Not a single complaint was or had been offered but the soldiers'
civility was enabled as surpassing any thing [the inhabitants] had met with
during the war." Satisfied that there was no cause for complaint in those
areas, and having received similar accounts from the area where the 1ˢᵗ Troop
of dragoons was quartered, Lee met with the three officers. Rudulph, Lewis,
and Irvine asserted that the complaint had originated with a "Mr. Tenbrook
and wife." Rudulph and Lewis were ill, and a local official arranged for them
to stay at the Tenbrook home until they recovered; Dr. Irvine stayed to attend
them. Lee noted that two witnesses, a militia officer and "another respectable
inhabitant," described the Tenbrooks as "notorious among their neighbors
for their ill nature, mutterings, and discontent." The three officers, Lee said,
"were subject to perpetual abuse from morning to night, for two days." One
officer, whom Lee did not name, finally had enough and told Tenbrook "that
unless he held his tongue he would throw him down his well." Except for
that outburst, Lee said he could not substantiate any of the accusations in
Brearley's letter. On the contrary, Lee insisted, the civilians in the area had
assured him of "the general happiness which had subsisted between the soldiers & the people." Lee also reminded Washington of the rigid discipline he
imposed upon his Legion, and that no one could claim that his troops were

"deficient" in that regard. Washington evidently agreed, and took no action on the matter.[38]

In addition to defending his officers and carrying out foraging operations, Lee attempted to strengthen his Legion with a portion of the new recruits being enlisted by the states. Bypassing the army's chain of command, Lee corresponded directly with the governors and complained that the Legion was not allocated enough of the new troops. "The small number [of men] due from this State can advantage us but little," he told Joseph Reed, the head of Pennsylvania's executive council. "Other States, I suppose will treat us in the same manner, and at the close of this campaign my small corps will be reduced to a mere party." Lee warned Reed that the Legion's strength might be so greatly diminished that it would be dissolved, and Lee would be "forced to relinquish a command I most sincerely love." However, he remarked stoically that he had "learned the art of being happy under my distress." Maryland governor Thomas Sim Lee tried to mollify the Legion commander, explaining that his state's legislature had directed that most of the recruits be assigned to fill Maryland's depleted infantry regiments, and that the numbers enlisted "will go but a little way in making good the deficiency." Governor Lee regretted that "there is no power with the Executive to furnish you with the proportion you expect" and repeated "how impossible it is to comply with your wish." The governor reassured Major Lee that "I respect your whole Corps and would labour with pleasure to serve them on this & every other Occasion where it can be done with propriety."[39]

Lee's worry that his Legion might be dissolved was not imaginary. Because the states were unable to find enough recruits to fill their Continental regiments, on October 3rd the Continental Congress began considering a recommendation from the Board of War that "all the separate light corps of the army, both horse and foot," be eliminated as of January 1st, 1781, and their men "incorporated with the troops of their respective states." Washington acted quickly to spare Lee's Legion, telling Congress that

> *"Major Lee has rendered such distinguished Services and possesses so many Talents for commanding a Corps of this nature, he deserved so much credit for the perfection in which he has kept his Corps, as well as the handsome exploits he has performed, that it would be a loss to the Service and a discouragement to merit to reduce him. And I do not see how he can be introduced into one of the [Virginia] Regiments in a manner satisfactory to himself."[40]*

The Marquis de Lafayette also attested to Lee's abilities, arguing that Lee deserved to be promoted because he possessed "superior abilities to his

Rank." Lafayette declared that Lee was "beyond compare the best officer of light infantry in the English, Hessian or American armies on this continent." Faced with such testimony, the delegates decided on October 21st that Lee's Legion, as well as the legion commanded by Charles Armand, would not be dissolved.[41]

While Lee was occupied with matters of supply, recruitment, and the possible dissolution of his Legion, a seemingly innocuous encounter in the woods near Tarrytown, New York, would soon draw him into the saga of the most famous act of treason in American history.

*****

The Plot to Capture Benedict Arnold

On September 23rd, three American militiamen patrolling a road in the Hudson River valley stopped a stranger dressed in a resplendent purple coat. When asked what he was doing, the stranger handed them a pass, signed by American major general Benedict Arnold, granting permission to "Mr. John Anderson" to travel "on public business." Something about the man sparked suspicion among the militiamen, who searched him and found a detailed description of the garrison and defenses of the American fortress at West Point, hidden in Anderson's boot. The militiamen turned their prisoner and the captured documents over to their commander, Lt. Col. John Jameson, who forwarded them to General Washington. The commander-in-chief had been attending a conference with French officers in Hartford, Connecticut, and was on his way to West Point to confer with Arnold. Arriving on September 25th, he found the major general inexplicably absent, and the state of West Point's fortifications far worse than Arnold had led him to expect. It was not until late in the afternoon that Alexander Hamilton handed Washington Jameson's note and the intercepted papers. The documents showed that Arnold, whom Washington considered one of his best combat officers, had been corresponding with British general Sir Henry Clinton, and was planning to defect to the British and surrender West Point. Arnold had fled to New York City when he learned of Anderson's capture.[42]

Up to the moment when he received the documents, Washington had maintained strong confidence in Arnold. Now the general felt personally betrayed. He announced Arnold's treason to the army in his general orders of September 26th:

> *"Treason of the blackest dye was yesterday discovered! General Arnold who commanded at Westpoint, lost to every sentiment of honor, of public and private obligation, was about to deliver up that important Post into the hands of the enemy. Such an event must have given the*

American cause a deadly wound if not a fatal stab. Happily the trea-
son has been timely discovered to prevent the fatal misfortune."[43]

The Americans soon learned that the civilian-attired "John Anderson" was
in fact Major John André, an aide to the British commander-in-chief. André
was tried by court martial, convicted of spying, and hanged on October 2nd.
During his captivity, André had impressed the Continental officers; Alexander Hamilton declared that André was a man of "excellent understanding,
well improved by education and travel," with "a peculiar elegance of mind
and manners and the advantage of a pleasing person." Even the fourteen
generals who sat as judges during André's trial were charmed. Major Benjamin Tallmadge, who attended the trial, observed that "I can remember no
instance where my affections were so fully absorbed in any man." André's
execution was carried out with great reluctance. American officers understood
that André was, like them, a soldier following orders. Washington even tried
to spare André by offering to exchange him for Arnold. General Clinton,
despite his own affection for André, rebuffed the offer.[44]

In contrast to their sympathy for André, Arnold's former comrades were
infuriated by his betrayal. "There are no terms that can describe the baseness
of his heart," said Washington, reverting to his usual restraint after overcoming his initial shock at Arnold's treason. Other officers denounced Arnold
with greater vigor. "How black, how despised, loved by none, and hated by all.
Once his Country's Idol, now her horror," Major General Nathanael Greene
wrote. Colonel Alexander Scammell, the army's adjutant general, bemoaned
"Treason! black as hell! That a man so high on the list of fame should be
as guilty as Arnold, must be attributed not only to original sin, but actual
transgression." Scammell noted that Arnold's defection gave rise to suspicion
among the Continental officers, each carefully watching his fellows for signs
of treasonous behavior.[45]

Henry Lee shared the sentiments of his fellow officers. Yet he was not satisfied with merely denouncing Arnold; he sought to punish him as well. After
his investigation helped to clear Major General Arthur St. Clair, one of the
officers suspected of harboring treasonous sentiments, Lee turned his attention to Arnold. He began to devise a plan to capture the traitor. Washington,
thinking along the same lines, summoned Lee to a meeting on October 14th
to discuss the matter. The general approved Lee's scheme and authorized him
to make preparations to put it into action.[46]

A few days later Lee sent Washington a report of his progress thus
far: "*I have engaged two persons to undertake the accomplishment
of your Excellency's wishes. ... The chief of the two persons is a ser-*

geant in my cavalry. To him I have promised promotion, the other is an inhabitant of Newark; I have had experience of his fidelity, and his connections with the enemy render him, with his personal qualifications very fit for the business. To this man I have engaged one hund. guineas, five hundd. acres of land and three negroes. ... The outlines of the scheme are that the Sergeant should join Gen. Arnold as a deserter from us, should engage in his corps now raising, and should contrive to insinuate himself into some menial or military berth about the Genls. person. That a correspondence should be kept up with the man in Newark, by the latter's visiting the former every two days. When the favorable moment arrives they should seize the prize in the night, gag him, and bring him across to Bergen woods. ... The Sergeant is a very promising youth of uncommon taciturnity, and invincible perseverance. ... I have instructed him not to return till he receives direction from me, but to continue his attempts, however unfavorable the prospects may appear at first."[47]

Washington approved Lee's proposal, pronouncing the plan "a good one." He agreed to the compensation Lee had promised, and turned the enterprise over to Lee with only one stipulation—that under no circumstances should Arnold be killed. "The idea which would accompany such an event would be that Ruffians had been hired to assassinate him," Washington explained. "My aim is to make a public example of him," Washington observed, adding that the operation required "the most inviolable secrecy."[48]

The sergeant whom Lee had chosen to pose as a deserter was John Champe of Virginia, and his civilian contact was a man named Baldwin. Lee arranged for Champe to desert on the night of October 20th, bringing the Legion's orderly book with him to hand over to the British as proof that his change of allegiance was authentic. At midnight Champe would take his horse without, he hoped, arousing the suspicion of the guards watching the Legion's mounts, and flee as fast as he could to the coast, where he would hail one of the British vessels patrolling the waters. If Champe was discovered, Lee would do what he could to delay pursuit. However, for the ruse to succeed, Lee would have to act as though Champe were an actual deserter.[49]

That night, Lee tried to sleep in his quarters. "Useless attempt!" he recalled, since he worried about Champe's ability to escape the vigilant pickets. Lee's fears proved well founded, for about half an hour after Champe left camp, he was spotted by a sentry on mounted patrol. When Champe refused to respond to the sentry's challenge and instead put spurs to his horse and fled, the soldier reported the encounter to his superior, who in turn informed Lee. To buy Champe a bit of time, Lee ordered a count made of the men and horses, which revealed Champe's absence. Lee had no choice but to order a pursuit, ordering the men to capture the deserter alive. The Legion dragoons left camp in a clatter of beating hooves, and caught up with Champe a short distance from the coast. Champe dashed into the marsh along the shore, leaped from his horse, and waded through the water, shouting for help. The crew of a nearby British galley observed the commotion and lowered a boat, while their cannon opened fire on the pursuing Legion troopers. The dragoons broke off their pursuit, and Champe was taken aboard the galley, where he told the vessel's officers the story he and Lee had prepared: he was tired of the hardships of military service and had been badly treated by his officers. The galley's commander sent him to New York City.[50]

On October 25th, Lee received word via Baldwin that Champe had made it to New York. "He was before Sir Henry Clinton and passed all the forms of the garrison," Lee informed Washington the same day. "He accidentally met Col. Arnold in the street which has paved a natural way for further acquaintance. The party entertain high hopes of success." After Clinton questioned Champe about his reasons for deserting and the condition of the rebel army, the British general pressed Champe to enlist in one of the many loyalist regiments. At first Champe resisted, explaining that he was tired of military service and that if he enlisted and was captured, he would be hanged as a traitor. This, too, was part of the plan, and eventually Champe gave in to Clinton and agreed to enlist in the loyalist regiment Arnold was organizing. As an inducement, Clinton allowed him to keep his rank of sergeant.[51]

Champe now began planning Arnold's capture. He watched the traitor carefully, noting his habits. Arnold returned to his quarters each night about midnight, visited the garden briefly, and then retired. Champe loosened several boards in the garden fence so that he and Baldwin could seize Arnold and drag him into the adjacent alley. Then they would carry him through the streets to the waterfront, as though they were two friends carrying home a third who had too much drink. At the docks, one of Baldwin's accomplices would be waiting with a boat to ferry Arnold to New Jersey. Champe managed to send word of the scheme to Lee, and asked the Legion commander to be at Hoboken on a specific night to receive Arnold.[52]

Lee rode to Hoboken with a detachment of Legion dragoons on the designated night, bringing along three extra horses: one for Champe, one for Baldwin, and the third for Arnold. The boat and its eagerly expected passenger did not arrive, however. General Clinton was preparing an expedition to Virginia, and Arnold's corps was part of the force designated to take part. To better supervise preparations, Arnold moved his headquarters, depriving Champe and Baldwin of any chance to implement their plan. They had passed up several earlier opportunities to act, in hopes that they would find more favorable circumstances later. Instead, Champe found himself aboard a British transport in mid-December, bound for Virginia and unable to communicate with Baldwin. Soon Baldwin sent word to Lee of what had happened, and the Legion commander realized that his efforts had failed. The British expedition went ashore at Westover, Virginia, on January 4th, 1781.

Champe promptly deserted. He did not realize that he would soon meet his commander and comrades once again; with the American situation in Georgia and the Carolinas still desperate, Washington had ordered Lee's Legion to the South.[53]

1   2 Washington to Lee, Sept. 25, 1779, Washington Papers, LOC.
3   Washington to Lee, Sept. 30, 1779; Washington to the Comte D'Estaing, Oct. 4, 1779, Washington Papers, LOC.
4   Lee, *Memoirs*, 137; Chernow, 366.
5   Washington to Lee, Oct. 7, 1779, Henry Lee Papers, Library of Virginia, Richmond (quotation); Washington to Louis Le Beque DuPortail and Alexander Hamilton, Nov. 11, 1779 (quotation), Washington to Jonathan Trumbull, Nov. 16, 1779, Washington Papers, LOC.
6   Washington to Horatio Gates, Nov. 17, 1779, Washington Papers, LOC; Washington, "Order of Troops Cantonment," Nov. 1779, Washington Papers, University of Virginia.
7   Washington to Lee, Dec. 20, 1779, Washington Papers, LOC.
8   Wright, 347; Washington to Charles Armand Tuffin, Dec. 23, 1779 (quotation); Washington to Lee, Dec. 28, 1779 (quotation), Washington Papers, LOC.
9   Washington to the President of Congress, Dec. 23, 1779, Washington Papers, LOC; Carl P. Borick, *A Gallant Defense: The Siege of Charleston, 1780* (Columbia: University of South Carolina Press, 2003), 21, 23-25; Lee to William Carr, Dec. 3, 1779, Henry Lee Letter, 22957, Library of Virginia (quotation). Clinton's expedition constituted the third British attack on Charleston. Clinton had been present, but his troops did not participate in, a naval attack on the city on June 28, 1776, in which Sir Peter Parker's fleet was repulsed. In May 1779, General Augustine Prevost invaded South Carolina to forestall an expected American attack on British forces in Georgia; Prevost reached the outskirts of Charleston before the arrival of General Benjamin Lincoln's army forced him to withdraw.
10   George Washington, Circular Letter to Matthias Ogden, Henry Lee, and other commanders in New Jersey, Jan. 8, 1780, Washington Papers, LOC.
11   Cecere, 131.
12   Washington to Lee, Jan. 16, 1780, and Jan. 21, 1789 (quotation), Washington Papers, LOC.
13   Washington to Lee, Jan. 7, 1780 (quotation); Lee to Washington, Jan. 17, 1780; Washington to the President of Congress, Dec. 7, 1779 (quotation), Washington Papers, LOC.
14   Cecere, 132; Washington to Lee, Jan. 30, 1780, Washington Papers, LOC.
15   Washington to James Duane, June 5, 1780; Washington to Lee, Sept. 2, 1780 (quotation), Washington Papers, LOC; Cecere, 132-133.
16   Borick, 35-37; Urwin, "Continental Light Dragoons," in Piecuch, ed., *Cavalry of the Revolution*, 15-16; Washington to Lee, Jan. 7, 1780 (quotation), Washington Papers, LOC.
17   Borick, 85, 94; Washington to the Board of War, March 30, 1780 (quotation); Washington to Lee, March 30, 1780 (quotation), Washington Papers, LOC.
18   Washington to Lee, April 9, 1780 (quotation) and April 13, 1780 (quotation), Washington Papers, LOC.
19   Royster, *Revolutionary People at War*, 312.
20   Lee to Joseph Reed, May 17, 1780, "Letters of General Henry Lee," 153 (quotation); Borick, 222-223.
21   Washington to Lee, May 20, 1780 (quotation); Washington to the Board of War, June 8, 1780 (quotation), Washington Papers, LOC.
22   Cecere, 136.
23   Washington to Lee, June 11, 1780, Washington Papers, LOC.
24   Washington to the Continental Congress, June 18, 1780, Washington Papers, LOC; Lee, *Memoirs*, 24

(quotation).
25 Cecere, 136; Lee to Joseph Reed, June 20, 1780, in "Letters of Lee," 153-154 (quotation).
26 Lee to Reed, June 20, 1780, in "Letters of Lee," 154.
27 Cecere, 137-138.
28 Cecere, 138.
29 Washington to the Board of War, June 21, 1780 (quotation); Washington to Lee, June 27, 1780 (quotation), Washington Papers, LOC.
30 Washington to Lee, July 11, 1780, Washington Papers, LOC.
31 Washington to Lee, July 16, 1780, Washington Papers, LOC (quotation); Notes to Washington's Letter to Lee of July 19, 1780, Washington Papers, University of Virginia (quotations).
32 Washington to Lee, July 19, 1780 (quotation); Washington to Lafayette, July 22, 1780, Washington Papers, LOC.
33 Washington to Lee, July 24, 1780, George Washington Letters, Library of Virginia.
34 Lee to Washington, July 25, 1780, Henry Lee Papers, Library of Virginia.
35 Lee to Joseph Reed, Aug. 6, 1780, in Lee, *Memoirs*, 25-26 (quotation); Washington to Reed, Aug. 26, 1780, Washington Papers, LC (quotation).
36 Washington to Lee, Aug. 22, 1780, and Aug. 24, 1789, Washington Papers, LOC.
37 Washington to Lee, Sept. 3, 1780, Washington Papers, University of Virginia.
38 Lee to Washington, Sept. 5, 1780, Washington Papers, University of Virginia.
39 Lee to Joseph Reed, Aug. 6, 1780, in Lee, *Memoirs*, 26 (quotation); Thomas Sim Lee to Henry Lee, Aug. 18, 1780, Lee Family Papers, VHS (quotation).
40 Cecere, 142-143.
41 Cecere, 143-144.
42 Chernow, 381-382.
43 Washington, General Orders, Sept. 26, 1780, Washinton Papers, LOC.
44 Chernow, 385-386.
45 Chernow, 386 (quotation); Royster, *Revolutionary People at War*, 290-291 (quotations).
46 Washington to Lee, Oct. 13, 1780, Washington Papers, University of Virginia.
47 Lee to Washington, undated letter, 1780, Washington Papers, LOC.
48 Washington to Lee, Oct. 20, 1780, Washington Papers, LOC.
49 Chernow, 387; John Bakeless, *Turncoats, Traitors and Heroes* (Philadelphia, PA: J. B. Lippincott, 1959), 307; William Buckner McGroarty, "Sergeant John Champe and Certain of His Contemporaries," *William & Mary Quarterly*, Second Series, Vol. 17, No. 2 (April 1937), 153; William Buckner McGroarty, "Captain Cameron and Sergeant Champe," *William & Mary Quarterly*, Second Series, Vol. 19, No. 1 (Jan. 1939), 50.
50 McGroarty, "Champe and His Contemporaries," 153; Bakeless, 307, 309-311; Lee, *Memoirs*, 399-403; Wilbur C. Hall, "Sergeant Champe's Adventure," *William & Mary Quarterly*, Second Series, Vol. 18, No. 3 (July 1938), 323, 325.
51 Lee to Washington, Oct. 25, 1780, Washington Papers, LOC (quotation); Hall, 326; McGroarty, "Champe and His Contemporaries," 155; Bakeless, 312-313.
52 Bakeless, 315-316; McGroarty, "Champe and His Contemporaries," 155.
53 Bakeless, 316-317; Hall, 340-341; Lee, *Memoirs*, 409-411; McGroarty, "Champe and His Contemporaries," 155.

CHAPTER FIVE

THE MARCH SOUTH AND THE RACE NORTH

On October 22nd, 1780, George Washington instructed Major Lee to prepare his Legion to march south to reinforce the beleaguered American army in the Carolinas. "I think it more than probable that your Corps will be ordered to the southward," Washington wrote. The commanding general ordered Lee to "send an Officer to Philadelphia to provide accoutrements and Clothing." The officer assigned this task, Washington said, should first report to headquarters where "I will give him a letter to the Board of War upon the subject." Washington also advised Lee to keep the possible movement and destination of the Legion secret.[1]

Lee dispatched Captain Michael Rudulph that same day to call upon the commander-in-chief, and Washington provided the captain with the promised letter. "I have concluded to send Major Lees Corps to the southward as soon as" the necessary equipment could be provided, Washington stated, and he informed the Board that Rudulph was bringing a list of the required items to Philadelphia. Washington shared his concern with the Board that the government's lack of funds would make it difficult to secure the supplies, but added that "when the consequence which this Corps will be of in our southern operations is taken into consideration, I am convinced every exertion will be made to forward them as expeditiously as possible." In an effort to insure Congress's cooperation, Washington also addressed a letter to South Carolina delegate John Mathews, stating that "Lees corps will also go to the Southward. I believe it will be found very useful. The corps itself is an excellent one and the officer at the head of it has great resources of genius."[2]

Congress approved Washington's order to send Lee and his Legion to the South on October 31st. The motion was made by Mathews, and seconded by Lee's former commanding officer, Theodorick Bland, who now represented Virginia in Congress. The delegates resolved "that the pressing emergency of our southern affairs requiring as speedy a reinforcement of cavalry as possible, Major Lee's corps be directed to proceed immediately on their route to join the southern army." Congress asked Lee to provide "an exact return" of the Legion's strength, along with a list of its "horses, arms, accoutrements and clothing." Lee was also instructed to leave an officer in Philadelphia to work with the Board of War to gather supplies and forward them to the Legion. On November 6th, Congress rewarded Lee with a much deserved promotion to lieutenant colonel. Lee's cavalry commander, Captain Henry Peyton, was promoted to major.[3]

Lee began his journey southward shortly afterward, and by November

Operations in the South, 1781

17th, part of the Legion had reached Head of Elk in Maryland, where they boarded boats that carried them to the southern shore of the James River in Virginia. Lee's troops encountered great difficulties in obtaining supplies and shelter. Captain James Armstrong informed Lee that when his troops arrived at Head of Elk, they "could find no one willing to give a soldier a night's quarters." Armstrong was forced to employ a combination of "many entreaties and some threats" before the inhabitants agreed to provide places for the troops to sleep. "The people here deny us every thing," Armstrong complained, noting that his men were short of canteens and eating utensils. The lack of public support was ascribed to "the exasperated feelings of the population caused by the calamities of war." On several occasions Lee had to use his personal funds to procure needed items for his soldiers.[4]

During his march, Lee attempted to add recruits to his Legion. He wrote to the governors of the first four states on his route, Pennsylvania, Delaware, Maryland, and Virginia, asking them to encourage their citizens to enlist in the Legion. These efforts, however, brought negligible results. When he arrived at the American army's camp at Cheraw in northeastern South Carolina on January 6th, 1781, the Legion numbered between 240 and 260 men.[5]

Both South Carolina Governor John Rutledge and Major General Nathanael Greene, the recently appointed commander of the Continental Army in the Southern Department, welcomed Lee's arrival. Shortly before Lee reached Greene's camp, the general had written optimistically to Brigadier General Francis Marion of the South Carolina militia that he hoped to give the British "a Stroke in a little time, as Colonel Lees Legion is near at hand." Greene knew Lee well, having served with him in the northern theater, and recognized the value of the Legion and its commander. Rutledge, who was with Greene, was favorably impressed when he met Lee and saw his troops. "I like [Lee] very much and expect great service from his corps," the governor wrote. On January 11th, after Lee expressed his wish to increase the Legion's cavalry by 150 men, Rutledge approved and issued a proclamation urging "active and spirited young men in this State to join" Lee's corps.[6] Even the special attention of a governor's proclamation failed to increase Lee's force. The Legion's strength waned over time as new recruits were never sufficient to make up for the losses from constant hard service.

*****

The Military Situation in the South—January 1781

Lee and his Legion faced a situation in the South unlike anything that they had experienced in the North. The British had made steady inroads in the region since their capture of Savannah in December 1778, and the surrender of General Benjamin Lincoln's army at Charleston in May 1780. In the weeks following Charleston's surrender, British columns had fanned out across Georgia and South Carolina, occupying strategic positions in both states. Having commanded the victory at Charleston, General Sir Henry Clinton sailed back to New York in early June of 1780, leaving Lieutenant General Charles, Earl Cornwallis, in command of British forces in the South. While Cornwallis had busied himself with administrative duties in Charleston, the Continental Congress appointed Major General Horatio Gates, hero of the American victory at Saratoga three years earlier, to replace Lincoln and rebuild the southern army. Gates proceeded to North Carolina and took command of the seven regiments of Maryland Continentals and one from Delaware commanded by Major General the Baron De Kalb, troops that Washington had sent from the northern army to reinforce Charleston, but who did not reach that city before its surrender. Gates marched with the Continentals into South Carolina, where he was joined by large militia forces from North Carolina and Virginia that brought his total strength to over four thousand men. He established contact with partisan forces that had been recently organized by Thomas Sumter and Francis Marion, and devised a plan to drive the British from the interior of South Carolina.[7]

Gates' plans for the reconquest of the South ended abruptly when he suffered a disastrous defeat at the Battle of Camden, South Carolina on August 16th, 1780. He had placed the militia on the left of his line, and they melted away in the face of a British frontal assault, leaving De Kalb's seasoned Continental troops to fight on alone. DeKalb fell mortally wounded, and many of the Maryland and Delaware troops were taken prisoner. Small bands of these tough Continental troops managed to escape through the swamps that were adjacent to the battlefield and make their way to Charlotte, North Carolina, eighty miles to the north. There they would start the process of trying to rebuild an army from the shattered remnants of DeKalb's former command. In the meantime, Gates' fate as Commander of the Southern Army was sealed by the Camden defeat and by his hurried retreat from the battlefield to Hillsborough, North Carolina, 180 miles away. Lee sensed injustice toward Gates, as he had in the earlier case of Charles Lee after the Battle of Monmouth, and he confided to a friend that "the unfortunate general has been most insidiously, most cruelly traduced." As with his earlier defense of Charles Lee, young Lieutenant Colonel Lee's opinion on Gates was distinctly in the minority, and his support did little to shield either General from their fate.[8]

Cornwallis followed up his Camden victory with a leisurely eighty-mile advance to Charlotte, and the conquest of North Carolina seemed all but inevitable. However, bands of hardy frontiersmen surrounded a force of British loyalists commanded by Patrick Ferguson at the Battle of King's

Mountain on October 7th, 1780, and killed or captured nearly every man. Cornwallis retreated back into South Carolina and took up winter quarters at Winnsboro.[9]

Meanwhile, Congress relieved Gates of his command on October 5th, ordered an investigation into his conduct, and asked Washington to name a replacement to head the southern army. Washington chose Nathanael Greene. While awaiting Greene's arrival, Gates made great strides in consolidating the surviving Maryland and Delaware troops into new units, restoring the soldiers' morale, and organizing a corps of light troops for rapid movement. His greatest achievement, however, was to lure his old Saratoga comrade, Daniel Morgan, out of retirement.

Morgan had resigned from the army after command of Washington's light troops had been given to another officer whom Morgan considered to be less qualified than he was. When Gates took command in the Southern Department, he convinced Congress to promote Morgan to brigadier general if he would return to active service, and when that task was accomplished, Gates convinced Morgan to accept the promotion and return to the field. Unfortunately for Gates, Morgan did not join the army in time to fight at Camden, but his skills would greatly benefit Greene.[10]

Greene took command of the Southern Army at Charlotte, North Carolina, on December 2nd, 1780. Washington had warned the Board of War earlier that "the southern service is a disagreeable one," and Greene soon found that the commander-in-chief's assessment was correct. He wrote Washington that "the difficulties of the Northern service" paled in comparison to the obstacles he faced in the South. Greene explained these difficulties in detail to an unnamed friend:

> *"I find the difficulties of subsisting an army far beyond all anticipation. Even here, where the inhabitants are generally well disposed, they will not gather in their crops from the field, because depositing their grain in their barns exposes it to be seized by their friends, or burnt by their enemies. It is hard to stand so much in need of friends, and be compelled to subsist ourselves by means so well calculated to convert our friends into enemies. But we have not a shilling of money, and must collect for subsistence by force, or disband. I have had an opportunity of learning the force of loyalists in these states, and the parts of the country in which they reside, and their numbers and zeal present a formidable obstacle to our future measures. On the other hand, the whig population has been greatly reduced by the numbers that have fled from the distress that friends and foes have heaped upon them. ... At present [the British] are in possession of all the fertile*

and populous parts of South Carolina, and ... we shall have to oper-
ate in a country that has been exhausted and depopulated. ... North
Carolina has not a man on foot, and Virginia only a few raw and
naked troops, and those enlisted for a short time. The fine troops of
Maryland and Delaware ... are now reduced ... to a handful. ...
The whigs will not serve ... if forced to take the field, will run away,
desert, or betray us. [11]

Although Greene had a clear understanding of the difficulties before him, he had no intention of allowing Cornwallis to seize the initiative. On December 16th, 1780, while he was at Charlotte, he ordered Morgan to take command of a "Flying Army" consisting of 320 Maryland and Delaware Continentals, 200 Virginia riflemen, and William Washington's 100 Continental cavalrymen and march into northwestern South Carolina. Morgan's assigned objectives were to bolster the sagging morale of South Carolinians in that part of the state, harass British and loyalist forces when opportunity offered, and procure provisions for his troops because sufficient supplies were not available around Charlotte. Greene also hoped that by dividing his army, Cornwallis might do likewise and give Greene or Morgan a chance to attack part of the British force. Greene marched to Cheraw, where supplies were more abundant, on December 20th, and the next day Morgan left Charlotte to begin his campaign. [12]

Henry Lee arrived at Greene's camp at Cheraw in early January, and his assessment of the military situation in the South mirrored Greene's pessimism. On January 7th, the day after his arrival at Cheraw, he wrote a long letter to his friend, General Anthony Wayne, providing "Mad Anthony" with "a true presentation of the position of affairs" in the South, a necessity, Lee asserted, because the "truth" regarding the military situation in that region "very seldom reaches either Congress, the general [Washington], or the public." He briefly noted that Gates' army had been completely routed at the Battle of Camden, although, in his view, Gates would have prevailed if the militia had not given way. The American victory at Kings Mountain, Lee noted, won honor for the militia but brought no long term benefits; most of the loyalist prisoners had escaped and again taken up arms with the British. Other small victories won by Francis Marion and Lieutenant Colonel William Washington, who had reconstituted a regiment of Continental light dragoons and returned to action, were no more than "petty advantages" that "do not tend to the promotion of grand designs. Not a single post of the enemy has yet been broken up; their communication with Charleston is uninterrupted." Most of Thomas Sumter's recent partisan operations had failed. Given the small number of regular troops under Greene's command and the chronic supply shortages,

Lee concluded that "I am confident nothing important can be accomplished by this army in its present state." Lee expressed similar views in a letter that he wrote to Joseph Reed two days later, adding that Cornwallis would easily be able to invade the coastal region of North Carolina and appeared to be preparing for such a move.[13]

In spite of the pessimistic view shared by Greene and Lee, the two leaders looked for opportunities to make inroads against the growing British dominance in the South. Lee's arrival gave Greene the strength he needed to strike a second blow in addition to Morgan's thrust into western South Carolina. This one would be led by Francis Marion and Lee, and directed against the British in the northeastern section of that colony. Marion was a lieutenant colonel in the South Carolina Continentals, and had been leading partisan operations against the British and loyalists in that area since the summer of 1780. He and his regiment had taken part in the defense of Charleston, but nearly two months before the city surrendered he was furloughed home to recuperate from an injury.

Invited to a party with other American officers, Marion had learned to his chagrin that the affair was an all-night drinking fest; when he tried to leave, he found that his host had locked all of the doors. Marion broke his ankle when he escaped by jumping from a second story window. The event proved beneficial to the American cause, however, as it saved Marion from being taken prisoner when the British captured Charleston. In December 1780, South Carolina governor John Rutledge rewarded Marion for his successful guerrilla operations with a promotion to brigadier general in the state's militia.[14]

Marion contemplated an attack on Georgetown, a small port at the mouth of the Pee Dee River in northeastern South Carolina. He hoped that the capture of the town and its stockpiles of clothing, salt, and ammunition would relieve the supply shortages that plagued the partisans. The British had fortified Georgetown and used it as a base from which they raided the neighboring countryside for provisions and assisted the loyalist militia in the battle against Marion's force. Greene was willing to support Marion in the venture, sending him ammunition and expressing a desire to give the British "a Stroke in a little time, as Colonel Lees Legion is near at hand." On January 9th, 1781, Marion informed Greene that eighty troops had departed Georgetown on various assignments, reducing the British garrison to only two hundred men. The enemy, Marion reported, stayed "close in their redoubt." He left some of his men to watch the garrison and prevent them from launching any raids, while other detachments gathered rice and cattle to keep those supplies out of British hands. The day after the Legion arrived at Cheraw, Greene ordered Lee to join Marion. Lee may also have

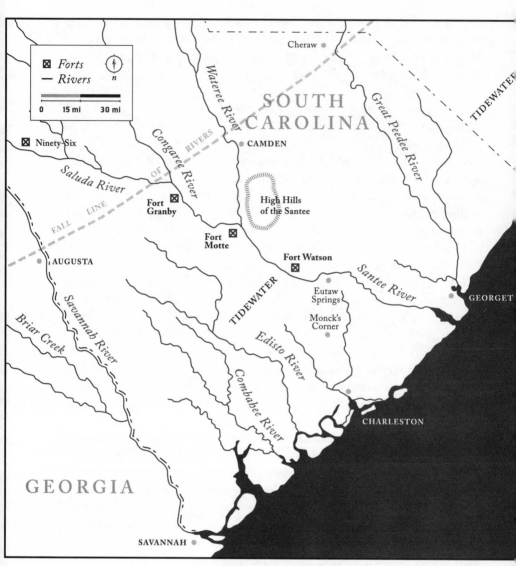

Lee's Operations in the South

recommended an attack on Georgetown. On January 12th, two days after Lee left Cheraw, Greene urged the Legion commander to act quickly. "The sooner you can carry into execution your project at George Town the better," Greene wrote. "Take your measures so as not to fail if possible, but if you should, with as little loss as may be; for a misfortune at this time would be little less than fatal."[15]

*****

The Attack on Georgetown

The Legion's march was slowed by heavy rains that flooded the many creeks and swamps on Lee's route. Nevertheless, Lee remained optimistic about the attack on Georgetown, telling Greene on January 16th that even though it would take the Legion several more days to reach Marion, "it is a very opportune moment to strike where I meditate." Meanwhile, Marion kept Greene informed of the Georgetown garrison's activities. On January 14th, he reported that some of his men under Colonel Peter Horry had skirmished with British troops led by the garrison's commandant, Colonel George Campbell, while Horry was driving off cattle and gathering boats. The partisan general worried that Campbell's foray was the first step in an attempt to link up with a party of 150 North Carolina loyalists under Hector McNeil, who had assembled at Drowning Creek near the border between the two Carolinas. McNeil, Marion warned, could then "collect a Large number of toreys from N. Carolina," and the combined British and loyalist force could operate unopposed in the border area, because if Marion moved against them it would leave the area around Georgetown and the Pee Dee River completely exposed to other British and loyalist troops. Marion's fears proved unfounded; four days later Campbell had withdrawn to Georgetown, nothing had been heard of McNeil, and one of Marion's detachments defeated a small party of the loyalist South Carolina Rangers. There appeared to be no remaining obstacles to an attacking Georgetown.[16]

Greene shared Marion's concerns over the several British and loyalist parties operating throughout eastern South Carolina. Learning that Colonel John Watson and two hundred British soldiers were at Nelson's Ferry on the Santee River, supported by some Hessian troops on the opposite bank, Greene advised Lee that while Georgetown remained the most important objective, the Legion and Marion should also examine the possibility of cutting off and attacking Watson's detachment. Greene also considered the possibility of sending troops from his own army to assist Marion in striking Watson, and on January 16th he asked the partisan commander to provide him information regarding possible routes of march and a location where Greene's and Marion's troops could unite. Later that same day, Greene suggested another operation:

a combined attack by some of Lee's and Marion's troops on McNeil's loyalists at Drowning Creek. Greene noted that the latter operation should only be undertaken if it would not interfere with the assault on Georgetown. Two days later, Greene abandoned the idea of sending some of his own troops to attack Watson and instead detached two hundred men to disperse McNeil's loyalists at Drowning Creek.[17]

By January 20th, the Legion still had not joined Marion's partisans, although Lee was close enough to dispatch an officer, Major John Rudulph, to meet with Marion. The conference did not go well. The Legion commander complained to Greene that Marion's reaction to Lee's plan for the attack on Georgetown was "not so favourable." Lee declared that he would cross the Pee Dee River and then "see further into things & measures." Perhaps piqued by Marion's negative reaction to his plan, Lee also informed Greene that he was sending all his wagons back to Cheraw because it was "repugnant to common sense" for light troops to operate with even a single wagon. Marion wrote to Greene the same day, noting only that he had spoken to "an Officer from Colo Lee." Yet Marion must have been equally dissatisfied with the results of the conference, because after explaining that the nature of the terrain made it virtually impossible for troops from Greene's army to surprise Watson's corps and discussing supply matters, Marion asserted that "should I join in duty with [Lee], I expect to command, not from the Militia Commission I hold, but from an elder Continental Commission." Marion said that he had raised the issue so that his authority "may not in any Juncture be Disputed." However, Marion stated that he would provide Lee with intelligence and cooperate with him if there were an "Opportunity to do any thing against the Enemy."[18]

Upon receiving Lee's letter, Greene crafted a careful reply, offering advice on the Georgetown operation while studiously avoiding any reference to the meeting between Rudulph and Marion. "The difficulties you say are greater than you expected in carrying into execution your plan of attack" against Georgetown, Greene observed. "Get good information before you attempt any thing. Your Corps is too valuable to throw away without some important object in view." Greene noted if Lee's attack failed, the British were not in a position to capitalize on it since it would take them eight to ten days to get reinforcements to the Georgetown area. The general reassured Lee that "I am fully perswaded of your zeal; and I have full confidence in your discretion." He also hinted that if Lee found that an assault on Georgetown was not feasible, another target was nearby. "Dont forget Watsons Corps upon the Santee. Perhaps all things considerd that may be the most inviting object."[19]

Lee and the Legion arrived at Marion's camp on Snow's Island on January 23rd, where Lee may have been surprised by the warm reception he received. The Legion, Lee declared, was "in excellent condition," and greatly impressed

Marion's ragged militiamen. One of Marion's officers, Colonel Peter Horry, described the arrival of Lee and his troops:

> *"Colonel Lee with his legion came up, to the inexpressible joy of us all; partly on account of his cavalry, which to be sure, was the handsomest we had ever seen; but much more on account of himself, of whom we had heard that, in deep art and undaunted courage, he was a second Marion. This, our high opinion of him, was greatly exalted [later] by his own gallant conduct."[20]*

The inauspicious first meeting between Marion and Major Rudulph of the Legion proved to have no effect on the relationship between Lee and Marion. The two officers apparently got along well from the moment they met, and Lee accepted Marion's authority without protest. Lee was disappointed to learn that Marion lacked "that sort of intelligence" regarding the post at Georgetown "necessary for the full execution" of Lee's planned attack, but Lee, declaring that "loss of time cannot be admitted," outlined a plan that he believed would succeed. He and Marion began making the necessary preparations, and the militia general ordered his detachments back to Snow's Island to assist in the operation. Before the end of the day they had agreed on how to proceed, and ninety infantrymen of the Legion accompanied by some of Marion's men set off down the Pee Dee River in flatboats, heading toward Georgetown.[21]

Lee and Marion examined Georgetown's fortifications and were unimpressed. "In his front," Lee wrote, Colonel Campbell "had prepared some slight defences, better calculated to repel a sudden, than resist a determined assault. Between these defences and the town … was an inclosed work … which constituted his chief protection." Aside from a small number of troops in the fort, Campbell had dispersed the remainder of his troops "in light parties in and near the town, looking toward the country." No preparations had been made to resist an assault from the Pee Dee River, and that stratagem was exactly what Marion and Lee intended. Lee's ninety infantrymen, commanded by captains Patrick Carnes and Michael Rudulph, had traveled down the Pee Dee and concealed themselves on an island throughout the day of January 24th. That night, Lee with the Legion cavalry and Marion and his partisans marched to Georgetown. The infantry would land between one and two o'clock on the morning of January 25th and begin the attack. When Lee and Marion heard the first shots, they would join the assault from the landward side of the town.[22]

The attack began well. Carnes and his troops came ashore at Mitchell's Landing, meeting no opposition and achieving complete surprise. The

Legion infantry marched on an embankment bordering a rice field and into Georgetown, where in accordance with orders they moved immediately to Colonel Campbell's quarters. The building was adjacent to an open area that the British garrison used as a parade ground, and Lee expected the town's defenders to try to assemble there. Carnes's men captured Campbell, killed his second-in-command, and then prepared to ambush the garrison when it turned out. Rudulph and his troops, who had landed shortly after Carnes, occupied their assigned position between the town and the small fort.[23]

Then the American plan began to unravel. Muddy roads slowed the march of Lee's and Marion's force, so that they arrived after Carnes and Rudulph had begun the attack. Lee blamed "the blunders of the guides" for preventing him from coordinating his assault with that of the Legion infantry. When Lee and Marion arrived, they charged into the town, and found the infantrymen properly positioned. The small British force in the fort had finally been alerted and held its ground, and the rest of the garrison did not react as Lee had expected. He described his "astonishment" at the British response in his memoirs:

> *"Not a British soldier appeared; not one attempted either to gain the fort, or repair to the commandant. Having discovered their enemy, the troops of the garrison kept close to their respective quarters, barricaded the doors, and determined there to defend themselves. The assailants were unprovided with the requisite implements for battering doors and scaling windows."*

The American troops also lacked artillery. Lee and Marion decided that an effort to storm the fort or the buildings would cost more casualties than the result would be worth. As dawn broke, they paroled Campbell and a few other captured officers and withdrew from the town. Lee reported one killed and two wounded among the Legion, while Marion did not record any casualties. Aside from the few prisoners, British losses were likewise small, with only two or three men killed. Lee expressed some frustration at having been "in some degree baffled in the important consequences" he had hoped to achieve.[24]

One of Marion's militiamen, William Dobein James, asserted that the attack's failure was the result of poor planning. James believed that if the Legion infantry had "pushed up directly to the redoubt" and seized it when they had the element of surprise, the entire town and garrison might have been taken. Instead, during the delay incurred by finding and capturing Campbell, the British troops were "alarmed and placed in a state of defence." Marion viewed the affair more optimistically, informing Greene that he and Lee had a "Little Success on Georgetown, which could not be greater without artillery." The partisan general was also impressed with Lee's military abilities, and declared that "Colo Lee's Interprising Genius promises much."[25]

In fact Lee was already hard at work planning other operations. The same morning that he withdrew from Georgetown, Lee dispatched Captain Joseph Eggleston with some of the Legion cavalry to cross the Santee River and destroy a British supply magazine at Thompson's Plantation. Marion assigned two detachments from his brigade to cooperate with Eggleston, and the militia succeeded in the mission after Eggleston was thwarted when he could not procure canoes to cross the river. Lee also considered a second assault on Georgetown but rejected the idea after learning that the garrison had been reinforced by troops sent from Charleston by sea. Another possibility Lee weighed was "an enterprise against Wilmington," North Carolina, where the British had a garrison. Marion preferred to move against a small party of forty troops defending Fort Watson at Wright's Bluff on the Santee. Lee agreed, and on January 27th Marion notified Greene that their forces were about to undertake the expedition. The planned attack had to be canceled, however, because although Lee did not yet know it, the situation elsewhere in the Carolinas had taken a serious turn, and Greene ordered Lee to rejoin the main army as soon as possible.[26]

*****

The Race to the Dan

On January 17th, while Lee and the Legion were still struggling through the flooded lowlands towards Marion's camp, Greene's strategy of dividing his army produced a major victory. As Greene had hoped, Daniel Morgan's foray into northwestern South Carolina induced Lord Cornwallis to divide his own army. The British general decided that Morgan's movements endangered the important British post at Ninety Six, and on January 1st he ordered his cavalry commander, Lieutenant Colonel Banastre Tarleton, to drive Morgan from the backcountry. Tarleton set out the next day with 550 infantry and cavalry of his own British Legion and 200 troops from the 1st Battalion of the 71st Regiment. Shortly afterward, Cornwallis sent Tartleton an additional 50 cavalrymen from the 17th Light Dragoons and 200 infantry from the 7th Regiment. Cornwallis expected Tarleton to drive Morgan toward the Broad River, where Cornwallis would march with the rest of the army to trap and destroy the American force. Morgan quashed the British plans with a decisive victory over Tarleton at the Battle of Cowpens on January 17th, 1781[27]

Greene learned of Morgan's victory on January 23rd and immediately sent the news to Marion, asking the partisan general to relay the information to Lee since Greene did not have time to write a separate letter to the Legion commander. Lee received the news with a mixture of joy and regret, telling Greene that "I congratulate you from my soul on the glorious victory obtained by Genl Morgan. I wish my fortune [at Georgetown] had been equally propitious, as then Lord Cornwalis must have been exceedingly distressed." Cornwallis was indeed distressed, and Greene hoped to capitalize on the victory at Cowpens by increasing the pressure on the British. He informed Lee on January 26th that he was setting out for Charlotte to confer with Morgan, plus South Carolina militia generals Andrew Pickens and Thomas Sumter, and General William Davidson of the North Carolina militia. Greene contemplated moving the entire army to the vicinity of Ninety Six, and if he did so, he wanted the Legion with him. Therefore he advised Lee to "be in readiness to act in concert with us."[28]

Greene's plans were rendered moot by Cornwallis, who finally marched on January 19th after he had learned of the defeat at Cowpens. The British army moved towards the battlefield, its commander hoping that Morgan had lingered in the area and might still be defeated and the seven hundred British prisoners released. Tarleton, scouting ahead of the main force, discovered that Morgan had left the Cowpens area. The wily Virginian realized that Cornwallis might try to retake the captives and had retreated across the Catawba River. Cornwallis changed the direction of his march and reached Ramseur's Mill, North Carolina, on January 24th. Morgan was only twenty miles away, and the British commander decided to speed his march by destroying all of the army's excess baggage and wagons, in effect converting the entire British force into light infantry. Cornwallis, unable to march because of heavy rains, spent three days burning all of the army's goods except ammunition, salt, and medical supplies.[29]

The British army began its pursuit of Morgan on January 28th. The next day, Morgan rode to Beattie's Ford on the Catawba River. "The enemy is within ten miles of [this] place in force," Morgan notified Greene, adding that he could see their vanguard. Fresh intelligence reported that Cornwallis had burned his wagons, and four British prisoners stated that their army was headed for Salisbury, deep in the interior of North Carolina. Recognizing the urgency in Morgan's message, Greene hastened to Sherrald's Ford on the Catawba and consulted with Morgan. The British army was eighteen miles away and advancing with determination. Greene realized that he had no choice but to abandon his other plans and concentrate his entire army in North Carolina. He promptly wrote to his second-in-command, Brigadier General Isaac Huger, who had remained with the troops at Cheraw, and ordered him to "hasten your march towards Salisbury as fast as possible." After explaining all the details regarding the movement of provisions, Greene instructed Huger: "Desire Lt Col Lee to force a March to join us."[30]

Unaware of the new orders, Lee replied that same day to Greene's earlier letter of January 26th, and another sent by Greene's adjutant, Colonel Otho

Holland Williams, who had pressed Lee to "join with dispatch." Lee replied that the Legion cavalry had been detached and he could not march to join the rest of the army until the mounted troops returned on February 2nd.[31] The long time lag in communications between Greene and the scattered elements of his army put the Americans at risk of being beaten in detail if Cornwallis was able to engage part of the Continental force before all of Greene's units could be united.

Cornwallis crossed the Catawba River on the morning of February 1st, and Greene worried that the British were marching so swiftly that they might reach Salisbury in the next day or two. Greene had summoned the North Carolina militia to his assistance, but they were still assembling and Greene did not consider his force sufficient to slow the British advance. He thus ordered Huger to march the troops from Cheraw up the east side of the Yadkin River toward Salisbury, where the river would protect them from a sudden British thrust. He also directed that the army's supplies be sent to the town of Guilford, where they would be farther from Cornwallis. "To have the baggage and Stores secure is the next great object to the salvation of the troops," he explained to Huger. Finally, Greene told Huger to order Lee to "move up" with his cavalry, letting the slower moving Legion infantry follow. Greene wanted Lee's cavalry to bolster the militia. "Had we a superiority in horse the Militia would be useful but for want of which the Militia dare not go within Miles of the Enemy," Greene observed.[32]

In an effort to avoid any further delays in Lee's joining the main army that might result from the slow channels of communication, Greene dispatched one of his aides, Major Ichabod Burnet, to Lee. Burnet reached the Pee Dee River at Mask's Ferry, North Carolina, on February 2nd and dispatched a letter to Lee. The only cavalry with Greene, Burnet wrote, were sixty men of Lt. Col. William Washington's Continental Light Dragoons, who were too few to challenge Banastre Tarleton's 250 British cavalrymen. Greene's "anxiety to collect the cavalry is very great," Burnet noted, as without "a superiority in cavalry" the militia "will not assemble or annoy the enemy." Burnet then did his best to explain the seriousness of the situation:

> *"If you knew the anxiety of General Greene, who is now exposing himself to collect the militia, which he expects only to accomplish by having a superiority of horse. Indeed our army cannot keep the field one moment after they cross the Yadkin, unless we have a superiority of cavalry."*

Burnet, clearly attuned to Lee's driving ambition, concluded his appeal with the observation that the campaign would give Lee a chance to obtain further glory, writing that unless Lee could join Greene "immediately" the Legion commander might "lose the opportunity of acquiring wreaths of laurels."[33]

Lee wrote to Greene on February 3rd, before he received Burnet's letter. The Legion commander had moved to Culp's Ferry on the Pee Dee River, about thirty miles south of Cheraw, but still had no idea of the serious threat that Greene faced. Lee told Greene that he had hurried to his present position, although he had to wait there another day for two troops of his cavalry to join him. He went on to describe the opportunities for successful operations south of the Santee River, going so far as to suggest that Greene detach troops and artillery to reinforce the Legion so that Lee could attack British posts in the area.[34]

If Lee did not develop an accurate picture of the true state of affairs and react quickly, he and his Legion were in danger of being cut off. The British army reached Salisbury on February 4th, where Cornwallis learned that Morgan's force was just ahead at Trading Ford, and had not yet crossed the Yadkin River. Cornwallis dispatched Brigadier General Charles O'Hara with a mixed force of infantry and cavalry to strike Morgan, but "owing to rain, darkness, and bad roads, the troops did not arrive at the Yadkin till near midnight," where they discovered that Morgan had crossed a few hours earlier, taking all the boats to the opposite shore. The river was too high to be forded, and O'Hara occupied high ground and the west bank. The American and British forces spent the next two days facing one another across the rain-swollen river.[35]

On the night of February 6th, with the rain having abated and the Yadkin falling, Morgan undertook a night march to Guilford Courthouse, the town that Greene had designated as a rendezvous point for the American army. The Continental troops marched forty-seven grueling miles on muddy roads to reach their destination. Huger arrived there with the force from Cheraw on the afternoon of February 7th. Greene's army had now completely assembled, with the notable exception of Lee's Legion. Lee, however, having finally learned of the crisis created by the British advance, had hastened northward and was moving closer to the rendezvous point at Guilford Courthouse. Huger informed Greene on February 8th that "Lee with the cavalry of his Legion is two miles and a half on this side of Bell's Mill. I have thought proper to halt him there 'till he received your orders." Lee's position was about thirty miles distant from the rest of the army, and Greene sent Lee orders to march during the night of the eighth to move closer to Guilford Courthouse.[36]

Lee finally arrived at Greene's headquarters on February 9th, where he was immediately assigned an important task. Greene had decided to organize a light corps comprising his best troops, who would act as a rear guard to protect the main army from Cornwallis while Greene conducted a retreat to Virginia. Greene believed Morgan was the officer most suited to command this elite corps, but the Virginian was suffering from sciatica and several other ailments and had requested a discharge to his home. Knowing that Lee was a close friend of Morgan, Greene asked the Legion commander to call on Morgan and try and persuade his fellow Virginian to remain with the army as commander of the light troops. Lee tried "many commonplace arguments," yet Morgan remained unmoved. Lee then suggested that Morgan's departure

> *"at that crisis might induce an opinion unfavorable to his patriotism, and prejudicial to his future fame; that the resignation of a successful soldier at a critical moment was often attributed, and sometimes justly, to an apprehension that the contest would ultimately be unfortunate to his country, or to a conviction that his reputation had been accidentally acquired, and could not survive the vicissitudes of war."*

This argument, Lee saw, "appeared to touch the feelings of Morgan," and he hesitated briefly before announcing that his physical condition would not allow him to continue in service. Greene reluctantly concurred and granted Morgan a leave of absence. Colonel Otho Holland Williams of Maryland received command of the light corps.[37]

Greene selected his best officers to serve under Williams: Lt. Col. John Eager Howard, another Marylander who had earned a silver medal from Congress for his distinguished leadership at the Battle of Cowpens; Lt. Col. William Washington, who had also shown outstanding skills and won a silver medal at Cowpens; and Lee. The light corps numbered 700 men, including the infantry and cavalry of Lee's Legion, and it would have to face Cornwallis's 2,400 veteran British soldiers. Cornwallis, unable to ford the Yadkin because of the high water level, had sent Tarleton with his cavalry and the 23rd Regiment of infantry upstream to search for a crossing. Tarleton encountered some American militiamen, who fled on his approach, and learned that the upper tributaries of the Yadkin could be forded. He informed Cornwallis, and the British general moved northward, crossed the streams, and reached the town of Salem, twenty-five miles from Guilford Courthouse, on February 9th. That same day Cornwallis learned that Greene had succeeded in uniting his army.[38]

Williams and his detachment left Guilford Courthouse on February 10th and moved northwest to Bruce's Crossroads near Reedy Fork Creek to take position between Cornwallis's army and Greene's as the latter marched in a northeasterly direction. "This was exactly the proper position for the light corps, and Williams judiciously retained it," Lee wrote. Williams hoped that

Cornwallis would believe that the light troops were directly behind Greene's army and follow them, drawing the British away from Greene's actual route. Cornwallis, "wishing to intercept the Americans, and force them to action," followed Williams. Uncertain whether Cornwallis had been deceived by his ruse, on February 11th Williams fell back from the crossroads and dispatched two parties of cavalry to find the enemy. The scouting parties informed Williams that Cornwallis was approaching, whereupon the Marylander ordered Lee and a troop of the Legion cavalry toward the British. Lee encountered Tarleton and the British advance guard at the crossroads and charged them; the Americans were repulsed, and according to Tarleton suffered "some loss." A British officer and some of his men attempted to pursue Lee's retreating dragoons, but Lee turned on them and captured the officer and three men. The prisoners informed Williams that "Ld Cornwallis & the whole British Army ... is close in our rear."[39]

Cornwallis continued to press Williams throughout the next day, and in a series of maneuvers forced the light corps from a strong position they had occupied at Chambers Mill. By sunset on February 12th the British were only twenty-two miles from Greene's army and only ten miles from Williams and his troops. The cavalry officers told Williams that "their Horses want refreshment exceedingly," and the infantrymen were "so excessively fatigu'd" that some were left behind every day, unable to keep up with their comrades. Lee later described the ordeal of the troops in his memoirs:

> "The duty, severe in the day, became more so at night; for numerous patrols and strong pickets were necessarily furnished by the light troops, not only for their own safety, but to prevent the enemy from placing himself, by a circuitous march, between Williams and Greene. Such a manoeuvre would have been fatal to the American army; and, to render it impossible, half of the troops were alternately appropriated every night to duty: so that each man, during the retreat, was entitled to but six hours' repose in forty-eight. Notwithstanding this privation, the troops were in fine spirits and good health; delighted with their task, and determined to prove themselves worthy the distinction with which they had been honored. At the hour of three, their toils were renewed; for Williams always pressed forward with the utmost dispatch in the morning, to gain such a distance in front as would secure breakfast to his soldiers, their only meal during this rapid and hazardous retreat. So fatigued was officer and soldier, and so much more operative is weariness than hunger, that each man not placed on duty surrendered himself to repose as soon as the night position was taken."[40]

Lee and his dragoons were enjoying their morning breakfast respite on February 13th when Isaac Wright, a local resident, rode into their camp to report that he had seen British cavalrymen only two or three miles from Lee's position. Lee ordered Captain James Armstrong and a detachment of mounted troops to accompany Wright back to the supposed location of the enemy and verify the information. After riding for more than three miles, which caused an angry Armstrong to accuse Wright of giving false information, Lee's horsemen encountered some dragoons of the British Legion, who immediately charged them. Armstrong and his men raced back to Lee's camp with the enemy in close pursuit. Lee, hearing carbine fire, prepared an ambush. Just as the British dragoons rode into the trap, several of them caught up with James Gillies, a bugler in Lee's Legion, and killed him with their sabers. The Legion troopers then opened fire, killing and wounding several British cavalrymen, and the remainder fled. Lee, infuriated by the death of Gillies, ordered one of his lieutenants to pursue the fugitives, and "to give no quarters" to any who tried to surrender. When his troops returned after having captured Captain David Miller and several other prisoners, Lee "reprimanded" the lieutenant "on the spot for disobedience of orders." He decided to hang Miller in retaliation for the death of Gillies, and the captain's life was spared only because more British troops were rapidly approaching, thus leaving Lee no time to conduct an execution. The prisoners were sent to Williams, and the Legion cavalry resumed its rearguard duties. Lee freely admitted that he had given orders to take no prisoners and to hang Miller, justifying his actions as retaliation for what he termed the "murder" of Gillies and other alleged atrocities committed by Tarleton's British Legion. Despite Lee's effort to defend his actions, this incident demonstrated the young lieutenant colonel's volatile temperament and how quickly he could flare into a violent rage when provoked by what he deemed an injustice.[41]

Williams continued to fall back, with Lee's cavalry acting as rear guard. The American light corps marched toward Dix's Ferry, hoping to lure Cornwallis farther away from Greene, who was headed to Irwin's Ferry on the Dan River. Cornwallis, however, learned from a captured American militiaman that Williams's movement was a ruse, and deftly changed direction. The British followed a trail that led directly toward Greene's army. Hours earlier, Lee had taken the same detour after he learned from local guides that it would allow the Legion to reunite with the light corps while reducing their march by "a considerable distance." Upon reaching Andrew Boyd's farm, Lee allowed his men to rest and partake of the food that Boyd offered them. Lee admitted that "the obscurity of the narrow road" that the Legion had taken "lulled every suspicion with respect to the enemy," and the Legion posted only a few sentries. Then, "to the surprise and grief of all, the pleasant prospect was instantly marred by the fire" of the sentries, Lee reported. General O'Hara's advance guard had arrived.[42]

Fortunately for Lee, the British were "equally surprised" by the unexpected encounter. O'Hara ordered his light infantry to form line of battle, a difficult task in the wooded terrain. Lee took advantage of the brief reprieve to order his infantry to move at a run across a bridge at the opposite end of the farmstead, while he deployed the Legion cavalry to fight a delaying action. As soon as the infantry cleared the bridge, the dragoons followed. O'Hara pursued, but his exhausted soldiers could not catch the Legion. Lee and his Legion only narrowly escaped defeat. Late in the day they rejoined Williams and the rest of the light corps at Harts Old Stores and the entire force continued to retreat.[43]

O'Hara, despite having already marched twenty-four miles that day, did not relent. Tarleton's dragoons, searching for the American camp, encountered some of the light corps' pickets after midnight and exchanged shots with them, causing Williams to rouse his troops and march several more miles during the early morning hours of February 14th. Shortly after dawn, Williams received a pessimistic message from Greene; the American general declared that he was preparing "for the worst."[44]

As Williams pressed on to Irwin's Ferry, the news became progressively better. At two p.m. Greene wrote to say that he had gotten most of the wagons across the Dan and that the Continentals were crossing. Greene wrote again at 5:30 in the afternoon, telling Williams that the whole army had reached safety in Virginia. The general added that he was waiting for the light corps, and prepared to give Williams and his troops "a hearty welcome." The light corps arrived during the night and everyone, including Lee's Legion, was safe on the Virginia side of the Dan by sunrise on February 15th.[45]

Cornwallis arrived a few hours later, but could not follow. His men were exhausted, and Greene had secured all the boats on the Virginia shore. The British general's gamble had failed despite the best efforts of his troops, as Cornwallis explained to the Secretary of State for the American Department, Lord George Germain:

> *"Nothing could exceed the patience and alacrity of the officers and soldiers under every species of hardship and fatigue in endeavoring to overtake [the Americans]: But our intelligence upon this occasion was exceedingly defective; which, with heavy rains, bad roads, and the passage of many deep creeks, and bridges destroyed by the enemy's light troops, rendered all our exertions vain."*[46]

On February 16th the British army began a slow withdrawal to

Hillsborough, North Carolina. Greene's troops enjoyed a period of rest and the unusual experience of adequate supplies. Lee summed up the importance of the Race to the Dan, asserting that "no operation during the war attracted the public attention than this … the safety of the South, hanging on its issue, excited universal concern." Had Greene not won the race, Lee believed, "all the country south of [the] James River … would soon be ground to dust and ashes" by the British. Greene, however, had won the race, and was already preparing to return to North Carolina and challenge Cornwallis once again.[47]

---

1   Washington to Lee, Oct. 22, 1780, Washington Papers, LOC.

2   Washington to the Board of War, Oct. 22, 1780; Washington to John Mathews, Oct. 23, 1780, Washington Papers, LOC.

3   Ford, ed., *JCC*, Oct. 31, 1780, 18:997 (quotation); Cecere, 145; Lee's Commission as Lieutenant Colonel, Nov. 6, 1780, Lee Family Papers, VHS.

4   Lee, *Memoirs*, 31-32.

5   Lee, *Memoirs*, 32. South Carolina Governor John Rutledge, who was at the American camp when the Legion arrived, put their number at 260, Robert D. Bass, *Swamp Fox: The Life and Campaigns of General Francis Marion* (Orangeburg, SC: Sandlapper Publishing, 1974), 132. General Nathanael Greene, commander of the Continental Army in the South, stated that Lee had 240 men, Nathanael Greene to Benjamin Harrison, Jan. 20, 1781, in Richard K. Showman and Dennis M. Conrad, eds., *The Papers of General Nathanael Greene*, Vol. 7 (Chapel Hill: University of North Carolina Press, 1994), 162. The discrepancy may have arisen from American officers' practice of counting only enlisted men, while Rutledge, a civilian, may have included officers in his tally.

6   Nathanael Greene to Francis Marion, Jan. 4, 1781, in Showman and Conrad, eds., *Papers of Greene*, 7:47 (quotation); Bass, *Swamp Fox*, 132 (quotation); Lee, *Memoirs*, 32 (quotation).

7   Jim Piecuch, *The Battle of Camden: A Documentary History* (Charleston, SC: History Press, 2006), 12, 13, 16; Jim Piecuch and John Beakes, *"Cool Deliberate Courage": John Eager Howard in the American Revolution* (Charleston, SC: Nautical & Aviation Publishing, 2009), 37.

8   Piecuch and Beakes, "Cool Deliberate Courage," 39-44; Lee to Anthony Wayne, Jan. 7, 1781, in Lee, *Memoirs*, 33 (quotation.).

9   Piecuch and Beakes, *"Cool Deliberate Courage,"* 44-45.

10 Piecuch and Beakes, *"Cool Deliberate Courage,"* 47-50; Piecuch, *Battle of Camden*, 143.

11 Washington to the Board of War, April 9, 1780, Washington Papers, LOC (quotation); Greene to Washington, Jan. 24, 1781, in Showman and Conrad, eds., *Papers of Greene*, 7:181 (quotation); Greene to Unidentified Person, Jan. 1-23, 1781, in ibid., 175-176 (quotation).

12 Piecuch and Beakes, *Cool Deliberate Courage*, 54-55.

13 Lee to Anthony Wayne, Jan. 7, 1781; Lee to Joseph Reed, Jan. 9, 1781, in Lee, *Memoirs*, 33-34 (quotations), 35-36.

14 Bass, *Swamp Fox*, 28, 29, 126.

15 William Dobein James, *A Sketch of the Life of Brig. Gen. Francis Marion and a History of his Brigade from Its Rise in June 1780 until Disbanded in December 1782* (Marietta, GA: Continental Book Co., 1948), 65; Marion to Greene, Jan. 1, 1781, in Showman and Conrad, editors, *Papers of Greene*, 7:36; Greene to Marion, Jan. 4, 1781, ibid., 7:47 (quotation); Marion to Greene, Jan. 9, 1781, ibid., 7:86 (quotation); Greene to Lee, Jan. 12, 1781, ibid., 7:104 (quotation) and 104n. regarding the possibility that Lee suggested attacking Georgetown; Lee, *Memoirs*, 223.

16 Lee to Greene, Jan. 16, 1781, in Showman and Conrad, editors, *Papers of Greene*, 7:136 (quotation); Marion to Greene, Jan. 14, 1781, ibid., 7:121 (quotation); Marion to Greene, Jan. 18, 1781, ibid., 7:143.

17 Greene to Lee, Jan. 15, 1781, in Showman and Conrad, editors, *Papers of Greene*, 7:123; Greene to Marion, Jan. 16, 1781, ibid., 7:131; Greene to Marion, Jan. 16, 1781, ibid., 7:132 Greene to Marion, Jan. 19, 1781, ibid., 7:145.

18 Lee to Greene, Jan. 20, 1781, in Showman and Conrad, editors, *Papers of Greene*, 7:164 (quotation); Marion to Greene, Jan. 20, 1781, ibid., 7:164-165 (quotations); Bass, *Swamp Fox*, 133 (quotation).

19 Greene to Lee, Jan. 21, 1781, in Showman and Conrad, editors, *Papers of Greene*, 7:166-167.

20 Lee, *Memoirs*, 223 (quotation); Peter Horry and Mason L. Weems, *The Life of General Francis Marion* (Philadelphia, PA: Joseph Allen, 1852), 195 (quotation). Although Weems often embellished his biographies, in this case Horry's words are consistent with other evidence and therefore probably accurate.

21 Lee to Greene, Jan. 23, 1781, in Showman and Conrad, editors, *Papers of Greene*, 7:177 (quotations); Lee, *Memoirs*, 223; Bass, *Swamp Fox*, 135; James, *Life of Marion*, 90.

22 Lee, *Memoirs*, 223 (quotation), 224; Bass, *Swamp Fox*, 135; James, *Life of Marion*, 90-91.

23 James, *Life of Marion*, 91; Lee, *Memoirs*, 224; Bass, *Swamp Fox*, 135-136.

24 Lee, *Memoirs*, 224 (quotation); Bass, *Swamp Fox*, 136-137; Lee to Greene, Jan. 25, 1781, in Showman and Conrad, editors, *Papers of Greene*, 7:197-198 (quotations).

25 James, *Life of Marion*, 91 (quotations); Marion to Greene, Jan. 27, 1781, in Showman and Conrad, editors, *Papers of Greene*, 7:207 (quotations).

26 Lee to Greene, Jan. 27, 1781, in Showman and Conrad, editors, *Papers of Greene*, 7:206-207; Lee to Greene, Jan. 25, 1781, ibid., 7:197 (quotation); Marion to Greene, Jan. 27, 1781, ibid., 7:207.

27 Piecuch and Beakes, *Cool Deliberate Courage*, 55-65.

28 Greene to Marion, Jan. 23, 1781, in Showman and Conrad, editors, *Papers of Greene*, 7:173; Lee to Greene, Jan. 27, 1781, ibid., 7:206 (quotation); Greene to Lee, Jan. 26, 1781, ibid., 7:202 (quotation).

29 Piecuch and Beakes, *Cool Deliberate Courage*, 71.

30 Piecuch and Beakes, *Cool Deliberate Courage*, 71; Morgan to Greene, Jan. 29, 1781, in Showman and Conrad, editors, *Papers of Greene*, 7:215 (quotation); Greene to Isaac Huger, Jan. 30, 1781, ibid., 7:219-220 (quotation).

31 Lee to Greene, Jan. 30, 1781, in Showman and Conrad, editors, *Papers of Greene*, 7:222.

32 Greene to Huger, Feb. 1, 1781, in Showman and Conrad, editors, *Papers of Greene*, 7:231.

33 Ichabod Burnet to Lee, Feb. 2, 1781, in Showman and Conrad, editors, *Papers of Greene*, 7:234-235.

34 Lee to Greene, Feb. 3, 1781, in Showman and Conrad, editors, *Papers of Greene*, 7:247-248.

35 Banastre Tarleton, *A History of the Campaigns of 1780 and 1781, in the Southern Provinces of North America* (London: T. Cadell, 1787), 227.

36 Piecuch and Beakes, *Cool Deliberate Courage*, 74; Huger to Greene, Feb. 8, 1781, in Showman and Conrad, editors, *Papers of Greene*, 7:259 (quotation); Greene to Lee, Feb. 8, 1781, ibid., 7:257.

37 Piecuch and Beakes, *Cool Deliberate Courage*, 75; Lee, *Memoirs*, 237 (quotations).

38 Piecuch and Beakes, *Cool Deliberate Courage*, 73, 74-75; Tarleton, 227-228.

39 Thomas J. Edmonds, *The Tactical Retreat of General Nathanael Greene* (Privately published, 2006), 2; Lee, *Memoirs*, 238 (quotation); Tarleton, 228 (quotations); Otho Williams to Greene, Feb. 11, 1781, in Showman and Conrad, editors, *Papers of Greene*, 7:283 (quotation).

40 Williams to Greene, Feb. 13, 1781, in Showman and Conrad, editors, *Papers of Greene*, 7:285-286 (quotations); Lee, *Memoirs*, 238-239 (quotation).

41 Edmonds, 3-4; Lee, *Memoirs*, 239-242 (quotations). In defending his order to give the enemy "no quarters," i.e. to take no prisoners even if British soldiers attempted to surrender, Lee specifically mentioned the "terrible slaughter" of Colonel Abraham Buford's Virginia Continentals at the Battle of the Waxhaws on May 29, 1780 (342). While Lee and other Americans believed that Tarleton's British Legion had murdered dozens of Buford's troops as they attempted to surrender, a careful analysis of the battle indicates that no such atrocity actually occurred. See Jim Piecuch, *The Blood Be Upon Your Head: Tarleton and the Myth of Buford's Massacre* (Lugoff, SC: Southern Campaigns of the American Revolution Press, 2010).

42 Lee, *Memoirs*, 243-244 (quotations); Edmonds, 5.

43 Lee, *Memoirs*, 244 (quotation); Edmonds, 5.

44 Edmonds, 6; Greene to Williams, Feb. 14, 1781, 4 a.m., in Showman and Conrad, editors, *Papers of Greene*, 7:287 (quotation).

45 Edmonds, 8; Greene to Williams, Feb. 14, 1781, 2 p.m., and second letter of 5:30 p.m., in Showman and Conrad, editors, *Papers of Greene*, 7:287.

46 Edmonds, 8; Charles, Lord Cornwallis to Lord George Germain, March 17, 1781, in Tarleton, 264 (quotation).

47 Edmonds, 9; Cornwallis to Germain, March 17, 1781, in Tarleton, 264; Lee, *Memoirs*, 247 (quotation).

CHAPTER SIX

GREENE'S RE-ENTRY TO NORTH CAROLINA AND
THE BATTLE OF GUILFORD COURTHOUSE

Nathanael Greene's troops enjoyed a few days of rest in their camp at Halifax, Virginia, protected from their British pursuers by the Dan River. The local inhabitants were friendly, and the Continental soldiers reveled in the rare luxury of having more than enough to eat. Lee recalled that the army's morale was high, "as if every man was conscious of having done his duty." The men visited friends, congratulated one another on their successful retreat, and recalled the dangers of their northward march.[1]

While his troops took advantage of their opportunity to relax, Nathanael Greene never stopped working to try to find a way to resume the offensive and strike a blow against Cornwallis. He wanted to keep pressure on the earl so that the British troops would not have the opportunity to recuperate, or to recruit supporters from among region's numerous loyalists, or to bring up supplies from the British base at Wilmington.

Greene's objective was to keep Cornwallis from establishing a strong position in North Carolina and use it as a base to invade Virginia. Greene knew that he needed many more troops to be able to compete with Cornwallis on the battlefield. He therefore wrote letters to state governors, militia officers across Virginia and the Carolinas, and Baron Friedrich von Steuben, the commander of Continental forces in Virginia requesting reinforcements.

In further preparation for the ordeal ahead, Greene also ordered William Washington and Lee to remount as many of their cavalrymen as possible with Virginia's thoroughbred horses. Washington in particular exceeded Greene's instructions, impressing several "prime stud stallions" worth up to $1,000 each, which forced Greene to caution him and Lee not to take such horses in the future and to act "with great delicacy." The horses' owners complained to Governor Thomas Jefferson, who informed Greene of their dissatisfaction. Greene admitted to Jefferson that he was "fatigued to death," but defended his officers' impressment of horses. "Superior Cavalry is of the greatest importance to the salvation of this Country and without them you would soon hear of detachments being cut to pieces in every quarter," Greene told the governor.[2]

The American commander had learned that a large and effective force of cavalry was essential to achieve military success in the southern theater. Over the next several months, Greene repeatedly emphasized the importance of cavalry in his correspondence. He reiterated to Jefferson in April that

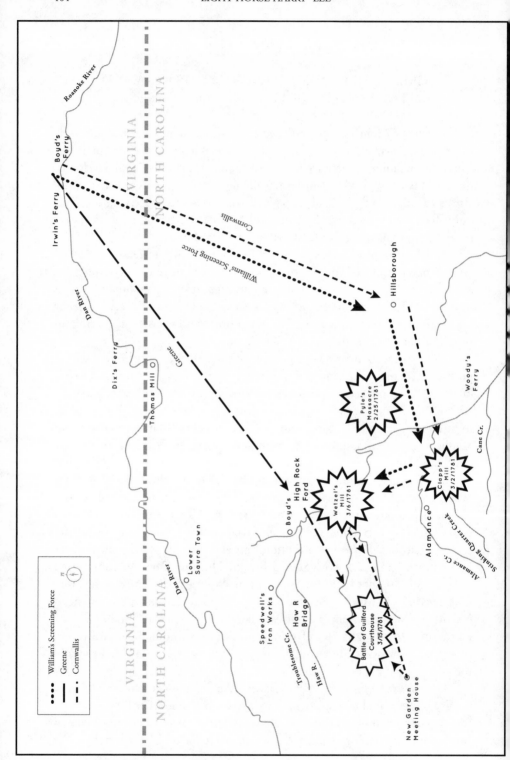

Concentrating the forces near Guilford Courthouse

"Nothing but light Horse can enable us, with the little Army we have, to appear in the field, and nothing but a superiority in Cavalry can prevent the Enemy from cutting to pieces every detachment coming to join the Army or employed in collecting supplies. From the open State of this Country their services are particularly necessary, and unless we can keep up the Corps of Cavalry and constantly support a superiority it will be out of our power to act or prevent the Enemy from overrunning the Country, and commanding all its resources."[3]

In a similar vein, Greene told Thomas Sumter that "if we are superior in Cavalry ... it will be almost impossible for [the British] to hold their posts, and utterly impossible to pursue us if we should find a retreat necessary." Likewise, he explained to the Marquis de Lafayette that "a good body of horse is every thing to an Army that is obliged to act upon the defensive, and you will have little to fear either from a skirmish or even a defeat if you are well covered with horse, but without [cavalry] you have everything to apprehend, as the most trifling disorder may be improved into a rout." Greene's emphasis on maintaining a strong mounted force yielded good results; Lee observed that his British opponent, Lt. Col. Tarleton,

"was obliged to use such horses as he could get; whereas his opponent had the whole South to select out of. The consequence was the British dragoons were mounted upon small, weak horses; those of the Legion on stout, active horses, and kept in the highest condition."[4]

Lee would need the advantage his better horses would provide, because he and the Legion would soon be returning to action. Lee himself was eager to take the field. Always anxious to get back into action, Lee had only been on the safe side of the Dan for two days when he wrote to Greene on February 16th proposing that he recross the river that evening and "hang on to the enemy." Greene was not yet ready for such a move, and waited two more days until the eighteenth before he ordered the Legion, along with two companies of Captain Andrew Oldham's Maryland Continentals, across the Dan to unite with a force of seven hundred militia under Brigadier General Andrew Pickens that had been trailing Cornwallis through North Carolina. Lee's mission, he explained, was to "rouse the drooping spirits" of the North Carolinians and "check the audacity" of the British and their supporters in the state. Greene saw Lee's move as part of a larger plan to bring Cornwallis to battle. "The moment the enemy move towards Hillsborough I shall fall into their rear," the American general told North Carolina governor Abner Nash.[5]

*****

Pyle's Massacre

Cornwallis fell back to Hillsborough, where on February 20th he "published a proclamation, inviting all loyal subjects to repair to the King's standard, and to take an active part in assisting him to restore order and constitutional government." Hundreds of loyalists responded by coming to Cornwallis's camp, but very few enlisted, even though some of their friends and neighbors were already serving in Lt. Col. John Hamilton's Royal North Carolina Regiment. The ragged appearance of the hungry and exhausted British soldiers after their long pursuit of Greene convinced some loyalists that Cornwallis was incapable of equipping or feeding them. Others, Tarleton noted, "declared, they soon expected [Greene's army] to return, and the dread of violence and persecution prevented their taking a decided part in a cause which yet appeared dangerous." Tarleton's British Legion was composed almost entirely of loyalists, and he understood their reluctance. He observed that the British had made no serious attempt since the war began to assist the loyalists in North Carolina, who over the previous five years had suffered "a variety of calamities which ... had not only reduced their numbers and weakened their attachment, but had confirmed the power and superiority of the adverse party."[6]

A few loyalists did accept commissions issued by Cornwallis and the former royal governor of North Carolina, Josiah Martin, who was with the British army. They then returned to their homes to recruit other supporters of the crown, but another loyalist officer had already achieved considerable success in building a sizeable militia force. Fifty-seven-year-old Doctor John Pyle of Chatham County had been appointed a colonel in North Carolina's royal militia by Governor Martin in 1775. Pyle had taken part in the loyalist uprising in early 1776 and was captured after the loyalists' defeat at the Battle of Moore's Creek Bridge on February 27th of that year. Imprisoned in Virginia, Pyle escaped and made his way home, where he was allowed to remain after taking an oath of allegiance to the state government. Now, with Greene's army in Virginia and Cornwallis apparently in control of North Carolina, Pyle finally saw an opportunity to take up arms once again in support of the king. He notified Cornwallis of his plan, and the British general promised to send troops to protect the loyalists while they assembled.[7]

Pyle recruited in the region between the Haw and Deep rivers, and quickly organized a substantial force of nearly 400 mounted militia. Greene and Cornwallis were both trying to increase the size of their forces by recruiting militia into their ranks, and Pyle's command represented an important potential addition to the British army's numbers.[8]

On February 23rd, Cornwallis detached Tarleton with 200 cavalry, 150 infantrymen from Lt. Col. James Webster's brigade, and 100 Hessian jaegers to form a junction with Pyle's force. Cornwallis had instructed Pyle to march to Hillsborough, or to find Tarleton and unite with him. It appears that no rendezvous point had been agreed upon, leaving Pyle and Tarleton to search for one another as the loyalist party marched toward Hillsborough. Tarleton crossed the Haw River on February 24th and "dispersed a party of American militia, who had united to counteract the intentions of the loyalists." From some captured militiamen, Tarleton learned that Continental troops were expected to arrive in the vicinity soon. He therefore dispatched a messenger to find Pyle and urge him to move quickly. Later in the day, Tarleton received more specific intelligence confirming that "Colonel Lee's cavalry" had also crossed the Haw River to link up with Colonel William Preston's corps of militia from the trans-Appalachian region of Virginia. It is not clear whether Tarleton was aware that Lee had already united his Legion with Pickens's militia the previous day. Lee's movement, according to the information Tarleton received, was "for the purpose of intimidating or dispersing the King's friends." Tarleton sent a second message to Pyle ordering him to hurry. If Tarleton could unite with Pyle quickly, the British Legion commander planned "to proceed against either Lee or Preston before they united," and he sent spies to monitor the movements of both of the American units.[9]

Pyle's men had been marching toward Tarleton, overcoming scattered opposition from various groups of North Carolina militia and capturing other militiamen who had completed their terms of service and were returning to their homes. Captain Joseph Hackney and "the whole of his company" were captured by Pyle's loyalists on February 19th and sent ahead under guard to Hillsborough, where they were imprisoned. Several days afterward, a group of militiamen including Philip Higdon, a Colonel Knowles, and a Lieutenant Hackney "were taken prisoners by the Tories commanded by a Doc't. Pyles an old man" and forced to accompany the loyalists. Militiamen Thomas Barnett and Solomon Geren were also captured, and Pyle evaded another North Carolina militia unit that had been ordered to halt what another participant, Daniel Smith, described as "great outrage … killing burning & plundering" by Pyle's men. Lee, however, attributed the destruction to Tarleton's detachment rather than to Pyle's loyalists.[10]

While Pyle skirmished and maneuvered across North Carolina, Lee had set out on his mission to gather intelligence for Greene, encourage the North Carolina militia to turn out, and to form a junction with Pickens. The Legion crossed the Dan River on February 19th and camped that night "within twenty five miles of Hillsborough." He ordered a party forward to scout the British position and try to procure information about their intentions. Lee told Greene that if Cornwallis moved toward Cross Creek, he would place the Legion "in their front" and fight a delaying action until Greene arrived with the rest of the American army. Such a battle would cost his corps many casualties, Lee conceded, and he expected Greene to replace the Legion's losses. Cornwallis, however, did not go to Cross Creek.[11]

This was the type of warfare at which Lee excelled: commanding independently and far to the front, where his skills at rapid movement, quick decisions, and bold action were essential to success. As one of Greene's early biographers described Lee's activities during this period,

> *"He was now in the very element of his talents. Better scope for the exercise of his partisan powers could not be coveted, and we find him every hour meditating or executing some new exploit. His communications, which were frequent and hurried, exhibit the greatest activity, zeal and intelligence. On the right, on the left, in the rear of the enemy, wherever service could be performed, or intelligence collected, we find him continually occupied, and forever changing his positions, to guard against surprise."* [12]

Lee was able to provide Greene with useful intelligence during this period, but he had difficulty finding Pickens and raising the North Carolina militia. On February 21st, Lee informed Greene that Cornwallis had reached Hillsborough the previous night, that the militia was assembling, and that the Legion would take "a position more advanced on the enemys right flank." Pickens, he added, was expected to arrive at any time. That belief was optimistic, as Pickens and Lee did not unite until the morning of February 23rd. The first meeting between the two forces almost turned disastrous when Pickens's men initially mistook Lee's Legion for Tarleton's British Legion. Lee's soldiers, like those of Tarleton's Legion, wore green uniform coats as a sign of their elite status. And although the coats were not identical, they were similar enough to confuse some of Pickens's men who nearly opened fire on Lee's Legion before they realized their error. Lee also expressed dissatisfaction with the failure of the people around Hillsborough to support him. He was, he told Greene, "much mortified with the timidity & treachery of the people in the vicinity." Instead of turning out to fight on the American side, "they swarm to the town, take the oath of allegiance to the King of G. Britain, & I verily beleive, would have mustered yesterday had not our troops visited their country."[13]

Pickens had experienced problems of his own with the militia. His force consisted of Georgians, South Carolinians, North Carolinians who had joined him on his march through that state, and Catawba Indians, the only Native nation in the South that supported the Americans. On February 19th,

Pickens had described to Greene "the difficulty in turning the Men out they seem to be much averse to the march so far to the Northward." One unit had stayed with Pickens only because they wanted to meet Greene and make a personal appeal to return to South Carolina. "The Georgians are daily scattering" and their officers did little to control the men, Pickens added. The next day, Pickens complained about the militia from the Salisbury district of North Carolina, telling Greene that they were in a "bad state," with the men "continually deserting and no persuasion can prevail with them." They were, Pickens declared, "among the worst Men" he had ever commanded.[14]

Greene sympathized with the problems that Pickens faced. "I am sorry the Militia desert you, but it is the practice of all Militia," the general observed. He confirmed the reports that Pickens had received regarding the location of the British army, adding that "Lt Col Lee with his Legion is in full pursuit," that Col. Otho Williams was "also on the march," and that the rest of the army "will cross the river in the Morning." Greene instructed Pickens to send a message to Col. Campbell telling him "to push on with all imaginable dispatch" with his Virginians. Pickens arrived at a point only eighteen miles from Hillsborough on February 21st and sent a small party toward the town to gather information. When the scouts failed to encounter any British troops, Pickens moved his entire force within ten miles of the town. Learning that Cornwallis had posted a small picket guard two-and-a-half miles outside Hillsborough, Pickens dispatched a party of forty volunteers under Georgia Colonel Hugh McCall to attack them. McCall surprised the pickets, killing or wounding eight and capturing ten British soldiers and several loyalists without any loss on the American side.[15]

Lee was displeased when he joined Pickens on February 23rd and learned of the affair. The Legion commander had detached some of his own troops to reconnoiter the British position, and McCall's attack alerted Cornwallis, so that Lee's scouts were unable to obtain any information. However, Lee shrugged off the disappointment and promised Greene that he and Pickens "shall exert ourselves to alarm the enemy by night, & to harrass them by day." According to Lee, that night Greene, "never avoiding toil or danger," rode "with a small escort of [William] Washington's cavalry … and overtook the advanced corps." Greene spent the night discussing his future plans with Lee and Pickens, announcing "his intention of repassing the Dan with the army in a few days," but telling his subordinates that he would keep the main army in the "upper country," too far away to support Lee and Pickens. After Greene left, the American force set out for Hillsborough to begin Lee's intended harassment of the British army.[16]

As their main force advanced toward Hillsborough, Lee and Pickens sent out reconnaissance parties, with instructions to remain concealed, observe the road ahead and report back from time to time with their findings. The route paralleled the road running from Hillsborough to the Haw River crossing, and the soldiers' progress was slow. Lee and Pickens decided to camp for the night. An officer who had been dispatched on the twenty-third to reconnoiter Hillsborough arrived in camp to report that all was quiet in and around the town, with no indications that a British movement was imminent. The scouting parties likewise returned to report that they had seen no one moving on the road. They did bring with them "a well-grown boy," nineteen-year-old Samuel Findley, who lived along Alamance Creek with his widowed mother. Upon learning that Lee was "much in want of a person to pilot him through that section of country," Findley, who was "well acquainted" with the area, obtained his mother's permission to accompany the Legion troopers. He eventually served with Lee for two months before returning home.[17]

Lee and Pickens resumed their march after breakfast on February 25th, still heading for Hillsborough. At about noon, militia Colonel William Moore met them and reported that a British detachment was in the area and believed to be heading toward the plantation of American militia general John Butler. Moore's account of the "numbers & conduct" of the British force led Lee to believe that they were "a foraging party." He and Pickens, guided by Findley, promptly changed direction, picked up the trail of the enemy on the Salisbury Road, and pursued the British, hoping to catch them at Butler's. As they pressed forward, the American commanders received new and disturbing information. Their quarry was not a foraging party, but a large force under Banastre Tarleton. Lee and Pickens also learned that Tarleton had already crossed the Haw River and expected "to be joined during the night by large bodys of enlisted Carolinians." Seeing an opportunity to "prevent by a timely stroke this junction," the American officers resumed their pursuit, crossing the Haw with "the utmost dispatch." Lee sent a messenger to the Legion infantry, which was some distance behind, informing them of his movements so that they would be ready "to secure our retreat in case of disaster."[18]

The American forces reached Holt's Plantation at about five o'clock in the afternoon, where Lee learned that Tarleton was only four miles away at O'Neal's Plantation. Lee and Pickens continued to push forward in an effort catch Tarleton's force, "it being our wish," Lee wrote, "to decid[e] the contest that evening." Pickens observed that "never was there a more glorious opportunity of cutting off a detachment than this." As the Legion cavalry and mounted militia rode through the countryside, Pickens found that most of the inhabitants of the area were loyalists:

> *"So very little was the expectation of an American party, the Inhabit-*
> *ants seemed prodigiously rejoiced, imagining we were a fresh party of*

British. We found them chiefly in arms and prepared to join Tarlton that evening." [19]

In his memoirs, written more than thirty years afterward, Lee related that the Legion cavalry's advance guard captured two British Legion officers in a farmhouse along their route. However, neither Lee nor Pickens mentioned this in their reports written shortly after the encounter with Pyle's loyalists, and Captain Joseph Graham wrote nothing of such an incident in his later account. Lee's memory was probably in error on this point, but it is clear that around this time Lee decided "to pass as a re-enforcement sent from Hillsborough to Lieutenant-Colonel Tarleton" and took position at the front of the American column. The troops marched with an officer and several Legion dragoons riding several hundred yards ahead. Given the loyalist sentiments of the area's residents that Pickens had noted, Lee's deception would help to prevent anyone from warning Tarleton of the Americans' approach. As Lee explained:

"This stratagem could not fail of imposing on the country people, however well acquainted they might be with the appearance of British troops, so far as respected the Legion, inasmuch as both cavalry and infantry were dressed in short, green coats, with other distinctions exactly resembling some of the enemy's light corps."

A South Carolina militiaman with Pickens later noted that Lee had taken measures to deceive any loyalists that his troops encountered. "Col. Lee's men were prepared with red (or Tory) plumes or feathers which they stuck in their caps," Manuel McConnell recalled. "We imitated them [loyalists] as much as possible." [20]

After continuing down the road for about three miles to the vicinity of Holt's Race Paths, the party riding in advance of the American force met "two well-mounted young countrymen." The Legion officer questioned them, and assuming that he and the troops behind him were Tarleton's, they replied that they were loyalists and had been sent ahead by Colonel Pyle to locate Tarleton's camp. Pyle and his men "had not complied with the orders they received" from Tarleton on the previous day to move quickly since there were enemy forces in the area.. Tarleton observed that, "being all equally ignorant of the customs of war," Pyle's loyalists proceeded at a leisurely pace. "Though forewarned of their danger," the men "thought fit to pay visits to their kindred and acquaintance before they repaired to the British camp: Inspired by whiskey and the novelty of their situation, they unfortunately prolonged their excursions," and as a result encountered Lee when at last they set out to meet Tarleton. [21]

The officer who met the two loyalists sent a dragoon to Lee with a report of what they had said, and then sent Pyle's officers, escorted by two cavalrymen, to the Legion commander. Before they arrived, Lee sent a message to Pickens ordering him to conceal his militia on the column's left. This, Lee wrote, "was readily to be done, as we were then in a thick wood." The messenger also told Pickens that Lee had "determined, in conformity with the concerted plan, to make an attempt with the Legion, of turning the occurrence to advantage."[22]

Lee greeted the loyalists "with much apparent cordiality," and he "listened with seeming satisfaction" as they told him of

> *the laudable spirit which had actuated Colonel Pyle and his associates, and which they asserted was rapidly spreading through the country. Finding them completely deceived (for they not only believed the troops they saw to be British, but overlooking what had been told them, they took them to be Tarleton's, addressing the commandant [Lee] as that officer). Lee sent one of them back with two dragoons to his van, thence to proceed to Colonel Pyle with Lieutenant-Colonel Tarleton's gratulations, and his request that he [Pyle] would be so good as to draw out on the margin of the road, so as to give convenient room for his much fatigued troops to pass without delay to their night position.*

The second loyalist remained with Lee, who sent an order to the officer commanding the advance guard "to halt as soon as he got in sight of the loyalists."[23]

Lee's officer did as instructed, and Lee soon joined him with the remainder of the Legion. Pyle's troops, in accordance with Lee's directions, had halted and moved to the right of the road. Colonel Pyle was at the opposite end of the line from the direction of Lee's approach, so that Lee rode past Pyle's entire command before he met up with the colonel.[24]

Pyle's men, had their "rifles and fowling pieces" slung over their shoulders with the muzzles pointed away from Lee's cavalry —they were not expecting a battle, This made them extremely vulnerable to attack because it was cumbersome to move their firearms off their shoulders and into firing position in any situation, but it was even more difficult if the fighting was hand-to-hand.[25]

As Lee led his column past the loyalists, Pyle's men "frequently uttered salutations of a friendly kind, believing us to be British." Soon the two forces were arrayed side-by-side in the road, with the Legion cavalry "in the most eligible situation for any vicissitude," Lee wrote.[26]

Lee reached the end of Pyle's column and had drawn astride of the loyalist commander when fighting broke out far down the line. Lee reported to Greene that the fighting began when "the enemy discovered their mistake on the near approach of our militia & commenced action." In his memoirs, he added that "the enemy's left, discovering Pickens's militia, not sufficiently concealed, began to fire upon the rear of the cavalry commanded by Captain Eggleston. This officer instantly turned upon the foe, as did immediately after the whole column." Pickens, however, indicated in his report to Greene that the Americans began the fighting. Pyle's men mistook the Americans for Tarleton's troops, Pickens wrote, and "Our men were in some measure under the same mistake, but soon found out" and attacked the loyalists.[27]

Whatever caused the fighting to break out, the combat was brutal, short and entirely in favor of Lee's men. Still convinced that the troops beside them were British, Pyle's men "made no preparation to resist." Some of the stunned loyalists cried out "that they were friends of King George," while others shouted "God save the King," "You are killing your own men," and similar declarations of their allegiance as Lee's dragoons and the mounted militia hacked at them with sabers. The assault was so fierce that North Carolina militia officer Joseph Graham recorded that some of the militiamen's "swords broke, others bent." Between twelve and fifteen of Pyle's men, realizing that "their professions of loyalty were to no avail," managed to unsling their rifles and fired wildly. The fusillade caused some of Lee's troopers to hesitate, but when they realized that the loyalists' "guns were empty," the American dragoons charged and "cut [them] down in a group together." Thomas Miles of the North Carolina militia claimed that Captain Dudley Reynolds killed Pyle, and in doing so saved the life of militia colonel William Moore. Militiaman Miles was incorrect. Pyle actually survived his wounds and managed to escape, supposedly by lying submerged in a nearby pond with only his nose above the water.[28]

The encounter lasted no more than ten minutes, and came to be known as "Pyle's Massacre." Many of the surviving loyalists fled, and the Americans did not pursue them. In his report to Greene, Lee stated that after the encounter "the night came on & we necessarily deferred farther operation." Pickens said the same when he wrote to Greene a day later. In fact, the Americans were in no condition to undertake a pursuit. Graham described the chaos that followed the massacre:

> "At the close of the action, the troops were scattered, mixed, and completely disorganized. General Pickens and Colonel Lee gave repeated orders to form, but the confusion was such that their orders were without effect. These officers appeared sensible of the delicate situation that they were in. If Tarleton, who was only two or three miles off, with

nearly an equal force, had come upon them at this juncture, the result must have been disastrous. Lee's men, though under excellent discipline, could with difficulty be gotten in order. The commandants exhibited great perturbation, until at length Lee ordered Major [John] Rudulph to lead off, and his dragoons to fall in behind them." [29]

As the American column finally began to leave the field, Lee remained at the rear of the Legion, and dispatched a sergeant to find a prisoner who could act as a guide. The sergeant returned with a man named Holt, "who had received a slight wound on the head, and who was bleeding freely." Upon delivering the prisoner, "the sergeant apologized to [Lee] because he could find none who were not wounded" among the captives. Lee questioned Holt about the terrain and roads. When Lee finished his interrogation, Holt, still believing that his attackers were Tarleton's troops, told Lee: "God bless your soul, Mr. Tarleton, you have this day killed a parcel of as good subjects as ever His Majesty had." Joseph Graham, whose militia was directly behind the Legion in the line of march and thus nearby, heard Lee's angry response. "You d------d rascal, if you call me Tarleton, I will take off your head," Lee shouted. Graham saw that Holt "appeared thunderstruck."[30]

Pyle's force was decimated in this encounter, and was eliminated as a factor in the fight for North Carolina. Cornwallis would not be able to count on Pyle for assistance, and word of the brutal defeat put an immediate damper on loyalist recruiting. Lee reported to Greene that "the greatest part of them were left dead on the field and wounded." Years later, he provided more detail in his memoirs, writing that "the conflict was….bloody on one side only. Ninety royalists were killed, and most of the survivors wounded." Pickens gave a similar estimate, stating that "nigh one hundred were killed and the greatest part of the others wounded." North Carolina's Joseph Graham reported that, on the day after the battle, American militia returned to the scene and "counted ninety-three dead, and there was the appearance of many more having been carried off by their friends. There were certainly many more wounded." He suggested that some of the injured loyalists may have pretended to be dead "for security." There have been various estimates of the number of Pyle's casualties, but many historians have accepted the number provided by Lee and essentially confirmed by Pickens.[31]

*****

Analysis of the Pyle Affair

This ten-minute encounter on a remote country road has been analyzed by a number of observers over the years, and the story has been clouded by differing eye-witness accounts provided by people who witnessed events from different locations at the scene of the fight. This tapestry is made more complex by the propaganda efforts of the American army, loyalists, and the British writers at the time; by the passage of time that affected the memories of witnesses who wrote their pension applications fifty years after the actual events; and by the work of historians, some of whom may have been affected by motivations other than pure historical accuracy.

Generally, the controversies related to the Pyle Affair address (1) what started the fighting? (2) did Lee have a plan all along to massacre Pyle's men? and (3) were atrocities committed?

It is clear from the various descriptions of the incident that Lee and Pickens did not have the luxury of time to plan the encounter, and therefore there was no opportunity to pull all of the troops together and brief them on the situation, or on Lee's objectives. Lee had one picture in his mind as he rode at the head of his column. The Legion cavalry who followed him had a different understanding and perspective, as did Pickens' militia in the woods, and the militia cavalrymen who were riding behind Lee's command. Lee stated at the time and in his memoirs that he believed that Pyle's men initiated the attack, and from his position opposite Pyle at the head of the column, that must have been how things appeared. Pickens, stationed with his militia in the adjacent woods, contradicted the Legion commander and stated that Lee's men started the fighting. Pickens could see things that Lee could not, just as Lee was the only officer who directly confronted Colonel Pyle at the start of the incident, and only he was in a position to describe that interaction.

Others observed the scene from different locations and therefore provided different accounts. Captain Joseph Graham, riding behind the Legion cavalry at the head of seventy North Carolina mounted militiamen armed with swords, stated that at first he believed Pyle's men to be some of Captain Joseph Dickson's American militia who had been on Graham's right. However, when he noticed that "these men had on cleaner clothes than Dickson's party, and that each man had a strip of red cloth on his hat," Graham turned to Captain Joseph Eggleston of the Legion, who was riding next to him and said: "That is a company of Tories; what is the reason they have their arms?" Eggleston then turned to a man he took to be one of Pyle's officers and asked: "To whom do you belong?" The loyalist replied that he was "a friend of His Majesty," and Eggleston "struck him over the head." Graham wrote that "the militia ... on this example being set, rushed on the Tories like lightning and cut away." Graham gave a slightly different version of events in his pension application, indicating that the militia and not Eggleston had begun the attack:

> *"none of Lee's men knew their [Pyle's loyalists'] character but Lee him-*
> *self, his men having so recently come to the south did not know the*

*distinguishing mark of the Tories, but when the [American] militia
came near and discovered the red strip of Cloth each man had in his
hat, [the American militia] made the first attack on them."* [32]

While Graham's story changed somewhat in the years between the actual
event and his pension application, he appears to have been the observer who
was closest to the actual start of the fighting, and therefore most probably has
identified the source most accurately—namely that Captain Eggleston of the
Legion cavalry or some unidentified members of the militia, unaware of any
intention Lee might have had to negotiate with Pyle, attacked his enemy as
soon as they were identified, and touched off fighting that quickly raged from
end-to-end of Pyle's line.

Some writers and pensioners have questioned Lee's intentions in the
encounter with Pyle, even suggesting that he planned the slaughter from
the outset. When the British commanders first heard of the affair, they were
quick to accept that their enemies were capable of great atrocities. The specter
of over ninety of their men lying dead in the road, with hardly any American
casualties, seemed to be evidence enough of some nefarious intent.

Some of the wounded loyalists managed to make it to the safety of the
British camp, and they were apparently still convinced that it was Tarleton's
men that had attacked them, because they "complained to Tarleton of the
cruelty of the dragoons." After learning the details of Lee's attack on Pyle,
Tarleton denounced the "inhuman barbarity" of the Americans. Cornwallis
described the event in similar terms, informing Lord George Germain that
Pyle's men "were most inhumanly butchered, when begging for quarter,
without making the least resistance." [33]

When Lee wrote his memoirs thirty years later, he explained why he and
his men had to act decisively in the incident, and in so doing, he inevitably
responded to the accusations that he had acted brutally in this affair:

> *"during this sudden rencounter, in some parts of the line the cry of
> mercy was heard, coupled with assurance of being our best friends;
> but no expostulation could be admitted in a conjuncture so critical.
> Humanity even forbade it, as its first injunction is to take care of your
> own safety, and our safety was not compatible with that of the sup-
> plicants, until disabled to offend."* [34]

One of the first writers after the war to condemn Lee's actions at Pyle's
Massacre was Charles Stedman, who had served in the British army as chief
commissary under Cornwallis, and whose "impartiality and respect for truth"
Lee had acknowledged. However, in the case of Pyle's Massacre, Lee thought

that Stedman had received misinformation and committed a "palpable mistake." In the rebuttal that Lee wrote in his memoirs, he first quoted Stedman's accusations concerning Pyle's men:

> *"they called out for quarter, but no quarter was granted; and between two and three hundred of them were inhumanly butchered while in the act of begging for mercy. Humanity shudders at the recital of so foul a massacre; but cold and unfeeling policy avows it as the most ef-fectual means of intimidating the friends of the royal government."*

Lee's memoirs then provide this rejoinder:

> *"The fire commenced upon us, and self-preservation commanded the limited destruction which ensued. Only ninety of the loyalists were killed; not between two and three hundred, as Mr. Stedman states; and less than ninety could not have been spared from the close condi-tion of the dragoons, and the necessity of crushing the resistance in-stantly. Had the officer or corps been capable of massacre, it was only necessary to have ordered pursuit, and not a man of the enemy would have escaped. So far from doing so, Lee resumed his march, leaving all that had dispersed to secure themselves without interruption."* [35]

Lee was only twenty-five-years-old at the time of the Pyle Affair, but he was a veteran soldier, having spent a significant part of the last five years in combat. He was accustomed to the weight of responsibility that goes with an independent command, and his usual assignment was far to the front and in the face of the enemy. The most senior leaders like George Washington and Nathanael Greene relied heavily on the young cavalryman, and would often make key decisions based on the information that he developed and sent back to them. He had suffered the gut-wrenching experience of having men who served under him killed in combat, and his own life and the lives of the men in his beloved Legion were on the line in this Pyle Affair. Pickens and Lee comprised a small advanced corps, and they were operating far from the support of their main army, and much closer, in fact, to the enemy's main force. They also thought that they had a chance to strike a successful blow at a despised British adversary, Banastre Tarleton, and they wanted to get on with that vital task. Lee and Pickens were therefore motivated to dispense with Pyle as quickly as they could—first, to protect themselves in case British forces in the area heard the ruckus and attacked; and, second, to get on as quickly as they could with the main task of cornering and defeating Tarleton. Lee and Pickens were focused on the serious work at hand, and it seems unlikely that leaders of this caliber would devote precious time in a tense situation like this to revenge killings.

Pension applications were submitted by Revolutionary War veterans over fifty years after the Pyle affair. While these documents can suggest important additions to our understanding of the actual event, they must also be evaluated in the context of older men who were struggling to provide written memories of events that had occurred a half-century or more earlier, and who probably had difficulty separating those distant facts from the effects of the shared stories and folklore that they had heard and accepted as fact in the intervening years.

In the only known account from someone who was with Pyle's force at the time of the attack, American militia prisoner Philip Higdon stated in his pension application submitted in 1834 that while he and the other captives were "marching with the Tories they were overtaken by Col Lee & a battle immediately commenced." Lee's guide, Samuel Findley, said in his pension application submitted in 1836 that the Americans "surprised" Pyle's men "in a lane." William Lenoir, another North Carolinian, recalled the onset of the action similarly, asserting in his pension application submitted in 1833 that the Americans "fell in with a body of Tories ... with whom they immediately engaged. [36]

In his pension application submitted in 1833, Thomas Boyd of the North Carolina militia declared that after Pyle "mustered his men on the side of the road in order to receive the supposed Colonel Tarleton," the American commanders "moved up with their mounted men (leaving the infantry some little distance behind in order for battle)." Upon reaching "the upper end of Colonel Pyles line," Boyd stated, the American horsemen wheeled and "facing to Pyles line, amidst shouts of long live King George from both parties, our troops drawing their swords attacked the Tories and cut them down." Boyd acknowledged in his pension application that he was in an infantry detachment that had been "some little distance behind" the main affair, and his memory fifty-two years after the event incorrectly recalled that William Washington co-led the American troops and had personally "cut out the eye of Pyles."[37]

Another North Carolina militiaman, Moses Hall, also described in his pension application submitted in 1835 what he seems to recall as a planned attack on Pyle's loyalists:

> *"Colonel Lee knew what he was about and so did Major [Joseph] Dixon. But ... my Captain Hall, perceiving they were Tories and thinking that Colonel Lee did not know it and was imposed upon by their cries of friendship and misunderstood them to be our friends in-*

*stead of the British, he called to Colonel Lee across the Tories' line and
told him, 'Colonel Lee, they are every blood of them Tories!' Colonel
Lee gave him a sign to proceed on with the execution of the command,
which was to march on until a different command was given. In a
few minutes or less time, and at the instant that they, the Tories, were
completely covered by our lines upon both flanks, or front and rear as
the case may have been, the bugle sounded to attack, and the slaughter
began."* [38]

In his pension application submitted in 1832, Samuel Eakin, a North
Carolinian who served under Pickens at the Pyle affair, gave a shorter but
similar account, asserting that the loyalists "were killed on orders being to give
them Blueford's play." The terms "Buford's Play" and "Tarleton's Quarter"
were commonly used by American troops after May 1780, and described the
brutal practice of taking no prisoners and killing all of the enemy's troops,
even if they were in the process of surrendering. Such acts were considered
legitimate retaliation, for it was widely believed on the American side that
Tarleton's men had massacred American soldiers in Abraham Buford's
command who were trying to surrender at the Battle of the Waxhaws on May
29th, 1780. [39]

Samuel Eakin described the affair as "a total rout and slaughter." Another
North Carolina militiaman related how he and the other American troops,
"drawing their swords attacked the Tories and cut them down ... a great
slaughter was made." Matthew Vandiver stated that the loyalists were "cut
to pieces," an assertion that William Lenoir verified was "literally" true. "I
never before witnessed the works of death carried to such an extent in so
short a time." Thomas Lofton of North Carolina declared, "Pyles with his
Tories being all either killed or wounded." Captain Graham added that "some
Catawba Indians ... who did not overtake us until the close of the action ....
were suffered to kill seven or eight wounded men with spears before they were
made to desist." [40]

Only one of the soldiers with Lee's force was injured in the slaughter,
although there were casualties among the American prisoners that Pyle had
in his column. When a handful of Pyle's men fired their rifles, one shot struck
the horse of William Moore, a mounted militiaman from North Carolina.
The horse fell and the impact as its body struck the ground dislocated and
fractured Moore's right knee. Moore was unable to extricate himself, but as
soon as the fighting ended, two of his comrades dismounted and rolled the
horse's body, freeing Moore. The injury was severe enough to end Moore's
military service, yet he was fortunate compared to several other Americans.
"The slaughter was indiscriminate," said Philip Higdon, one of the captured

militiamen with Pyle. "Several of the prisoners were killed among the number was the unfortunate Col Knowls." Solomon Geren "was retaken from the Tories" and sent home soon afterward "in consequence of a wound he had received" from his liberators. Like Higdon and a few other prisoners, Thomas Barnett was more fortunate, and recorded that he was "Rescued by Lee's troop of Horse," apparently escaping the incident without injury.[41]

Lee asserted in his memoirs that the loyalist survivors dispersed "in every direction" and were not captured because there was no pursuit; however the pension applications of militiamen John Efland and Joseph Hall indicate that some prisoners were taken, and some were treated with great brutality. Efland reported that he was one of those later assigned to guard "the prisoners made by Col. Lee in the battle ... with the Tories under Pyle." Moses Hall stated that "a considerable number" of Pyle's men were taken prisoner, and that "the evening after our battle with the Tories," some of his fellow militiamen invited him to view the captives. Hall described what happened next:

> "We went to where six were standing together. Some discussion taking place, I heard some of our men cry out, 'Remember Buford,' and the prisoners were immediately hewed to pieces with broadswords. At first I bore the scene without any emotion, but upon a moment's reflection, I felt such horror as I never did before nor have since, and returning to my quarters [was] overcome and unmanned by a distressing gloom."

Hall's memory may have been strengthened by the searing recollection of the deep emotions he described, and may indicate that some units on the American side did kill unarmed loyalist prisoners during the affair. It is significant that Hall indicated that the people who invited him to view the captives were his fellow militiamen, and it will be seen in some subsequent encounters that militia troops sometimes wreaked brutal vengeance on their enemies. However, there is no evidence here that Lee's disciplined regular troops were among the perpetrators.[42]

In spite of all the various observations and accusations about Lee's intentions during Pyle's Massacre, careful reading of the report that Lee wrote in the field on the night of the encounter and the one Pickens wrote the next day clearly indicate that both men were intently focused on attacking Tarleton, and that Pyle's militia was a distraction. Pickens was enthused by the opportunity to confront Tarleton, and was "pushing on with the utmost hope and our Men in the highest spirits" to bring his old adversary to battle. Just a little over five weeks earlier, Pickens had played a key role in the Battle of Cowpens, where the Americans under Daniel Morgan had utterly destroyed another detachment commanded by the same Tarleton. He knew that the

British cavalryman could be beaten, and he was bristling for a fight. Pickens was therefore disappointed that the engagement with Pyle "blasted" their "sanguine expectations" of defeating Tarleton. Ever ambitious for striking the dramatic blow and achieving his share of glory, Lee must also been driven by the vision of tangling with the notorious commander of the British cavalry, in every sense his green-jacketed rival.

Lee provided additional insight into the importance they placed on Tarleton in his memoirs, offering his (perhaps too optimistic) observation that the destruction of Tarleton's partisan corps "would probably have led to the termination of the war in the South." Pickens and Lee realized that defeating Tarleton's detachment while it was separated from the main British army would be a tremendous victory, and they were anxious to achieve that important objective.[43]

Accordingly, Lee wrote to his commander, Nathanael Greene, on the night of the massacre (February 25th), that he had moved past Pyle in the guise of British troops "that no time might be lost in reaching Col Tarleton," verifying that he had no intention of engaging in combat with the loyalists. Three decades later, in his memoirs, he added that when he reached Pyle, he had intended to "make known to the colonel his real character ... with a solemn assurance of his and his associates perfect exemption from injury and with the choice of returning to their homes" or joining the Americans. Lee noted that he actually reached and greeted Pyle, and "was in the act of consummating his plan" when fighting broke out.[44]

*****

The Impact of Pyle's Massacre

Greene and Pickens realized that this engagement had an important effect on the campaign to defeat Cornwallis, and neither leader expressed concern with the level of violence. Pickens was focused on attacking Tarleton, and he complained to Greene that the unexpected encounter with Pyle's loyalists had dashed his hopes of catching Tarleton's detachment, but he also realized that "this Affair ... has been of infinite Service. It has knocked up Toryism altogether in this part."

Greene based his understanding of the incident on the reports he received from Lee and Pickens, and informed George Washington that the Legion and accompanying militia had intended to march past Pyle's column and continue their pursuit of Tarleton, but that the militia had frustrated that plan by opening fire on Pyle's men. "The whole of the enemy were routed in a few minutes, and the greater part of them left dead on the ground," Greene wrote. He later told Major General Baron Friedrich von Steuben that Lee's troops "made a dreadful carnage" of Pyle's men. The American general believed that the blow would demoralize North Carolina's loyalists and hinder British efforts to recruit them. "It [Pyle's Massacre] has had a very happy effect on those disaffected Persons, of which there are too many in this Country," he wrote to Thomas Jefferson. Greene observed in a letter to Pickens that "the defeat of the Tories was so happily timed, & in all probability will be productive of such happy consequences, that I cannot help congratulating you on your success."[45]

The short and bloody affair called Pyle's Massacre had helped him in his quest to gain a numerical advantage over Cornwallis and increased his chances of victory, if he could entice the British army into a standup battle.

*****

Guilford Courthouse—Preliminary Maneuvers

Pickens reported that after Pyle's Massacre "Colonel Lee and myself determined to retire to some plantation for part of the night and attack them (Tarleton) by day break in the morning." At the same time that Lee and Pickens were planning to advance on him, Tarleton had learned of the massacre from some of Pyle's stragglers, and had sent out scouts who found an American encampment. As Tarleton was preparing to move forward and attack the camp, he received orders from Lord Cornwallis to rejoin the main British army. The British general had decided to concentrate his forces after learning that Greene's army had crossed the Dan River and moved back into North Carolina on February 22nd. Lee, who was only three miles from Tarleton's camp, detached a party to observe the British and intended to attack them on the twenty-sixth. Lee's command was strengthened by the arrival of Colonel Preston's Virginia militia during the night, and now Lee, Pickens and Preston were all were looking to strike a successful blow against Tarleton. However, Lee's scouts did not report Tarleton's withdrawal until an hour and a half after the British marched, and although the American force immediately pursued them as far as the Haw River, they found that Tarleton's rear guard had crossed "but a small time before" the American advance guard reached the crossing. Lee and Pickens called off the pursuit, believing that Tarleton's detachment had too much of a head start to be caught.[46]

Greene, encouraged by the large numbers of troops that were on the way to reinforce his army, had left the safety of Virginia and led his troops back into North Carolina to challenge Cornwallis, completing the crossing of the Dan River on February 23rd. The American commander was disappointed at both the "scarcity of provision" in Guilford County and "the loose and irregular manner in which the Militia of this Country take the field." As he had done during the Race to the Dan, Greene organized a screening force to operate between his army and the British. Once again Colonel Otho Williams commanded the force, which consisted of Continental light infantry under Lt. Col. John Eager Howard, Lee's Legion, William Washington's Continental dragoons, and militia units led by Pickens and Preston. Cornwallis responded to Greene's approach by leaving Hillsborough on February 26th and occupying a position near Alamance Creek the next day.[47]

For the next two-and-a-half weeks, the two armies probed and prodded each other as they maneuvered across the north-central region of North Carolina. Joseph Graham referred to this as "their game of checkers." (The map on page 104 will help the reader follow these movements.) There were frequent encounters between the advanced parties and screening forces of the two armies, as both Greene and Cornwallis sought to gain a position that would offer the best advantage in a major battle. Lee was once again in the saddle as a key element of the screening force, far to the front and in daily contact with the enemy, where he could gather essential information and be among the first to parry any British attempts to break the screen and get at Greene's army. Greene told Baron von Steuben, commander of the Continental forces in Virginia, of his reliance on his mounted troops: "I am superior in Cavalry, and therefore can approach them (the British) without risquing more than circumstances may make necessary."[48]

Williams started to move the screening force toward to the British army, but at first he was uncertain of their exact position or Cornwallis's intentions. At dusk on February 28th he was struggling to verify conflicting reports, one that indicated that the British were on the west side of the Haw River and the other stating that they were on the east side. He dispatched a party of militia to investigate the latter account and ordered Lee with the Legion and all of the other cavalry to cross to the west side of the Haw and probe two or three miles in that direction. Williams warned Greene that it was possible that Cornwallis was playing "Hide & Seek" to try and force the American army to battle. On March 1st, Williams learned that the British army was about three miles south of the American screening force. The Continental infantry and Washington's cavalry had just encamped on the southern side of Alamance Creek, while the rest of the American detachment remained north of the stream.[49]

*****

Clapp's Mill

Williams planned to attack the British at dawn the next morning. "I do not think Lord Cornwallis knows our situation, or if he does, I'm sure he does not know our numbers and may dispise us," Williams explained to Greene. He added that "if we make a brisk, unexpected attack ... our advantage may be considerable." Lee disagreed, and, accustomed to communicating directly with the commanding general, suggested to Greene that it would be "more prudent" to wait until the British army marched and then strike them. If the British suspected that the Americans might attack, the screening force could "be much worsted," and "the spirits of the militia would be broke, & very little good derived in future from them."[50]

Ignoring Lee's objections, Williams ordered Lee and the Legion, along with Major Thomas Rowland's rifle battalion and some of Pickens's militia including Catawba Indians, to advance toward the British in the early morning hours of March 2nd. The total strength of the American force was about eight hundred men. Tarleton's British Legion was engaged in foraging operations that morning about three miles from their army's camp when Captain Richard Hovenden spotted some of Lee's dragoons. Hovenden rode forward to get a closer look and saw infantry following the cavalry. He ordered the foragers to abandon the provisions they had gathered and return to camp, then notified Tarleton of the Americans' approach. Tarleton immediately assembled his cavalry, some mounted infantry, the light infantry company of the Guards Brigade, and a contingent of infantrymen from Lt. Col. James Webster's brigade, and marched to find the American force. Because the rough terrain was not well suited for cavalry operations, Tarleton placed Capt. Francis Dundas's light infantry in his front, followed by Webster's infantry with the cavalry in the rear.[51]

Lee's troops advanced through wooded terrain near Clapp's Mill, and they had covered about a mile when Capt. Joseph Graham's North Carolina militiamen, pushing through a thick expanse of trees on the American left, "encountered a large party of the Enemy drawn up in position." Confused fighting erupted as the separate American units engaged the British at different times and places. In the center, both flanks of Tarleton's advance company were hit by fire from the dragoons of Lee's Legion under Captain Michael Rudulph, who were posted behind a barn, and from militiamen in the woods. Rowland's mounted riflemen on Lee's right similarly came under flanking fire from British troops and "had not time to dismount and did not return the fire so brisk as [Williams] expected." A bayonet charge by some of the British troops from Webster's brigade drove Rowland's men back. The Catawbas likewise were struck by British volleys and fled. Graham's militia fired "3 or 4 rounds" before they "gave way" and began to retreat. In the center, the Legion infantry and some of the militia "were making a handsome defence" but with their flanks exposed were forced to retreat. Williams ordered Lee to break off the action and fall back to their starting point, where the remainder of the screening force was "drawn up to support us." Unable to unleash a cavalry charge upon the retreating Americans because of the "thick woods and high rails" of farm fences, Tarleton did not pursue. British casualties in this fifteen-minute skirmish at Clapp's Mill totaled 21 killed and wounded; American losses are unknown but at least 10 men were killed and Williams estimated that "10 or 12" were wounded. Actual casualties were probably higher. Graham reported 2 killed, 3 wounded, and 2 captured in his company alone.[52]

The next day, March 3rd, Lee wrote to Greene requesting reinforcements. If he was "to skirmish daily," Lee said, the Legion would require three hundred militiamen to support its operations. Lee also suggested that Greene might examine the soldiers assigned to guard duty with the main army, identify those who were capable of serving as dragoons, and reassign them to the Legion cavalry. Such a measure might provide up to fifty additional cavalrymen, Lee believed. While awaiting Greene's reply, Lee offered the commanding general further advice on strengthening the Legion and also undertook some steps of his own. On March 4th, he informed Greene that he had "bargained" with the commander of a militia company that was acting with the Legion, and that its captain had agreed to provide "twelve riflemen to act with me for three months, on condition that the remainder be discharged." Lee added that he had heard that a company of mounted militia had joined the main army, and asked Greene to order them forward to the Legion's camp. "As they will be useless," Lee explained, "my sole object is ... to get their best horses for the use of my cavalry, & permit them to return home." Greene replied on March 5th, stating that he had ordered 170 mounted militia from Halifax County to be attached to the Legion. "I am not a little embarrassed for want of more perfect information respecting the enemies movements and intentions," Greene observed. He suggested that if possible Lee should hire a spy to go into the British camp, and that the Legion should do its best to discover what Cornwallis intended. "My dear Sir I depend greatly upon you for information," Greene concluded.[53]

Lee continued to support his commander with his advice on the army's future operations. On March 5th he wrote:

> *"I take the liberty to trouble you with my opinion on our present prospects briefly. If you have assembled what troops you expect, loose no time in moving to a position near Cain Creek or Rocky River, or near Deep River in the above direction. Cornwallis is pinched for subsistence, & depends for support from the country laying on the three mentioned creeks. You may readily march & assume a strong position at such a distance as will prevent his reaching you in one days march. Your light horse acting near your army & under your immediate direction will act with zeal, & can do more, than in their present situation. I* [here Lee is referring to what he would do were he in Greene's place] *would not decline fighting his Lordship having worried him on his first days march, & would so regulate the hour of*

meeting as to bring the night on me in due season. Being disastrous you may escape in the night. He cannot if unfortunate, turn it to his advantage."

Lee urged Greene to carry out this plan quickly because the forage in the area was "nearly all destroyed, the want of which will oblige you to withdraw further from him [Cornwallis] soon."[54]

*****

Weitzel's Mill

While Greene, Williams and Lee were trying to assess British intentions, Cornwallis at that time was looking for ways to take the offensive. Greene and the main American army were north of the Haw River near Guilford Courthouse, while Williams and the screening force were some distance south along Reedy Fork Creek, the separation making it difficult for the two main elements of Greene's army to cooperate. Cornwallis received intelligence on March 5th that the screening force "remained near us; and ... they were posted carelessly at separate plantations for the convenience of subsisting." At three o'clock on the morning of March 6th, Cornwallis marched to strike the screening force, "and to attack General Greene, if an opportunity offered." Colonel Williams was unaware of Cornwallis's intentions. He informed Greene that morning that the British army, seven miles away, "remains where it was." Williams did not expect Cornwallis to move, declaring that "while Lord Cornwallis keeps his present position, like a Bear with his stern in a corner, I cannot Attack him" without risking heavy losses.[55]

Banastre Tarleton and his Legion led the British column, supported by the Guards' light infantry and Hessian jaegers. They were followed by Lt. Col. James Webster with the Hessian regiment Von Bose, the Guards Brigade, and Colonel John Hamilton's Royal North Carolina Regiment. Aided by a heavy fog that concealed their movements, the British crossed Alamance Creek and approached to within two miles of the Americans before they were detected by an officer whom Williams had dispatched to reconnoiter. When the officer informed Williams that the British were moving along a road to the left of the American screening force, the Marylander got his troops "instan[t]ly in motion" toward Weitzel's Mill on Reedy Fork Creek. The mill was ten miles away, and if the British reached it first, they would be between Williams and Greene, giving Cornwallis an opportunity to defeat the screening force and then turn on Greene.[56]

Williams assigned Lee's Legion and Colonel William Campbell's Virginia militia to act as a rear guard and delay the British while the rest of the screening force "moved on briskly to the Mill." Tarleton stated that "the

British dragoons soon pushed Colonel Lee's cavalry from their advanced situation," but Lee and Campbell, whose riflemen harassed the British flanks, slowed the British just enough to allow the Americans to get safely across Reedy Fork. Nevertheless, Williams reported that his troops "were so closely press'd by Coll Webbsters Brigade & Lt. Coll Tarltons Legion that I found it absolutely necessary to leave a covering party" on the southern bank of the creek. Williams assigned Colonel William Preston to command the rear guard, which included Preston's militiamen along with those of Campbell and Pickens, supported by Lee's Legion and William Washington's Continental dragoons. When Tarleton reached the field, he halted and reported the situation to Cornwallis.[57]

The British general ordered Webster to "form his brigade into line with the light company of the guards and the yagers." Webster then advanced while the rest of the army remained in column on the road behind him. The British troops poured a heavy fire into the ranks of the militia, which Preston's men at first "return'd with great Spirit." However, the militia's resistance did not last long. As the British pressed forward, the militiamen fell back in some confusion. According to Tarleton,

> "the enemy did not oppose the right wing of the British so steadily as the left: the 23d and 71st [regiments] moved forwards to the creek without any great impediment; and the ardent bravery of the 33d and the light company of the guards soon dislodged them from their strong position."

Clouds of smoke from the gunfire blanketed the battlefield, and from his position north of the creek, Capt. Joseph Graham was able to discern the militia "running down the hill from under the smoke. The ford was crowded, many crossing the watercourse at other places. Some, it was said, were drowned."[58]

Continental troops under Lt. Col. John Eager Howard were posted on a hill overlooking the creek and provided covering fire for the retreating militia. As soon as all of his men were across, Williams ordered a retreat, "the ground on this side being very unfavourable," he explained. Webster led the British troops across the creek and in a charge up the hill they "dispersed the Americans so effectually," Tarleton said, "that the cavalry could only collect a few stragglers." The British cavalry pursued, skirmishing with Lee's and Washington's mounted troops until it became clear that Tarleton's dragoons were too few to accomplish anything further. Cornwallis lost about thirty men killed, wounded, and captured. American losses were at least ten killed and twelve wounded, although Tarleton gave an estimate of more than one hundred, mostly militiamen. There is some evidence to support the higher figure, as later that day most of the militia under Pickens and Preston departed for home, complaining that they and their comrades had been sacrificed at Weitzel's Mill to protect the Continental troops.[59]

The departure of a large number of American militiamen would have provided Cornwallis with an advantage had he chosen to press forward. After learning of the fighting at Weitzel's Mill, Greene fell back to the north side of the Haw River, and Cornwallis learned of the American move when a British Legion dragoon captured an American courier. The information sparked a heated debate among Cornwallis and his officers, as Tarleton urged the earl to continue the army's march to High Rock Ford on the Haw and interpose his troops between Greene's army and the reinforcements that were approaching from Virginia. Other officers advised the earl to withdraw to the southwest toward Deep River. Cornwallis chose the latter, and the British army marched away from Greene. The American general moved to High Rock Ford to forestall the possibility that the British might get between his army and the reinforcements marching from Virginia to join him, as Tarleton had suggested. Meanwhile, Cornwallis marched to New Garden.[60]

Like Tarleton, Lee also had advice to offer his commander. On the evening of March 6th, Lee took the liberty of assessing Greene's options:

> *"I think three things are left for you, the one to move to the position recommended in my letr of yesterday, the other to cross the Dan, or to move up to the mountains, the third, to attack the enemy. ... I hope you will not be under the necessity of re-crossing the Dan. If you move towards the back country, I advise that a party be detached into the rear of the enemys late camp to efface every impression which the enemys advance may have on the minds & exertions of the Torys."*

Lee added that the mounted militia should be employed to carry out the latter operation, as they "can be better spared than your regular dragoons."[61]

Two days later, Lee was scouting the British army's movements and sending Greene both intelligence and additional advice. He informed Greene that he had parties of dragoons "close to the enemy" and the rest of the Legion nearby within "supporting distance." Cornwallis, Lee believed, was going to march along Buffalo Creek to Cross Creek and then to the British base at Wilmington. The British troops were collecting supplies and destroying what they could not use or carry with them to prevent Greene from drawing subsistence from the area. Lee advised Greene to move "directly" to the head of Cane Creek and "press forward" with the entire American army, because the British acted "with so much caution & move in such compact order as to prevent light partys injuring them."[62]

Greene replied on March 9th, confirming reports that Lee had heard earlier that the screening force had been reincorporated into the main army. To replace it, Greene explained that he would form "two parties of observation," one commanded by William Washington to operate on the army's right and the second under Lee to act on the left, each reinforced by three to four hundred riflemen. Colonel William Campbell's Virginians would be assigned to Lee's party. Greene instructed Lee and Washington, "either seperately or conjunctively as you may agree, to give the enemy all the annoyance in your power." With regard to the advice Lee had offered, Greene stated that "the intentions of the enemy is by no means fully explained." The general believed that Cornwallis wished to avoid a major battle, and did not think that the British would march to Cross Creek. "But let him march by what route he will," Greene wrote, "you will observe his motions with great attention and give me the earliest information."[63]

Lee set about gathering intelligence even before he received Greene's orders. On March 9th he informed Greene that Cornwallis had marched toward Guilford Courthouse, where British troops destroyed a cache of American weapons. Lee expected Cornwallis's further movements to indicate where the British army was headed, either to "Cross Creek, the Cheraw Hills, or Salisbury." He reported the next day that Cornwallis had camped the previous night at Gorrell's Plantation, and that he remained uncertain of the enemy's ultimate destination. However, he had heard that loyalists were "collecting provisions for them along the road to Cross Creek." Then Cornwallis changed direction suddenly on the tenth and marched back toward Guilford Courthouse. At six o'clock on the morning of March 11th, Lee notified Greene that Cornwallis was only two-and-a-half miles from Guilford Courthouse. "I cannot account for this mysterious conduct in his Lordship," Lee observed. "It appears to me that his Lordship & army begin to possess disagreeable apprehensions." Throughout the previous day, Lee had tried "to bring on a skirmish" with the British, though without success. He had, however, managed to capture a total of ten prisoners and sent them to Greene. Lee also sent additional advice, suggesting that the commanding general move the army closer to the British, and if a battle resulted, Greene had "good reasons to expect success."[64]

Cornwallis eventually moved to Dillon's Mill to procure cornmeal for his hungry soldiers. Lee remained close to the British army, seeking information, and on the morning of March 12th Tarleton's cavalry attacked Lee's camp, driving back the Legion's cavalry patrols and firing on the pickets. Lee withdrew, and later in the day reported that the British army had not moved. Cornwallis subsequently marched to New Garden, and Greene advanced to Guilford Courthouse.[65]

*****

Guilford Courthouse—The Battle

During the preceding days, large numbers of troops had joined Greene's army. A regiment of 400 Maryland Continentals, two regiments of Continental troops from Virginia numbering some 900, about 1,200 North Carolina militia, and another 1,400 from Virginia increased Greene's strength to approximately 4,400 men. He now outnumbered Cornwallis by a margin of at least two-to-one, and was ready to give battle. On March 14th, Greene occupied a strong position near Guilford Courthouse to await a British attack.[66]

Cornwallis welcomed the opportunity to fight his opponent at last. The British commander had only two options, "to commence his retreat, or prepare for a general action." When he learned on March 14th that Greene's army was at Guilford Courthouse, he decided to attack it. Before sunrise on March 15th, Cornwallis sent his baggage train to Bell's Mill on Deep River, escorted by 20 British Legion dragoons, 100 infantrymen, and Lt. Col. John Hamilton's Royal North Carolina Regiment. The need to send such a strong guard to protect the baggage in a potentially hostile region left Cornwallis with no more than 2,000 men available for action. Nevertheless, the earl was optimistic about his prospects for success. He set his army in motion northeastward on the New Garden Road, with Tarleton's British Legion, the Guards' light infantry, and Hessian jaegers as the advance guard, followed by Lt. Col. Webster's brigade and then the brigade of Major General Alexander Leslie.[67]

At six o'clock the previous evening, Greene had ordered William Washington to take position on the Salisbury Road about two miles in front of the army's position at Guilford Courthouse, and Lee to "guard the Newgarden road upon our left." The American general felt certain that Cornwallis would not attack the next day, yet wished to be prepared for that eventuality. "I am perswaded the enemy will not move in the Morning," Greene told Lee. "If they should it will be to attack us. ... Dont get surprised, nor let us be so."[68]

Lee sent forward a small party of dragoons under Lt. James Heard to observe the British camp during the night and obtain as much information as they could about the enemy's movements and intentions. British patrols impeded their efforts, but at about 2 a.m. they heard the supply wagons leaving the British camp. Heard sent this information to Lee along with his belief that the baggage train's departure signaled a "general movement" by the British army. Lee forwarded the report to Greene, who then ordered Lee to probe down the Salisbury Road and try to learn what Cornwallis was doing. Lee set out with his cavalry in the lead, followed by the Legion infantry, Campbell's riflemen, and a company of Virginia Continentals. After a march of two miles, Lee met

Heard's detachment retreating north on the Salisbury Road, with Tarleton not far behind. A short time earlier at New Garden Meeting House, Heard's dragoons had fired without effect on the British vanguard and hurried away, leading Tarleton to conclude that he had driven in the American pickets.[69]

Lee decided not to engage the British with his cavalry because his supporting infantry was still some distance behind, so he ordered his dragoons to fall back. Tarleton saw the maneuver and sent his cavalry forward in a charge against a foe he presumed was fleeing. The road down which Lee retreated was bordered by tall fences on both sides, and Lee realized that the situation might enable him to block the British. He ordered Captain James Armstrong's troop at the rear of his column to turn about and meet Tarleton's charge. A brief but intense skirmish ensued, during which "the whole of the enemy's section was dismounted, and many of the horses prostrated; some of the dragoons killed, the rest made prisoners," Lee wrote. The Americans suffered no casualties. Tarleton retreated "with celerity" toward his supporting infantry, and Lee pursued.[70]

The British cavalry fell back and took "a secondary road" to New Garden Meeting House, where Tarleton "expected to meet the infantry of Cornwallis's advance guard." Lee stayed on the main road, and reached the meeting house first, where the Legion encountered Captain John Goodricke of the Guards with his light infantry at about 7:30 a.m. The Guards greeted the Americans with a "close and general fire" that brought down several of Lee's dragoons. In the chaos, one of the Legion soldiers, Peter Rife, watched as Lee's horse, a "fine chestnut-sorrel, high-spirited, like his master, and of superior qualities for that business, was so good that [Lee] lost him." The Legion charged from the east, and the morning sunlight glinting off the bayonets and polished metal accoutrements of the British troops produced "such a flash of light" as the dragoons' horses approached "that it frightened them and caused a momentary disorder. Lee's horse threw his rider and got away from him." Fortunately one of Lee's dragoons observed his commander's fall, dismounted, and gave Lee his horse. While the Legion cavalry staggered under the Guards' fire, Captain Michael Rudulph reached the scene with the Legion infantry, and soon after was joined by Campbell's riflemen. Additional British troops also hurried up to assist the Guards: first the jaegers, and then infantrymen of the 23rd Regiment. Realizing that he was outnumbered, Lee ordered his infantry to withdraw to the north while the Legion cavalry screened their movement. The Americans fell back less than a mile to a crossroads, where Lee decided to make a stand. Rough terrain made the location unsuitable for cavalry operations, so the infantry of Lee's Legion and the militia battled the British and Hessian foot soldiers for perhaps a half hour. The light infantry of the Guards and British Legion eventually drove back the troops in the center of Lee's line. Lee decided to retreat, and as his force withdrew Campbell's militiamen "were dispersed with considerable loss." The British did not pursue, Tarleton noted, as it was now clear "that General Greene was at hand." Losses in the early morning fighting amounted to between 30 and 40 British soldiers, with an equal or slightly higher number of American casualties [71]

When Lee encountered British infantry advancing along the Salisbury Road, he correctly concluded that Cornwallis planned to attack and informed Greene that the enemy was approaching. Replicating the tactics that Daniel Morgan had employed at Cowpens, Greene posted the North Carolina militia in front as the army's first defensive line. The Virginia militia took position about three hundred yards to their rear on higher ground, and at the crest of the rising terrain, another three hundred yards farther back, Greene deployed the Virginia Continentals on his right and the Marylanders on his left in a third line. William Washington's cavalry, supported by Captain Robert Kirkwood's Delaware Continentals and Colonel Charles Lynch's Virginia riflemen, protected the right flank. Lee's Legion and Campbell's riflemen would guard Greene's left when they rejoined the army, and both Washington and Lee had orders to fall back to support the second and third lines as the British troops advanced, since Greene did not expect the militia to withstand the onslaught of Cornwallis's veteran troops.[72]

After breaking off the action on the Salisbury Road, Lee posted his troops as instructed on the left flank of Greene's front line. Cornwallis reached the American position at mid-morning and deployed his army for an assault, intending to make his main effort on Greene's left because the woods that sheltered both flanks of the American first line were thinner there. The earl placed Leslie's troops on his right, with the Hessian Regiment Von Bose on the flank and the 71st Regiment of Scottish Highlanders between the Hessians and the Salisbury Road. Leslie had the 1st Battalion of Guards in reserve. On the British left, Webster commanded the 33rd Regiment on his flank and the 23rd Regiment to their right. Cornwallis held the 2nd Battalion of Guards, the Guards Light Infantry and Grenadiers, the jaegers, and Tarleton's British Legion in general reserve astride the road.

About 11 o'clock, the American artillery opened fire when British troops appeared, and the British artillery replied. During the bombardment, Lee rode along the front line, encouraging the North Carolina militiamen. One witness described Lee as being "in a great rage for battle," telling the North Carolinians "that it would be sufficient if they would stand to make two fires." Lee was apparently brandishing his saber, as the militiaman believed that there "appeared to be blood on his sword." Another man heard Lee shout above the roaring cannonade that he had "given Tarleton hell this morning" and that their country depended on their performance in the coming battle.

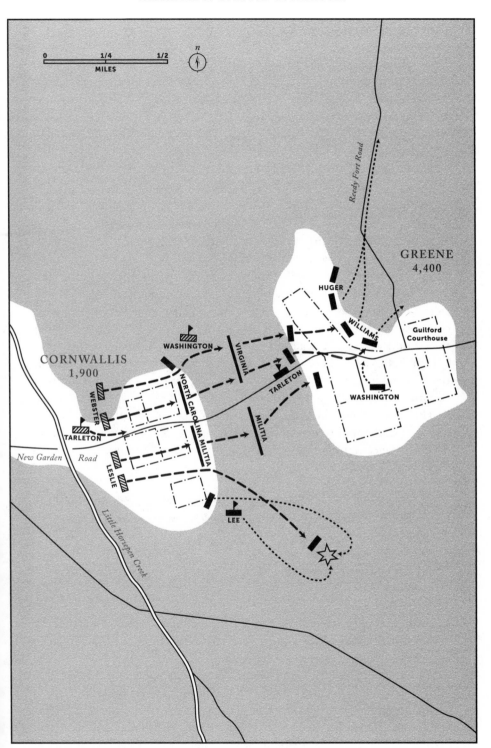

The Battle of Guilford Courthouse

Peter Rife provided a more detailed account, stating that when Lee's cavalry

> *"arrived at the scene of action, cool as the morning was, their horses*
> *were all in a foam of sweat, and were nearly broke down; but Col.*
> *Lee rode along the front line from one end to the other, exhorting*
> *them to stand firm, and not to be afraid of the British; for he swore*
> *that he had whipped them three times that morning, and could do it*
> *again."*[73]

Cornwallis opened his assault a few minutes after noon, and the American militia opened fire almost immediately, although the British were still well beyond effective musket range. Major Johann Du Buy led the Hessian regiment, the trees at first shielding his troops from the fire of Campbell's riflemen. When they were within a hundred yards of the North Carolinians in their front and Campbell's Virginians to their right, the Hessians came under heavy fire and suffered significant losses. All along the line the British troops answered with volleys of their own, and after some further exchanges of musketry most of the North Carolinians fled. Freed from the threat to their front, the Hessians angled to their right and advanced against Lee's Legion and Campbell's riflemen. Brigadier General Charles O'Hara ordered the 1st Battalion of Guards forward to take post on the right of the Von Bose Regiment and support the Hessians.[74]

This initial slight shift in the direction of the British attack resulted in Lee's and Campbell's troops falling back at an angle away from the rest of the American line, and fighting in isolation from the rest of Greene's army. As Tarleton explained:

> *"The [British] right wing, from the thickness of the woods and a jeal-*
> *ousy for its flank, had imperceptibly inclined to the right, by which*
> *movement it had a kind of separate action after the front line of the*
> *Americans gave way, and was [eventually] engaged with several bod-*
> *ies of militia and riflemen above a mile distant from the center of the*
> *British army."*

Lee explained in his memoirs that the British adroitly exploited the collapse of the North Carolina militia to create a "chasm in our order of battle" which "threw the corps of Lee out of combination with the Army, and also exposed it to destruction." In Lee's explanation, he and Campbell were driven in a southeasterly direction and were eventually pushed too far back for them to be able to support Greene's army, or be supported by it. Lawrence E. Babits and Joshua B. Howard theorize that perhaps "the British managed to exploit

a terrain feature separating" the covering party from the rest of Greene's force,
"and that Campbell and Lee, following level ground, drifted away from the
main army's flank."[75]

Some of the North Carolina militiamen who had not fled delayed the
advance of the Von Bose Regiment, and thus the 1st Battalion of Guards
initially fought alone against Lee's Legion infantry and the Virginians. This
left the Guards' left flank temporarily unsupported, and Major Alexander
Stuart's Virginians raked them with a heavy fire, forcing them to fall back. The
Virginians pursued, and were repulsed when the Guards rallied. The Guards
then renewed their attack, only to be beaten back a second time. Again Stuart's
militia counterattacked, and again the Virginians failed to dislodge the British
battalion. The Guards advanced a third time and drove off Stuart's men, but
this time they found their right flank exposed to Lee's and Campbell's troops.
The Americans attacked, and Stuart's militia returned to the fight and struck
the Guards' front. The elite British troops were decimated.[76]

Fortunately for the remaining Guards, the Hessians arrived in time to save
them from complete destruction. Having at last overcome the remaining
North Carolinians, the Von Bose Regiment moved forward to the Guards'
left. The Virginia militiamen saw the Hessians approaching, but mistook
them for Continental troops because the Hessians also wore blue uniform
coats. By the time the Americans realized their mistake and opened fire, the
Hessians reached the Guards Battalion and gave them the protection they
needed to rally. The two units soon renewed their push into the dense forest,
while Lee and Campbell fell back slowly, and sent flanking parties to harass
the advancing enemy. Some of these Americans worked their way behind the
British, so that the Hessians and Guards often found themselves under fire
from all sides. The separate battle on the American left flank raged for half an
hour or more, with the Guards and Hessians suffering severe losses.[77]

On March 10th, just five days earlier, Greene had instructed Lee that the
mission of the Corps of Observation comprised of his Legion and Campbell's
riflemen was to guard the army's left flank. The opening scenes of the Battle
of Guilford Courthouse had pushed his command away from that mission,
and he explained in his memoirs that his objective was to break away from
the fight on the American left and regain his position on the flank of the
Continentals in the third line. When he thought the fighting in his front had
diminished and one British unit inclined back toward the main battlefield, he
"dispensed with his cavalry, heretofore held in the rear to cover retreat in case
of disaster, ordering it to close with the left of the Continental line, and there
to act until it should receive further orders."

When he and Campbell were able to push back the remaining Von Bose
regiment, Lee "hastened with his infantry to rejoin his cavalry upon the flank

of the Continentals, the point so long and vainly contended for." In his memoirs, Lee states that he and his infantry, "supported by the van company of the riflemen" did battle with what he identified as the battalion of Guards commanded by Norton as he moved toward the third line, pushing his foes back upon the von Bose regiment. With that accomplished, all obstacles were removed and "Lee pressed forward, followed by Campbell, and joined his horse close by Guilford Court-House." The memoirs may have mis-identified the unit that Lee and his infantry fought as they moved toward their post on the flank of the Continental line, and, as subsequent events will show, some or all of Campbell's command was left alone and without cavalry protection to face British and Hessian troops southeast of the main battlefield, where they had fought since the opening stages of the battle.[78]

While Lee and Campbell were struggling with the British in the woods to the southeast and Lee was trying to move his command to his assigned position on the left flank of the Continentals, Cornwallis defeated Greene in the main engagement. After heavy fighting, the rest of the British army had overcome the Virginia militia in Greene's second line and engaged the Continentals in the third American line. A bitter contest ensued, in which the inexperienced 2nd Maryland Regiment was routed. Although the veteran 1st Maryland managed to defeat the 2nd Battalion of Guards in a clash with bayonets at close quarters, Lt. Col. James Webster's troops on the British left threatened to outflank the Virginia Continentals, causing Greene to order a withdrawal. The American commander may not have been aware that Lee and Campbell were still engaged some distance away, but Cornwallis knew that the fight on his right continued. The earl ordered Tarleton to take his cavalry southward and assist Leslie's troops.[79]

Tarleton led his cavalry along the Hessians' and Guards' route of advance, encountering many of their wounded comrades and some who were prisoners under guard, apparently captured by the American harassing parties. "The prisoners were quickly rescued from the hands of their captors, and the dragoons reached General Leslie without delay," Tarleton stated. When the British Legion cavalry arrived, Leslie ordered the Guards and Hessians

> *"to fire a volley upon the largest party of the militia, and, under the cover of the smoke, Lieutenant-colonel Tarleton doubled round the right flank of the guards, and charged the Americans with consider-able effect. The enemy gave way on all sides, and were routed with confusion and loss. Thus ended a general, and, in the main, well-contested action."*

Major Du Buy later asserted that Tarleton's arrival and charge saved the

Von Bose Regiment from annihilation. The Guards were probably saved as well.[80]

Greene ordered a retreat along Reedy Fork Road, which was protected by a rear guard of Colonel John Green and his regiment of Virginia regulars. Lee arrived in the vicinity of the Courthouse after the last American units had departed, so he led his Legion up the great Salisbury road until he found a path by which he could rejoin Greene and the main army. [81]

Cornwallis held the field at Guilford Courthouse, but his victory had been costly. His official report listed 93 dead, 413 wounded, and 26 missing, more than one-fourth of his army. Greene reported 57 Continentals killed, 111 wounded, and 161 missing, along with 22 militiamen killed, 73 wounded, and 885 missing, most of whom had fled for home. The actual number of dead and wounded among the militia was certainly higher. Greene had also left his four cannon on the field, temporarily depriving his army of artillery. In general orders the next day, Greene recognized Lee, Campbell, and other officers for their "Gallant Behaviour." In his official account of the battle submitted to Congress, Greene again praised his two cavalry commanders, writing that "the Corps of observation under Washington and Lee were warmly engaged and did great execution."[82]

Two days after the battle, Lee tried to re-connect with Campbell:

> *"I am very happy in informing you that the bravery of your Battalion displayed in the action of the 13th (actually the 15th), is particularly noticed by the General. It is much to be lamented that a failure took place in the line, which lost the day, separated us from the main body, and exposed our retreat. I hope your men are safe, and that the scattered will again collect. Be pleased to favor me with a return of your loss, and to prepare your men for a second battle."*

Campbell, however, had decided to resign his commission and return home to southwestern Virginia.[83]

✶✶✶✶✶

Review of Lee's Performance at the Battle of Guilford Courthouse

Lee's actions at the Battle of Guilford Courthouse have been the subject of considerable discussion, most of which arose long after the guns had gone silent. The stalwart infantry commander John Eager Howard, who fought there with a portion of the Maryland Line, stated that Lee's "post at Guilford was on the left but he was not there when Tarleton charged the riflemen." Howard does not mention that the other Continental cavalry unit commanded by William Washington had left its assigned post on the right during the battle, and supported Howard and his Marylanders in the fight with a battalion of British Guards on the left flank. In moving away from his assigned post, Washington had inevitably left Lynch's riflemen on the right with reduced cavalry support, which, fortunately, did not result in any calamity for those troops. Lee's move on the left flank had similarities to that of Washington—he made the on-the-spot decision to use the mobility of his command to try to achieve an advantageous position on the battlefield which, as Lee explained in his memoirs, he viewed as his assigned post on the left of the Continental line. Washington's move happened at a propitious time, contributed to a positive result, and did not result in undue harm to the riflemen he had left behind. In the uncertainties of battle, the outcome of Lee's actions proved less beneficial for the American cause, but it appears that he used good battlefield judgment, performed bravely in the face of the enemy and was striving to achieve an appropriate military objective.[84]

Criticisms published by people who were not in the fight began over fifty years after the battle with William Johnson's 1822 publication of *Sketches of the Life and Correspondence of Nathanael Greene*. Johnson's work included some positive sentiments about Lee's performance as a commander of the Legion in its partisan warfare activities, but regarding the Battle of Guilford Courthouse, he asserted that, whatever Lee's intentions, he did not make it to the third line in time to affect the fighting there, that he should have made the move earlier, and that his path of retreat separated him from Greene. While these examples identify some situations in which Lee did not fully achieve his objective, Johnson's observations take little account of the challenges and unpredictability of combat operations, and of the energetic and decisive actions that Lee took as a combat leader.

For example, Lee in all probability was separated from Greene at the end of the battle because a large segment of the British army stood between the two forces. Lee's actions seem wholly consistent with good battlefield judgment in this case—he found a safe path to rejoin the main army without taking the risk of having his small and valuable force annihilated. Johnson's other observations also seem to lack a detailed understanding of how decisions are made in the crucible of actual combat operations, and how events in that uniquely complex and dangerous setting are sometimes determined by completely unpredictable factors.[85]

Johnson's work was published several years after Lee's death and elicited a vigorous defense from his son, Henry Lee IV (called "Black Horse Harry" for some notorious indiscretions) in 1824. Johnson was a Democratic Republican and an appointee of President Thomas Jefferson to the United States Supreme Court. Some observers such as Francis D. Cogliano believe that Johnson was recruited to discredit Lee, who had been a staunch Federalist and political opponent of Jefferson during his lifetime.[86]

Even more intense criticism of Lee came one hundred years after the battle with the 1881 publication of Lyman C. Draper's *King's Mountain and Its Heroes.* Supported by citations of long-deceased Revolutionary War soldiers William C. Preston, a commander of rifle troops, and William R. Davie, Greene's senior commissary officer. Draper avowed that Lee had abandoned William Campbell and his riflemen, leaving them vulnerable to assault by Tarleton, and that Campbell was furious at Lee for enabling Tarleton to inflict significant casualties on his men.

Campbell did resign and return home to western Virginia a few days after the battle, which Draper and others have attributed to Lee's actions at Guilford Courthouse, although there is no known contemporary documentation of Campbell's actual justification for his resignation. Campbell was a fine soldier and an excellent leader of rifle troops, as his performance at King's Mountain, Weitzel's Mill, and Guilford Courthouse made abundantly clear. However, militia commanders and units left the southern army for many different reasons all the time, and it was such a frequent occurrence that Greene left an extensive record of his frustration in this regard, such as his lament to Virginia Governor Thomas Jefferson:

> *"The Militia indeed have flocked in from various quarters, and seemed to promise me as much as I could wish; but they soon get tired out with difficulties, and go and come in such irregular Bodies that I can make no calculations on the strength of my Army, or direct any future operations that can ensure me the means of success."*[87]

Perhaps reflecting his own separation from his family, Greene once opined to his friend Joseph Reed, a former member of George Washington's staff now serving as President of the Pennsylvania Council, that "Our Army is in good spirits; but the Militia are leaving us in great numbers, to return home and kiss their wives and sweet hearts." A militia leader as dedicated to the cause and as effective as the valiant Andrew Pickens missed the Battle of Guilford Courthouse because a week earlier he took his Georgia and South Carolina troops back to South Carolina, responding to their complaints about being too far from home. Some went home for other reasons, such as groups of riflemen who complained after the skirmish at Weitzel's Mill (where both Lee and Campbell were engaged) that they were "made to be a sacrifice by the Regular Officers to screen their own troops." [88]

Sentiments like these from the riflemen give insight into the relationship between officers of the Continental Army and even the finest of the militia troops. The Continental troops had signed up for long-term commitments, and leaders like George Washington and Nathanael Greene had completely devoted their lives to victory in the war effort. It seems completely understandable that these leaders came to rely primarily on the men who they knew would stand with them in any situation, men like Lee whose first thought after a Battle like Guilford Courthouse was how to get at the retreating enemy, not when they could go home. Lee's stated urge during the battle was to get to his post and to defend the left of the extremely valuable units of the Continental line, which he described in his memoirs. This attitude seems entirely consistent with the belief that the regular troops that Lee was determined to protect, the stalwart Marylanders commanded by men like Otho Holland Williams, John Eager Howard and their brother officers, were a very valuable asset that required maximum protection. Large numbers of militia troops made it possible for Greene to stand and fight at Guilford Courthouse, and militia leaders like Andrew Pickens and William Campbell made invaluable contributions to the war effort. Nonetheless, victory in the Revolution would not have been possible without the veteran Continental troops that formed the solid core of the American army—steady, dependable officers and men like Lee and his Legion that Greene and other senior leaders knew were indispensable to the success of their cause.

There is considerable background information and supporting documentation about the ongoing disputes between the militia and the regulars, but there is no known record where William Campbell expressed anger at Lee for his actions at Guilford Courthouse. In fact, Campbell wrote to Reverend Charles Cummings on March 28th, 1781, thirteen days after the battle, describing the early portions of the engagement and his cooperation with Lee's Legion in unremarkable terms, although he did not hesitate to criticize others, lamenting about the North Carolina militia that "many of them never fired their Guns, and almost the whole of them threw away their Arms and fled with the greatest precipitation." Campbell likewise described the end of the battle unremarkably as "The Enemy followed us no farther than the Heights just above Guilford C. House, and our Army retreated in good Order to Speedwell Furnace which is about ten Miles below, there the most of the Troops who were dispersed in the Action were assembled the next day."

Campbell's description of the results of the battle reflects his optimism for the American cause, and, by inference, his pride in the contribution that he and his men made at Guilford Courthouse and elsewhere to that success. He did not express directly any dissatisfaction with Lee regarding Tarleton's charge in the waning moments of the fighting, and, in fact, the letter casts no aspersions on Lee at all, although there are many opportunities in the narrative to do so. Campbell wrote with a veteran soldier's hard, realistic understanding of the number of casualties at Guilford Courthouse, and about the prospects for victory in the South, knowing full well that men like Lee would be in command:

"The return of our kill'd and wounded does not amount to more than 250 men; that of the Enemy is said from the last Accounts to be near 1000, among whom are some of their principal officers—Colo Loveless & Major Stuart of the Regiment of Guards are killed, General O'Hara mortally wounded, and the favorite Tarleton shot through the Hand. We have no Officer higher than a Major killed, and only one of that Rank. General Stephens was shot through the thigh.

Tho we lost the Battle, our Army is now as formidable as at the first, and such another victory must ruin the Enemy. Their Numbers after the last Action were not more than 1700 effective Men, and I could not learn they had any Expectation of a Reinforcement. Our Affairs, in my Opinion, are in a more favorable train to the Southward, than they have been since the reduction of Charles Town, and I flatter myself the destruction of the British Army to the Southward is at hand, which will, and that alone, restore peace to all the Southern department."

Campbell's references to casualties and his naming of Tarleton are open opportunities to transition to criticism of Lee if he chose to do so, and he did not. He did include in his final paragraph that "I have resigned my Commission as Colo of Washington County, as I thought I could not hold it longer with honor," but he provides no specifics in justifying that action. Some writers have apparently attributed his reason to dissatisfaction with Lee, however, Campbell did not take the opportunity to pen that accusation. Even the 1881 critic Lyman Draper was honest enough to acknowledge that "at this late day, it is difficult to determine if Lee was excusable, or culpable, for the course he pursued."[89]

The most conclusive evidence that there was no raging Lee-Campbell controversy in the wake of the battle is that neither Lee nor Greene wrote one word in defense of the Legion commander at the time. If the controversy had been public, Lee's sensitivity to criticism and his tendency toward arduous and voluminous defense would have surely left some documentation in its wake. Campbell died a little over five months after the battle, on August 22nd, 1781, while supporting Lafayette against Cornwallis in the Yorktown campaign. Some have surmised that Campbell would have tried to pursue his disagreements with Lee after the war, but he left no record of such an intent before his unfortunate and untimely death.

If the final judgment goes to the general who commanded at the Battle of Guilford Courthouse, Nathanael Greene's report to the President of Congress expressed his entire satisfaction with Lee's performance. [90]

*****

Nathanael Greene's Assessment

Three days after the battle, Nathanael Greene analyzed the results of the Battle of Guilford Courthouse for his friend Joseph Reed, President of the Pennsylvania Council:

> *"We were obligd to give up the ground, and lost our Artillery. But the enemy have been so soundly beaten, that they dare not move towards us since the action; notwithstanding we lay within ten Miles of them for two days......I have never felt an easy moment since the enemy crossed the Catabaw until since the defeat of the 15th; but now I am perfectly easy, being perswaded it is out of the enemies power to do us any great injury."* [91]

The battle had given Greene increasing confidence that his little army could eventually prevail against his British adversaries. When he published the General Orders that recounted the outcome of the battle to his men, he included in his praise the "Gallant behavior of the Corps of Observation consisting of Detachments of Cavalry and Infantry commanded by L[t.] C[ol]. [William] Washington & the Legion commanded by L[t]. C[ol]. [Henry] Lee in Conjunction with the Rifle men & Light Infantry commanded by Colls [William] Campbell & [Charles] Lynch."[92]

Greene was a leader who continually looked for an opportunity to strike a blow at his enemy, and he sensed that the mauling his army had inflicted on Cornwallis at Guilford Courthouse had given him an important opening. To find and pursue the enemy, he would rely upon Lee to operate far to the front, in an independent command, with orders to "follow their rear" and "provide the earliest intelligence." Greene knew that he could depend upon his young Legion commander to exercise the judgment, vigilance, rapid movement, and tireless activity that would be needed to accomplish that vital mission.[93]

---

1   John Buchanan, *The Road to Guilford Courthouse: The American Revolution in the Carolinas* (New York: John Wiley & Sons, 1997), 360; Lee, *Memoirs*, 251 (quotation).
2   Buchanan, 360, 362 (quotation); John S. Pancake, *This Destructive War: The British Campaign in the Carolinas, 1780-1782* (University: University of Alabama Press, 1985), 174 (quotation); Greene to William Washington, Feb. 16, 1781, and Greene to Lee, Feb. 17, 1781, in Showman and Conrad, editors,

Papers of Greene, 7:298, 301-302 (quotation).

3   Greene to Thomas Jefferson, April 28, 1781, in Dennis M. Conrad, editor, *Papers of Greene*, Vol. 8 (1995), 166.

4   Greene to Thomas Sumter, April 15, 1781, and Greene to the Marquis de Lafayette, June 9, 1781, in Conrad, editor, *Papers of Greene*, 8:100-101 (quotation), 367 (quotation); Lee, *Memoirs*, 274 (quotation).

5   Piecuch and Beakes, *Cool Deliberate Courage*, 83; Lee to Greene, Feb. 16, 1781, and Greene to Abner Nash, Feb. 17, 1781, in Showman and Conrad, editors, *Papers of Greene*, 7:298 (quotation), 303 (quotation); Buchanan, 362; Lee, *Memoirs*, 253 (quotation).

6   Tarleton, 229, 230-231 (quotations); Cornwallis's Proclamation, Feb. 20, 1781, in Tarleton, 256-257; Piecuch and Beakes, *Cool Deliberate Courage*, 82.

7   John T. Hayes, *Massacre: Tarleton and Lee, 1780-1781* (Fort Lauderdale, FL: Saddlebag Press, 1997), 71; Tarleton, 231-232.

8   Lawrence E. Babits and Joshua B. Howard put Pyle's force at "nearly 400." This is a credible and recent estimate, based on a careful study of all available documentation. Tarleton estimated their strength at 200, while Henry Lee stated in a report to Greene that Pyle had 350 men. In his memoirs, Lee gave a higher figure of 400. Andrew Pickens told Greene that Pyle's force consisted of 200 to 300 men. Greene, in a letter to George Washington, wrote that Pyle led "upwards of 200" loyalists. Joseph Graham, a North Carolina militia captain whose troops were with Lee's Legion, calculated Pyle's strength at more than 300. Several eyewitnesses to the subsequent massacre of the loyalists gave estimates of their numbers that ranged from 300 to 500. Most historians accept a figure in this range; John Buchanan uses 400 in his account of Pyle's Massacre; John S. Pancake states that the loyalists numbered 300 to 400. Lawrence E. Babits and Joshua B. Howard, *Long, Obstinate, and Bloody: The Battle of Guilford Courthouse* (Chapel Hill: University of North Carolina Press, 2009), 38 Tarleton, 232; Lee to Greene, Feb. 25, 1781, Andrew Pickens to Greene, Feb. 26, 1781, Greene to George Washington, Feb. 28, 1781, in Showman and Conrad, editors, *Papers of Greene*, 7:348, 7:355, 7:370 (quotation); Lee, *Memoirs*, 256; Graham's estimate appears in Hayes, 91; in their respective pension applications, Samuel Eakin put Pyle's strength at 500, S3317, Oct. 16, 1832, Jonathan Harris gave an estimate of 400-500, W4979, Aug. 16, 1833, Thomas Barnett stated that there were 300 loyalists, S8041, May 28, 1833, Thomas Lofton's estimate was 500, S17114, Dec. 10, 1832, David Cockerham said there were 400, S8240, Aug. 15, 1832, Thomas Boyd gave a figure of 300, S17286, Aug. 20, 1833, and William Lenoir calculated that Pyle had 300 or 400 men, S7137, May 1, 1833, all pension applications from National Archives, Washington, DC; Buchanan, 363; Pancake, 173;. Charles Royster also puts Pyle's numbers at three hundred, Royster, *Light-Horse Harry Lee*, 37..

9   Tarleton, 232 (quotations); Jeffrey Bright and Stewart Dunaway, *Pyle's Defeat, The Most Comprehensive Guide: Case Closed* (Privately published, 2011), 108-109.

10 Barnett, S8041; Joseph Hackney, Pension Application S6973, Sept. 19, 1832 (quotation); Philip Higdon, Pension Application S10839, Dec. 12, 1834 (quotation); Solomon Geren, Pension Application W80, Sept. 15, 1832; Daniel Smith, Pension Application S7550, Dec. 28, 1835; Lee, *Memoirs*, 254.

11 Lee to Greene, Feb. 20, 1781, in Showman and Conrad, editors, *Papers of Greene*, 7:324.

12 William Johnson, *Sketches of the Life and Correspondence of Nathanael Greene, Major General of the Armies of the United States in the War of the Revolution*, 2 vols. (Charleston, SC: A. E. Miller, 1822), 1:449.

13 Lee to Greene, Feb. 21, 1781, and Feb. 23, 1781, in Showman and Conrad, editors, *Papers of Greene*, 7:330 (quotation) and 336 (quotations); Buchanan, 362. Regarding the similar uniforms worn by Lee's and Tarleton's legions, see Bright and Dunaway, 25.

14 Pickens to Greene, Feb. 19, 1781, in Showman and Conrad, editors, *Papers of Greene*, 7: 320 (quotations) and 325 (quotations). On the presence of the Catawbas, see Hayes, 93, and Matthew Vandiver, Pension Application S9500, Feb. 22, 1833.

15 Greene to Pickens, Feb. 21, 1781, Pickens to Greene, Feb. 21, 1781, and Feb. 23, 1781, in Showman and Conrad, editors, *Papers of Greene*, 7:327 (quotations), 331, 341.

16 Lee to Greene, Feb. 23, 1781, and Feb. 25, 1781, in Showman and Conrad, editors, *Papers of Greene*, 7:336 (quotation), 347; Lee, *Memoirs*, 253-254. In his memoirs, Lee stated that after Greene's departure the advanced corps began to pursue Tarleton, but Lee's original correspondence dated Feb. 25 clearly states that he and Pickens were en route to Hillsborough when they learned of Tarleton's movements.

17 Lee, *Memoirs*, 254 (quotation); Samuel Findley, Pension Application R14168, Nov. 19, 1836, (quotations).

18 Lee, *Memoirs*, 254; Lee to Greene, Feb. 25, 1781, and Pickens to Greene, Feb. 26, 1781, in Showman and Conrad, editors, *Papers of Greene*, 7:347-348 (quotations), 355 (quotation); Findley, R14168.

19 Lee to Greene, Feb. 25, 1781, and Pickens to Greene, Feb. 26, 1781, in Showman and Conrad,

editors, *Papers of Greene*, 7:348 (quotation), 355 (quotations).

20 For the account of the capture of the two British Legion officers, see Lee, *Memoirs*, 255-256. The initial reports of the attack on Pyle's loyalists are Lee to Greene, Feb. 25, 1781, and Pickens to Greene, Feb. 26, 1781, in Showman and Conrad, editors, *Papers of Greene*, 7:347-348 and 355, 358. Graham's account can be found in Hayes, 89-94. Lee, *Memoirs*, 256 (quotations); Manuel McConnell, Pension Application S2773, Sept. 18, 1832 (quotations).

21 Lee, *Memoirs*, 256 (quotation); Tarleton, 232 (quotations); Findley, R14168.

22 Lee, *Memoirs*, 256.

23 Lee, *Memoirs*, 256-257.

24 Lee, *Memoirs*, 257.

25 Lee, *Memoirs*, 257-258.

26 Lee, *Memoirs*, 257 (quotation); "Moses Hall's Account," 1835, in Hayes, 96 (quotation).

27 Lee to Greene, Feb. 25, 1781, and Pickens to Greene, Feb. 26, 1781, in Showman and Conrad, editors, *Papers of Greene*, 7:348 (quotation), 355 (quotation); Lee, *Memoirs*, 258.

28 William Falls, Pension Application S6834, Nov. 21, 1832 (quotation); Boyd, S17286 (quotation); Robert Luckey, Pension Application W4368, Oct. 30, 1832 (quotation); Graham, "Narrative," in Hayes, 92 (quotations); Hall, "Account," in Hayes, 97; Graham, S6937; Thomas Miles, Pension Application R7168, May 27, 1833; Carole Watterson Troxler, *Pyle's Defeat: Deception at the Racepath* (Graham, NC: Alamance County Historical Association, 2003), 72; Buchanan, 364.

29 Lee to Greene, Feb. 25, 1781, and Pickens to Greene, Feb. 26, 1781, in Showman and Conrad, editors, *Papers of Greene*, 7:348 (quotation), 355; Graham, "Narrative," in Hayes, 93 (quotation).

30 Graham, "Narrative," in Hayes, 94.

31 Lee to Greene, Feb. 25, 1781, and Pickens to Greene, Feb. 26, 1781, in Showman and Conrad, editors, Papers of Greene, 7:348 (quotation) and 355 (quotation); Lee, Memoirs, 258 (quotation); Graham, "Narrative," in Hayes, 91 (quotations). Different estimates of Pyle's casualties were made by various observers. North Carolina militia officer Joseph Graham wrote that when the Americans left the field after the slaughter ceased, "it appeared as though three hundred might be lying dead." Samuel Eakin thought that four hundred loyalists were killed. Pyle and everyone with him were "all either killed or wounded," according to Thomas Lofton. "The greater part of [Pyle's] men (265 it was said) was killed," William Falls recalled later. Another North Carolina militiaman, David Cockerham, asserted that the Americans "killed and crippled about three hundred" loyalists and "took about thirty prisoners." William Gaulden thought that the total number killed and captured was 150. Jonathan Harris declared that Lee's troops "took a number of those who escaped death during the engagement prisoners," while William Rutledge insisted that the Americans killed "nearly all that were in the action & took no prisoners." Carole Watterson Troxler argues that the evidence points to a death toll of about two hundred. Graham, "Narrative," in Hayes, 91 (quotations;) Eakin, S3317; Lofton, S17114 (quotation); Falls, S6834 (quotation); Cockerham, S8240 (quotation); William Gaulden, Pension Application W7509, April 15, 1833; Harris, W4979 (quotation); William Rutledge, Pension Application S4171, Sept. 25, 1832 (quotation;) Troxler, 36-37. Historians who accept Lee's estimate of ninety dead loyalists include Hayes, 105; Babits and Howard, 38; Buchanan, 364; and Royster, *Light-Horse Harry Lee*, who gives a figure of one hundred, 37.

32 "Joseph Graham's Narrative," in Hayes, 89-91 (quotations); Joseph Graham, Pension Application S6937, Oct. 30, 1832 (quotation).

33 Tarleton, 232 (quotations); Cornwallis to Germain, March 17, 1781, in Tarleton, 265 (quotation). Carole Watterson Troxler tentatively identified sixty survivors, many of whom may have been wounded as their names appeared on British hospital lists after the massacre. Troxler, 64.

34 Lee, Memoirs, 259.

35 Lee, Memoirs, 259.

36 Higdon, S10839 (quotation); Findley, R14168 (quotation); Lenoir, S7137 (quotation).

37 Boyd, S17286.

38 Hall, "Account," in Hayes, 96-97.

39 Eakin, S3317. Although actual evidence of the atrocities attributed to Tarleton is virtually nonexistent, at the time most Americans believed the massacre story to be true, and even those who did not nevertheless encouraged that belief in order to stiffen resistance to the British. For a detailed account of the Waxhaws incident, see Piecuch, *Blood Be Upon Your Head*. Royster, *Light-Horse Harry Lee*, believes that the massacre occurred "without Lee's direct order," 37, but also mentions another militiaman's account that supports the view that Lee planned the attack on Pyle, along with historian Christopher Ward's opinion that the attack was "a piece of strategy fully matured and intentionally executed, whose outcome shocked its author," 38.

40 Eakin, S3317 (quotation); Boyd, S17286 (quotation); Vandiver, S9500 (quotation); Lenoir, S7137

(quotation); Lofton, S17114 (quotations); Graham, "Narrative," in Hayes, 93 (quotation).
41 William Moore, Pension Application S183, Aug. 20, 1820; Graham, "Narrative," in Hayes, 92; Higdon, S10839 (quotation); Geren, W80 (quotation); Barnett, S8041 (quotation).
42 Lee, *Memoirs*, 258 (quotation); John Efland, Pension Application S6814, Aug. 18, 1832 (quotation); Hall, "Account," in Hayes, 97-98 (quotation).
43 Lee to Greene, Feb. 25, 1781, and Pickens to Greene, Feb. 26, 1781 in Showman and Conrad, editors, *Papers of Greene*, 7:347-348, 355-358 (quotations); Lee, *Memoirs*, 258 (quotation).
44 Lee to Greene, Feb. 25, 1781, in Showman and Conrad, editors, *Papers of Greene*, 7:348 (quotation); Lee, *Memoirs*, 257-258 (quotations).
45 Buchanan, 364; Lee, *Memoirs*, 258 (quotation); Pickens to Greene, Feb. 26, 1781, Greene to Pickens, Feb. 26, 1781, Greene to George Washington, Feb. 28, 1781, Greene to Thomas Jefferson, Feb. 29 [28], 1781, Greene to Friedrich von Steuben, Feb. 29 [March 1?], 1781, in Showman and Conrad, editors, *Papers of Greene*, 7:353 (quotation), 355 (quotation), 358 (quotation), 367 (quotation), 370 (quotation), 376 (quotation).
46 Pickens to Greene, Feb. 26, 1781 in Showman and Conrad, editors, *Papers of Greene*, 7:355-358 (quotation);Tarleton, 233, 257; Lee to Greene, Feb. 25, 1781, and Pickens to Greene, Feb. 26, 1781, in Showman and Conrad, editors, *Papers of Greene*, 7:348, 358 (quotation).
47 Greene to George Washington, Feb. 28, 1781, in Showman and Conrad, editors, *Papers of Greene*, 7:369 (quotations); Buchanan, 365; Babits and Howard, 43; Piecuch and Beakes, *Cool Deliberate Courage*, 84; Tarleton, 234.
48 William A. Graham, *General Joseph Graham and his Papers on North Carolina Revolutionary History* (Raleigh, NC: Edwards & Broughton, 1904), 341; Greene to Friedrich von Steuben, March 11, 1781, in Showman and Conrad, editors, *Papers of Greene*, 7:427 (quotation).
49 Otho Williams to Greene, Feb. 28, 1781, (second letter of that date) and March 1, 1781, in Showman and Conrad, editors, *Papers of Greene*, 7:373 (quotation), 378.
50 Williams to Greene, March 1, 1781, and Lee to Greene, March 1, 1781, in Showman and Conrad, editors, *Papers of Greene*, 7:378 (quotations), 379 (quotations).
51 Williams to Greene, March 2, 1781, in Showman and Conrad, editors, *Papers of Greene*, 7:381; Graham, S6937; Tarleton, 234-235; Babits and Howard, 43.
52 Graham, S6937 (quotations); Williams to Greene, March 2, 1781, in Showman and Conrad, editors, *Papers of Greene*, 7:381 (quotations); Babits and Howard, 43-44; Tarleton, 235-236.
53 Lee to Greene, March 3, 1781, and March 4, 1781, Greene to Lee, March 5, 1781, in Showman and Conrad, editors, *Papers of Greene*, 7:384 (quotation), 392-393 (quotation), 395 (quotations).
54 Lee to Greene, March 5, 1781, in Showman and Conrad, editors, *Papers of Greene*, 7:398.
55 Babits and Howard, 45; Tarleton, 237; Cornwallis to Germain, March 17, 1781, in Tarleton, 266 (quotations); Williams to Greene, March 6, 1781, in Showman and Conrad, editors, *Papers of Greene*, 7:406-407 (quotations); Lee, *Memoirs*, 265.
56 Tarleton, 237; Babits and Howard, 45-46; Buchanan, 367; Williams to Greene, March 7, 1781, in Showman and Conrad, editors, *Papers of Greene*, 7:407 (quotation).
57 Lee, *Memoirs*, 265-266; Tarleton, 237; Buchanan, 367; Babits and Howard, 46; Williams to Greene, March 7, 1781, in Showman and Conrad, editors, *Papers of Greene*, 7:407 (quotations).
58 Tarleton, 237-238 (quotations); Williams to Greene, March 7, 1781, in Showman and Conrad, editors, *Papers of Greene*, 7:407 (quotation); Buchanan, 367 (quotation).
59 Williams to Greene, March 7, 1781, in Showman and Conrad, editors, *Papers of Greene*, 7:407-408 (quotation); Tarleton, 238 (quotation); Babits and Howard, 46-47.
60 Tarleton, 338-239; Buchanan, 368.
61 Lee to Greene, March 6, 1781, in Showman and Conrad, editors, *Papers of Greene*, 7:405.
62 Lee to Greene, March 8, 1781, in ibid., 7:412.
63 Greene to Lee, March 9, 1781, in ibid., 7:415.
64 Lee to Greene, March 9, 1781, March 10, 1781, and March 11, 1781, in ibid., 7:417 (quotation), 7:424 (quotation), 7:427-428 (quotations).
65 Lee to Greene, March 12, 1781, (two letters of this date), in ibid., 7:428, 429; Buchanan, 368; Babits and Howard, 49-50.
66 Babits and Howard, 220-221; Buchanan, 368-369.
67 Tarleton, 270 (quotation); Babits and Howard, 219-220
68 Greene to Lee, March 14, 1781, in Showman and Conrad, editors, *Papers of Greene*, 7:430.
69 Lee, *Memoirs*, 272-273; Tarleton, 270; Babits and Howard, 51.
70 Babits and Howard, 52-53; Lee, *Memoirs*, 273-274 (quotations).
71 Babits and Howard, 53-54 (quotations), 56; Caruthers, 154 (quotations); Tarleton, 270-271

(quotations).
72 Babits and Howard, 52; Piecuch and Beakes, *Cool Deliberate Courage*, 86.
73 Babits and Howard, 77-78 (quotations), 79, 94, 96, 105; Piecuch and Beakes, *Cool Deliberate Courage*, 87; Caruthers, 155 (quotation).
74 Babits and Howard, 96, 102-103, 108, 112, 114.
75 Tarleton, 275 (quotation); Lee, *Memoirs, 278 (quotations);* Babits and Howard, 115 (quotation).
76 Babits and Howard, 130-131.
77 Babits and Howard, 131, 133-134, 136.
78 Greene to Lee, March 10, 1781, in Showman and Conrad, editors, *Papers of Greene,* 7:421. (Note: The authors believe it is clear from the context that the word "enemies left flank" in the text should be "army's left flank."); Lee, *Memoirs,* 278 (quotations), 281 (quotations).
79 Piecuch and Beakes, *Cool Deliberate Courage*, 89-92.
80 Tarleton, 275-276 (quotations); Babits and Howard, 137.
81 Babits and Howard, 165, 168.
82 Piecuch and Beakes, *Cool Deliberate Courage*, 92-93; Greene's Orders, March 16, 1781, and Greene to Samuel Huntington, March 16, 1781, in Showman and Conrad, editors, *Papers of Greene,* 7:431, 433, and 433-435 (quotations).
83 Lee to Col. William Campbell, March 17, 1781, in Robert W. Gibbes, editor, *Documentary History of the American Revolution, consisting of Letters and Papers relating to the Contest for Liberty Chiefly in South Carolina, Vol. 3,* 42-42.
84 John Eager Howard to unnamed Revolutionary historian, undated letter, Rocky Mount Collection, DuPont Library, Stratford Hall, Virginia (quotation).
85 Johnson, *Life of Greene*, 2:14.
86 Cogliano, Francis D. *Thomas Jefferson: Reputation and Legacy* (Edinburgh, Scotland: Edinburgh University Press, 2006), 64.
87 Greene to Thomas Jefferson March 10, 1781 (quotation), in Showman and Conrad, editors, *Papers of Greene,* 7:420.
88 Greene to Joseph Reed, March 18, 1781 (quotation), in Showman and Conrad, editors, *Papers of Greene,* 7:450; Greene to Pickens, March 8, 1781, in Showman and Conrad, editors, *Papers of Greene,* 7:410; Pickens to Greene, March 5, 1781, in Showman and Conrad, editors, *Papers of Greene,* 7:399; Charles Magill to Thomas Jefferson, 10 March, Boyd, *Jefferson Papers,* 5:115 (quotation), cited in Otho Williams to Greene, March 7, 1781, n3, Showman and Conrad, editors, *Papers of Greene,* 7:408.
89 William Campbell to Charles Cummings, March 28, 1781 (quotations). Printed from the original manuscript in the New York Public Library. *Bulletin of the New York Public Library, Volume IX, January to December 1905. Astor, Lenox and Tilden Foundations.* New York. 1905; Lyman C. Draper, *King's Mountain and Its Heroes: History of the Battle of King's Mountain, October 7th 1780, and the Events which Led to It* (Cincinnati, OH: Peter G. Thompson, 1881), 395 (quotation).
90 Greene to Samuel Huntington, President of the Continental Congress, March 16, 1781, in Showman and Conrad, editors, *Papers of Greene,* 7:435
91 Greene to Joseph Reed, March 18, 1781, in Showman and Conrad, editors, *Papers of Greene* 7:450-451.
92 Greene's General Orders, March 16, 1781 (quotation) in Showman and Conrad, editors, *Papers of Greene* 7:431-433.
93 Greene to Lee, March 19, 1781 (quotations), in Showman and Conrad, editors, *Papers of Greene* 7:454.

CHAPTER SEVEN

THE "WAR OF POSTS"

After the Battle of Guilford Courthouse, both armies paused to recuperate from the intense fighting while the commanders pondered their next moves. The British army, despite having driven the Americans from the field, had suffered crippling losses. In addition to caring for their own 413 wounded, the British also had to treat more than 100 wounded Americans who had been left on the battlefield. The task was made even more difficult by a relentless downpour that drenched the ground for two days after the battle. Brigadier General Charles O'Hara of the Guards, who had himself been wounded twice, wrote that

> *"I never did, and hope I never shall, experience two such days and Nights as those immediately after the Battle, we remained on the very ground on which it had been fought covered with Dead, with Dying, and with hundreds of wounded, Rebels as well as our own—a violent and constant Rain that lasted above Forty hours made it impracticable to remove or administer the smallest comfort to many of the Wounded."*[1]

Sergeant Roger Lamb of the 23rd Regiment, the Royal Welsh Fusiliers, described the scene at Guilford Courthouse in similar terms:

> *"The wounded of both armies were collected by the British, as expeditiously as possible after the action; it was, however, a service that required both time and care, as from the nature of the action, they lay dispersed over a great extent of ground. Every assistance was furnished to them, that in the then circumstances of the army could be afforded; but, unfortunately the army was destitute of tents, nor was there a sufficient number of houses near the field of battle to receive the wounded. The British army ... had no provisions of any kind whatever on that day, nor until between three and four in the afternoon of the succeeding day, and then but a scanty allowance .... The night of the day on which the action happened was remarkable for its darkness, accompanied with rain, which fell in torrents. Near fifty of the wounded, it is said, sinking under their aggravated miseries, expired before morning. The cries of the wounded, and dying who remained on the field of action during the night, exceeded all description."*[2]

On March 16th, Cornwallis sent a letter to Greene under a flag of truce, assuring the American commander that "every possible Attention shall be paid" to the wounded Americans, but informing Greene that he lacked the resources to "give them sufficient Assistance." The earl asked Greene to "send immediately Surgeons to take care of them, & a Supply of Necessaries & Provisions." Greene replied that he had already dispatched a surgeon, and that he would send medical supplies as well. Lee was also concerned about the wounded and missing soldiers of his Legion; Greene's official report listed the Legion's casualties as 3 killed, 9 wounded, and 7 missing. Bypassing the chain of command, Lee wrote directly to Tarleton, asking that the British officer see to the care of Lee's wounded soldiers as well as the Virginia riflemen who had fought alongside them. Tarleton "graciously answered that he would do so with pleasure."[3]

Cornwallis tried to portray the battle in the best light possible in his report to London. He praised the behavior of his troops, and declared that he would have pursued Greene's army the day after the battle had the march not been prevented by the fatigue of his troops, the need to care for the wounded, and "the total want of provisions" in a region where food supplies were scarce. He also observed that "a great number" of his wounded soldiers "will soon recover." Nevertheless, his plans indicated the extent of the damage to his army. "I shall … leave about seventy of the worst of the wounded cases at the New-garden Quaker meeting house, with proper assistance," Cornwallis wrote, "and move the remainder of the army to-morrow morning to Bell's mill." From there the British army would proceed toward Wilmington, where the troops could be resupplied. Although he did not state it explicitly, Cornwallis and his battered army were going to retreat.

General O'Hara did not attempt to drape his own account of the battle in a veil of false optimism. He asserted that the Race to the Dan and the Battle of Guilford Courthouse had "totally destroyed this Army," without gaining any advantage for the British. "I wish [the campaign] had produced one substantial benefit to Great Britain. On the contrary, we feel at the moment the sad and fatal effects of our loss" at Guilford Courthouse, O'Hara wrote. His pessimism was shared by many members of Parliament, who found that the positive tone of Cornwallis's letter was contradicted by the accompanying report of British casualties. "Another such victory would ruin the British army," proclaimed Charles James Fox, a member of the House of Commons, who had long opposed the war.[4]

Cornwallis began his retreat on March 18th, 1781 with the intention of taking post at Cross Creek. After crossing Deep River, the British found an abundance of supplies and camped for a few days at Ramsey's Mill. Meanwhile, Greene's army had recovered from its exertions. The Americans had withdrawn about thirteen miles from the battlefield to the appropriately named Speedwell Ironworks on Troublesome Creek. Greene's loss in killed and wounded had been far less than that of the British, but the flight of the militia during and after the battle reduced total American strength by about one-third. In a letter to Joseph Reed, Greene complained of the militia's lackluster performance, noting that they "are leaving us in great numbers, to return home to kiss their wives and sweethearts." Nevertheless, after contemplating the results of the campaign, Greene believed that American prospects were improving. "I have never felt an easy moment since the enemy crossed the Catabaw until since the defeat of the 15th; but now I am perfectly easy, being perswaded it is out of the enemies power to do us any great injury," he explained to Reed. "Indeed I think they will retire as soon as they can get off their wounded."[5]

When Greene learned that Cornwallis had left Guilford Courthouse, he ordered Lee to follow the British army and procure "the earliest intelligence" of its movements. The American general suspected that Cornwallis would go "directly" to Colston's Plantation on the Pee Dee River, but alerted Lee to the possibility that the earl might choose to "go by the way of Cross Creek." Greene also expressed his opinion that "the enemy are greatly embarassed" and had left seventy of their most severely wounded men behind so that they could move "free from the encumberment." The American army would march for "the head waters of Rocky River" on the morning of March 20th, Greene added. Lee replied with a suggestion that it would be advantageous to attack the British army while it was strung out along its line of march, and Greene responded that he concurred.[6]

Lee's Legion, supported by the riflemen formerly commanded by Colonel William Campbell, followed Cornwallis to the British army's camp on Deep River. There was some skirmishing between Lee's advance parties and the British rear guard; Tarleton reported that "the day before the King's troops arrived at Ramsey's, the Americans insulted the yagers in their encampment," and that later, while the British troops constructed a bridge across Deep River, "the light troops of the Americans again disturbed the pickets." The encounters were evidently minor, as Lee later wrote that "nothing material occurred between the adverse van and rear corps," and added that Cornwallis did not "even make any serious attempt to drive from his neighborhood the corps of Lee." The Legion commander attributed the earl's inactivity to the "effects of his dear-bought victory" at Guilford Courthouse.[7]

Unlike Cornwallis, Greene eagerly sought another battle. He wrote to Lee on March 21st and explained that the army was advancing more slowly than expected because of a shortage of provisions and the soldiers' need to prepare new cartridges. Again Greene asked for intelligence of the British army's movements and urged Lee to prepare his command for battle. Greene stated that he planned "to fight the enemy again," declaring that "Lord Cornwallis must be soundly beaten before he will relinquish his hold" on North Carolina. To maintain pressure on the British, Greene authorized Lee to "attempt any thing which promises an advantage." In a second dispatch, Greene informed Lee that he was sending forward Lt. Col. William Washington with his Continental dragoons to cooperate with the Legion.[8]

The next day, Greene informed Lee of his plans to bring Cornwallis to battle. The army would march from its camp at Buffalo Creek at six o'clock on the morning of March 23rd, Greene wrote. He continued:

> *"It is my intention to attack the enemy the moment we can get up with them. I am agreed in opinion with you that Lord Cornwallis dont wish to fight us, but you may depend upon it, he will not refuse to fight if we push him. You will push their rear all you can. Col. Washington has the same directions. We shall force a march in order to get up with the enemy at Deep River."*

Despite Greene's aggressive intentions, the American army's progress was delayed by bad weather, muddy roads, and shortages of provisions, and the intended attack could not be made. Greene therefore ordered Lee to try to detain Cornwallis at Ramsey's Mill by preventing the British from completing the bridge. After scouting the position, Lee determined that an attack on the bridge would be "of easy execution." The span was guarded by only two hundred men, and Lee believed that he could surprise them and then unleash his men on the bridge with "axes and fire," causing enough damage to hold Cornwallis in position for at least one more day. On the night of March 26th Lee and the Legion made a wide detour, crossed Deep River ten miles upstream from the bridge, and hastened forward to attack the British detachment guarding it. However, on reaching the scene Lee found that the British troops at the bridge had been reinforced. Lee canceled the attack, and the next morning the British departed toward Cross Creek. Lee pressed so closely behind the British rear guard that the Legion seized the bridge before the enemy could destroy it. Greene arrived the next day, March 28th, with the main army.[9]

*****

Greene's Decision to Return to South Carolina

On the last day of March, Cornwallis reached Cross Creek on the Cape Fear River, where he expected to find support and ample provisions among the loyalist Scottish Highlanders who inhabited the area. Instead he discovered, "to my great mortification, and contrary to all former accounts, that it was impossible to procure any considerable quantity of provisions, and that there was not four days forage within twenty miles." Upon his arrival at the Scottish settlement, Cornwallis received a letter from Major James Craig, commander of the British garrison at Wilmington; Craig's report only increased the earl's consternation. Cornwallis had intended to refit his army with supplies sent upriver from Wilmington by boat, but Craig's letter explained that such an operation was impossible. Cornwallis reviewed the reasons in a letter to Lord George Germain, noting that "the distance by water [from Cross Creek to Wilmington] is upwards of one hundred miles, the breadth [of the river] seldom above an hundred yards, the banks high, and the inhabitants on each side generally hostile." Given these circumstances, Cornwallis decided that he had no choice but to retreat all the way to Wilmington. The British army arrived there on April 7th. During their march, Lt. Col. James Webster, one of Cornwallis's most capable subordinates, died of the wound he had received at Guilford Courthouse.[10]

Banastre Tarleton disagreed with his commander's decision. He believed that Cornwallis did have an option other than a withdrawal to Wilmington, and that Cornwallis had chosen the wrong course. Tarleton argued that "an instant movement from Cross creek towards Camden" in South Carolina "would have been an advisable measure." In his memoirs, Tarleton discussed the factors that justified such a maneuver:

> "The comparative situations of the British and American armies, the state of [affairs in] South Carolina, the dismantled [i.e., defenseless] condition of Charles town, and the remembrance of the second object of the campaign, which was to secure old possessions, strongly suggested and recommended such an expedition; and it may be deemed unfortunate that so eligible a plan was not carried into execution."[11]

Like Tarleton, Greene recognized the strategic value of South Carolina. After reaching Ramsey's Mill, the American general halted his pursuit of Cornwallis. He ordered Lee and a detachment of North Carolina militia to follow the British army at a discreet distance, so that Cornwallis would not suspect Greene's real intentions. Greene revealed his plans to George Washington in a letter written on March 29th:

> "If the Enemy falls down towards Wilmington they will be in a position where it will be impossible for us to injure them. In this critical and distressing situation I am determined to carry the War immediately into South Carolina. The Enemy will be obliged to follow us or give up their posts in that State. If the former takes place it will draw the

War out of this State and give it an opportunity to raise its proportion of Men. If they leave their posts to fall they must lose more [in South Carolina] *than they can gain here. If we continue in this State the Enemy will hold their possessions in both. All things considered I think the movement is warranted by the soundest reasons both political and military. The Manoeuvre will be critical and dangerous; and the troops exposed to every hardship. ... I expect to be ready to march in about five Days.... I am persuaded the movement will be unexpected to the Enemy.*"[12]

The next day, Greene wrote to General Thomas Sumter seeking the partisan leader's assistance in raising the South Carolina militia to assist the Continental Army, and to procure food for Greene's troops. Greene reiterated the reasons for his decision, telling Sumter that the army's return to South Carolina "will oblige the Enemy to give up their prospects in this State, or their posts in South Carolina; and if our Army can be subsisted there we can fight them upon as good terms with your aid as we can here." The Continental commander also asked Sumter to order South Carolina's other partisan commanders, Andrew Pickens and Francis Marion, "to collect all the Militia they can to co-operate with us." The army would arrive in the vicinity of Camden by about April 20th, Greene noted.[13]

In his memoirs, Lee claimed that it was he who suggested to Greene that the army return to South Carolina, and that the general simply accepted his proposal. While there is evidence that Lee did make such a proposal to Greene—the Legion commander was never shy about offering advice to his superiors—the surviving documents clearly indicate that the plan to march to South Carolina, and the decision to carry out that plan, originated with Greene. Lee's advice may have helped Greene reach his decision, but that was the extent of Lee's contribution. The assertion that Greene admitted that Lee had conceived the idea of returning to South Carolina when the commanding general later told the Legion commander that he had "run every hazard to promote *your plan of operations*" is inaccurate. In the letter, Greene was clearly referring to the support he had provided to Lee's operations against the British garrison of Fort Watson while the Continental Army threatened the main British position at Camden. Lt. Col. John Eager Howard of the 1st Maryland Continentals observed long after the war "that Lee suggested the movement from Deep River to Camden I think probable but that it had not occurred to the active mind of Greene, I can not believe."[14]

Lee's own correspondence from the period reinforces the view that it was Greene who first proposed the plan of returning to South Carolina. "As you have been pleased to honor me with your confidence, I take the liberty to communicate to you my Sentiments respecting your plan of operations," Lee wrote to Greene on April 2nd. The Legion commander declared that "I am decidedly of opinion with you that nothing is left for you," except to strike the British in South Carolina. "This conduct may eventually undo the Successes gained by the enemy the last campaign, & must probably render abortive" any effort by Cornwallis "to establish himself" in North Carolina. Lee noted that "thousands of difficultys oppose your success," yet there were no other promising options. The greatest obstacle Greene faced, Lee observed, was that "no General ever commanded troops worse appointed or worse supplied, than those which form your present army," and the coming campaign would "require the utmost wisdom" to achieve success.[15]

*****

Lee's Campaign Against the British Forts in South Carolina

Having determined to march his army to the southward, Greene decided to detach Lee and his Legion to operate with South Carolina's partisan forces, once again placing Lee in the environment best suited to his military talents. Greene briefly debated whether to send Lee to assist Thomas Sumter's troops in northwestern South Carolina or Francis Marion's militia in the northeastern part of the state. Greene chose to send Lee to join Marion, expecting the two officers to work together as they had in the operations against Georgetown four months earlier. Howard later explained Greene's reasoning:

> "Lee objected to be put under Sumter's command, and Greene well knew that the service would not be promoted by it, for Sumter and Lee were both very tenacious of command and would not have acted cordially together—Marion and Pickens were very different in that respect, they were not capricious about command and they did not object to any things proposed by Lee which was for the good of their Country—This will account for the cordiality with which those officers acted with Lee."[16]

On April 4th, Greene sent Lee orders for the next phase of the campaign. He instructed the Legion to march toward Cross Creek to deceive Cornwallis into believing that Greene was continuing to pursue the British army. Before reaching Cross Creek, however, Lee was to change direction, cross the Pee Dee River, and attempt to "effect a surprise upon the enemies posts on the Santee." Greene recommended Fort Watson as the objective where success appeared most likely. Anticipating Lee's needs, Greene stated that he had detached Captain Edward Oldham's company of Maryland Continentals to reinforce the Legion. The general then concluded with a series of warnings.

He reminded Lee that "our force is small, and ... we cannot afford to waste men without a valuable object in contemplation." He added that if Cornwallis pursued the American army into South Carolina, "it will not be advisable for you to be seperated from us." Finally, Greene asked Lee to "remember that you command men, and that their powers may not keep pace with your ambition."[17]

Greene then dispatched Captain James Conyers to Francis Marion with a letter requesting that the partisan officer support the main army with "a considerable force." The letter did not include specific details of Greene's plans; that information would be relayed verbally by Conyers. On April 6th Greene's army marched from its camp at Ramsey's Mill, heading southward. Following his instructions, Lee reached the Pee Dee River on April 10th and sent Greene an intelligence report. The Legion would cross the river the next morning, Lee wrote, noting that "the posture of affairs is favourable." Lt. Col. John Watson and a British detachment estimated at five hundred men with two artillery pieces was believed to be "near Brittons Ferry" on the Pee Dee, and Marion's partisans were said to be near Watson. Lee observed that he had some doubts as to the reliability of the information.[18]

Lee' arrival proved fortuitous, because Marion's force was in serious trouble. Lt. Col. Francis, Lord Rawdon, had mounted a major campaign against the partisans in early March, dispatching two forces, one under Watson and a second under Major John Doyle, into northeastern South Carolina. Marion focused his attention on Watson's larger force and engaged in constant skirmishing with the British and loyalist troops, but while Marion was thus distracted, Doyle found the location of Marion's base on Snow's Island. On March 29th Doyle's troops easily overwhelmed the small detachment Marion had left to guard the post, killing seven Americans and wounding fifteen. Doyle's men then destroyed all of the carefully accumulated stocks of muskets, ammunition, and other supplies before withdrawing. William Dobein James, one of Marion's soldiers, described the destruction as "a most serious loss."[19]

Marion broke off the fight against Watson, who marched to Georgetown, and raced to strike Doyle. He detached Colonel Hugh Horry with some of the partisans, and when they attacked Doyle's men, the British withdrew. However, the loss of their base, the casualties they had suffered, the news that the troops under Watson and Doyle had burned the homes of nearly one hundred of Marion's men, and reports that loyalist leader Micajah Ganey had his militia back in the field demoralized the partisans. Marion's force "began to disintegrate." By early April Marion had only seventy men left under his command, the remainder having given up the fight and returned home. Reports that Ganey's loyalist militia had reinforced Watson with four hundred men further discouraged the Americans. Marion summoned his handful of troops and proposed that they "retreat into the upper parts of North-Carolina." The officers and men unanimously agreed.[20]

Shortly afterward, a scout arrived in Marion's camp with surprising news. Baker Johnson informed the partisan commander that he had seen "a great number of continental troops, horse and foot," approaching. James recorded the effect that the report of the Legion's imminent arrival had on Marion's men:

> *"The news was sudden and unexpected, and to men now in a state of desperation nothing could be more transporting. Scarce was there an eye but what was suffused with tears of joy. All sufferings appeared now to be at an end, and that balm of the soul hope began to revive."*

A few minutes later, Johnson's report was confirmed by the arrival of the Legion infantry's vanguard.[21]

Lee arrived with the remainder of the Legion on April 14th, and he and Marion promptly set to work planning their future operations. Marion suggested that their combined force move against Watson's corps, which had reached Georgetown. Lee disagreed, arguing that the attempt would draw the Legion too far away from Greene's army, leaving Lee unable to comply with the order to reinforce Greene should Cornwallis pursue the Americans. Lee preferred to follow Greene's advice and strike at Fort Watson. "Gen. Marion must have given up his point with much reluctance," James observed, "for he was afterwards heard repeatedly to regret that his orders did not permit him to pursue Col. Watson." However, Marion's shortage of ammunition as a result of the loss of his stores at Snow's Island would have constrained lengthy field operations, whereas the capture of Fort Watson and its supplies would allow the partisans to replenish their stocks of gunpowder and lead. Thus Marion finally agreed that Fort Watson should be their first target.[22]

Despite Greene's efforts to keep American maneuvers a secret, Rawdon had learned of his and Lee's movements. Rawdon wrote to Lt. Col. Nisbet Balfour, the British commandant of Charleston, on April 12th to report that an escaped loyalist prisoner had brought news that Greene was marching toward South Carolina. The next day, Rawdon sent the additional information that "Lee passed the Pedee two days ago and I conjecture will join Marion." On April 15th Rawdon confirmed that Greene's objective was Camden. In response to this information, Balfour wrote to Cornwallis and asserted that "the force now at Camden is not equal to clear the country and drive Greene back without your assistance." Although he was unwilling to directly advise his commanding officer regarding future movements, Balfour was strongly hinting that he thought Cornwallis should return to South Carolina.[23]

Balfour's plea went unheeded by the earl. He had already decided to march northward to Virginia, where he planned to unite his battered army with a 5,500-strong British expeditionary force operating near the Chesapeake Bay. Cornwallis had explained his thinking to his superior, General Henry Clinton, in a letter of April 10th, declaring that "until Virginia is in a manner subdued, our hold on the Carolinas must be difficult, if not precarious." But even as he assured Clinton that a march to Virginia would help secure British control of South Carolina, Cornwallis privately knew that he was jeopardizing the British position there. He conceded to Balfour that although the British might be "so unfortunate as to lose some of the Outposts and the Country of S. Carolina," at least "Charleston is not in danger." On April 25th, Cornwallis led his army out of Wilmington and headed northward to Virginia. Lee and Greene would no longer have to worry about the earl interfering with their operations.[24]

*****

Fort Watson

Lee and Marion wasted no time once they had reached a decision, and they set out for Fort Watson on April 15th. The post had been constructed by the British in late December 1780 or early January 1781 atop an Indian mound some thirty to forty feet high along the Santee River. The fort guarded both the river and the road by which supplies were shipped overland from Charleston to the key British post at Camden. If this line of communications was severed, Camden and the British post farther west at Ninety Six would be untenable, for as Lord Rawdon noted, the Camden garrison was dependent upon this route "for subsistence, for military stores, for horses, for arms, and for ... re-enforcements" sent from Charleston. Lt. Col. Watson supervised the fort's construction, and to protect the supply line with the limited number of troops available, he made the post as strong as possible. "We scarp'd it, stockaded it at Top, abattis'd it at bottom," Watson wrote. Marion noted that there were three rows of abatis, and that the ground surrounding the fort had been cleared of trees to deprive attackers of cover. Watson assigned Lt. James McKay and forty men to garrison the position.[25]

"At four in the Afternoon" of April 15th, "a party of the Enemy's Horse & foot appeared in the Skirts of the wood on our front," McKay recorded in a journal he kept of the siege. He ordered out a party that briefly skirmished with the Americans, losing one man mortally wounded, but he recalled the detachment when Lee and Marion raised a white flag. The bearer of the flag brought a message demanding the fort's surrender, but McKay summarily rejected the demand, telling the American officer that "if they wanted [the fort], they must come and take it." When the American officer returned to his superiors with the message, Lee and Marion ordered their troops to open fire.

In the ensuing engagement one of the defenders was wounded and several Americans fell. During the fighting the Americans managed to set fire to the fort's hospital and capture the nurse; however, McKay had already evacuated the sick men. Lee and Marion called off the attack, and decided instead to force the fort to surrender by cutting off the garrison from its water supply. Lee believed that the defenders "might be readily and effectually excluded" from access to a loop of the Santee River known as Scott's Lake, and once denied water, "a surrender of the garrison could not have been long delayed."[26]

Marion and Lee had correctly assessed the situation, because the next day McKay noted that there were "no Provisions or Water in the Works." Both sides occasionally exchanged fire, inflicting a few casualties, and on the night of April 17th McKay assigned a party to begin digging a well. The next day they had found water and McKay was able to allocate a half pint per man. That night, despite a lack of entrenching tools, McKay noted that the Americans "broke ground within one hundred Yards of our Works" and captured some baggage stored outside of the stockade.[27]

Lee, dissatisfied with the lack of progress, decided that artillery was necessary to bombard the fort and force its surrender. He wrote to Greene requesting a field piece. The commanding general replied on April 19th, stating that the main army was within two miles of Camden and after reconnoitering Rawdon's defenses, did not think he could spare any artillery. "The risque of sending it would be too great as we cannot afford a sufficient guard [to accompany the cannon], the Garrison of Camden being much greater than I expected," Greene explained. He suggested that if Lee could send troops to escort the artillery piece, and if "no intelligence comes" that Cornwallis was marching southward, Greene would "send a piece immediately." The next day, Lee sent another request to Greene, this time asking for one hundred riflemen and another company of Continentals. Later in the day, Lee dispatched another letter to his commander, declaring that he was "unhappy with the delay of the field pieces" and insisting that if he had artillery, "this post could be reduced in five moments." He also advised Greene not to worry about Cornwallis, asserting that "you will not hear of him in ten days time."[28]

The British garrison at Fort Watson continued to hold out and to pursue their efforts to obtain water and supplies. With their well running dry on April 19th, McKay ordered the men to dig deeper, and that night he dispatched two militia men who evaded Lee's and Marion's sentries and hurried to Nelson's Ferry where they hoped to find provisions and summon relief for the besieged garrison. Meanwhile the Americans and British continued to exchange fire, and Lee's and Marion's men did their best to dig approach trenches. They made enough progress to enable them to capture the remaining British baggage on the night of the nineteenth. By the following day Fort Watson's defenders had dug the well deep enough to insure an adequate supply of water, and during the night constructed a "covered Passage" to protect the well from American fire. Also that night, three barrels of pork and four of flour were brought through the American lines into the fort, perhaps by the same militiamen whom McKay had dispatched the previous night.[29]

Marion and Lee by this time "despaired of success," Lee wrote; however, one of Marion's officers devised a plan that the two commanders found promising. Major Hezekiah Maham proposed the construction of a log tower, similar to the siege towers employed by the ancient Romans, that would be higher than Fort Watson's stockade. Riflemen at the top of the tower would have a clear shot at the defenders, thus rendering the fort untenable. Lee and Marion endorsed the plan, and sent detachments to scour the nearby farms for the axes needed to build the structure. During the night of April 20th nearby trees were felled and the troops began to assemble the tower. Lee described it as "a large strong oblong pen, to be covered on the top with a floor of logs, and protected on the side opposite to the fort with a breastwork of light timber." The next day, Lee and Marion sent a flag of truce and asked McKay for permission to bury the American dead lying in the fields between the lines, but because the American commanders refused to cease "Firing during the time, their request was denied." That afternoon, McKay was surprised to see the Americans bringing forward "a Wooden Machine which they had built, & were busy in raising a Scaffold made of Rails ... nearly level with the top of our Works for their Marksmen to pick off our Centinels." During the night, McKay attempted to counter the tower by "raising a Traverse ... & sinking our ditches."[30]

April 22nd passed with intermittent firing while the Americans continued to work on their structure, which they named a "Maham tower" after its inventor. On the morning of April 23rd the tower was complete and the top parapet occupied by a party of riflemen. Covered by the riflemen's fire, some of Marion's militia and the infantry of the Legion advanced "and began to pull away the abbatis" surrounding the fort. The defenders, pinned by rifle fire from the tower, were unable to oppose the attacking party as it secured a lodgment on the mound. McKay claimed that Lee and Marion then summoned him to surrender, although both American officers asserted that it was McKay who raised a white flag. Given his journal entry recording that he was "reduced to the disagreeable necessity of Capitulating, by the Cowardly & Mutinous behaviour of A majority of the Men—having grounded their Arms & refused to defend the Post any longer," it appears more likely that McKay initiated the surrender.[31]

Since Marion reported the capture of five officers and seventy-three enlisted men, the garrison must have been strengthened after Watson established the post. The surrender terms paroled the British officers and men to Charleston, while the loyalist militiamen were held as prisoners of war. In a letter to Greene, Marion praised Lee for his "advice and indefatigable diligence" during the siege, and described their efforts as a "tedious operation against as strong a Little post as could be made on the most advantageous spot that could be wished for." Lee seems to have originally had little faith in the effectiveness of the Maham tower. Unaware that Greene had in fact dispatched a six-pounder cannon with an infantry detachment, but that the escort party had gotten lost and returned to Greene's camp with the gun, Lee complained to Greene on the morning of April 23rd that he was "miserable to find … that no field piece is on the way" and told his commander that he was squandering "great & certain advantages" by refusing to send artillery. When Fort Watson surrendered later in the day, Lee dispatched a second letter to Greene apologizing for his earlier message and expressing his wish to continue acting with Marion, along with his willingness to be placed under Marion's command.[32]

While Lee and Marion had been besieging Fort Watson, Greene had been attempting to capture Camden. The American commander hoped to lure Lord Rawdon and the town's garrison out of their strong defenses, and between April 19th and 22nd Greene maneuvered around Camden and sent detachments to attack the outlying fortifications, but Rawdon stayed put. On the evening of April 23rd Greene occupied a strong position on Hobkirk's Hill, about a mile north of Camden, in hopes that Rawdon would attack the American army. Rawdon did so on April 25th, concealing his march by moving through thick woods to strike the American left flank. After heavy fighting, the smaller British force drove Greene's troops from the hill. Greene retreated about five miles; his aide Captain William Pierce informed Lee of the defeat and Greene's determination to continue his efforts to capture the town. Unaware that Fort Watson had surrendered, Pierce told Lee that "General Greene wishes you to be on your guard, as [the British] may probably detach a party to releive the fort in consequence of their success."[33]

Rawdon, however, was not in a position to detach troops to operate against Lee and Marion. The loss of Fort Watson had cut the supply line from Charleston. The British could not forage for supplies in the vicinity of Camden with the American army nearby, and on May 2nd Rawdon reported that he had only two weeks' supply of provisions remaining in the town. Although Watson finally arrived in Camden on May 7th and Rawdon attempted to attack Greene with his reinforced army, Greene wisely avoided battle. Unable to destroy Greene's army and learning that Lee and Marion were threatening yet another British fort in his rear, Rawdon was forced to evacuate Camden. The last British troops left on May 10th after destroying much of the town, and Greene's army entered Camden later that same day.[34]

After capturing Fort Watson, Marion and Lee had divided their forces in an effort to prevent Lt. Col. Watson and his detachment from reinforcing Rawdon at Camden. The stores of ammunition taken in the British fort were "a Sufficient Supply" to allow his force to continue operations, Marion noted, and he and Lee tried to anticipate Watson's line of march. The British column eluded them, however, leaving the two officers "mortified with the result of their unceasing exertions." Greene was similarly unhappy, telling Marion that Watson's junction with Rawdon was "rather an Unfortunate Circumstance. ... Our force divided & the Enemies collected puts matters upon an Unmilitary footing."[35]

Marion accepted Greene's assessment of the military situation, but he was less tolerant of Greene's efforts to procure horses from Marion's militia. The dispute originated in a seemingly innocuous request that Greene sent to Lee in a letter of April 24th. "Don't neglect to get all the good Dragoon horses you can meet with, and give Certificates for all both to Whig & tory," the general instructed Lee. Three days later, Greene sent Marion the same instructions, adding that some of the horses were needed by Lt. Col. William Washington's Continental dragoons. Lee continued to correspond with Greene on other matters, and it was not until May 2nd that he replied to Greene regarding the army's need for horses. The Legion commander told Greene that Marion could provide 150 dragoon horses "from his Militia, most of them impressed horses," and at the very least could "spare 60 which would be a happy supply." Lee observed, however, that the horses could not be provided unless Marion was willing to part with them.[36]

Acting on Lee's information, Greene wrote to Marion on May 4th and reminded the partisan commander that he had raised the matter of horses several times without result. He asked Marion to provide as many horses as possible, remarking that

> *"I am told the Militia claim all they take from the Tories: and many of the best horses are collected from the Inhabitants upon this principle. I cannot think the practice warranted either in justice or policy. If the object of the people is plunder altogether, Government can receive but little benefit from them. The horses would be of the highest importance to the public in the regular service."*[37]

Greene's letter reached Marion just as he and Lee were beginning their operations against their next objective, Fort Motte, and the partisan general was so angered that he threatened to resign his command. Not only had Greene accused him of withholding horses needed by the regular army, but the American commander had also insinuated that Marion permitted his men to plunder the property of anyone they deemed a loyalist. Marion dashed off a heated reply:

> *"I acknowledge that you have repeatedly mention the want of Dragoon horses & wish it had been in my power to furn[is]h them but it is not nor never had been. The few horses which has been taken from [loyalists] has been kept for the service & never for private property, but if you think is best for the service to Dismount the Malitia now with me I will Direct Col Lee & Capt Conyers to do so, but am sertain we shall never git their service in futute. This woud not give me any uneasyness as I have somtime Determin to relinquish my command in the militia as soon as you arrived in it & I wish to do it as soon as this post is Either taken or abandoned."*

Marion added that as soon as Fort Motte was captured, he would call upon Greene and seek permission to travel to Philadelphia, where he perhaps intended to bring his grievances before the Continental Congress.[38]

One of Greene's greatest skills as a leader was his ability to compromise with his subordinates when necessary. Knowing Marion's importance to the success of the American campaign, Greene astutely soothed the partisan commander's injured feelings:

> *"I shall be always happy to see you at head Quarters; but cannot think you can seriously mean to solicit eave to go to Philadelphia. It is true your task has been disagreeable; but not more so than others. It is now go[in]g on seven years since the commencment of this war. … Your State is invaded, your all is at stake. What has been done will signify nothing unless we persevere to the end. I left a family in distress and every thing dear and valuable to come & afford you all the assistance in my power, and if you leave us in the midst of our difficulties while you have it so much in your power to promote the service it must throw a damp upon the spirits of the Army to find that the first Men in the State are retiring from the busy scene. … My reasons for writing so pressingly respecting the Dragoon [horses] was from the distress we were in. It is not my wish to take the horses from the Militia if it will injure the public service, the effects and consequences you can better judge of than I can. You have renderd important services to the public with the Militia under your command; and done great honor to yourself and I would not wish to render your situation less agreeable with them unless it is to answer some very great purpose and this I perswade my self you would agree to from a desire to promote the common good."*[39]

Marion replied on May 11th, insisting that he was "very serious in my intention of relinquishing my Malitia Command." He attributed this desire to his inability to accomplish anything of significance with the small number of men under his command. Marion also made a minor concession on the issue of horses, informing Greene that he was sending the commanding general a horse for his personal use and promising that "as soon as it is in my power to procure more I will send them." The dispute over the horses thus came to an end, and despite Marion's assertion that he was serious about resigning, the partisan leader continued to serve until the end of the war.[40]

If Marion suspected that it had been Lee who told Greene about the alleged surplus of militia horses, there is no direct evidence that he ever raised the issue with the Legion commander. However, Lee was clearly aware of Marion's dissatisfaction and complained to Greene about the South Carolinian. Lee had been "deceived in [Marion]," he declared. "He is inadequate & very discontented—this discontent arises from his nature." Nevertheless, the two officers continued to cooperate effectively.

At this point in their relationship, Marion must have understood that it was Lee's nature to propose one plan after another to Greene, and that the young lieutenant colonel's intentions were good though he was often overly zealous. Even Greene found that Lee's advice strained his patience. On April 28th, Lee had written to headquarters, criticizing Thomas Sumter's failure to reinforce Greene and asking permission to cross the Santee River and "pursue the conquest of every post & detachment in that country." If Greene did not approve his request, Lee asserted that the only option remaining was "the storming of Cambden" and wrote that if Greene made such an assault he wished to participate with the Legion. Should Greene consider his army too weak to attack the town, Lee suggested that the main army "keep up appearances" at Camden and perhaps summon Marion there, while the Legion and other partisan units and detachments acted "vigorously between the Santee & Savannah rivers." Exasperated with this deluge of advice, Greene replied that he agreed "with the necessity of pushing our operations on the west side of the Santee ... but the means are wanting." He reminded Lee that if Marion and the Legion separated, "you will both be exposed." He concluded with a mild rebuke, telling Lee that "you write as if you thought I had an army of fifty thousand Men."[41]

*****

Fort Motte

Greene added some additional advice, proposing that "the [British] posts upon the Santee & Congaree should be our great object." Lee and Marion agreed, and after failing to prevent Watson's detachment from reaching

Camden, they set out to attack Fort Motte, a British post that guarded McCord's Ferry on the Congaree River. Lee noted that the position was "the principal depot of the convoys from Charleston to Camden, and sometimes of those destined for Fort Granby and Ninety-six." Situated atop 245-foot-high Buckhead Hill, the fortifications had been built around the three-story plantation home of Rebecca Brewton Motte. The British had encircled the house with a nine-foot palisade, and an "earthen rampart" at least ten feet wide sloped away from the top of the palisade's exterior to a ditch that was over seven feet wide and six feet deep. About twenty feet outside the ditch a row of abatis encircled the fort. The defenses also included two blockhouses at "opposite corners of the fort." The strength of the position was undermined to some degree by its small size; the fort measured only 120 feet on each side and the palisade walls were only a few feet from the house. The space between the building and stockade was so narrow that the defenders had been forced to dig a well outside the walls to provide water for the garrison.[42]

Fort Motte was held by more than 180 troops. Captain Donald McPherson commanded 80 British officers and enlisted men of the 84th Regiment, 59 Hessians, about 45 loyalists, and a few dragoons who had escorted a recently arrived supply convoy. The defenders had an artillery piece, but it had not been mounted on a carriage and therefore could not be fired. Lee and Marion arrived at Fort Motte on the morning of May 6. They enjoyed a considerable numerical advantage over the garrison; Lee's Legion mustered 100 cavalrymen and almost 150 infantry, while Marion commanded another 150 militia. They also had artillery—the six-pounder cannon that Greene had not been able to send in time to assist in the siege of Fort Watson had finally arrived. The American troops took position at several points between two and three hundred yards from the fortifications.[43]

While Marion's riflemen and the six-pounder kept up a covering fire on Fort Motte's defenders, Lee impressed Rebecca Motte's slaves and others from neighboring plantations and set them to work alongside his own troops digging an approach trench toward the north side of the fort. The work continued for several days without success. On May 10th, Lee informed Greene that the fort "still holds out" in spite of "every exertion" on the part of the attackers. A surrender demand had been sent in that day under a flag of truce, but McPherson had vowed to continue resistance. Lee expressed his certainty that the post could be captured unless Rawdon arrived to "drive us away." The Legion commander hoped that Rawdon would "not evacuate Camtden for two weeks," unaware that the last British troops had left the town that same morning.[44]

Marion updated Greene on the progress of the siege on May 11th, stating that "our approaches here is almost up to the Enemys abbattis. Today we shall make Lodgement at the foot of their work & make no Doubt we shall carry the post." The partisan commander had learned that Rawdon had evacuated Camden, and he had also received accurate intelligence that the British were marching toward Nelson's Ferry on the Santee River. The news led Marion and Lee to hurry their work on the approach trench, and the Legion soldiers and slaves labored ceaselessly during the night of May 10th and throughout the next day. Their efforts appeared to have been insufficient, however, because on the night of May 11th Rawdon's army camped on hills along the Santee, close enough to Fort Motte that the British campfires could be seen by both the attackers and the besieged garrison. Lee wrote that "the illumination of [Rawdon's] fires gave the joyful annunciation of his approach to the despairing garrison." Encouraged by their belief that relief was at hand, the defenders continued their resistance the next day, leading Marion to observe that the fort was "Obstinate and strong." He predicted it might take as much as another day to capture the post, and remained unconcerned with Rawdon, as reports continued to confirm that the British army was not heading toward Fort Motte.[45]

By noon on May 12th the American approach trench was only sixty feet from the Motte house. Lee and Marion decided to hasten the fort's surrender by setting the building on fire with flaming arrows. After McPherson rejected another demand for his surrender, the American officers set their plan in motion. According to Lee, Rebecca Motte herself agreed to the destruction of her home and even provided the bow and arrows, "imported from India," used by the Americans. The midday sun had already heated the shingles of the plantation house, facilitating the work of the fire arrows. Lee described the events that ensued:

> *"The first arrow struck, and communicated its fire; a second was shot at another quarter of the roof, and a third at a third quarter; this last also took effect; and like the first, soon kindled a blaze. McPherson ordered a party to repair to the loft of the house, and by knocking off the shingles to stop the flames. ... The fire of our six-pounder, posted close to one of the gable-ends of the house, soon drove the soldiers down; and no other effort to stop the flames being practicable, McPherson hung out the white flag."[46]*

As soon as the defenders surrendered, both victors and vanquished joined together and extinguished the fire before it could destroy the house. That night Rebecca Motte served the officers of both sides "a sumptuous dinner," but there were limits to the camaraderie between the Americans and their prisoners. Thirty years later, Lee's bitterness was still apparent when he recounted his attitude toward the fort's garrison after they surrendered:

> *"Mercy was extended, although policy commanded death, and the obstinacy of McPherson warranted it. ... McPherson was charged with having subjected himself to punishment, by his idle waste of his antagonist's time; and reminded as well of the opportunities which had been presented to him of saving himself and his garrison from unconditional submission, as of the cogent considerations, growing out of the posture of affairs, which urged the prevention of useless resistance by exemplary punishment. ... Powerfully as the present occasion called for punishment, and rightfully as it might have been inflicted, not a drop of blood was shed."*[47]

Lee's account was not quite accurate, because some of his men decided to execute several of the captured loyalists. According to Levi Smith, the commander of the loyalist contingent in Fort Motte, Lee's men ignored a Lt. Fulker's pleas for mercy and hanged him "on Mrs. Motte's gatepost," then executed two other loyalist prisoners, John Jackson and Hugh Maskelly. Smith was the next prisoner selected for execution, and was dangling from the hangman's rope when Marion was informed of what was happening. Marion rushed out of the house where the officers were dining, saw the scene, and ordered that Smith be cut loose immediately. Cornet William Harrison of the Legion dragoons remarked casually that the men were "only hanging a few Tories." Marion repeated the order, which was obeyed. The partisan general, observing the dissatisfaction on the faces of the Legion cavalrymen, declared "I'll let you know, damn you, that I command here and not Colonel Lee!" Lee provided a different version of events, writing that Smith was "very obnoxious, and his punishment was loudly demanded by many of the militia serving under the brigadier; but the humanity of Marion could not be overcome." Marion's timely intervention saved Smith's life and quite possibly prevented additional executions. Aside from the three loyalist prisoners hanged by Lee's men, the British suffered no casualties in the siege. On the American side, two of Marion's officers were killed and it is likely that the attackers also suffered some additional casualties.[48]

*****

Fort Granby

The loss of Fort Motte represented another severe blow to the British. Lord Rawdon learned of the post's surrender when he arrived at Nelson's Ferry, and observed that "the stroke was heavy upon me as all the provisions had been forwarded from Neilson's to that post." The British army continued its retreat.

Greene, on the other hand, saw an opportunity to eliminate the British forts in the South Carolina backcountry one by one. On May 13th, having learned of Fort Motte's surrender, Greene ordered Lee to "march immediately with the van of the Army for the post at Fryday's Ferry [Fort Granby] commanded by Major Maxwell and demand an immediate surrender of that post. ... if he shall obstinately persist in holding the post he must abide the consequences." Greene added that he was depending on Lee to act swiftly. The Legion marched promptly upon receiving Greene's orders. Marion and his partisans did not accompany the Continentals; instead they crossed the Santee to rest and prepare to strike Georgetown.[49]

Fort Granby was a formidable position, but it proved to be an easy conquest for Lee, even though General Thomas Sumter's militia had failed to force its surrender earlier in the month. Sumter had left a detachment to watch the fort and had moved on to attack another British post at Orangeburg when Lee's Legion arrived at Fort Granby on the evening of May 14th. Lee found that the position was strong. The fort, built around a house as Fort Motte had been, stood on the Congaree River guarding Friday's Ferry, and Lee described it as "completely finished, with parapet encircled by fosse and abatis, and being well garrisoned." He recognized that "it could not have been carried without considerable loss," unless he resorted to the time-consuming methods of a siege. Lee, however, did not want to wait, so during the night "the enemys position was reconnoitered, labourers collected, & the line of approaches determined on." A position was also prepared for Lee's artillery piece within "point blank shot of the fort." The next morning Lee summoned Major Andrew Maxwell to surrender. The two met and after a brief discussion the loyalist officer agreed to surrender the post on the condition that the garrison be paroled and allowed to take the supplies and the soldiers' personal baggage with them. Lee agreed, and Maxwell and his garrison of three hundred loyalists, sixty British troops, and some Hessians turned over the fort to the Americans without having made any resistance.[50]

Lee's success angered Sumter, who considered himself and his militiamen entitled to the supplies and baggage that Lee had permitted the garrison to keep. On May 14th Sumter had written to Greene demanding that Lee be recalled from Fort Granby. Greene disagreed, and when Sumter learned of the surrender terms, he sent the commanding general his resignation. Although he must have been extremely frustrated at the frequent threats to resign coming from the militia generals, Greene refused to accept Sumter's resignation and asked him to continue serving. The South Carolinian, though still dissatisfied, complied with Greene's request and retained his command. In a further effort to mend relations with the cantankerous Sumter, Greene asked Lee to apologize to the militia general, and to turn over the slaves captured in Fort Granby to

Sumter. Greene then notified the South Carolinian that "such of the negroes as were taken at this Garrison … belonging to the Tories or disaffected you will apply to the fulfilling your contracts with the ten months Troops."* This was in accordance with a practice established by Sumter of giving slaves as enlistment bounties to his recruits, a policy known as "Sumter's Law."[51]

Several days after the surrender of Fort Granby, Lee's soldiers were accused of diverting some of the supplies, which were supposed to have been kept by the garrison, for their own profit. On May 21st Greene wrote to Lee stating that "some of your Legion behaved greatly amiss at the fort at Fryday's Ferry. They sold the Arms and a large quantity of cloth." Greene did not hold Lee responsible for his men's alleged misbehavior, instead telling the Legion commander that "this is only meant as a hint to have them watched narrowly." Lee did not mention the incident in his reply to Greene the next day, but wrote a note on Greene's letter stating: "Not my Legion but some of the detachmt from the army," referring to Captain Edward Oldham's company of Maryland Continentals that had been with him at the capture of Fort Granby.[52]

*****

The Capture of Augusta

Although the controversies over Fort Granby's supplies gave Lee and Greene more trouble than had been involved in the actual capture of the British post, neither man allowed the dispute to deflect them from their major objectives. Rawdon's evacuation of Camden and Lee's capture of three key forts had left only two significant British forces in the southern backcountry, one at Ninety Six in South Carolina and the other in and near Augusta, Georgia. When Greene received Lee's dispatch reporting the capture of Fort Granby, the commanding general put his army in motion toward that post. Greene left his men camped at Ancrum's Plantation on the Congaree River and rode to Friday's Ferry to confer with Lee. Both men were delighted with the progress of their campaign, and discussed future operations. Lee described the state of military affairs at the time along with Greene's plans:

> *"in less than one month since General Greene appeared before Camden, he had compelled [Rawdon] to evacuate that important post, forced the submission of all the intermediate posts, and was now upon the Congaree, in the heart of South Carolina, ready to advance upon Ninety-Six* (the only remaining fortress in the State,

---

* Greene use every available means to win the war, even the horrid system of slavery that existed at that time. See footnote 51.

besides Charleston, in the enemy's possession), *and to detach against Augusta, in Georgia; comprehending in this decisive effort, the completion of the deliverance of the two lost States, except the fortified towns of Charleston and Savannah.*"[53]

Greene confirmed his plans in writing on May 15th. He ordered Lee to "march immediately for Augusta," where he would find General Andrew Pickens. Working together, the two officers were to "demand the Surrender" of the British posts there. "Perform the March as soon as you can without injury to your troops, and make vigorous exertions for the reduction of those posts," Greene instructed. Hoping to avoid a repetition of the contentions that followed the capture of Fort Granby, the commanding general advised Lee that if the British posts surrendered, Lee should "take special care that none of the Stores are plunder'd." Greene noted that he and the main army would march to attack the British at Ninety Six. Greene also wrote to Pickens, informing him of the main army's movements and that Lee was on the way to Georgia.[54]

Lee thought it possible that he might encounter some of Rawdon's troops or a detachment from the garrison at Ninety Six while on his march to Augusta, so he asked Greene to assign Captain Oldham's company to reinforce the Legion. Greene demurred because he had already assigned Lee additional troops: Major Pinketham Eaton's North Carolina infantry battalion and a six-pounder cannon. The Legion commander therefore decided that speed was his best protection and his troops covered seventy-five miles in three days. To sustain this pace required driving his troops forward until late in the evening, giving them a few hours of rest and then resuming the march before dawn. "Relieving the fatigued infantry by occasionally dismounting his dragoons and mounting his infantry" also aided the Legion's rapid movement, Lee reported.[55]

On May 21st, Greene sent Lee further instructions. Unaware that the Legion had reached the vicinity of Augusta on the eighteenth, Greene advised Lee that when he arrived he should "Cultivate a good understanding with General Pickens and the Militia" and act quickly to subdue the British garrison. When Greene received word the next day that Lee had already reached his destination, he was amazed. "Your early arrival at Augusta astonishes me," the general wrote. "For rapid marches you exceed Lord Cornwallis and every body else. I wish you may not have injured your troops." In fact the Legion was in good condition when it reached the American militia positions near Augusta. Eaton's North Carolinians and the artillery marched into the militia camp on May 19th. There Lee consulted with Pickens to determine the course of their future operations.[56]

The commander of the British forces at Augusta, Lt. Col. Thomas Brown, was a South Carolina loyalist. He led a formidable force that included his own regiment, the King's Rangers (also known as the East Florida Rangers) composed of southern loyalist refugees, a detachment of the 3rd Battalion of New Jersey Volunteers, about one hundred Georgia loyalist militiamen under Colonel James Grierson, and an estimated two hundred slaves, some of whom worked as engineers while others were armed. In addition, Brown served as one of two British Indian agents in the South and an estimated three hundred Cherokees, Creeks, and Chickasaws (including women and children) were at Augusta to confer with him. Altogether, Brown mustered some four hundred loyalist troops supported by four pieces of artillery, and could also count on the support of at least three hundred slaves and Indian warriors.[57]

Brown was alert to the American threat; Georgia militia under colonels Elijah Clarke and James Jackson had been hovering near Augusta since late April, and by May 1st Brown estimated their numbers at nearly six hundred. That day he wrote to the Hessian officer who commanded the British garrison at Savannah, Colonel Friedrich von Porbeck, and asked for reinforcements. Von Porbeck declined, claiming that he could not spare any troops. Georgia's royal governor, Sir James Wright, pleaded with von Porbeck on Brown's behalf, asking the Hessian colonel to send a hundred men to Augusta. When von Porbeck again refused, Wright dispatched some of the loyalist militia from the Georgia lowcountry to assist Brown, but American militia intercepted them and forced them to turn back. While Brown waited for reinforcements that never came, he tried to keep the Americans off balance, launching a raid that captured four hundred horses and killed several American militiamen.[58]

*****

Fort Galphin

Brown's success did little to offset the growing number of Americans gathering around Augusta, as Pickens arrived with his South Carolina militia and Lee approached with the Legion and Eaton's North Carolina Continentals. After Lee and Pickens discussed the situation, they decided to make their first move against Fort Galphin, located about twelve miles southeast of Augusta on the South Carolina side of the Savannah River at Silver Bluff. The post, called Fort Dreadnought by the British, had been the home of George Galphin, an Indian trader and American agent to the southern Natives. The British had confiscated Galphin's property as punishment for his support of the rebellion, and his estate made an ideal defensive position. The property included a two-and-a-half story brick house, warehouses, slave quarters, and other buildings, all surrounded by a stout brick wall. Nearly two hundred men defended the position, including a company of the King's Rangers under

Captain Samuel Rowarth, Captain Thomas Hanlocke's detachment of the New Jersey Volunteers, loyalist militiamen, armed former slaves, and some boatmen who had recently conveyed a large quantity of supplies to the fort. The goods were destined for Augusta, but the nearby American forces had forced the boats to halt at Fort Galphin and offload their cargo.[59]

Lee set out for Fort Galphin on May 20th with the Legion dragoons and a detachment of his infantry, supported by two regiments of South Carolina militia commanded by colonels Samuel Hammond and William Hardin. The Americans reached the fort the next morning, the men "fatigued" from their forced march and the day "sultry beyond measure," according to Lee. He decided not to risk storming the fort and instead concocted a ruse that, if successful, would take the defenders by surprise. Lee detached some of Hammond's and Hardin's men to watch the road to Augusta in case Brown learned of the American presence at Fort Galphin and dispatched reinforcements. The Legion cavalry and infantry concealed themselves in "the pine barrens which skirted the field surrounding the fort." While the troops waited for the operation to commence, they suffered greatly. Lee wrote that

> *"for many miles not a drop of water had been procurable; and the extreme heat of the scorching sun, rendered more oppressive by the necessary halt under the pines, without any liquid whatsoever to revive sinking nature, produced a debility forbidding exertion."*[60]

Despite the difficulties confronting his men, Lee knew that the quickest way to relieve their problems was to capture the fort as rapidly as possible. He ordered the militia still with him to dismount and attack the fort from a direction opposite the position of the Legion. Lee was certain that Fort Galphin's defenders would sally from the post to counterattack, "as was the custom," and when they did so, the militiamen were to flee. The garrison, Lee expected, "would eagerly pursue them," and this would give the Legion an opportunity to take the fort. Everything worked as Lee had anticipated. The South Carolinians attacked, and Rowarth led his troops from the fort in a charge. The militia fled with the loyalists in pursuit, and as soon as Rowarth's force was a safe distance from the fort, Captain Michael Rudulph led the Legion infantrymen and one troop of dragoons in a rush from among the pines, racing through the open gates and leaving the dazed defenders who remained inside the walls with no choice but to capitulate. Rowarth, cut off and outnumbered, also surrendered. British casualties totaled four men killed and 187 captured, and a few of Rowarth's Rangers escaped to Augusta. Only one American died, lost not to enemy fire but to heat stroke. Inside Fort

Galphin the Americans found a valuable trove of supplies, including "guns, ammunition, blankets, tools, and medicine," much of the spoils intended as gifts for Britain's Indian allies. "This success not only deprived Browne of a very important portion of his force, but yielded to his enemy an abundance of supplies much wanted by the army," Lee observed.[61]

The next day Lee informed Greene of his victory and promised to reunite his force with Pickens's militia and put into effect "the most vigorous operations" necessary for the "recovery of Augusta." Greene was pleased with his subordinate's success, and he told Lee that "your exertions merit my warmest approbation."

To avoid the disputes that had followed the capture of Fort Granby and the contention with Thomas Sumter over the supplies taken at that post, Greene gave Lee lengthy instructions on how the captured goods were to be distributed, as well as regarding the Legion commander's relations with Andrew Pickens:

> *"The Stores taken I have given General Pickens power to distribute as he may think best calculated to answer the just claims of the Militia and the good of the service at large: If you have appropriated any part of the Stores to the use of your Corps, which I hope you have not, as it will increase prejudicial jealousies, let the things received be part of the continental proportion. I am happy to hear that you and General Pickens are upon a perfectly good footing; and I beg you will cultivate it by every means in your power. He is a worthy good Man and merits great respect and attention; and no Man in this Country has half the influence that he has."*[62]

Once Fort Galphin had been secured, Lee decided to rest his infantry "for a few hours" before marching to Augusta. Meanwhile, he sent Major Joseph Eggleston ahead with the Legion dragoons. Eggleston's orders were to make contact with the American militia commanders, "make himself thoroughly acquainted with the enemy's situation" so that he could brief Lee on the defenses at Augusta, and then to carry a flag of truce to Lt. Col. Brown. Eggleston was to inform the loyalist officer of Fort Galphin's capture, and attempt to open negotiations for the surrender of Augusta. However, Brown rebuffed Eggleston. Lee believed that Brown "either discredited the information contained in the summons, or, immutable in the decision he had taken, would not answer the letter addressed to him, and forbade the renewal of such communication." It appeared that the Americans would not be able to talk Brown into surrendering—they would have to take Augusta by force.[63]

*****

Fort Cornwallis

The British had done a thorough job of fortifying the town. Northwest of Augusta, about a hundred yards from the Savannah River, they had constructed the main defensive work, Fort Cornwallis. The surrounding ground had been cleared to provide the defenders an unobstructed view for eight hundred yards in all directions, the sole exception being a blind spot along the riverbank. About one-half mile south of Fort Cornwallis stood a secondary defensive work, Fort Grierson. This consisted of little more than a trench and stockade around the home of loyalist militia colonel James Grierson, who commanded the local Tories serving with Brown. Each fort contained two pieces of artillery, but Fort Grierson's location had a serious weakness. Just east of the post ran a deep gulch known as Campbell's Gully that connected Alligator Pond to the Savannah River, and an approaching enemy could advance through the gully to within easy storming distance of the fort.[64]

When Lee joined Pickens at Augusta on May 22nd, he was impressed by the strength of Brown's position. He described Fort Cornwallis as "judiciously constructed, well finished, and secure from storm." In a letter to Greene, Lee added that the "connexion of Brownes and Griersons forts" made the situation "difficult" for the attackers, and that only the 110 infantrymen of his Legion were suited for "sieges and storms." Lee also noted that he and Pickens were facing a highly capable opponent in Brown. "So vigilant and resolute was the active and sagacious officer opposed to them," Lee wrote, that the Americans could not proceed "with the wished-for celerity." Brown did not sit idly waiting to be besieged. On the night of May 19th, he led some of his men in a raid against the nearby American militia, catching the Georgians and South Carolinians by surprise and dispersing them. Brown claimed that his troops killed ninety Americans in the attack, and captured eighty horses. The next night Brown planned another raid, but was forced to cancel the operation because Grierson deployed his militia in a failed attempt to ambush American militiamen who had been probing Campbell's Gully just outside Fort Grierson.[65]

The arrival of Lee's Legion and other militia units had raised the strength of the besiegers to between fifteen hundred and seventeen hundred men, allowing Lee and Pickens to invest both British forts with plenty of troops available for offensive operations. The two American commanders recognized that Fort Grierson, made vulnerable by the proximity of Campbell's Gully, should be their first target. During the night of May 23rd Lee and Pickens organized an elaborate assault on the British post. A battery was constructed, and at daylight its artillery piece, a four-pounder belonging to Elijah Clarke's Georgia militia, opened fire on Fort Grierson. Clarke and Pickens led their men in a charge from the northwest, spearheaded by a regiment in which every second soldier had been issued an axe to chop down the fort's stockade. The axe-wielding Americans leaped from their position in the gully and began hacking at the logs, while Clarke's and Pickens's militia charged. From the southwest, a second force consisting of Major Pinketham Eaton's North Carolina Continentals and Major James Jackson's Georgia militia made a simultaneous attack. Lee and his Legion, along with his six-pounder cannon under Captain Samuel Finley, moved into the gully. Anticipating that Brown would sally from Fort Cornwallis to assist Grierson, Lee wanted to move into position to block such a move. If Brown stayed within his fortifications, Lee would support Eaton's force. Lee detached Captain Joseph Armstrong with a troop of Legion cavalry to enter the town of Augusta during the assault and eliminate the few British outposts there.[66]

Grierson immediately realized that he could not hold out for long against such a large number of determined attackers. He ordered his men to escape to the Savannah River and make their way down the bank to the safety of Fort Cornwallis. Brown saw the loyalist militiamen abandoning the fort and ordered the two artillery pieces in Fort Cornwallis to provide covering fire. Finley's six-pounder replied. Then Brown led his infantrymen to Grierson's assistance, as Lee had expected, and the Legion checked Brown's attack. Many of Fort Grierson's defenders were shot down or captured as they escaped, but many including Colonel Grierson reached safety in Fort Cornwallis. Dr. Thomas Taylor, who was in Fort Grierson, reported British losses as "16 men kill'd several wounded & about 40 Prisoners." Pickens agreed that forty prisoners had been taken, although he estimated the number of loyalist dead at "about thirty."

The Americans also captured Fort Grierson's two artillery pieces, while Armstrong's dragoons "drove the enemys outposts from the town, and took possession of their redoubts, thus," Pickens declared, "we are fully masters of the Country & Town and have circumscribed Colonel Brown to one fort." This achievement had cost the Americans relatively few casualties. Pickens reported two men of his command wounded, while other units did not record their losses. However, Major Eaton was mortally wounded and died later that day.[67]

Several of the wounded men captured at Fort Grierson needed treatment, and because Lee observed that the required items were "not to be found in the American camp," a loyalist officer asked permission to go into Fort Cornwallis and procure the items there. Lee consented, and to his surprise Brown "returned a very polite answer by the prisoner." After Eggleston had been rebuffed earlier, Lee had not expected the British commander to engage in any communication with the Americans. Brown, however, explained that he thought Eggleston had come as a representative of the militia, and specifically of Colonel Elijah Clarke, whom Brown abhorred. Now that he was aware that Continental officers were present, he was willing to reopen communications with them. Lee stated that he and Pickens "were very much gratified" at the news, and later criticized the "spirit of hate and revenge" displayed by the Georgia militia in their encounters with loyalists, which had caused Brown to halt all communication with Clarke. Lee clearly felt a growing admiration for his stubborn and skillful adversary.[68]

The Americans began digging approach trenches as Lee and Pickens decided to resort to the standard tactics of a siege. Lee added a variation, however; he ordered construction of a Maham tower, the same device that had proven so effective at Fort Watson. When the tower was completed, Lee intended to mount his six-pounder on the top platform and rake Fort Cornwallis with artillery fire. Inside Fort Cornwallis, Brown's men were also engaged in some extensive digging, and though Lee could see "the heaps of fresh-dug earth in various directions," the Legion commander could not guess what Brown's intentions were.[69]

Brown attempted to delay the Americans' work on the siege approaches by mounting a series of night raids on the enemy trenches. During the night of May 28, Brown led a detachment of his Rangers and some Indians in an attack on the American trenches near the Savannah River. "By the suddenness and vigor of his onset," Lee wrote, Brown "drove the guard before him." Captain George Handy rushed forward at the head of a company of Legion infantry and "after an obstinate conflict" forced the attackers to withdraw. Fearing that such assaults might inflict serious damage on the American forces, Lee decided that the defense of the siege trenches could no longer be entrusted to the militia. Instead, he divided the Legion infantry into two units, ordered the men relieved from all other duty, and assigned them to guard the trenches at night. It was a wise decision, because Brown sallied out again on the following night with a larger force. Captain Michael Rudulph of the Legion met the assault, which had targeted the same point in the American lines as the one attacked the previous night. "For a long time the struggle was continued with mutual pertinacity," Lee observed. Finally Rudulph managed to organize a bayonet charge that drove the Rangers and Indians back inside Fort Cornwallis.[70]

The Americans finished cutting the timber for the Maham tower on May 30th, and began assembling the structure that night only 150 yards from Fort Cornwallis. Despite being within range of the fort's two cannon, the workers were sheltered by several abandoned houses that stood between them and the fort's ramparts. Throughout the day of May 31 the besiegers labored to complete the tower. By the end of the day the top of the tower was "nearly on a level with the enemy's parapet," and the troops "began to fill its body with fascines, earth, stone, brick, and every other convenient rubbish, to give solidity and strength to the structure," Lee wrote. Other American soldiers worked to extend their trenches "to connect them with the tower." Accurately gauging the aggressive nature of their opponent, Lee and Pickens expected Brown to make a prompt effort to destroy the tower, which seemed especially likely after the loyalist commander spurned another surrender demand sent to Fort Cornwallis that day. Therefore Pickens and Lee ordered the lines around Augusta "doubly manned," with militiamen packed into the trenches along with the North Carolina Continentals formerly commanded by Eaton and infantry from the Legion.[71]

Brown reacted as expected. Several hours after darkness had fallen, part of the garrison emerged from Fort Cornwallis and attacked the Americans near the riverbank. The British troops drove Clarke's Georgia militia from their trenches, and Captain Michael Rudulph counterattacked with the Legion infantry to restore the situation. Brown's troops were forced to withdraw after a hard fight, but the assault had been only a diversion. As soon as the forces were engaged, Brown personally led a larger force from the opposite side of Fort Cornwallis toward the Maham tower. The loyalists rushed forward and plunged into the trenches. Lee noted that "for awhile the militia of Pickens contended with vigor, but at length were forced by the bayonet out of the trenches." Captain Samuel Handy, posted with two companies of Legion infantry to guard the tower, left one company to protect the structure and counterattacked with the other. Pickens sent his militia back into the fray, and bitter hand-to-hand fighting ended with Brown and his troops falling back to their fort.[72]

The next morning both Lee and Pickens reported on the progress of the siege to Greene, expressing their dissatisfaction with the slow pace of operations. Lee explained that "the strength of this post, the uncommon inertness & disorder of our [militia] assistants, the inferiority of our regulars in point of number, & the judicious conduct of the enemy will render the issue of these operations later than you can wish or expect." He expressed his hope that the American forces would be able to gain a decisive advantage "tomorrow or the next day," and thus Lee could not for the present comply with Greene's request, made through the commanding general's aide Major Ichabod Burnet, that Lee and his Legion reinforce the main army at Ninety Six. Pickens described the situation to Greene in similar terms:

"We are carrying on Works against Fort Cornwallis with what expedition we can though I think our progress is but very Slow. Yesterday Lt Colo Lee and myself Summon'd Colo Brown to Surrender,

but his Answer was that it was his duty and inclination to defend the Post to the last extremity, and as there is reason to think he will make an obstinate defence, and the Season of the year making it so very necessary that as many of the Militia as possible Should be at their farms, I would be happy if the Service would admit of Sending us two hundred regular troops, which if done immediatly would greatly facilitate the reduction of this Post. "

Evidently Pickens was not aware that Greene could not spare any troops to assist in the siege of Augusta, and to the contrary had already asked for Lee's assistance at Ninety Six.[73]

Greene replied to both of his subordinates on June 3rd. "I am sorry to find that you are in want of some additional force to complete the reduction of Fort Cornwallis," he told Pickens, and expressed similar disappointment to Lee. Greene promised to send reinforcements to Augusta as soon as his army received additional troops who were reported to be on the march from Charlotte to Ninety Six. Concerned that Lee might grow frustrated with the slow progress of the siege and opt to assault Fort Cornwallis, Greene cautioned him that "if you are obligd to storm the place it ought to be attempted with a force adequate to the purpose, otherwise a failure may produce disagreeable consequences. "[74]

Lee continued to show great patience as the siege operations plodded forward. The Maham tower was finished on June 1st; its top platform stood higher than the parapets of Fort Cornwallis and a log embrasure had been completed to protect the six-pounder. A ramp was then constructed to allow the cannon to be dragged up to its position, and that task was accomplished on the morning of June 2nd. Brown, too, had been at work, filling sandbags to raise the height of his parapets, constructing a lateral earthwork within the fort as protection against fire from the tower, and building a new artillery platform in the southwestern corner of Fort Cornwallis, where he mounted his two pieces of cannon in a position to fire on the tower.

Captain Finley opened fire with the American six-pounder shortly after it was positioned atop the tower, and Brown's return fire was ineffective. By noon both of the British guns had been dismounted and put out of action, and the only secure area inside Fort Cornwallis was the portion protected by the lateral earthen traverse.[75]

With his chances for successful resistance rapidly ebbing, Brown resorted to two desperate gambles. On the night of June 2 he sent a Scottish sergeant into the American lines posing as a deserter. The sergeant was taken to Lee and reported on the conditions inside Fort Cornwallis. Lee then asked him: "in what way could the effect of the cannonade be increased?" The alleged deserter declared that he knew the location of the fort's powder magazine, and from the tower he could direct the American artillery fire toward it. Lee was initially deceived and sent the sergeant to Captain Finley. Upon further reflection, Lee grew skeptical of the deserter's motives and changed his mind, ordering the sergeant placed under guard. It was a wise decision, because the sergeant was acting under Brown's orders to destroy the tower if he found a way to do so. Also that night, Brown sent parties from Fort Cornwallis to burn the empty houses between the fort and the American lines. All but two of the buildings were soon consumed by flames. Lee and Pickens had intended to use the houses as posts from which covering fire could be provided in the event they decided to storm the British fort. It seemed strange to them that the raiders had left two of these buildings standing.[76]

No material change in the situation occurred on June 3rd. The Americans sent Brown yet another demand to surrender, and again Brown refused. Meanwhile, the six-pounder atop the Maham tower continued to blast away at Fort Cornwallis. Pickens reported that two redoubts for riflemen were nearly completed within fifty yards of the ditch surrounding the British fort in preparation for an assault the next day. Lee, too, believed that victory was near at hand, although he criticized the militia for "the unmaterial aid which we receive" from them. In the early morning hours of June 4, American troops began moving into position. Pickens sent some of his militiamen into the empty houses between the lines and some of the defenders saw the Americans enter the buildings, but did not see them leave. Brown made his last gamble. At approximately 3 a.m., Lee wrote, "we were aroused by a violent explosion, which was soon discovered to have shattered the very house intended to be occupied by the rifle party before daybreak." Chunks of shattered wood rose forty feet into the air and rained down across the field. Now Lee knew the reason for the mysterious piles of earth he had seen inside Fort Cornwallis, and why Brown had spared the house from the torch the previous night. The British had tunneled under the building, filled the cavern with explosives, and planned to detonate the charge when the house was full of American troops. But they had acted on inaccurate information and set off the blast too early.[77]

On the morning of June 4th, the American Continentals and militia deployed in assault formation. Before attacking, Lee and Pickens decided to offer Brown another opportunity to capitulate. Brown by now was fully aware that his position was untenable, yet he was reluctant to complete the surrender on that date, since it was the birthday of King George III. In order to delay the negotiations, Brown replied that he was willing to surrender his garrison on the same terms that the British army had granted the American defenders of Charleston in May 1780. Lee and Pickens suggested some modifications, Brown countered with further suggestions, and by the time terms were agreed to, the morning of June 5th had arrived. Agreeing to Brown's request that his troops be allowed to march from the fort with their arms, drums beating, Lee and Pickens declared that "the judicious and gallant defence made by the garrison entitles them to every mark of military respect." While the other loyalist officers and troops marched from Fort Cornwallis and stacked their arms, Captain Joseph Armstrong of the Legion escorted Brown to Lee, where the two apparently discussed matters cordially. Brown defended the Scottish sergeant whom he had sent to Lee in the guise of a deserter, and Lee, conceding that the Scotsman had acted as a soldier under orders, freed him from confinement. Armstrong reported to Lee that other Americans, especially the militiamen, were eager to exact vengeance on Fort Cornwallis's defenders and Brown in particular. Lee, declaring that the murder of Brown would be stain on the victory, ordered Armstrong to take Brown into his custody and protect the loyalist officer.[78]

Long after the war, Brown recalled Lee's efforts with gratitude:

> "From Colonel Lee, who commanded the Continental Legion, a gentleman of the most honourable and liberal sentiments, and from his officers, the King's troops experienced every security and attention; from the militia, under a General Pickens, every species of abuse and insult. Colonel Lee and his officers exerted themselves in an uncommon degree, and took every possible precaution to protect the prisoners from violence. The King's Rangers were paroled, and quartered at a gentleman's house, with a guard of Continental dragoons, under the command of Captain Armstrong. The militia prisoners were confined to a stockade fort, where General Pickens and his militia were quartered. After Colonel Lee marched from Augusta, Colonel Grierson, who had rendered himself peculiarly obnoxious to the enemy by his spirited and unwearied exertions in the cause of his country, was under the custody of the main guard, about ten paces from General Pickens' quarters. His spirit and unshaken loyalty in every change of fortune, marked him out as a proper victim to sacrifice to their savage resentment. One of General Pickens' men, named James Alexander, entered the room where he was confined with his three children, shot him through the body, and returned unmolested by the sentinel posted at the door, or the main guard. He was afterwards stripped, and his clothes divided among the soldiers, who, having exercised upon his dead body all the

rage of the most horrid brutality, threw it into a ditch without the fort. Thus fell the brave, unfortunate Colonel Grierson ... not by the shot of an unseen marksman, but under the eye of General Pickens, by the hand of a bloody, sanctioned, and protected villain, in shameful violation of a solemn capitulation."[79]

Grierson's murder on June 6th occurred in his own house, and another American militiaman, Andrew Shulus, also shot and wounded loyalist Major Henry Williams. Some accounts state that Lee had already left Augusta when the murder occurred, but Doctor Thomas Taylor, who was present, asserted that Lee was still in the town and had been warned that Grierson was in danger. After stating that "Col. Grierson was basely murdered in the very midst of the rebel Troops," Taylor noted that "a sham Pursuit was made for a few Minutes after the Murderer but he was permitted to escape." Regarding Lee's role in the incident, Taylor wrote:

"Col Lee indeed & his officers express'd abhorrence of the Fact but to my certain knowledge he refus'd to prevent it, for that very Morning I sent to see that gallant unfortunate Man [Grierson] & upon my carrying him a drink of Water some of the miscreants about bestow'd on us both the bitter Curses; he told me that his Life was threatened & if not remov'd from the Place where he then was he was certain the Threat would be executed. He therefore begg'd me to represent the matter thro' Col: Brown to Col: Lee which I did but in vain."[80]

Grierson's death raised the estimated British death toll in the siege to 53, while American losses were reported as 16 dead and 35 wounded, 8 of whom died later from their injuries. Pickens denounced the murder, as did Greene, who offered a reward of one hundred guineas for the capture of the assailant. However, despite the fact that the murderer's name was known, Alexander was never captured and his crime went unpunished.[81]

*****

The Siege of Ninety Six

Nathanael Greene and his army, numbering just over a thousand men, had arrived at Ninety Six on May 22nd. Lord Rawdon had ordered the post evacuated when the British were forced to abandon their position at Camden, but American troops intercepted Rawdon's messengers, and the defenders of the post never received the evacuation order. The British had fortified the position by constructing a stockade around the town. On the east side

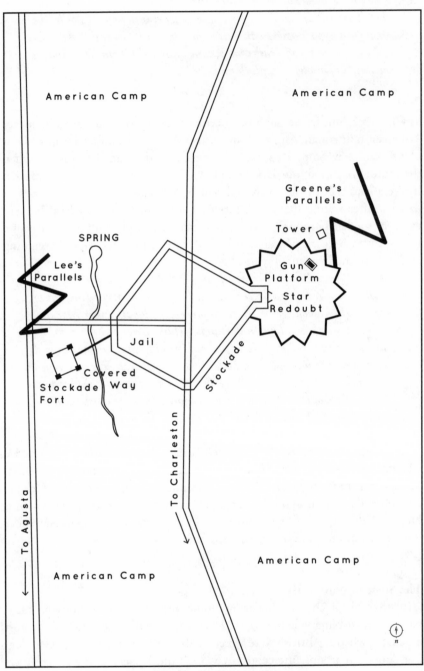

The Siege of Ninety-Six

of the stockade, a multi-pointed earthwork called the "Star Fort" bolstered the defenses. To the west of the stockade, a deep ravine sheltered a spring that provided water to the inhabitants and garrison. A covered way ran from the stockade to the spring and to a smaller wooden fort on the opposite side of the ravine. The defenders of Ninety Six consisted of 350 New York and New Jersey loyalists and 200 loyalist South Carolina militiamen. Their commander, Lt. Col. John Harris Cruger, was a former New York politician who had proved himself to be a skillful and resolute officer.[82]

Under the direction of Greene's engineer officer, Polish-born and European-trained Colonel Tadeusz Kosciuszko, the Americans were engaged in a slow and frustrating siege. Kosciuszko believed that the Star Fort was the key to the British defenses, and had directed his siege approaches toward that position. Like Brown at Augusta, Cruger had sallied frequently from his defenses to disrupt the American working parties. Cruger had also rejected an American surrender demand on June 3rd.[83]

Lee arrived at Greene's camp on June 8th, creating an inadvertent incident as the Legion approached. As he marched northward toward Ninety Six, Lee divided his column to utilize both roads leading to the town. One of the roads passed within sight of the British fortifications, and the officer assigned that route also had the task of guarding the prisoners captured at Augusta. When the prisoners appeared, Cruger was enraged. He thought that the captives had been intentionally displayed either to intimidate Ninety Six's defenders or "to insult the feelings of the garrison." Cruger ordered his artillery to open fire, but fortunately no prisoners or guards were injured. When Lee learned of the incident, he "severely reprimanded" the officer "for the danger to which his [error] had exposed the corps."[84]

After meeting with Greene to discuss the progress of the siege, Lee and the Legion were assigned to "the enemy's left [which] had been entirely neglected" in favor of the operations against the Star Fort. Lee quickly assessed the situation and recognized that the key to the capture of Ninety Six was the post's water supply, not the Star Fort. Dismissing Kosciuszko as an officer "very moderate in talent" whose operations against Ninety Six amounted to a series of "blunders," Lee was convinced that if the garrison had "been deprived of the use of the rivulet in the beginning of the siege, [Cruger] would have been forced to surrender." On June 11th Lee asked Greene for permission to attack and burn the small stockade fort on the west side of the ravine. Such an operation would give the Americans control of that side of the gully and make it impossible for Cruger's troops to obtain water.[85]

Greene approved the operation, and the next day Lee undertook the effort. Taking advantage of the darkness provided by an approaching storm, Lee assigned "a sergeant with nine privates of the Legion infantry, furnished with combustible matter … to approach the stockade in the most concealed direction." Greene provided a diversion by opening fire with his artillery and feigning preparations for an attack on the Star Fort. The Legion sergeant led his party forward, sometimes crawling on their bellies to avoid detection, until they reached the ditch outside the small fort. At that point their luck ran out, and the defenders spotted them as they attempted to set fire to the stockade. A hail of musketry killed the sergeant and five of his men, and the four survivors fled.[86]

The Americans continued the tedious work of digging approach trenches, unaware that on the same day that Lee attempted to burn the small fort west of the ravine, a loyalist had succeeded in riding through the American lines and delivering important news to Cruger. Rawdon had been reinforced by three new British regiments that had recently landed in Charleston, enabling him to undertake a march to relieve the garrison. This report greatly bolstered the morale of the garrison. Greene began receiving reports of Rawdon's approach on June 13, but although he ordered Thomas Sumter and Lt. Col. William Washington to delay Rawdon, the American general was not wholly convinced that Rawdon was marching to Ninety Six until the night of June 16th. More bad news arrived the next day, when Greene learned that Sumter had incorrectly guessed which route Rawdon would take, thus allowing the British army to bypass the militia and march virtually unimpeded to Ninety Six.[87]

Greene now faced the choice of either lifting the siege or of risking an assault on the post in hopes of capturing it before Rawdon arrived. The American general decided to storm the Star Fort with elements of the Maryland and Virginia Continentals, while Lee's Legion, reinforced by Captain Robert Kirkwood's Delaware Continentals, attacked the small fort that Lee had earlier tried to burn. "A furious Cannonade preluded the attack," Greene reported, and at noon the assaulting columns surged forward. The defenders of the Star Fort repulsed the Americans and inflicted significant losses on the storming party, but on the opposite side of the field, Lee's Legion and Kirkwood's troops overwhelmed the defenders of the small stockade and occupied the post. Lee apparently began to probe down the covered way toward the main stockade; however, after the failure of the assault on the Star Fort, Greene ordered Lee "to desist from farther advance" and simply hold the captured fort. That evening, Greene praised "the judicious and alert behaviour of the Legion and those Commanded by Captain Kirkwood, directed by Lt Colonel Lee, [who] met with deserved success." Yet their achievement was not enough, and having failed to capture Ninety Six, Greene ended the siege and withdrew the next day.[88]

Rawdon arrived at Ninety Six on June 21st, after an agonizing march in blistering weather that caused over forty British soldiers to die of heat stroke.

Upon reaching the post, he learned that Greene had withdrawn behind Bush River, sixteen miles away. The British army set out in pursuit the following night, hoping to fight and defeat Greene's army, but the Americans fell back another twenty-four miles and Rawdon called off the pursuit. Recognizing that Ninety Six was untenable, Rawdon ordered the town evacuated. Greene had begun to march toward Charlotte, but when he learned that Ninety Six had been abandoned, he changed direction and pursued the retreating British army to Orangeburg. The Americans caught up with Rawdon on July 12th and Greene initially planned to attack. However, he wrote, "we found [the enemy] so strong and advantageously posted that we had little hopes of succeeding" in an assault. Greene's troops had marched over three hundred miles in the summer heat since leaving Ninety Six, and were in poor condition for battle. He decided to suspend active operations and encamp at the High Hills of Santee, where the army could recover from the long and difficult campaign before undertaking new operations.[89]

But Lee, as usual, remained busy during this period. On June 20th he suggested to Greene that his Legion could be made "doubly servicable" if his infantry could be mounted and issued sabers and "carbines with bayonets." The simple change would increase the number of cavalrymen available, Lee asserted, without reducing the strength of the infantry. Greene ignored the suggestion, and during the American army's withdrawal from Ninety Six Lee shifted his focus to gathering intelligence. On June 22nd he reported Rawdon's arrival at Ninety Six and his intention to evacuate the post, and three days later Lee informed Greene of the British army's location and activities. As Rawdon withdrew, Lee kept his Legion "on the left flank and rear of the retiring army," seeking an opportunity to strike a blow. His chance came on July 3rd near the Saluda River. Aware that the region provided an abundance of supplies, Lee predicted that Rawdon would send out foraging parties that would be vulnerable to a surprise attack. The Legion commander dispatched two troops of dragoons under Major Joseph Eggleston and Captain John Armstrong to a likely farm on the evening of July 2nd, and the next morning they encountered a British foraging party "consisting of fifty or sixty dragoons and some wagons." The Legion dragoons waited for the enemy to approach and then charged, capturing three officers and forty-five enlisted men.

Lee continued to observe the British army until mid-July, when Greene ordered the Legion to the vicinity of Charleston to reinforce Thomas Sumter's militia. Unlike the rest of Greene's Continentals, Lee and his Legion would have to postpone their badly needed rest, and instead continue their fast-moving, hard-hitting fight against the British forces wherever they were to be found.[90]

1 Babits and Howard, 173; Pancake, 381 (quotation); Piecuch and Beakes, *Cool Deliberate Courage*, 93..

2 Roger Lamb, *An Original and Authentic Journal of Occurrences during the Late American War from Its Commencement to the Year 1783* (Dublin, Ireland: Wilkinson & Courtney, 1809), 357-358.

3 Cornwallis to Greene, Mar. 16, 1781, and Greene to Cornwallis, Mar. 17, 1781, in Showman and Conrad, editors, *Papers of Greene*, 7:443 (quotation), 444; Babits and Howard, 224; Lee, *Memoirs*, 275n. (quotation).

4 Cornwallis to Germain, March 17, 1781, in Tarleton, 307-310 (quotations); Piecuch and Beakes, *Cool Deliberate Courage* (quotations).

5 Tarleton, 279; Babits and Howard, 170, 175; Greene to Joseph Reed, Mar. 18, 1781, in Showman and Conrad, editors, *Papers of Greene*, 7:450-451 (quotation).

6 Greene to Lee, Mar. 19, 1781 (two letters of this date), in Showman and Conrad, editors, *Papers of Greene*, 7:454 (quotations from first letter).

7 Tarleton, 279 (quotations); Lee, *Memoirs*, 287, 288 (quotations).

8 Greene to Lee, Mar. 21, 1781 (two letters of this date), in Showman and Conrad, editors, *Papers of Greene*, 7:456 (quotations), 457.

9 Greene to Lee, Mar. 22, 1781, in Showman and Conrad, editors, *Papers of Greene*, 7:461 (quotation); Lee, *Memoirs*, 289-290 (quotations).

10 Buchanan, 383 (quotation); Cornwallis to Germain, Apr. 18, 1781, in Tarleton, 322-323 (quotation).

11 Tarleton, 281.

12 Pancake, 190; Greene to George Washington, Mar. 29, 1781, in Showman and Conrad, editors, *Papers of Greene*, 7:481 (quotation).

13 Greene to Thomas Sumter, Mar. 30, 1781, in Conrad, editor, *Papers of Greene*, Vol. 8 (1995), 12-13.

14 Lee, *Memoirs*, 319-320; Howard to unnamed, undated letter, Rocky Mount Collection (quotation).

15 Lee to Greene, Apr. 2, 1781, in Conrad, editor, *Papers of Greene*, 8:28.

16 Howard to unnamed, undated letter, Rocky Mount Collection.

17 Greene to Lee, Apr. 4, 1781, in Conrad, editor, *Papers of Greene*, 8:46. On the same day, before receiving Greene's letter, Lee wrote to Greene asking that Oldham's company be sent to aid the Legion. Lee to Greene, Apr. 4, 1781, ibid., 47.

18 Greene to Marion, Apr. 4, 1781, Greene's Orders, Apr. 5, 1781, and Lee to Greene, Apr. 10, 1781, in Conrad, editor, *Papers of Greene*, 8:47 (quotation), 54, 78 (quotations).

19 Bass, *Swamp Fox*, 156-157; John W. Gordon, *South Carolina and the American Revolution: A Battlefield History* (Columbia: University of South Carolina Press, 2003), 142-143; James, 104 (quotation).

20 Bass, *Swamp Fox*, 158-159 (quotation); James, 105-106 (quotation).

21 James, 107.

22 Lee, *Memoirs*, 330; James, 108-109 (quotation).

23 Lord Rawdon to Nisbet Balfour, Apr. 12, 1781, Apr. 13, 1781, Apr. 15, 1781, Balfour to Cornwallis, Apr. 26, 1781, in Ian Saberton, editor, *The Cornwallis Papers: The Campaigns of 1780 and 1781 in the Southern Theatre of the American Revolutionary War*, Vol. 4 (Uckfield, East Sussex, UK: Naval & Military Press, 2010), 173, 174 (quotation), 177 (quotation).

24 Piecuch and Beakes, *Cool Deliberate Courage*, 99-100.

25 Leland G. Ferguson, "Archeology at Scott's Lake: Exploratory Research, 1972, 1973," Institute of Archeology and Anthropology, University of South Carolina, Columbia, 1975. Provided courtesy of Charles B. Baxley, 6, 17 (quotation); Lee, *Memoirs*, 332; Rawdon (Marquis of Hastings) to Lee, June 24, 1813, in ibid., 615 (quotation), Marion to Greene, Apr. 23, 1781, in Conrad, editor, *Papers of Greene*, 8:139.

26 James McKay, "Journal of the Blockade at Scots Lake," Apr. 15, 1781, in Ferguson, 94 (quotations); Lee, *Memoirs*, 331 (quotation).

27 McKay, "Journal," in Ferguson, 94.

28 Greene to Lee, Apr. 19, 1781, Lee to Greene, Apr. 20, 1781 (two letters of this date), in Conrad, editor, *Papers of Greene*, 8:117-118 (quotations), 124-125, 125 (quotations).

29 McKay, "Journal," in Ferguson, 94.

30 Lee, *Memoirs*, 332 (quotations); McKay, "Journal," in Ferguson, 95 (quotations).

31 Bass, *Swamp Fox*, 177-178; Lee, *Memoirs*, 332; James, 110 (quotation); McKay, "Journal," in Ferguson, 95 (quotation); Marion to Greene, Apr. 23, 1781, in Conrad, ed., *Papers of Greene*, 8:140.

32 Marion to Greene, Apr. 23, 1781, Lee to Greene, Apr. 23, 1781 (two letters of this date), in Conrad, editor, *Papers of Greene*, 8:138 (quotations), 139, 140-141 (quotations); Bass, *Swamp Fox*, 177; "Capitulation of Fort Watson, Scots Lake," Apr. 23, 1781, in Ferguson, 95-96.

33 Piecuch and Beakes, *Cool Deliberate Courage*, 100-105; William Pierce to Lee, Apr. 25, 1781, in Conrad, editor, *Papers of Greene*, 8:146 (quotation).
34 Piecuch and Beakes, *Cool Deliberate Courage*, 108-109.
35 Marion to Greene, Apr. 23, 1781, and Greene to Marion, May 7, 1781, in Conrad, editor, *Papers of Greene*, 8:142 (quotation), 219 (quotation); Lee, *Memoirs*, 343 (quotation).
36 Greene to Lee, Apr. 24, 1781; Greene to Marion, Apr. 27, 1781; Lee to Greene, May 2, 1781, in Conrad, editor, *Papers of Greene*, 8:143 (quotation), 161, 192 (quotations).
37 Greene to Marion, May 4, 1781, in Conrad, editor, *Papers of Greene*, 8:198-199.
38 Marion to Greene, May 6, 1781, in Conrad, editor, *Papers of Greene*, 8:214-215.
39 Greene to Marion, May 9, 1781, in Conrad, editor, *Papers of Greene*, 8:231.
40 Marion to Greene, May 11, 1781, in Conrad, editor, *Papers of Greene*, 8:242.
41 Lee to Greene, Apr. 28, 1781; Greene to Lee, Apr. 29, 1781, Lee to Greene, May 8, 1781, in Conrad, editor, *Papers of Greene*, 8:171 (quotations), 172-173 (quotations), 223 (quotation).
42 Greene to Lee, Apr. 29, 1781, in Conrad, editor, *Papers of Greene*, 8:173 (quotation); Lee, *Memoirs*, 345 (quotation); Steven D. Smith, James B. Legg, Tamara S. Wilson, and Jonathan Leader, *"Obstinate and Strong": The History and Archaeology of the Siege of Fort Motte* (Columbia: South Carolina Institute of Archaeology and Anthropology, 2007), 13, 15, 21-22 (quotations). Copy provided courtesy of Charles B. Baxley.
43 Smith, et al, 21-23.
44 Smith, et al, 23; Lee, *Memoirs*, 345-346; Lee to Greene, May 10, 1781, in Conrad, editor, *Papers of Greene*, 8:237 (quotations).
45 Marion to Greene, May 11, 1781 and May 12, 1781, in Conrad, editor, *Papers of Greene*, 8:242 (quotation), 246 (quotation); Lee, *Memoirs*, 346 (quotation).
46 Smith, et al, 25; Lee, *Memoirs*, 346-348 (quotations).
47 Smith, et al, 26; Lee, *Memoirs*, 348 (quotations).
48 Smith, et al, 26-27, 28-29; Bass, *Swamp Fox*, 194-195 (quotations); Lee, *Memoirs*, 348-349 (quotations).
49 Rawdon to Cornwallis, May 24, 1781, in Saberton, editor, *Cornwallis Papers*, 5:289 (quotation); Greene to Lee, May 13, 1781, in Conrad, editor, *Papers of Greene*, 8:249 (quotation); Lee, *Memoirs*, 349; James, 121-122.
50 Lee, *Memoirs*, 349 (quotation); Lee to Greene, May 15, 1781, in Conrad, editor, *Papers of Greene*, 8:263-264 (quotations); Gordon, 152-153. A fosse is a ditch surrounding a fortified position.
51 Conrad, editor, *Papers of Greene*, 264n, 266n, 278n; Thomas Sumter to Greene, May16, 1781, and Greene to Sumter, May 17, 1781 (two letters of this date) in ibid., 274, 277, 278 (quotation).
52 Greene to Lee, May 21, 1781, and Lee to Greene, May 22, 1781, in Conrad, editor, *Papers of Greene*, 8:290 (quotation), 293.
53 Lee, *Memoirs*, 352-353.
54 Greene to Lee, May 16, 1781, and Greene to Pickens, May 16, 1781, in Conrad, editor, *Papers of Greene*, 8:272.
55 Lee to Greene, May 16, 1781, in Conrad, editor, *Papers of Greene*, 8:273; Lee, *Memoirs*, 353 (quotation), 354; Steven J. Rauch, "Prelude to Augusta: The Capture of Fort Galphin, 21 May 1781," in *Southern Campaigns of the American Revolution*, Vol. 3, No. 5, May 2006, 22.
56 Greene to Lee, May 21, 1781, and May 22, 1781; Lee to Greene, May 22, 1781, in Conrad, editor, *Papers of Greene*, 8:290 (quotation), 291 (quotation), 293.
57 Steven J. Rauch, "'A Judicious and Gallant Defense': The Second Siege at Augusta, Georgia, 22 May-5 June 1781," *Southern Campaigns of the American Revolution*, Vol. 3, Nos. 6-8, June-Aug., 2006, 36; Edward J. Cashin, *The King's Ranger: Thomas Brown and the American Revolution on the Southern Frontier* (New York: Fordham University Press, 1999), 133.
58 Cashin, 130-131.
59 Lee to Pickens, May 22, 1781, in Conrad, editor, *Papers of Greene*, 8:293; Rauch, "Prelude to Augusta," 22, 24.
60 Lee, *Memoirs*, 354 (quotations); Cashin, 131.
61 Lee, *Memoirs*, 354-355 (quotations); Cashin, 131 (quotation); Rauch, "Prelude to Augusta," 22.
62 Lee to Greene, May 22, 1781, and Greene to Lee, May 29, 1781, in Conrad, editor, *Papers of Greene*, 8:293 (quotation), 326 (quotation).
63 Lee, *Memoirs*, 355.
64 Rauch, "Judicious and Gallant Defense," 33; Cashin, 132; Thomas Taylor to John Wesley, Feb. 28, 1782, in Robert S. Davis, Jr., editor, "A Georgia Loyalist's Perspective on the American Revolution: The Letters of Dr. Thomas Taylor," *Georgia Historical Quarterly*, Vol. 81, No. 1 (Spring 1997), 136.
65 Cashin, 132 (quotation); Lee, *Memoirs*, 360 (quotations); Lee to Greene, May 24, 1781, in Conrad,

editor, *Papers of Greene*, 8:309 (quotations).

66 Rauch, "Judicious and Gallant Defense," 35-36; Cashin, 132; Pickens to Greene, May 25, 1781, in Conrad, editor, *Papers of Greene*, 8:311.

67 Cashin, 132-133; Rauch, "Judicious and Gallant Defense," 36-37; Taylor to Wesley, Feb. 28, 1782, in Davis, editor, "Letters of Taylor," 136 (quotation); Pickens to Greene, May 25, 1781, in Conrad, editor, *Papers of Greene*, 8:311 (quotations).

68 Lee, *Memoirs*, 360-361.

69 Lee, *Memoirs*, 361.

70 Cashin, 134; Rauch, "Judicious and Gallant Defense," 38-39; Lee, *Memoirs*, 361-362 (quotations).

71 Lee, *Memoirs*, 362-363 (quotations); Rauch, "Judicious and Gallant Defense," 40; Pickens to Greene, June 1, 1781, in Conrad, editor, *Papers of Greene*, 8:335.

72 Lee, *Memoirs*, 363 (quotation); Rauch, "Judicious and Gallant Defense," 40.

73 Lee to Greene, June 1, 1781, and Pickens to Greene, June 1, 1781, in Conrad, editor, *Papers of Greene*, 8:334 (quotations), 334-335 (quotation).

74 Greene to Lee, June 3, 1781, and Greene to Pickens, June 3, 1781, in ibid., 8340 (quotation), 342 (quotation).

75 Lee, *Memoirs*, 363-364; Cashin, 134.

76 Lee, *Memoirs*, 364-365 (quotation); Cashin, 135; Rauch, "Judicious and Gallant Defense," 42.

77 Lee to Greene, June 4, 1781, and Pickens to Greene, June 4, 1781, in Conrad, editor, *Papers of Greene*, 8:346 (quotation), 347; Cashin, 135; Lee, *Memoirs*, 366 (quotation).

78 Cashin, 135-136 (quotation); Rauch, "Judicious and Gallant Defense," 44; Lee, *Memoirs*, 367-370.

79 Thomas Brown to David Ramsay, Dec. 25, 1786, in George White, ed., *The Historical Collections of Georgia* (New York: Pudney & Russell, 1854), 617-618.

80 Taylor to Wesley, Feb. 28, 1782, in Davis, editor, "Letters of Taylor," 136-137.

81 Cashin, 137; Rauch, "Judicious and Gallant Defense," 44-45.

82 Piecuch and Beakes, *Cool Deliberate Courage*, 115.

83 Ibid., 115-116.

84 Lee, *Memoirs*, 371.

85 Lee, *Memoirs*, 371-373.

86 Ibid., 373-374.

87 Piecuch and Beakes, *Cool Deliberate Courage*, 117-118.

88 Lee, *Memoirs*, 375, 377 (quotation); Piecuch and Beakes, *Cool Deliberate Courage*, 118; General Greene's Orders, June 18, 1781, and Greene to Samuel Huntington, June 20. 1781, in Conrad, editor, *Papers of Greene*, 8:408 (quotation), 420 (quotation).

89 Piecuch and Beakes, *Cool Deliberate Courage*, 118-119.

90 Lee to Greene, June 20, 1781, June 22, 1781, June 25, 1781, June 29, 1781, and July 3, 1781, in Conrad, editor, *Papers of Greene*, 8:430 (quotations), 442, 456, 475-476, 486-487; Lee, *Memoirs*, 380-381 (quotations), 387.

CHAPTER EIGHT

THE BATTLE OF EUTAW SPRINGS
AND LEE'S FINAL MONTHS OF MILITARY SERVICE

While most of Greene's army proceeded to their camp at Midway Plantation in the High Hills of Santee by easy marches, Lee and his Legion moved to the South Carolina lowcountry near Charleston.

Thomas Sumter had proposed to attack the various British detachments posted in a loose defensive arrangement several miles outside the city, and Greene had assented. Greene placed Lee's Legion and Francis Marion's militia brigade under Sumter's command, and Sumter ordered Lee and Marion to converge on Moncks Corner by different routes. The American commander ordered Sumter to act quickly. "No time is to be lost, therefore push your operations night and day," Greene told the militia general on July 14th. "Keep Col Lee and General Marian advised of all matters from above and tell Col Lee to thunder even at the gates of Charlestown. I have high expectations from your force and enterprise."[1]

Sumter's objective was the British 19th Regiment under Lt. Col. James Coates, one of the units that had arrived at Charleston the previous month. Coates had marched from Charleston to support the troops under Lord Rawdon and Lt. Col. John Harris Cruger, who had retreated from Ninety Six on separate routes. Coates's own command consisted of approximately 600 men of the 19th Regiment, and he had been recently reinforced by 150 mounted South Carolina Rangers led by Major Thomas Fraser and an artillery piece. Sumter commanded more than 1,000 men, and Marion's and Lee's units added several hundred more. The resulting operations became known as the "Dog Days Expedition" because they were carried out during the "dog days" or hottest part of the summer.[2]

Lee struck the first blow on July 15th when he encountered part of Rawdon's supply train near Dorchester. The Legion attacked and captured the four unguarded wagons, taking them along with all of the draft horses. Unfortunately for Lee, three of the wagons were empty, but the fourth was loaded with artillery ammunition. Although Fraser was nearby with his Rangers, the loyalist cavalrymen did not attempt a counterattack. Lee hoped that if the campaign went as planned, Rawdon would not be able to "execute his wishes" and get back to Charleston without a serious engagement.[3]

That same day, some of Sumter's troops, a mounted detachment under Colonel Wade Hampton, by-passed Moncks Corner and rode unopposed all the way to the Quarter House on the Cooper River, just outside Charleston. There Hampton's troops dispersed a handful of British cavalry and burned four

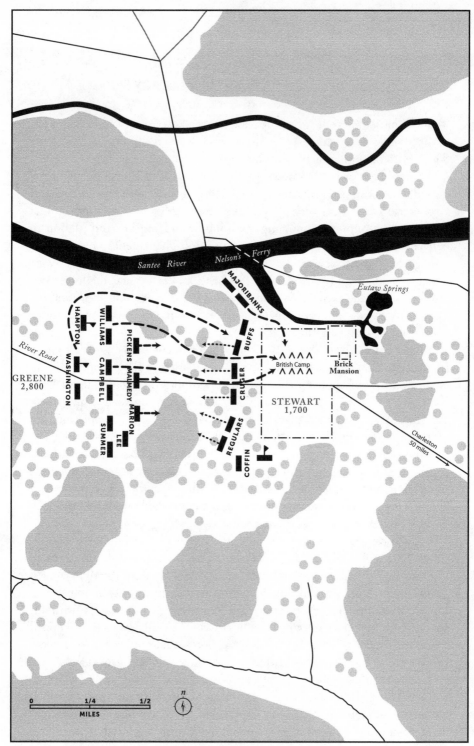

The Battle of Eutaw Springs

ships laden with supplies for Rawdon's soldiers. Only one American was killed in the raid, which caused a brief panic in Charleston. The next day a party of Marion's men commanded by Colonel Peter Horry arrived at Moncks Corner. Coates ordered Fraser to attack them, but the Americans easily repulsed the loyalists' mounted charge, killing twelve Rangers while suffering no losses of their own. Coates reinforced Fraser with some infantry and made a second attack, and Sumter, who had arrived on the scene, ordered Horry to fall back. With American forces seeming to threaten him from every direction, Coates withdrew from Moncks Corner on the night of June 16th.[4]

Sumter had planned to attack Moncks Corner on the following morning, but Coates thwarted that move by retreating. The first notice the Americans received of the British withdrawal came late in the night. "Coates decamped in silence," Lee noted, "setting fire to the church which had been used as a magazine, for the purpose of destroying stores which could not be withdrawn." When the flames burned through the roof of Biggin Church, the fire could be seen in the American camp. Lee wrote that "the troops were called to arms, and with great celerity moved upon Monk's Corner." There they found that the British had withdrawn to the east bank of the Cooper River. Sumter promptly ordered Lee and his Legion to set out in pursuit, supported by Wade Hampton's South Carolina cavalry with some of Marion's infantry and mounted militia to follow. "The attempt proved abortive," Lee observed when he reached the river, because the British had too great a head start and "crossed … some hours before our detachment reached it."[5]

At four o'clock on the morning of June 17th, Sumter entered the abandoned British post with the bulk of his force. He found "the Church[,] Stores &ct Burnt, some Waggons left unconsumed & a little Baggage which seemingly they had not time to throw into the flames." Uncertain as to the route Coates had taken, Sumter decided to proceed slowly until he "coud hear from Colos Lee & Hampton."[6]

Undeterred by his failure to intercept Coates at the Cooper River, Lee got his men across and continued the pursuit. He hoped to catch the British before they could cross Quinby Creek, which "was only passable" at Quinby Bridge. Lee's determination was rewarded; having pressed on for eighteen miles since leaving Moncks Corner, at about 9 a.m. the Legion's vanguard caught up with the British. After marching all night, Coates had halted at daybreak to allow his men some rest. Most of the British troops had crossed Quinby Creek, but Coates left his wagons and a rear guard of about one hundred infantrymen on the other side, about a mile from the bridge. As a precaution, Coates positioned his artillery piece to cover the bridge. When Lee's scout returned and described the British deployment, the Legion commander decided to attack immediately. He took personal command of the Legion cavalry and Hampton's mounted troops on the right, and assigned Major Eggleston to direct operations on the left. Lee's plan was to lead a frontal assault to draw the attention of the British soldiers while Eggleston outflanked them. When the British saw the Americans moving into position, they deployed in line of battle.[7]

Lee described the ensuing action:

> *"The instant the enemy had formed, the charge was sounded, and the horse rushed upon them with drawn swords in full gallop. On our approach the enemy's order to fire was distinctly heard from right to left, which not taking place caused some inquietude, lest it was intentionally reserved to render it more fatal. Contrary to expectation this was not the case. The suppression of their meditated fire was not a feint; but the line, terrified at the novel and menacing attitude of the horse close upon it, hoped to secure their safety by this inoffensive conduct; and, without discharging a single musket, threw down their arms and begged for quarters."*[8]

Some of the British soldiers in the rear guard escaped to warn Coates; however, Lee's horsemen moved much faster. Leaving the prisoners with some of Hampton's militia, Lee resumed his push toward Quinby Bridge. Captain James Armstrong and his troop led the line of march, and when they reached the bridge, they found that the British had already loosened the planks so that they could render the span impassable as soon as the rear guard was across. Furthermore, the British cannon was aimed directly at the bridge. Armstrong halted and sent a message back to Lee, stating that he had caught up with Coates but he neglected to add that the British were on the opposite side of Quinby Creek. Upon hearing the report from Armstrong's aide, Lee became angry, and as he put it, "warmly reminded [Armstrong] of the order of the day, which was to fall upon the foe without respect to consequences." Lee recalled that Armstrong was "stung with this answer."[9]

Armstrong dutifully charged, a maneuver so sudden and unexpected that the British troops did not have time to respond. The British artillerymen abandoned their gun and many of the infantry fled without firing. Coates rallied many of his men, and soon the Legion dragoons came under musket fire. The second troop of Legion cavalry commanded by Lt. George Carrington came up and hesitated at the bridge. "Some of the loose planks were dashed off by Armstrong's section, which, forming a chasm in the bridge, presented a dangerous obstacle," Lee explained. Nevertheless, Carrington ordered his dragoons to have their horses jump the gap, and the riders succeeded. The next troop in Lee's order of march, that of Captain Ferdinand O'Neal, halted at the bridge, perhaps because Carrington's horses had dislodged additional planks and made the gap too wide for the horses to leap. Lee arrived soon afterward, realized that it was impossible to get any more of his men across, and instead assigned O'Neal's troopers to try to replace the planks. Despite their efforts, they found that it was impossible to retrieve enough planks from the deep water and muddy bottom of Quinby Creek.[10]

Armstrong and Carrington, outnumbered, battled the British infantry for as long as they could. "It was the most daring thing I ever heard of," one British officer recalled. He watched as Armstrong and Coates dueled with their sabers. When another Legion dragoon rode up to aid Armstrong, a British musician named McPherson cast aside his clarinet, picked up a musket, and shot down the American cavalryman. As the situation stabilized, many of the British fugitives regained their courage and returned to the fray. Armstrong and Carrington, recognizing the futility of their situation, withdrew upstream into woods that sheltered them from British fire. Lee and O'Neal lacked such cover. When Armstrong and Carrington retreated, Coates directed his efforts against O'Neal's troop on the opposite side of the creek. The British gunners returned to their piece, and the Legion soldiers across the creek were raked with musketry and cannon fire. Several were wounded. "Having only sabres to oppose to the enemy's fire, and those sabres withheld from contact by the intervening chasm," Lee wrote, he "was forced to draw off from the vain contest, after several of his dragoons had been wounded." Some of the Legion dragoons who had crossed the bridge had also been wounded, and at least two killed. One of Marion's regiments under Colonel Hezekiah Maham had also arrived and two of his militiamen were wounded before the fighting ended.[11]

Coates fell back to the Shubrick Plantation, a short distance from Quinby Bridge. He posted his troops in the main house and the numerous outbuildings and prepared to meet the Americans if they continued their pursuit. Lee indeed intended to continue pressing the British, and since the bridge was irreparable, he dispatched scouts to reconnoiter Quinby Creek to see if they could find another place to cross. One of the scouts returned to report that he had found a ford upstream, and Lee sent a message to Marion, advising the partisan general to direct his march toward the crossing point. When Lee and Marion reached the plantation late in the afternoon, they found the British position exceedingly strong. "Posted in the house, the outhouses, and along the yard and garden fences, with his howitzer in front and under cover of the house, Lieutenant-Colonel Coates found himself safe," Lee observed. He and Marion examined the British line, and agreed "that no point of [Coates's] position was assailable with probable hope of success."[12]

Thomas Sumter preferred a more aggressive response. He arrived at Shubrick's Plantation soon after Lee and Marion had decided an attack on the British would be futile, and he agreed that the British defenses were strong.

"Their position was the most Advantageous that cou'd have fallen in their way, lodged in a long line of Houses on an Emminence," he wrote. Yet the unfavorable tactical situation did not deter Sumter, who ordered an immediate assault. Lee and Marion suggested that he wait for the American six-pounder cannon, which had been left at Biggin Church, but Sumter overruled them. He positioned Marion's brigade on the American left, his own brigade in the center, and although neither he nor Marion described Lee's position, the Legion infantry was probably posted on the right of the line, with Colonel Hugh Horry's regiment of Marion's brigade between Sumter's troops and the Legion. At 5 p.m. the combined American force, numbering about six hundred men, charged.[13]

Marion reported that the ground in front of his brigade and Horry's regiment "was intirely open" and British fire soon forced both elements of Marion's command to halt. "I marched my men to a fence about fifty yards of the Enimy under a very heavy fire, we soon made them take shelter in and behind the houses, but was fired on from the stoop of the Houses & through the doors windows & Corners," Marion wrote. Meanwhile, Colonel Thomas Taylor of Sumter's brigade, who had been ordered to push forward to a fence in front of the plantation house, reached his objective after suffering significant losses. The battle raged for almost an hour, with the Americans unable to advance farther. The British "stuck so close to the Houses," Sumter noted, that the American cavalry could not be committed to aid the infantry. Marion fought until his ammunition was "Intirely Expended" and then withdrew. Sumter likewise claimed that none of his men "left the field till their Ammunition was intirely Exhausted." Lee's infantry probably left the field when the other units withdrew; they may have been posted so far on the American right that they saw little action, because Lee made no mention of the battle in his memoirs.[14]

Sumter attempted to portray the American repulse at Shubrick's Plantation as a victory, but his own subordinates showed otherwise by their actions. Colonel Taylor vowed that he would never serve under Sumter again. After the battle, some of Marion's militiamen openly denounced Sumter and departed for home. Neither Lee nor Marion made any public comment, but both officers left the field with their troops that night, marching fifteen miles before making camp. It was the last time either would serve under Sumter's command. American losses amounted to about thirty killed and another thirty wounded, while British casualties were six killed and thirty-eight wounded. Lt. Col. Nisbet Balfour, commandant of the British garrison at Charleston, praised Coates's performance at Quinby Bridge and Shubrick's Plantation:

"The 19th Regiment … repulsed in the handsomest manner a charge

which was made on it and compell'd the enemy's cavalry to give way. Thus circumstanced, Colonel Cootes put his regiment in a strong position at Shubrick's House near Hugger's Bridge ... from which the enemy twice endeavour'd to force him but were driven back with loss. "[15]

After separating from Sumter, Lee marched the Legion to the High Hills of Santee to join Greene's army and provide some much needed rest for his men and horses. Lee described the army's experience in camp and also assessed the progress of the campaign:

"The troops were placed in good quarters, and the heat of July rendered tolerable by the high ground, the fine air, and good water of the selected camp. Disease began to abate, our wounded to recover, and the army to rise in bodily strength. Enjoying the period of rest, the first experienced since Greene's assumption of the command, it was natural to meditate upon the past scenes. Nor were such meditations less instructive than agreeable. The wisdom of the general was manifest; and the zeal, patience, and firmness exhibited by the troops could not be denied."

Lee concluded that, despite occasional defeats, the campaign had been an overwhelming success, the Americans having regained nearly all of Georgia and the Carolinas.[16]

During the American army's stay at the High Hills, Lee and the soldiers of the Legion met an old comrade, Sergeant John Champe. Having failed in his efforts to capture Benedict Arnold, Champe had accompanied Arnold's expedition to Virginia in December 1780. Seizing the first opportunity to desert from the British army, Champe made his escape in late May of 1781. He then traveled across Virginia and North Carolina, down the Congaree River, and finally arrived at Greene's camp, where he reported to Lee. The Legion commander mustered his troops, and with Champe standing beside him revealed the truth about the sergeant's pretended desertion from the Legion. Lee then introduced the sergeant to General Greene, who provided Champe with a horse and funds, along with orders to return to the north and report to George Washington. Champe left camp, and although he hoped to return to service with Lee's Legion, Washington forbade it, knowing that if Champe were captured by the British he would be executed either for desertion or as a spy.[17]

Lee later wrote that "the period of tranquility and of rest still continued in the camp of Greene, undisturbed by the din of war," had little effect on the "anxious mind and faithful heart" of the commanding general. The Legion commander could well have written of himself in those same terms, because Lee also found it impossible to remain idle. Instead, he contributed to Greene's "anxious mind" by devising new plans and submitting them to the general. Having learned of the operations taking place in Virginia, where the Marquis de Lafayette and a small American army were feebly trying to counter the operations of Lord Cornwallis and his much larger British force, Lee suggested on July 29th that "if your Cavelry could effect a junction with the Marquis it is not improbable but an advantageous action might take place, before the British army could reach their fortified town." Lee also proposed that Greene order Pickens to provide one regiment of his militia and Lt. Col. William Henderson to provide another two from the South Carolina state troops, to be trained as Continental soldiers. He also recommended that when colonels Peter Horry and Hezekiah Maham had recruited their regiments to full strength that their forces be added to Greene's army, along with another five hundred men from Sumter's militia. With these additions, Lee believed that the army would be strong enough to drive the British from the southern states. "I am confident that the close of October would bring about decisive advantages in favor of America, Let Cornwallis return or not," Lee concluded.[18]

Greene replied the same day, stating that he had been attempting the very things Lee had suggested with regard to the militia. "But it is difficult to make men see their true interest where it is opposed to their present ease," Greene observed. "I wish it was practicable to get the State troops to join the Army, but be assurd it would prove so fully my opinion of a certain person to give such an order, as not only to prevent farther exertions, but even opposition." Greene was referring to Thomas Sumter, who had been sulking since his defeat at Shubrick's plantation and showed no inclination to cooperate with the Continental commander. On the contrary, Greene feared that any effort on his part to assert more control over Sumter's troops might cause the irascible South Carolinian to do his utmost to thwart Greene's efforts.[19]

Apparently Lee offered Greene some additional advice in person that day; the Legion commander suggested that he take his troops to Haddrell's Point, across the Cooper River from Charleston. The British had confined many American prisoners of war there, and perhaps Lee hoped to free them. Greene rejected the plan and offered an alternative. "I have no great opin[ion] of the affair at Hadrales Poi[nt]," Greene remarked, "and at this time I should no[t] chuse to have your Corps low down in the Country or muc[h] fatiged, until I hear farther from Virginia." If Lee insisted on returning to action, the general suggested that Orangeburg was "a better object," adding that "you are at lib[erty] to go down your self for inquiry." When Lee suggested a second time on July 30th that he "had an idea that the enemys post at Haddrells Point might be struck at advantageously," Greene ignored the proposal.[20]

Lee asserted in his memoirs that on August 2nd, Greene ordered him to prepare for an attack on the British post at Wilmington, North Carolina. According to Lee, Greene believed that the operation could succeed if the Legion could conduct the march in secret and strike with the element of surprise. Lee therefore dispatched Captain Michael Rudulph "with a small party from the Legion infantry" to gather intelligence and procure boats for crossing the Cape Fear River. Rudulph carried out his mission and returned to report that a sufficient number of canoes was available to ferry the troops across the river, while the horses could swim. He also added that the British garrison of three hundred men was "inadequate to man" the town's defensive works. Greene ordered Lee to proceed northward by way of Camden to disguise his true objective, but canceled the expedition when he learned that a French fleet was off the coast. Lee said that the arrival of the French naval force convinced Greene that the British would be forced to evacuate Wilmington, making Lee's foray unnecessary. South Carolina governor John Rutledge also pressured Greene to refrain from sending troops out of the state, expecting the French to assist Greene in capturing Charleston.[21]

None of the surviving correspondence supports Lee's assertion. However, Greene did state in an August 12th letter to North Carolina governor Thomas Burke that "I have long had it in contemplation to attempt something against Wilmington; but my force and situation has put it out of my power." There is also an unusual gap from July 30th to August 5th during which Lee and Greene either did not exchange letters, or none of their letters survived. It is possible that the preparations for the Wilmington expedition were discussed during this period, and that in order to preserve secrecy Lee and Greene communicated verbally. Lee recorded that after the cancellation of the Wilmington attack, Rudulph was "directed to return" from North Carolina, "holding nevertheless secret his visit to Cape Fear."[22]

On August 5th, having procured Greene's permission to resume operations against British forces in South Carolina, Lee left the army's camp with the Legion cavalry. No known record of Greene's specific orders survives, nor did Lee explain the purpose of his mission, although it appears that the Legion's task was to monitor the movements of British forces.

Lt. Col. Alexander Stewart had assumed command of the British field army in South Carolina, replacing Lord Rawdon, the Irish nobleman whom illness had forced to sail for Europe. Rawdon had been without doubt the most capable of the British officers in the state.

Stewart had marched his troops west of the Santee River, trusting that the broad waterway would protect him from Greene's army, in an effort to procure supplies as well as to reassert some semblance of royal control over the South Carolina interior. Stewart had left Orangeburg on July 29th and by August 4th had reached McCord's Ferry on the Congaree River, about forty miles south of Camden and only twenty miles from Greene's camp.[23]

By August 8th, Lee and his Legion had fought two skirmishes with detachments from Stewart's army. When Lee and sixty of his troops encountered a British convoy of thirty-two wagons guarded by three hundred men, he attacked and drove off the loyalist cavalrymen, but the infantry stood firm—"regular and cool" in Lee's words, and the Legion pulled back with fifteen captured enemy dragoons. Cornet George Carrington's troop of the Legion captured another twenty British cavalrymen in an engagement near Orangeburg. However, sixty mounted loyalists appeared and attacked Carrington and his twelve men, who were forced to flee. In the chaos, seventeen of the British prisoners managed to escape. Lee described his operation thus far as consisting of "much toil" that yielded "very little success."[24]

*****

The Battle of Eutaw Springs

Lee believed that Stewart's northward probe might enable Greene to lure the British army farther from its base at Charleston, cut it off, and destroy it. In his August 8th letter to Greene, relating his recent activities, Lee observed that Stewart was at Thompson's Plantation near McCord's Ferry, that the British numbered less than fifteen hundred men, and that the Legion commander did "not beleive they have any intention of retiring. I rather think they will advance up to the Congaree. If you was to retrograde to Cambden or a little beyond it I believe it would induce them to venture farther into the country." Lee added that he was at Howell's Ferry on the Congaree, ten miles from Stewart, and that the region contained an abundance of supplies along with two flatboats that would enable Greene's army to cross the river and interpose his force between Stewart's force and its escape routes.[25]

Greene replied with lavish praise for Lee's soldiers:

> *"The officers and men of the Legion behave so well upon all occasions, and are so repeated successful, and have renderd such essential service to the public; from which they have justly had so many public and private acknowledgements, that it hardly remains in the power of language to add to their glory. For when I say that Capt Rudulph and Mr Carrington displayed great spirit[,] address and good conduct in the two rencounters, I only repeat what has been frequently said to them, either in particular or in general with others of the Legion. The services of the Corps so multiplies my obligation, and increases the*

confidence of the Army, that I fear I shall never be able to discharge the obligations, or support the spirits of the Army should any misfortune attend you at a critical hour."

Then, having dispensed these accolades, Greene rejected Lee's advice to try and draw Stewart farther north. "I am not of opinion that a retrograde movement will induce the enemy to cross the River in force; nor do I believe they will fight us if we cross," he declared.[26]

Lee replied that his officers and men were grateful for Greene's approval, and then proposed a different and far more dangerous maneuver. Lee announced that he intended to cross the Congaree River "& may probably reach Chs Town gates." He asked Greene to forward the Legion infantry to support the dragoons, and told the general that if he disapproved of Lee's plan, Greene should inform him "instantly." Greene did not respond until two days later. He was clearly unhappy with Lee's impetuous idea of marching to Charleston, and made an effort to explain his situation. Referring to Lee's earlier proposal of moving the main army against Stewart, Greene explained that he was "not less sorry ... than you are" that he had too few troops to attempt the maneuver. He agreed that "the position of the enemy puts them much in our power," and added that he was awaiting reinforcements. "I mean to wait a few days longer and then take my measures decidedly. Before this I wish you not to go below," Greene instructed, rejecting Lee's suggestion to raid as far as Charleston's fortifications.[27]

Greene's mention of the possibility of moving against Stewart if the American army was reinforced caused Lee to abandon his Charleston scheme and renew his push for a strike at the British field army. Lee conceded that it was not worth attacking Stewart with an insufficient force, because a partial American victory might only result in a British withdrawal with their army intact. He stressed again the great opportunity that lay before Greene if the American general could assemble enough troops to crush Stewart's force. The British troops were "much discontented," Lee wrote, adding that five of their deserters were currently in his camp. Lee estimated that Stewart had no more than sixteen hundred men, and said that this figure was probably too large. The Legion commander also made an eloquent appeal to Greene to embrace his plan to attack the British:

"I do not believe there ever was so glorious an opportunity of giving a fatal stab to the British tyrant, as the present day presents. I am exceedingly distressed with my apprehensions that you will not collect a sufficient force in due time. At present there is no appearance of Colo Stuarts moving; all the waggons are gone to Orangeburgh to meet a

convoy with provisions & men from Chs Town. "[28]

Greene's answer, dated August 14th, indicated that the general was becoming convinced of the merit of Lee's plan, and was now seriously considering a move against Stewart. After informing Lee that the Legion infantry had been ordered to join him, but had been delayed by high water levels in the rivers, Greene went on to express his increasing support for Lee's proposal:

> *"Your account of the strength and temper of the British Army at Col Thomsons, I believe is pretty just; and agrees with other accounts given by deserters. Nothing can be more unfortunate than not to be in a condition to improve so good an opportunity as the present affords, of giving the enemy a deadly blow. I have a good mind to put all to the hazard with the regular troops; and I believe our force if we commit the Cavalry would be compentent to the attack; but the loss must fall heavy on the regular force, and should we meet with a check, or defeat, the consequences would be very disagreeable. I think we should out number the enemy with our collective force including the horse and State troops. Six or eight hundred Militia would make the business easy and success certain; and the loss of the regular force not very considerable. What makes me more anxious to give battle is, I have some apprehensions of General Lesslie's coming from Virginia with a reinforcment."* [29]

On August 17th, Lee informed Greene of his intention to postpone the Charleston raid. Instead, he intended "to cross the river tomorrow to exercise my men" and to procure intelligence. Realizing that his efforts to persuade Greene to take the offensive against Stewart's army were making headway, Lee added: "Was you but able, it would be great to strike Stuart before his friend [Major General Alexander Leslie] arrives." The next day, Lee forwarded to Greene the intelligence he had gathered, including reports that discontentment still prevailed in Stewart's camp and that General Leslie had brought no significant reinforcements with him to Charleston. Lee also expressed disappointment at his failure to capture a British supply convoy on the preceding day.[30]

Lee achieved a minor success on August 20th, capturing eight British soldiers, although three of them were not fighting men but officers' servants. In his report of the incident, Lee took the opportunity to ask Greene if he intended to carry out a movement against Stewart. He provided a new tally of British strength, calculating that Stewart now led 1,700 infantry and 100 cavalry. Soon after dispatching this message, Lee received Greene's letter of

August 17th. The document has never been found, but its contents prompted Lee to press his plan to strike Stewart with renewed vigor. "I consider no attempt so easy & so ready as the ruining of Stuarts army provided you can get a force in your opinion adequate to the effort," Lee wrote.[31]

The next day, Greene informed Lee that he had decided to follow the Legion commander's advice and begin the operation to attack Stewart. "The Army marches to morrow by the way of Camden for the Congaree," Greene told Lee. "You know the object; therefore be prepard. Send some person down the Country to try to learn whether Mr Stewart is likely to be reinforced in a short time." Greene explained his decision to march via Camden, a route that would take his army on a wide detour to the northward, by noting that the American army would have the advantage of better roads, an easier crossing of the Congaree River, and would be marching toward supplies and reinforcements that were on the way from North Carolina.[32]

Once Greene had embraced Lee's plan, he worked diligently to assemble enough troops to take the offensive against the British army. On August 15th he ordered the French officer commanding the Salisbury District militia in North Carolina, Colonel Francois Lellorquis, Marquis de Malmedy, to gather as many men as possible and march them to Camden. Greene also requested assistance from Generals Andrew Pickens and Francis Marion and their brigades of South Carolina militia, and from Lt. Col. William Henderson with his South Carolina state troops, men who had enlisted for longer terms of service than the militia and were at least theoretically better trained and disciplined than the loosely organized and independently minded men of the militia units. Lee, however, did not see any difference between the state troops and militia, remarking that "such has been the Management of the state troops that they are really injurious. They are not a whit better disciplined than Militia & you get no aid from either class."[33]

Despite Greene's efforts, there were many delays. The American army did not march as planned on August 22nd; instead Greene informed Lee that "arrangments and reinforcements have been wanting nor are they by any means in that forwardness I could wish." The commanding general instructed Lee to "have your Legion as strong as possible to second the attempt for depend [on] it, we must have victory or ruin, nor will I spare any thing to obtain it." Greene finally got his army in motion on August 23rd and reached Camden the next day. There he met Malmedy and four hundred North Carolina militiamen. Greene planned to cross the Wateree River on August 25th, but suffered yet another setback when it took longer than expected to ferry the army's baggage across the river. He complained to Lee of his frustration in trying to coordinate his army's movements with those of the other American forces. "The tardiness with which every body moves who were expected to join us almost makes me repent that I have put the troops in motion," the general lamented. "Near 200 of the North Carolinia regulars who ought to have been here four days past is not likely to be here for four or five to come. ... General Pickens has not been heard of." Greene told Lee that he did not "shrink at difficulties, but our prospects are not flattering."[34]

The American situation soon changed for the better, as various unit commanders began reporting to Greene. On August 25th Lt. Col. Henderson informed Greene that he was marching to join the main army with 370 state troops, although one-third of them were unarmed. Henderson added that while he had not heard directly from Andrew Pickens, he had heard various accounts that Pickens and his militia were on their way to unite with Greene and were only a few days' march away. Francis Marion sent word of his brigade's location on September 3rd, and Pickens finally communicated with Greene on September 5th. Greene ordered the two generals to meet the army near Eutaw Springs. Stewart, short of supplies and having learned of Greene's approach, had withdrawn his army to the southeast. Lee, who had continued to hover close to the British force, had followed Stewart and on September 1st sent Greene intelligence that the British had camped at Eutaw Springs the previous night. The British army remained there while Greene marched toward them, gathering forces en route. The American army, all its forces gathered together at last, camped at Burdell's Tavern on the night of September 7th. Stewart, only seven miles away at Eutaw Springs, had no idea that Greene's army was in the area.[35]

In addition to gaining the advantage of surprise, Greene had also succeeded in obtaining a significant numerical superiority over the British army. The Americans had six regiments of Continental infantry: two each from Maryland, Virginia, and North Carolina. Lee's Legion numbered 90 infantry and 120 cavalry, and Lt. Col. William Washington commanded an estimated 70 Continental dragoons augmented by an unknown number of mounted militia. Capt. Robert Kirkwood's two companies of Delaware infantry and a detachment of four artillery pieces and their crews completed Greene's Continental force. These units were supported by South Carolina state troops and militia and Malmedy's North Carolina militia, giving Greene a minimum strength of 2,773 men.[36]

The British force that lay just ahead was now only half the strength of Greene's army. Lee's August 20th estimate that the British numbered about 1,800 men had been extremely accurate. A field return prepared on the morning of September 8th showed that Stewart had 1,945 men of all ranks fit for duty, not including an unspecified number of loyalist militia who "did not fire a Shot the whole day," most fleeing at the start of the battle. In addition,

Stewart had unwittingly weakened his army before the engagement began; because he was not aware of Greene's presence, he had dispatched 310 men at daybreak to gather sweet potatoes from nearby plantations to feed the poorly supplied British soldiers. The majority of these foragers were captured before they could rejoin their comrades, leaving Stewart with only 1,396 men to meet Greene's attack.[37]

At four o'clock on the morning of September 8th, Greene put his army in motion to attack Stewart. The cavalry and infantry of Lee's Legion led the column in company with Lt. Col. William Henderson's South Carolina state troops, which like the Legion contained both infantry and mounted units. The troops had been marching for two hours when two American deserters reached the British camp and told Stewart that Greene's army was only a few miles away. Stewart ordered his cavalry commander, Major John Coffin, to take his 50 dragoons and 140 light infantry toward Burdell's tavern to investigate the deserters' claims. Coffin marched four miles and at about 8 a.m. encountered the American vanguard. Believing that the enemy troops were only militia and could be easily routed, Coffin promptly ordered a charge. The British dragoons rode into a storm of musket fire from Lee's and Henderson's infantrymen, while Lee ordered the Legion cavalry to outflank Coffin. The British retreated hastily back to their camp. After Coffin left the field, the British foraging parties began making their way to the road to investigate the gunshots. Stumbling into the American column, many of the British soldiers surrendered, though a few made a brief, futile resistance before laying down their arms.[38]

Lee had effectively prevented Coffin from obstructing the army's march, but Greene had lost the element of surprise. When Coffin returned to report that the Americans were approaching, Stewart deployed his troops in line of battle. On his right flank, at an angle of almost ninety degrees to the rest of his line, Stewart posted the flank battalion of Major John Marjoribanks, comprised of the light infantry and grenadier companies of each of Stewart's infantry regiments. The flank battalion occupied the south bank of Eutaw Creek and was screened by thick brush. Facing west and adjacent to Marjoribanks's left flank was the 3rd Regiment, then the 63rd and 64th regiments, Lt. Col. John Harris Cruger's loyalist battalion, and the loyalists of the Provincial Light Infantry. In reserve Stewart held Major Henry Sheridan's New York Volunteers and Lt. Col. Isaac Allen's New Jersey Volunteers, along with a detachment of the British 84th Regiment and Coffin's cavalry. Perhaps reflecting his own lack of command experience in battle, Stewart placed Cruger in command of his army's front line. This was an almost unprecedented action by a British officer, as most regular officers lacked confidence in the abilities of loyalist commanders.[39]

While Stewart positioned his troops, Lee and Henderson led their men forward and engaged the British pickets. The Americans quickly came under fire from the British artillery, and Lee sent a message to Greene requesting that cannon be hastened forward. Greene had anticipated the need for fire support and Captain William Gaines hurried up with his two three-pounders. Lee's and Henderson's soldiers drove in the British picket line, keeping Stewart's men occupied while Greene brought the rest of his army on the field and positioned his units. Greene kept the South Carolina state troops on his left flank at the northern end of the line. Next to them he placed Pickens and his South Carolina militia, Malmedy's North Carolina militia, and Marion's South Carolinians. Greene then shifted Lee's Legion to the south, where they occupied the right flank position. Again replicating the tactics that Daniel Morgan had employed at the Battle of Cowpens, Greene formed a second line with the two Maryland Continental regiments on the left, the two regiments of Virginia Continentals in the center, and the two new and untested North Carolina Continental regiments on the right. The second line incorporated artillery made up of two six-pounders under Captain William Brown. The two companies of Delaware Continentals and William Washington's cavalry were held in reserve.[40]

When Greene completed his deployment, Stewart saw that the American forces extended well beyond the British left flank. He therefore ordered all of his reserve infantry forward to the left of the main line, leaving only Coffin's cavalry in reserve. The units barely had time to reach their new positions before Greene ordered his front line to attack. The militia surged forward into a hail of musket fire, and demonstrating an unusual degree of toughness, halted and exchanged numerous volleys with their veteran adversaries. Greene wrote after the battle that "the Militia fought with a degree of spirit and firmness that reflects the highest honor upon this class of Soldiers." After lengthy combat, however, Malmedy's North Carolinians began to fall back. Greene saw the militiamen wavering and ordered the North Carolina Continentals under General Jethro Sumner forward. The regulars replaced Malmedy's men in the American front line. Fighting continued with neither side able to gain the advantage, except on the British right where the flank battalion poured a withering fire into the flank of Henderson's state troops. Henderson asked Greene for permission to charge Marjoribanks, but the general refused, perhaps fearing that the attack would leave the American left flank exposed.[41]

The battle continued until Sumner's inexperienced North Carolina Continentals could not stand the volleys of British musket fire any longer. The troops wavered and then began to withdraw, leaving the flanks of Pickens's and Marion's militia exposed. Under fire from front and flank, the

South Carolinians also fell back. The British and loyalist troops sensed victory and, much to the chagrin of Cruger, launched an impromptu counterattack, driving back the remnants of Greene's first line at bayonet point.[42]

Greene responded calmly to the apparent disaster, waiting for the fleeing North Carolina Continentals and South Carolina militiamen to get clear of the second American line before ordering the Virginia and Maryland Continentals to charge with fixed bayonets. Greene reported that the surging Continentals "pressed on with such unshaken resolution that they bore down all before them. The Enemy were routed in all quarters." Shocked by the unexpected American counterattack, the British and loyalist troops turned and ran. Many were taken prisoner. Lee, watching the action unfold, led the Legion infantry in an attack on the British left flank, scattered his shaken opponents, and continued his charge northward across the entire length of the battlefield toward a brick house that had been behind the right flank of the original British line.[43]

With Stewart's army on the brink of annihilation, the course of the battle shifted yet again. Before the battle, Stewart had instructed Major Sheridan of the New York Volunteers that if the British were driven back, Sheridan and his troops should occupy the brick house and "check the enemy should they attempt to pass it." As the British line collapsed, Sheridan carried out the order, and many troops from other British units also took refuge in the brick house, slamming the door almost in the faces of Lee's infantrymen and securing the building.

Marjoribanks withdrew his battalion down the creek bed and took up a new position with part of his force still arrayed along the creek where they could fire into the American left flank, and the rest in a palisaded garden between the brick house and the creek. Greene brought up his two six-pounders, and impressed into service the two British six-pounders abandoned by their crews during the retreat. The American artillerymen tried to batter down the walls of the brick building, but the cannonade had no effect, so the gunners moved their pieces forward. They had no chance to discover whether the bombardment might work at shorter range; British and loyalist soldiers firing from the windows of the house shot down some of the artillerists and their supporting infantrymen. The surviving members of the gun crews and the infantry withdrew out of range, and a party of British troops sallied from the house and rolled the guns close to the walls, thus depriving Greene of his heavy artillery.[44]

Greene, seeing Stewart and Cruger reforming their men in the distance, tried to bypass the defenders in the brick house by ordering some of his troops through the tents of the British camp that stood south of the house. The rows of tents, supporting ropes and stakes, and camp equipment broke up the

ranks of the advancing Americans, and as they emerged in a trickle from
between the tents sharpshooters in the house killed and wounded several,
forcing the remainder to take shelter behind the tents. Greene or his second-
in-command, Colonel Otho Holland Williams of Maryland, ordered Lt. Col.
John Eager Howard to push some of his Maryland Continentals forward
between the house and the camp. Howard managed to assemble about thirty
men and led them past the house. "Here I discovered the enemy formed, horse
& foot ... East of the house," Howard wrote. "I was immediately wounded
& retired."[45]

With the British rallying, Greene turned to his last reserves: Robert
Kirkwood's Delaware infantry and the cavalry of William Washington and Lee's
Legion. Greene ordered Washington and Kirkwood to attack Marjoribanks
and drive him from the creek bank, but Washington charged without waiting
for the infantry. The British flank battalion, protected from Washington's
sabers by the thick brush, fired volley after volley into the dragoons as
they wheeled their horses and rode back and forth, unsuccessfully seeking
an opening in the scrub growth. Washington was wounded and captured,
and the surviving cavalrymen broke off the action before Kirkwood arrived.
Greene redirected Kirkwood to the British camp, where the Delaware troops
were pinned down with the other Americans there.[46]

Washington's repulse meant that the outcome of the battle rested in the
hands of the Legion cavalry. Greene dispatched his aide, Captain Nathaniel
Pendleton, with orders for Lee to attack Coffin's loyalist dragoons and outflank
the British left. Pendleton recorded that

> "When Coffin's Cavalry came out, Gen. Greene sent me to Col. Lee
> with orders to attack him. When I went to the corps Lee was not
> there, and the order was delivered to Major Egleston, the next in
> command, who made the attack without success. The truth is, Col.
> Lee was very little, if at all, with his own corps after the enemy fled.
> He took some dragoons with him, as I was informed, and rode about
> the field, giving orders and directions, in a manner the General did
> not approve of. Gen. Greene was, apparently, disappointed when I
> informed him Col. Lee was not with his Cavalry, and that I had
> delivered the order to Major Egleston."

Eggleston charged as instructed, but for perhaps the only time in the many
engagements fought between Coffin and the Legion cavalry, the outnumbered
loyalists checked Eggleston's attack and then forced the Legion dragoons to
retreat. Coffin followed up his success by charging the American infantry,
and Stewart ordered his reorganized infantry forward. Sheridan led his men

from the brick house to join the assault and Marjoribanks also committed his troops to the counterattack. Seeing his exhausted troops withdrawing, and with no good tactical options remaining after a grueling four-hour battle fought in blistering heat, Greene ordered his army to withdraw to Burdell's Tavern.[47]

Losses on both sides were severe. The official American report listed 138 men killed, 378 wounded, and 41 missing, and as was typical of such reports, it probably understated casualties incurred by the militia. Stewart stated that his losses in the main battle were 84 killed, 351 wounded, and 257 missing, along with an additional 147 men from the foraging parties who did not return to the army. Most of the latter were captured; the combined number of soldiers reported missing by Stewart is virtually identical to the figure of four hundred British prisoners Greene said were captured by the American army. Lee's Legion had not been spared. Lee noted that "my Legion lost every fourth man engaged, which is the proportion of loss in the army."

Despite having been forced to withdraw from the battlefield, Greene emerged from the struggle more successfully than did his adversary. The British army was so badly mauled that on the night of September 9th Stewart withdrew to the vicinity of Charleston, and except for a few raids to seize provisions, British forces never again ventured beyond the safety of their defenses near the South Carolina coast.[48]

*****

Controversy Surrounding Lee's Role at Eutaw Springs

After the Battle of Eutaw Springs, many Americans, both officers and enlisted men, shared the disappointment that Lee expressed to a friend: "You will feel for our mortifying disappointment, after carrying victory for two miles by an intrepidity never before exhibited so generally, during the war." Yet some of these Americans believed that the person responsible for their mortifying disappointment was not Alexander Stewart, or John Harris Cruger, or Nathanael Greene. They instead placed the blame squarely on the shoulders of Henry Lee. The bitter disappointment still evoked strong feelings from Lee himself when he penned his memoirs thirty years later:

> *"The conclusion of this battle was as unexpected to both armies as it was mortifying to ours. The splendor which its beginning and progress had shed upon our arms became obscured, and the rich prize within our grasp was lost. Had our cavalry contributed to its aid, as heretofore it never failed to do, a British army must have surrendered to Greene on the field of battle. But they were unfortunately brought into action under difficulties not to be conquered; and the critical moment passed*

before it concentrated." Lee then accused an unnamed member of
Greene's staff of issuing an unauthorized order to his cavalry, which
had taken them from a position where they could have made an
effective charge under his command. Based on the subsequent
written comments of Nathaniel Pendleton, it seems clear Pendleton
felt that it was he whom Lee accused, which sparked controversy
between the two. [49]

Since the cavalry of Lee's Legion was one of Greene's key mounted forces,
Lee would inevitably become part of the debate over what went wrong at the
end of the Battle of Eutaw Springs. Lt. Col. Howard wrote long after the war
that "at the Eutaws [Lee's] post was on the right and had he been there with
his horse collected, when we broke the enemy and have made a charge upon
them at that critical moment, we should have obtained a victory." Howard
added that while he was engaged with his Marylanders on the American left,
Lee "passed me alone enquiring for the artillery which he moved on to the
house with the Legion infantry." Howard's account implies that Lee taken
it upon himself to assume command of the artillery, and that it was he who
ordered the guns into position so close to the brick house that they were
captured. Howard's commentary does not mention that Lee accompanied the
Legion infantry in its very effective work on the battlefield, bringing him to
the initial attacks on the brick mansion on the British right, while the bulk
of the Legion cavalry remained on the other side of the battlefield, on the
American right. Colonel Otho Williams, in an account of the battle written
in consultation with other officers who participated, including Howard
and Colonel Wade Hampton, acknowledged Lee's personal role in the early
American success in this battle:

> *"Under the approach of the second line, the advanced left of the British
> army had commenced a retrograde movement, in some disorder. This
> was confirmed by the good conduct of Col. Lee. The Legion Infantry
> had steadily maintained its order in its position on the extreme right
> and the advance of the British left having exposed its flank, the
> Legion Infantry were promptly wheeled, and poured in upon them a
> destructive enfilading fire; then joining in the charge, the British left
> wing was thrown into irretrievable disorder."*

Williams also stated that Lee's decision to remain with his infantry may have
contributed to the American cavalry missing its opportunity to turn the battle
on the right into a rout, stating that:

"Cavalry are the military means for rendering disorder [in a retreating army] irretrievable. It is obvious, that at this point of time, the Legion Cavalry might have been turned upon the British left with very great effect. Their position was highly favorable to such a movement, and their Infantry was up close with the enemy to afford support. Why this was not done, has never been explained; we can only conjecture, that it was prevented by one or both of two causes known to have existed on that day. Col. Lee was generally absent from it during the action, and bestowing his attention upon the progress of his Infantry; and Captain Coffin was in that quarter, attending on the retreat of the British left."[50]

Greene biographer and Lee critic Judge William Johnson cited the observations of Nathaniel Pendleton for his criticism of Lee at the Battle of Eutaw Springs, quoting Pendleton with the accusation: "The most incorrect of all Colonel Lee's historical memoirs, are those which relate to the movements of the army previous to, and at the battle of the Eutaw Springs." Pendleton was from a prominent Virginia family, and served as one of Greene's aides during most of the war. He settled in Georgia after the war, and was appointed to a federal judgeship. His personal involvement in the Yazoo land scandal and an affair with the widow of Nathanael Greene prompted his relocation to New York, where Alexander Hamilton befriended him. Pendleton acted as second to Hamilton in his fatal duel with Aaron Burr in 1804. When Lee's son, Henry Lee IV, wrote his 1824 defense of his father against the aspersions of William Johnson, he stated that Pendleton had not publicly criticized his father's actions at Eutaw Springs until ten years after the publication of Lee's memoirs in 1812 and four years after his death in 1818.[51]

Major Samuel Hammond of the South Carolina provided additional insight into Lee's activities on the Eutaw Springs Battlefield. He recalled that during the battle, Lt. Col. Richard Campbell, the senior officer of the two Virginia Continental regiments, had been mortally wounded. When Lee learned that Campbell was incapacitated, Hammond asserted, Lee proceeded to the regiments' position and attempted to assume command of the units. Hammond claimed that he witnessed Lee engaged in this argument with his fellow officers in the midst of the battle.[52]

Lee wrote in his memoirs that toward the end of the battle he waited for the Legion cavalry to join him for a final assault, and finally observed Captain James Armstrong approaching with his troop. He ordered Armstrong to advance, but had only traveled a short distance when Armstrong "told him that only his section was up." Lee claimed to have been surprised by the news, and remarked that *"this unlooked-for intelligence was not less fatal to the bright prospect of personal glory, than it was to the splendid issue of the conflict. Not a single doubt can be entertained, had the cavalry of the Legion been in place, as it ought to have been, that Coffin would have been carried, which must have been followed by the destruction of the British army."*[53]

According to Lee, at the time he ordered Armstrong to advance, Eggleston and the rest of the Legion cavalry had already been sent into action and repulsed. He attributed their defeat to "encountering the same sort of obstacle experienced by [William] Washington," that is, an impenetrable barrier of brush. Again, Lee's version conflicts with all other accounts, which indicate that the terrain where Coffin's cavalry repulsed Eggleston's Legion dragoons was clear. Lee declared that:

"Had Eggleston not been drawn from his post by orders officiously communicated to that officer as from the general, when in truth he never issued such orders, Lee would have been joined by his cavalry, ready to inflict the last blow, so clearly within his power."

This version argues that Pendleton was acting on his own when he issued the order for the Legion cavalry to charge, and that Greene never gave such a command. Once again, Lee's statement contradicts every other account. Thirty years after the battle, when Lee wrote his memoirs, it is clear that the criticism of his behavior at Eutaw Springs still pained him, and he sought to justify his actions there while simultaneously shifting blame for his alleged errors to others.[54]

If Greene did have any negative feelings about Lee's behavior at Eutaw Springs, he never publicly criticized his subordinate. To the contrary, he praised Lee effusively in his official report to Congress. "Lt Colo Lee had with great address, gallantry, and good conduct, turned the Enemy's left flank, and was charging them in rear at the same time the Virginia and Maryland Troops were charging them in front," the commanding general wrote. He also noted the Legion's gallantry in the opening action against Coffin's detachment.[55]

On the surface, there was nothing in the report that should have angered Lee. However, he may have taken offense at Greene's remark concerning the final phase of the battle, where the general mentioned William Washington's repulse and added that "the Legion [was] baffled in an attempt upon the right." Perhaps Lee believed that he had been unjustly denied credit for conceiving the plan to attack Stewart, since he had in fact been the first to suggest such an operation and had worked diligently to persuade Greene to adopt the idea. Whatever the reasons for Lee's discontent, they would continue to fester until his anger burst forth, leading to a lengthy and occasionally heated correspondence with Greene and ultimately, to Lee's resignation from the army.[56]

To the great disappointment of Lee, Greene and other American leaders, the Battle of Eutaw Springs did not end in the overwhelming victory that seems to have been possible if a well-timed cavalry charge could have been conducted in the waning moments of the fight. Nonetheless, after this battle the British army did not again launch a major offensive in the South.

Lee fought hard at Eutaw Springs, from the very start of the battle until the final shots were fired. His leadership of the Legion infantry in the early stages of the fight was masterful, but took him away from a location where he had direct personal control of the Legion cavalry, although he left the cavalry in the very capable hands of his subordinate Eggleston. He was seen roaming the battlefield at different times and places. Unfortunately, to Lee's everlasting regret and as a deep blow to his pride in his command, the Legion cavalry was not able to make that last stirring charge that would have sealed the fate of the British army on that field. Of course, that other gallant cavalryman William Washington could not make that charge either, having committed his own tactical errors early in the fight, and leading his command to substantial losses while he was personally wounded and captured. Battlefields are complex, fast-moving, and uniquely dangerous environments where events rarely proceed in a predictable manner. Even the finest soldiers fall prey to uncertainty and error in this demanding crucible.

Lee wanted desperately to play a key role in his country's fight for independence, and he anguished over the missed opportunity at Eutaw Springs for the rest of his life. But those who study this man should not let the pens of his critics nor the bitter disappointments of a day like September 8th, 1781, overshadow the Legion commander's tremendous accomplishments, on that day, or on the many others that comprised his military service. Nathanael Greene did not forget. He was soon to write to his young friend and fellow soldier about the Battle of Eutaw Springs that "There was no man that deserved greater credit than you that day."[57]

*****

Activities After the Battle of Eutaw Springs

On the day after the battle, Greene demonstrated his continuing confidence in Lee by dispatching the Legion commander with his cavalry and Francis Marion's militia to occupy a position "between Eutaw and Charles Town, to prevent any reinforcements from coming to the relief of the Enemy, and also to retard their march should they attempt to retire," giving the main army a chance to strike Stewart from the rear if he withdrew. During their march, Lee and Marion learned that Major Archibald McArthur and six hundred British troops were on their way to join Stewart. The American officers decided to move south and strike McArthur. Pushing their exhausted men forward, Lee and Marion reached the location where they intended to intercept McArthur's force, only to learn that Stewart had retreated from Eutaw Springs during the night of September 9th. This put the American detachment at risk of being trapped between the two British forces, so Lee and Marion withdrew.[58]

Stewart and McArthur united their forces on the morning of September 10th. Lee had kept the Legion cavalry nearby, concealed in the woods, and followed the British army. Later in the day he sent Captain Ferdinand O'Neal's troop to attack the British rear guard, and the dragoons captured several British cavalrymen. The Legion continued to follow the British column, capturing stragglers, some of whom gave Lee information that led him to believe that he could cut off and capture Stewart's rear guard. He therefore pressed forward with two troops of the Legion cavalry while Major Eggleston set out on a circuitous route to outflank the enemy. When Eggleston tried to strike the British rear guard posted on the road, his dragoons became bogged down in thick brush and "were roughly handled," having several men wounded. Observing Lee approaching with the rest of the Legion cavalry, the officer commanding the British rear guard ordered a hasty withdrawal after his men fired their volley at Eggleston's troop. The fleeing British abandoned several wagons, but when Lee rode up he discovered to his consternation that the wagons were filled with wounded soldiers. "The success turned out to be useless, for the miserable wounded supplicated so fervently to be permitted to proceed" that Lee allowed them to do so. The Legion rejoined Marion. Meanwhile, Greene had decided to return to the High Hills of Santee where his wounded and sick could recover. Lee arrived there on September 18th.[59]

Lee noted that "nearly one-half of the army was disabled by wounds or fever," and he did not escape the illness raging through Greene's camp. He told a friend on October 2nd that "I have been exceeding ill of a fever which took me while below," during his pursuit of Stewart. "I followed the army in a litter," Lee admitted, "the heat of the weather, & the exertions in the field of Eutaw brought [the fever] on me."[60]

*****

Lee's Journey to Virginia

By October 7th, Lee had recovered and was about to undertake a new mission. George Washington had marched southward from New York with a combined American and French army to trap Lord Cornwallis at Yorktown, Virginia. Washington had asked Greene for information on the military situation in the Carolinas and Georgia, and Greene hoped to induce Washington to shift his operations to those states after Cornwallis had been defeated. Greene believed that the person best suited to make the case for an increased focus on the South was Washington's friend Henry Lee. "As your Excellency desires the most perfect information of the state of matters in this quarter," Greene wrote to Washington, "I have sent Lieutenant Colonel Lee who … is fully acquainted with every thing in this department." Greene asked Washington to inform Lee of the commander-in-chief's future "plan of operations and present prospect of giving full & ample freedom to the Southern States."[61]

Lee arrived at Yorktown in time to witness the surrender of the British army on October 19th. "No spectacle could be more impressive than the one now exhibited," he remarked when recalling how the British troops had marched between the ranks of the victorious American and French soldiers and lain down their arms. After the surrender, Lee spent at least two weeks visiting relatives and friends in Virginia. While he undoubtedly enjoyed these social calls, Washington grew increasingly frustrated at his absence. On October 31st, Washington wrote to Greene stating that

> "I have delayed writing further, waiting the Return of Colo Lee, who, I am informed has taken a tour to Port Royal [Virginia]. It now becoming uncertain whether I shall see him again or not, I commit my Information to paper by another Conveyance."[62]

Lee finally returned to Washington's headquarters in early November, collected the letters the commander-in-chief wanted him to deliver to Greene, and returned to South Carolina. He arrived at Greene's headquarters at Buckshead Creek, sixty miles northwest of Charleston, about November 21st. Greene apparently was not upset with Lee's long absence, because three days later the general appointed him to command all of the cavalry in the southern army.[63]

With the onset of cooler weather, Greene renewed his operations against the British. The American army left its camp and marched toward Charleston. By December 2nd, after a skirmish near Dorchester, the British abandoned that post and withdrew to the Quarter House, a more secure position closer to Charleston. Lee was again ill and could not participate in the campaign. Greene asked his aide, Colonel Lewis Morris, to "tell Col Lee not to think of joining us as our movements are rapid. I hope he has got better but I fear a long, lingering disorder will persecute him." When Lee recovered, Greene intended to provide him "with a detachment of infantry" in addition to the army's cavalry and use this force to protect the region between the Ashley and

Edisto rivers from British raids.[64]

Lee informed Greene on December 4th that he was "perfectly recovered" from his illness and ready to return to duty. Morris suspected that Lee was not as fit as he proclaimed himself to be, telling Greene that Lee was with the army again and insisting that he was ready for active service, "or at least he thinks so." The general decided to accept Lee's assurances that his health was restored, and on December 7th sent him detailed instructions regarding his new responsibilities:

> *"You will take command of the Dragoons of the 3rd Regiment [formerly commanded by William Washington] and the detachment of infantry under Major Eggleston which with your own Legion you will employ in covering the Country from the ravages of the enemy between the Ashley and the Edisto. But if any Military object invites your attention in any other quarter you are not confind to this particular district but at liberty to improve it returning again as soon as you can. You will appoint a forage Master and Commissary for your command and prevent as much as possible any unnecessary waste of provision and forage. As the reputation and interest of the American Arms are greatly interested in preventing the Inhabitants from being plundered and more especially the Negroes from whom the enemy get all their best intelligence and who will be either more or less useful to them as they are treated well or ill by us, you are desird to pay particular attention to this matter to check it all in your power. As to the mode and manner of imploying your party I have such entire confidence in your judgment and Activity that I leave you perfectly at liberty to act according to circumstances."[65]*

Lee marched his troops to the vicinity of a British post on the Stono River and captured seven prisoners, but decided that his position was too exposed and fell back on December 10th. He had received a report that the British force guarding Johns Island south of Charleston, commanded by Lt. Col. John Harris Cruger, had been reinforced by "all the cavalry" and a Hessian detachment and intended "to drive me from this district." Lee reassured Greene that he would take no risks unless "justified by situation," and asked how Greene planned to reinforce him in the event such a British attack occurred.[66]

The next day Lee's cavalry captured a British soldier who provided a detailed description of the British units on Johns Island. Cruger commanded his own regiment, Isaac Allen's New Jersey battalion, 150 Hessians, the remnants of the Prince of Wales American Regiment, some provincial infantry, 50 dragoons, and a three-pounder cannon. Based on the prisoner's report, Lee estimated Cruger's strength at a total of five hundred infantry, plus the dragoons and artillery piece. No longer feeling threatened by this force, Lee began to consider attacking the British on Johns Island. "If Cruger could be taken which in my opinion is not the most hazardous, & the citizens would aid us, [Charleston] would soon fall," Lee told Greene. He added that he had also "entered a conspiracy to fire the forage" in Charleston; "it is in stacks & under the care of a small guard." However, the plot was never carried out.[67]

*****

The Attack on Johns Island

Once Lee had concluded that an attack on Johns Island could prove decisive in driving the British from Charleston, he continued to press Greene to approve the assault. "I must repeat my opinion that if Cruger & his command could be taken, that it would be in your power to oblige the enemy to give up Chstown or Savannah, or both," he told the general on December 12th. "I can readily pass over to the island, but my force is inadequate to the attempt." Lee suggested that Greene support the attack by moving his army "near Dorchester." Lee conceded that "the enemys galleys &c will be a difficulty in our way, but may be overcome." When he did not receive a reply from Greene, Lee wrote the general again on December 15th and reminded him of his proposal. Lee explained that his cavalry would not be able to cross from the mainland to the island, and asked Greene to send the Virginia Continental regiments to replace the dragoons in the assault force. He reiterated his opinion that the attack would serve as "a corner stone of most important operations."[68]

Lee's assessment of the importance of Johns Island to the British garrison of Charleston was accurate. The British used the island as pastureland for large herds of cattle that provided meat for their troops, and also raised "long forage" there for their cavalry horses. General Alexander Leslie, who after the surrender at Yorktown had replaced Lord Cornwallis as the British commander in the South and established his headquarters at Charleston, likewise recognized the importance of Johns Island. He promised his superior, General Sir Henry Clinton, that he would hold the coastal islands as long as possible because they provided "the only hopes of supplies" for his troops. Leslie posted most of his infantry at the eastern end of the island, closest to Charleston, and the cavalry more than six miles away at the opposite end. There were only two fords across the Stono River leading to the island that could be waded at low tide, and one of these was rendered nearly impassable by large rocks. At the other ford, called New Cut, Leslie stationed two armed galleys to guard against an American attempt to cross.[69]

Another officer recently assigned to Greene's army, Lt. Col. John Laurens, embraced Lee's plan. Laurens, the son of wealthy South Carolina planter and Revolutionary leader Henry Laurens, had formerly been a member of George Washington's staff. After the surrender at Yorktown, Laurens had journeyed to his home state and taken a similar position with Greene. However, the young and ambitious Laurens preferred the activity of command in the field to the duties of a staff officer. Greene could not assign him to such a role without affronting other officers with more seniority. When Greene finally decided to approve Lee's plan for the attack on Johns Island, he assigned Laurens to command the operation, thus providing Laurens with the opportunity he sought while avoiding any problems that would certainly arise if Greene appointed the South Carolinian to a position in one of the existing Continental units.[70]

On December 20th, Lee informed Greene that "my attention is now wholly taken up with preparing for the enterprize against Johns Island. If the enemy do not exceed 400, Laurens & my self will be adequate to the attempt provided you could assemble sufficient force to take a position to cover us." Lee noted that Major James Craig, former commander of the British garrison at Wilmington, North Carolina, which had been withdrawn in November, had joined Cruger on the island. The mention of Laurens was a clear indication that Lee had won his fellow officer's support for the operation. Laurens himself confirmed it, sending a letter to Greene along with Lee's message. In it, Laurens stated that in a day or two Lee would have all the intelligence needed to plan the Johns Island attack, and declared that he was eager to participate in an assault that "promises such important consequences."[71]

Greene remained skeptical of Lee's plan, and explained his reluctance to approve the operation in a letter of December 21st. Nonetheless, the general gave Lee permission to carry out the attack:

> "I am afraid you are too confident of your strength, and have too much contempt for the enemies. You are to remember the place you are going upon is an Island. I hate all Island[s] for Military operations where we have not the command of the water. You will remember also that the tide will govern your going on and coming off; which may make a very material difference in the risque. To this you are to add the contiguity of the enemies whole force, and the great facility with which they can transport troops to Johns Island. It is out of our power also to cover you by a land March until ammunition arrives. Should we take a position for the purpose and the enemy advance upon us, we must retire having nothing to defend our selves with. But if after

fully considering and attending to all these matters you are of opinion the enterprise is warranted and remain desirous of attempting it I will give you all the aid in my power and you have my consent to make the attempt; for you know I am no enemy to enterprise; and yet I think the thing may be over done; and shou'd we meet with a misfortune and the measure have an appearance of rashness it will be laid hold on by our domestic enemies, and afford our common enemy a great triumph. It is true the object of the present case is important; but if you get cut off, and we driven back, the consequences would be dreadful from the effect it would have upon the Country. You know I have the highest confidnce in your judgment and that of Col Laurens; and therefore I am willing to encourage whatever you think prudent to attempt."[72]

The general's cautious approval was enough for Lee and Laurens, who set to work to put their plan into action. Lee's successful attack under similar conditions at Paulus Hook in 1779 undoubtedly bolstered his confidence in the operation, but difficulties arose in procuring accurate intelligence of the British positions and strength. Lee noted that "some weeks were assiduously devoted to the acquiring of a clear comprehension of this arduous and grand design, with an exact knowledge of the complicated means necessary to its execution." On December 27th, Lee informed Greene that he had spent the previous day observing the portion of the Stono where the British galleys were positioned, and concluded that any problems in "crossing or re-crossing the troops in case of victory" could be overcome. He noted that while it would not be "absolutely necessary" to capture one or both of the galleys, it would be "desirable." Lee wrote that he expected to make the attack on December 30th, when the tides would be especially favorable.[73]

The discovery that the British had a substantial force on James Island, which is immediately to the north of Johns Island, forced Lee and Laurens to cancel the December 30th assault. While awaiting another favorable opportunity to strike, the two officers continued to reconnoiter the British position. The intelligence reports they received changed frequently, with several accounts stating that the British garrison on Johns Island had been reinforced. The British cavalry occasionally made forays to the mainland, and in one such raid on December 30th Major John Coffin with "a considerable body of horse" attacked and defeated Captain James Armstrong's troop of Legion cavalry, capturing Armstrong and six other dragoons. During this period Cruger was called back to Charleston and Major Craig assumed command of the British forces on Johns Island. Greene warned Lee that if the British fortified Johns Island, "it will preclude our enterprise altogether."[74]

On January 11th, 1782, Laurens finally wrote to Greene stating that he and Lee had decided to make their attack on the fourteenth. Their information on the British garrison, including Laurens's personal observation from across the Stono, appeared to confirm that there were no more than four hundred troops on Johns Island. They had obtained solid information regarding the position of the main British camp and the pickets guarding the road leading inland from the ford. Satisfied that they had done all they could to be ready for the operation, Lee and Laurens began moving their forces closer to the enemy in preparation for the assault.[75]

Laurens and Lee planned to send two infantry columns across the ford, one commanded personally by Lee and the other by Major James Hamilton. Lee led his troops into the marsh at one o'clock on the morning of January 14th, when the tide had ebbed. The always reliable Captain Michael Rudulph led the advance, and as his troops passed between the two British galleys guarding the ford, the Legion infantrymen could hear the sentries on the vessels calling "all's safe." Soon all of Lee's force had crossed the waist-deep river and awaited the arrival of Hamilton's troops. Unfortunately, several hours passed and Hamilton did not appear; his column had gotten lost in the darkness, and by the time it reached the ford at New Cut, the tide had reversed. Laurens, who had been waiting on the mainland, ordered Lee and his soldiers to return before rising water trapped them on Johns Island. Lee withdrew, still undetected by the British galleys, through water that was chest deep.[76]

All of the American officers involved in the plan were disappointed by the result. "Thus was marred the execution of an enterprise surpassed by none throughout our war in grandeur of design, and equaled by few in the beneficial effects sure to result from its successful termination," Lee lamented. In response to the unsuccessful assault, General Leslie evacuated Johns Island, but Greene found that to be small consolation. "We have got territory but we mist the great object of the enterprise, which is the more to be regreted as we find the plan would have succeeded equal to our most sanguine wishes," Greene wrote. In his report to Congress, the general declared that "the failure of the enterprise was not a little mortifying to me, but much more so to Laurens and Lee. Had it succeeded it would have been both important and splendid."[77]

*****

Lee's Anguished Farewell to Military Service

The failure of the attack on Johns Island was indeed mortifying to Lee. More than two weeks before the attempt was made, the Legion commander had expressed a desire for a "leave of absence" when the operation was finished. Greene had replied on December 28th, 1781, writing that "there are few things you can ask in my power to grant, but I would readily consent to; but I confess I shall grant you leave of absence with great reluctance." Lee did not raise the issue again until January 26th, 1782, and this time he was more insistent:

> *"I must at length ask permission to absent myself from the army. Disquietude of mind and infirmity of body unite in giving birth to my request. The first arises from the indifference with which my efforts to advance the cause of my country is considered by my friends, the persecution of my foes, and my consciousness that it is not in my power to efface the disagreeable impression. The second owes its birth to the fidelity with which I have served, and is nourished by my continuance in the same line of conduct."* [78]

Lee's complaints echoed those he had made when he was charged with misconduct after the raid on Paulus Hook. He believed that he was surrounded by enemies who sought to destroy his reputation. Greene did his best to reassure his youthful subordinate when he replied the next day:

> *"I have beheld with extreme anxiety for some time past a growing discontent in your mind and have not been without my apprehensions that your complaints originated more in distress than in the ruins of your constitution. What ever may be the source of your wounds I wish it was in my power to heal them. You say your friends are not disposed to do justice to your exertions. If you mean me and any thing appears in my conduct to confirm it, it has been owing to error in judgment or accident and not to a disinclination."*

Greene went on to recount his friendship for Lee since they first campaigned together, and his desire to do justice to Lee's reputation. With regard to Lee's complaint that Americans did not appreciate his service, Greene observed that "I believe few Officers either in America or Europe are held in so high a point of estimation as you are." Greene agreed that some people disliked Lee, but attributed such feelings to "ignorance and malice." The general also noted that any effort he might make to enhance Lee's reputation might be seen as partiality and do more harm than good.[79]

Lee professed his friendship for Greene when he replied, and apologized for writing anything that Greene might have construed as personal criticism. Lapsing into self-deprecation, The Legion commander declared that "I am candid to acknowledge my imbecility of mind" and repeated his request to leave the army. While awaiting Greene's decision, he continued to supervise his troops in their regular duties and send intelligence reports to headquarters.

By February 12th, Greene had relented and given permission for Lee to return to Virginia. The general told his departing friend that "should the war rage here, I shall call for you in a few months." Lee replied that if Greene summoned him back into service, "I will come at the risk of every thing in this world." He said that he would not call on Greene or his other comrades before leaving: "the ceremony of parting from you & my friends in the army is so affecting, that I wish to decline it personally."[80]

On February 17th, Lee sent Greene what he described as the last of his "official communications" and expressed his hope that the two men would continue a "private correspondence." Greene, however, had grown tired of Lee's complaints. Although the general described Lee as "an officer of the highest merit and singular zeal for the public service" in a letter written on February 18th, that same day he sent Lee a far less positive message. Apparently referring to comments that Lee had not made in writing, Greene told his departing subordinate that he was sorry "that your disgust increases and that you harbour sentiments respecting me no less groundless than unfriendly." The general raised the issue that had been the root of Lee's anger: "You say you think you have been injured in my public report of the battle of the Eutaws." Greene advised Lee to read every one of his official reports, and he would find only praise. Then Greene addressed another of Lee's complaints. "You say no Officer has been treated so cruelly as you have except General [Charles] Lee." This, Greene asserted, was "strange indeed." Greene recounted how his name had not been mentioned in several of George Washington's battle reports, even when the Rhode Islander thought he had merited such a distinction, yet he had continued to serve without taking offense. Greene reassured Lee that he still held the young officer in high esteem, but it was clear that he had run out of patience with Lee's complaints.[81]

Lee and Greene exchanged a few more letters, with the former continuing to air his complaints interspersed with self-deprecating comments—"I am much mortified at the trouble which my stupid conduct gives you," Lee wrote on one occasion, while Greene made it clear that his report had nothing to do with the criticism of Lee's performance at Eutaw Springs. "In the affair at Eutaw what ever idle reports operated to your prejudice it was long before my public letter made its appearance," the general declared. The once warm relationship between the two officers had been badly damaged because Lee still considered himself unjustly criticized for his performance at the Battle of Eutaw Springs.[82]

The Continental Congress passed a resolution on April 15th praising Lee's contributions to the American cause. He was 26 years old. The delegates stated that they "entertain[ed] a high sense of the spirited and military conduct of Lt. Col. Henry Lee especially while serving in the Southern Army under the command of Major General Greene, and that this resolution be published" in Greene's general orders. This tribute should have put to rest any concerns Lee had about his reputation. He had always striven to win glory on the battlefield, and he had won many honors and much praise from men like Greene and Washington during the war. He would remain the only individual who was not a general officer to be awarded a gold medal by the Continental Congress, and now that body had officially commended his achievements in the southern theater. Lee's sensitivity to criticism and his appetite for praise and glory were immense, but perhaps Congress's recent action gave him some comfort as his military service ended, and after six years of arduous campaigning he returned to civilian life as a war hero, to resume his position with other members of the Lee family in the upper echelon of Virginia society.[83]

1   Lee, *Memoirs*, 387; Pancake, 216; Greene to Sumter, July 14, 1781, in Conrad, editor, *Papers of Greene*, Vol. 9 (1997), 8 (quotation).
2   "Headnote on the Dog Days Expedition," in Conrad, editor, *Papers of Greene*, 9:13; Pancake, 216; Gordon, 160.
3   Lee to Greene, July 15, 1781, in Conrad, editor, *Papers of Greene*, 9:13.
4   Pancake, 216; Gordon, 160; "Headnote," Sumter to Greene, July 25, 1781, Greene to Thomas McKean, July 26, 1781, in Conrad, editor, *Papers of Greene*, 9:14, 80, 82-83.
5   Lee, *Memoirs*, 387-389.
6   Sumter to Greene, July 17, 1781, in Conrad, editor, *Papers of Greene*, 9:50-51.
7   Lee, *Memoirs*, 389 (quotation); "Headnote on the Dog Days Expedition," in Conrad, editor, *Papers of Greene*, 9:14-15.
8   Lee, *Memoirs*, 389-390.
9   Lee, *Memoirs*, 390 (quotations); "Headnote on the Dog Days Expedition," in Conrad, editor, *Papers of Greene*, 15.
10   Lee, *Memoirs*, 390-391 (quotation); "Headnote on the Dog Days Expedition," in Conrad, editor, *Papers of Greene*, 15.
11   Lee, *Memoirs*, 391 (quotation); "Headnote on the Dog Days Expedition," and Marion to Greene, July 19, 1781, in Conrad, editor, *Papers of Greene*, 14-15 (quotation), 47.
12   Lee, *Memoirs*, 391-392 (quotation); Gordon, 161.
13   Gordon, 161; Sumter to Greene, July 17, 1781, and Marion to Greene, July 19, 1781, in Conrad, editor, *Papers of Greene*, 9:47-48, 52 (quotation).
14   Gordon, 161-162; Pancake, 216; "Headnote on the Dog Days Expedition," Marion to Greene, July 19, 1781, and Sumter to Greene, July 17, 1781, in Conrad, editor, *Papers of Greene*, 9:16, 48 (quotations), 52 (quotations).
15   Pancake, 216; Gordon, 162; Lee, *Memoirs*, 392; "Headnote on the Dog Days Expedition," in Conrad, editor, *Papers of Greene*, 9:17; Nisbet Balfour to Henry Clinton, July 20, 1781, in Saberton, editor, *Cornwallis Papers*, 6:249 (quotation).
16   Lee, *Memoirs*, 393-394.
17   McGroarty, "Sergeant John Champe," 156; Hall, "Sergeant Champe's Adventure," 341.
18   Lee, *Memoirs*, 446 (quotations); Lee to Greene, July 29, 1781, in Conrad, editor, *Papers of Greene*, 9:101 (quotations).
19   Greene to Lee, July 29, 1781, in Conrad, editor, *Papers of Greene*, 9:102-103.
20   Greene to Lee, July 29, 1781 (second letter of this date), Lee to Greene, July 20, 1781, in ibid., 9:104 (quotations), 114 (quotation).
21   Lee, *Memoirs*, 447-448.
22   Greene to Thomas Burke, Aug. 12, 1781, in Conrad, editor, *Papers of Greene*, 9:166 (quotation); Lee, *Memoirs*, 448 (quotation).

23   Lee to Greene, Aug. 5, 1781, in Conrad, editor, *Papers of Greene*, 9:133; Pancake,215-216, 217; Jim Piecuch, "The Evolving Tactician: Nathanael Greene at the Battle of Eutaw Springs," in Gregory D. Massey and Jim Piecuch, editors, *General Nathanael Greene and the American Revolution in the South* (Columbia: University of South Carolina Press, 2012), 222-223.
24   Lee to Greene, Aug. 8, 1781, and Greene to Thomas Burke, Aug. 12, 1781, in Conrad, editor, *Papers of Greene*, 9:150 (quotations), 168.
25   Lee to Greene, Aug. 8, 1781, in ibid., 9:151.
26   Greene to Lee, Aug. 9, 1781, in ibid., 9:152-153.
27   Lee to Greene, Aug. 10, 1781, and Greene to Lee, Aug. 12, 1781, in ibid., 9:162 (quotations), 170 (quotations).
28   Lee to Greene, Aug. 13, 1781, in ibid., 9:177.
29   Greene to Lee, Aug. 14, 1781, in ibid., 9:181.
30   Lee to Greene, Aug. 17, 1781, and Aug. 18, 1781, in ibid., 9:195-196 (quotations), 203.
31   Lee to Greene, Aug. 20, 1781 (two letters of this date), in ibid., 9:214, 214-215 (quotation).
32   Greene to Lee, Aug. 21, 1781, in ibid., 218.
33   Piecuch, "Evolving Tactician," in Massey and Piecuch, 223-224; Lee to Greene, Aug. 20, 1781, in Conrad, editor, *Papers of Greene*, 9:215 (quotation).
34   Greene to Lee, Aug. 22, 1781, and Aug. 25, 1781, in Conrad, editor, *Papers of Greene*, 9:222-223 (quotations), 239 (quotations); Piecuch, "Evolving Tactician," in Massey and Piecuch, 224.
35   Piecuch, "Evolving Tactician," in Massey and Piecuch, 224; Lee to Greene, Sept. 1, 1781, in Conrad, editor, *Papers of Greene*, 9:278.
36   Piecuch, "Evolving Tactician," in Massey and Piecuch, 226-227.
37   Piecuch, "Evolving Tactician," in Massey and Piecuch, 226, 227-228; Alexander Stewart to Cornwallis, Sept. 26, 1781, in Saberton, editor, *Cornwallis Papers*, 6:168 (quotation).
38   Piecuch, "Evolving Tactician," in Massey and Piecuch, 227, 228.
39   Ibid., 228, 229.
40   Ibid., 228-229.
41   Ibid., 229.
42   Ibid., 229.
43   Ibid., 230.
44   Ibid., 230-231; "Col. Howard's Notes on Johnson," 1808, Henry Lee Papers, VHS; Lee, *Memoirs*, 470.
45   "Howard's Notes on Johnson," Henry Lee Papers, VHS; Piecuch, "Evolving Tactician," in Massey and Piecuch, 230-231.
46   Piecuch, "Evolving Tactician," in Massey and Piecuch, 230-231.
47   Ibid., 231-232; Otho Holland Williams, "Battle of Eutaw. Account Furnished by Col. Otho Holland Williams, with additions by Cols. W. Hampton, Polk, Howard and Watt," in Gibbes, editor, *Documentary History of the American Revolution, consisting of Letters and Papers relating to the Contest for Liberty Chiefly in South Carolina*, 3 Vols. (New York: Appleton, 1857), 3:154-155 (quotation).
48   Piecuch, "Evolving Taction," in Massey and Piecuch, 232; Lee to unnamed, Oct. 2, 1781, in "Henry Lee on the Southern Campaign," George F. Scheer, editor, *Virginia Magazine of History and Biography*, Vol. 51, No. 2 (Apr. 1943), 149 (quotation).
49   Lee to unnamed, Oct. 2, 1781, in Scheer, editor, "Lee on the Southern Campaign," 149; Lee, *Memoirs*, 473 (quotation).
50   "Howard's Notes on Johnson," Henry Lee Papers, VHS (quotations); Williams, "Battle of Eutaw," in Gibbes, editor, Documentary History, 3:150 (quotation), 151 (quotation).
51   Johnson. *Life of Greene*, 2:221 (quotation); Thomas Fleming, *Duel: Alexander Hamilton, Aaron Burr, and the Future of America.* (New York: Basic Books, 1999), 60; Henry Lee, IV. *The Campaign of 1781 in the Carolinas, with Remarks Historical and Critical on Johnson's Life of Greene* (Philadelphia, PA: E. Littrell, 1824) 475.
52   Piecuch, "Evolving Tactician," in Massey and Piecuch, 231.
53   Lee, *Memoirs*, 471-472.
54   Ibid., 471, 473.
55   Greene to Thomas McKean, Sept. 11, 1781, in Conrad, editor, *Papers of Greene,* 9:329, 331(quotation).
56   Greene to McKean, Sept. 11, 1781, in ibid., 9:331-332.
57   Greene to Lee, Oct. 7, 1782, in Johnson, *Life of Greene*, 2:235.
58   Greene to McKean, Sept. 11, 1781, in ibid., 9:332 (quotation); Lee, *Memoirs*, 475.
59   Lee, *Memoirs*, 475-477.
60   Lee, *Memoirs*, 477 (quotation); Lee to unnamed, Oct. 2, 1781, in Scheer, editor, "Lee on the Southern

Campaign," 150 (quotation).
61 Greene to Washington, Oct. 7, 1781, in Conrad, editor, *Papers of Greene*, 9:430.
62 Lee, *Memoirs*, 512 (quotation); George Washington to Greene, Oct. 31, 1781, in Conrad, editor, *Papers of Greene*, 9:504 (quotation).
63 Greene to Arthur St. Clair, Nov. 21, 1781, and General Orders, Nov. 24, 1781, in Conrad, editor, *Papers of Greene*, 9:604, 617.
64 Lee, *Memoirs*, 521; Greene to Lewis Morris, Jr., Dec. 2, 1781, and Greene to Otho Williams, Dec. 2, 1781, in Conrad, editor, *Papers of Greene*, 9:648 (quotation), 649-650 (quotation).
65 Lee to Greene, Dec. 4, 1781, Morris to Greene, Dec. 4, 1781, and Greene to Lee, Dec. 7, 1781, in Conrad, editor, *Papers of Greene*, Vol. 10 (1998), 6 (quotation), 7 (quotation), 12-13 (quotation).
66 Lee to Greene, Dec. 10, 1781, in ibid., 10:31.
67 Lee to Greene, Dec. 11, 1781, in ibid., 10:34-35.
68 Lee to Greene, Dec. 12, 1781, and Dec. 15, 1781, in ibid., 10:44 (quotations), 59 (quotations).
69 Lee, *Memoirs*, 524 (quotation); Greene to Lee, Jan. 1, 1782, Greene to John Rutledge, Jan. 16, 1782, in Conrad, editor, *Papers of Greene*, 10:145n. (quotation), 207n.
70 Lee, *Memoirs*, 550-551.
71 John Laurens to Greene, Dec. 20, 1781, and Lee to Greene, Dec. 20, 1781, in Conrad, editor, *Papers of Greene*, 10:83 (quotation), 84 (quotation).
72 Greene to Lee, Dec. 21, 1781, in ibid., 10:85.
73 Laurens to Greene, Dec. 22, 1781, and Lee to Greene, Dec. 27, 1781, in Conrad, editor, *Papers of Greene*, 10:89, 123 (quotations); Lee, *Memoirs*, 526 (quotation).
74 Lee to Greene, Dec. 29, 1781, and Dec. 31, 1781 (three letters of this date), Greene to Lee, Jan. 1, 1782, in Conrad, editor, *Papers of Greene*, 10:135, 142 (quotation), 144 (quotation); Lee, *Memoirs*, 524, 529.
75 Laurens to Greene, Jan. 11, 1782, in Conrad, editor, *Papers of Greene*, 10:183; Lee, *Memoirs*, 529-530.
76 Greene to John Rutledge, Jan. 16, 1782, in Conrad, editor, *Papers of Greene*, 10:206; Lee, *Memoirs*, 533-534 (quotation).
77 Lee, *Memoirs*, 534 (quotation); Greene to Rutledge, Jan. 16, 1782, and Greene to John Hanson, Jan. 23, 1782, in Conrad, editor, *Papers of Greene*, 10:206 (quotation), 244 (quotation).
78 Lee to Greene, Dec. 28, 1781, Greene to Lee, Dec. 28, 1781, Lee to Greene, Jan. 26, 1782, in Conrad, editor, *Papers of Greene*, 10:126 (quotation), 127 (quotation); 264-265 (quotation).
79 Greene to Lee, Jan. 27, 1782, in ibid., 10:268-269.
80 Lee to Greene, Jan. 29, 1782 and Feb. 13, 1782, Greene to Lee, Feb. 12, 1782, in ibid., 10:282-283 (quotation), 358 (quotation), 361 (quotation). For Lee's military service in this period, see Lee to Greene, Jan. 27, 1782, Jan. 30, 1782, Feb. 3, 1782, Feb. 7, 1782, and Feb. 10, 1782, in ibid., 10:271, 284-285, 309, 332, 350
81 Lee to Greene, Feb. 17, 1782, Greene to John Hanson, Feb. 18, 1782, Greene to Lee, Feb. 18, 1782, in ibid., 10:375 (quotations), 377 (quotation), 378-379 (quotations).
82 Lee to Greene, Feb. 19, 1782, Greene to Lee, Mar. 12, 1782, in ibid., 10:389 (quotation), 487 (quotation).
83 Ford, editor, *Journals of the Continental Congress*, Apr. 15, 1782, 22:183.

CHAPTER NINE

LEE'S LIFE AFTER THE WAR

During the rare occasions when he had been granted wartime leave, Henry Lee had courted and eventually became engaged to his second cousin, Matilda Lee. She was the daughter of his father's cousin Phillip Ludwell Lee, who had died in 1775. After leaving Greene's army in February 1782, Lee journeyed to Matilda's plantation, Stratford Hall in Westmoreland County, Virginia. They were married that April. The newlyweds initially shared the residence with Matilda's sister Flora, their mother, Elizabeth Steptoe Lee, and her new husband Richard Fendall. The Fendalls and Flora soon moved to Alexandria, Virginia, leaving Henry Lee as the master of Stratford Hall, since Matilda's mother and sister entrusted him with full responsibility for managing the estate.[1]

Although Lee claimed he would seek refuge in family life, with no further thought of military affairs, he found the attraction of his former career difficult to put aside entirely. In May 1783, a group of Continental Army officers organized the Society of the Cincinnati at Fishkill, New York. The group was intended to be a fraternal organization to allow former American officers to maintain friendships after the war and assist one another when necessary. The founders of the Society decided to form chapters in each state, as well as in France. They also agreed that membership would be inherited, passing to the eldest son of each of the original members and henceforward to future generations. The Virginia chapter of the Society met for the first time at Fredericksburg on October 6th, 1783, and elected five delegates to represent them at the Society of the Cincinnati's first general meeting, scheduled to convene at Philadelphia in May 1784. Lee attended the Fredericksburg gathering, and was chosen to represent the state at the national meeting, an indication of the high regard he enjoyed among his fellow former officers.[2]

Lee probably did not believe that he was doing anything more than joining a social group comprised of his former army comrades, but the formation of the Society of the Cincinnati quickly became a contentious political issue. To many Americans, who had despised the hereditary aristocracy of Great Britain, the Society seemed to be the foundation for the creation of an American aristocracy. Americans feared that the Society's members and their descendants, like the noble families of Britain, would unite and use their prominence to dominate the new government. Such fears were not limited to simple farmers and craftsmen. Revolutionary leaders such as Thomas Jefferson, Benjamin Franklin, and John Adams criticized the Society. Adams called the creation of the Cincinnati "the deepest piece of cunning yet attempted ... the first

223

step taken to deface the beauty of our temple of liberty." The furious debate among the Founders over the Society of the Cincinnati proved unnecessary, for while the Society survives to the present day, it played a very minor role in public affairs throughout its existence. However, by joining the Society and accepting an important role in the Virginia chapter, Lee was inadvertently choosing sides in the political battles that would increase to fever pitch over the subsequent two decades and rend the politics of the new United States into bitter party factions.[3]

*****

Lee Embarks on a Political Career

In 1785 Lee was elected to represent Westmoreland County in the Virginia state legislature. Later that year, his fellow legislators chose him to represent Virginia in the Continental Congress, and he arrived in New York to take up his new responsibilities on February 1st, 1786. He played an important role in securing passage of the Northwest Ordinance of 1787, the legislation that established the basis upon which future states would be added to the Union, created procedures for settling the region that later became Ohio, Indiana, Illinois, and Michigan, and declared slavery illegal in those territories.[4]

Like most former Continental Army officers, Lee believed that the system of government under the Articles of Confederation was inadequate for the newly independent United States. He therefore supported the call for a gathering to revise the Articles, a meeting that became the Constitutional Convention of 1787. Lee avidly supported the new Constitution, and was elected a delegate to Virginia's ratification convention in 1788. During the debates, Lee aligned himself with the Federalists, as the supporters of the Constitution became known, and joined his former commanding officer Theodorick Bland, Edmund Randolph, and other prominent Virginians in arguing for ratification of the document. The Federalists faced formidable opposition from some of the state's most distinguished Revolutionary leaders, including Patrick Henry, Lee's own cousin Richard Henry Lee, and George Mason, who had attended the Constitutional Convention but refused to approve the new system of government. These men argued that the new central government created by the Constitution was too powerful, and lacked protection for the people's liberties in the form of a bill of rights. The Federalists triumphed after a long and bitter debate, and Virginia ratified the Constitution.[5]

Lee's success at the ratification convention was followed by a swift fall from political grace. During his third term in the Continental Congress, he voted against a bill demanding that Spain open the Mississippi River and the Spanish port of New Orleans to American shipping. While it is unlikely that Spain would have conceded to the demand, the legislation was symbolically important to Virginia, which then included all of the land that later became the state of Kentucky. Settlers in Kentucky needed access to the Mississippi and New Orleans to export their surplus crops, and were suffering economically from Spain's rigid policy. Lee's vote against challenging Spain assumed a suspicious character when it was learned that he had accepted a loan of $5,000 from the Spanish government (which he never repaid). The Virginia state legislature, angry at both Lee's vote and the insinuation that it had been purchased by Spanish officials, removed him from the Continental Congress.[6]

The voters of Westmoreland County and the surrounding area were less troubled by the affair, and in 1789 elected Lee to the state legislature. In November 1792, his transgression in the Spanish matter apparently forgotten, Lee was elected to the first of three consecutive terms as governor of Virginia. Even as his political career resumed its ascent, however, Lee suffered several personal tragedies. In 1790 his wife Matilda died in childbirth along with their fourth child. Two years later, Lee's eldest son Phillip also died. Lee was so upset that for a time he considered going to France to serve in the revolutionary army there. He corresponded with his old comrade, the Marquis de Lafayette, on the possibility, and then sought the advice of his friend and former commander, George Washington:

> "Bred to arms, I have always since my domestic calamity wished for a return to my profession, as the best resort for my mind in its affliction. Finding the serious turn, which the French affairs took last year, I interposed with the Marquis [Lafayette] to obtain a commission in their army, and at the same time made the same application in another way. … I am informed, that a major-general's commission will be given to me on my appearance in Paris, and that probably it would be sent to me. I have detailed this to you, merely that your mind might be fully informed, inasmuch as the step I may take will be to me all-important I am consequently solicitous for the best advice, and this I am persuaded you can give."[7]

Washington's carefully worded reply subtly discouraged Lee's proposal to join the French army. After noting that he could say nothing in his public capacity as president of the United States, Washington added that "as a private man, I am unwilling to say much." The president observed that "much speculation would be excited" if the governor of such an important state as Virginia suddenly left office to serve a foreign nation. Washington also reminded Lee of the difficulties facing the French. Further pressure came from

Charles Carter; Lee had been courting his daughter, Ann, and Carter refused to permit his daughter to marry a man intent on leaving the country to serve in a foreign army. The objections of Washington and Charles Carter convinced Lee to renounce his plan to go to France. Carter then gave his consent to the wedding, and Henry Lee married Ann Carter on June 18th, 1793.[8]

*****

The Whiskey Rebellion

As a Federalist, Lee generally supported the policies of George Washington's administration. Even before the first president was selected, Lee had been among those urging Washington to accept the office. "Without you, the govt can have but little chance of success, & the people of that happiness which its prosperity must yield," Lee had written to his former commander. Washington had indeed accepted the office, but soon found himself plagued by both an Indian war in the Northwest and internal political divisions between the Federalists and the emerging opposition party, the Democratic-Republicans, led by Thomas Jefferson and James Madison.[9]

The British government had ceded all of its territorial claims between the Appalachian Mountains and the Mississippi River to the United States in the 1783 treaty that ended the Revolutionary War. However, the Indian nations in the Northwest denied that Britain had any right to cede that land, and formed a confederation of tribes to oppose American encroachment. Washington dispatched two expeditions to defeat the Indians; the first in 1790 suffered a serious defeat, and the second, under General Arthur St. Clair, was disastrously routed a year later. Washington sought a new commander who could achieve a victory, and considered Lee for the position. Madison contacted Lee about the possibility of him assuming command of the army in the Northwest even though he was still serving as governor. Lee replied on January 29th, 1792:

> *"Were I called upon by the President to command the next campaign, my respect for him would induce me to disregard every trifling obstruction which might oppose my acceptance of the office. … As a citizen, I should hold myself bound to obey the will of my country, in taking any part her interests may demand of me. Therefore, I am under a bias in favor of obedience to any claim which may be made of me."*

Lee added, however, that he would not serve if he was forced to carry out any actions that might be detrimental to the interests of his own state. "No consideration on earth could induce me to act a part, however gratifying to me, which could be construed into disregard or forgetfulness of this

Commonwealth," he declared. There are echoes of this sentiment in statements made by his sixth son Robert E. Lee when he refused command of the Union armies almost seventy years later at the outset of the Civil War.[10]

After careful consideration, Washington decided that appointing Lee to the command would arouse jealousies among other former Continental officers who had been senior in rank to Lee during the Revolution. There was, the president wrote, "but little ground to hope, that either the Military talents which [Lee] has displayed in the course of the War, or his present dignified Station, would reconcile any of them to act a Subordinate part." Washington explained his decision to Lee in a letter of June 30th:

> *"I conceived few men were better qualified for such a command than you. ... I have no hesitation in declaring to you that the bias of my inclination was strongly in your favor; but, that the result of my enquiries, direct and indirect, of Military, and indeed of other characters (who were well disposed to see you in nomination) was, that if you were appointed to the Command it would be vain to look for Senior Officers to act subordinately; or if they consented, it would be so grudgingly as, more than probably, the seeds of Sedition would be coeval with the formation of the Army."*

Instead of Lee, Washington appointed General Anthony Wayne to command the Legion of the United States. On August 20th, 1794, Wayne resoundingly defeated the Indians at the Battle of Fallen Timbers, forcing the Native nations to surrender their land claims in Ohio and part of Indiana.[11]

While Wayne was preparing his expedition against the northwestern Indians, Washington faced a new threat to federal authority in western Pennsylvania. In 1790, Secretary of the Treasury Alexander Hamilton had convinced Congress to approve his revenue program to put the new federal government on a sound financial footing. The legislation included an excise tax on distillers of alcoholic beverages, a measure that created severe problems for small farmers in western Pennsylvania. Unable to transport their surplus corn easily or otherwise preserve it, they distilled it into whiskey, which was then used as a form of currency in the barter economy of the frontier, where little actual cash circulated. These farmers also lacked the cash to pay the excise tax, and their protests escalated as federal officials became more insistent on payment of the tax. By 1794 the farmers had begun harassing excise collectors, shutting down the courts, and staging protest marches including one that brought seven thousand farmers into the streets of Pittsburgh. Resistance to the excise tax soon spread to the western counties of Maryland and Virginia.[12]

At first Washington was reluctant to act, but Hamilton, ever eager to demonstrate and expand the power of the federal government, convinced the president that unless the administration used force to uphold its authority, the Constitution would be meaningless. Washington agreed to call the militia of several states into federal service to suppress the rebellion, and took personal command of the army. Hamilton became second-in-command. Among the governors whom Washington contacted to obtain militia was Henry Lee. Denouncing the "lawless and outrageous conduct" of the rebels, Lee pledged to support the president. Lee joined the federal forces in Pennsylvania at the head of a force of Virginia militiamen, acting on his authority as commander-in-chief of his state's militia as well as under a federal commission as an officer of the so-called "Army of the Constitution." Hamilton was pleased to note on Lee's arrival that the Virginian was "all zeal."[13]

When the federal army marched into western Pennsylvania in the autumn, the Whiskey Rebellion evaporated. The troops faced no resistance. Several opponents of the excise tax were arrested, and twenty were brought to Philadelphia and tried for treason. Only two were convicted, and Washington pardoned both men. The president had left the army and returned to resume his duties early in the campaign, and other officers soon followed, leaving Lee in command. Lee originally maintained his headquarters at Fort Cumberland, but by November he had relocated to Pittsburgh. A challenge to federal authority had been suppressed without bloodshed, and supporters of the administration considered the campaign a noteworthy success. Lee was included among those receiving accolades for their participation; one observer noted that "there are no complaints of governor Lee having been inexorable or inhumane," and that President Washington praised Lee and the army for their "enlightened zeal for the constitution." However, when Lee returned to Virginia, he found that he had paid a high price for his service against the frontier rebels.[14]

The federal government's response to the Whiskey Rebellion increased the antagonism between Hamilton's Federalists and Jefferson's and Madison's Democratic-Republicans. Lee already disliked Jefferson, and had seized an opportunity to discredit him a year earlier. In August, Lee had written to Washington that a "very respectable gentleman" told him of a conversation the unidentified informant had with Jefferson in which the latter inquired whether the president was too attached to Great Britain and the monarchical principles of the British government. Lee asserted that "the conversation astonished me and is inexplicable to me as well as derogatory to your character." Washington dismissed Lee's concerns, but Jefferson and Madison believed that the president's response to the Whiskey Rebellion, guided by Hamilton, indicated that federal authority was becoming too extensive. Jefferson dismissed the whole operation in Pennsylvania with the sarcastic remark that "an insurrection was announced and proclaimed and armed against, and marched against, but could never be found." Madison harbored greater fears, warning that the Federalists were establishing a precedent for the use of the federal army to enforce the laws whenever they deemed it necessary.[15]

The Virginia legislature agreed with Jefferson and Madison, and expressed dissatisfaction with Lee's role in the rebellion. They first considered a vote of censure against Lee, but then decided that his decision to leave the state and join the federal army had constituted a voluntary relinquishment of his office. The legislature declared the governor's office vacant and elected a replacement. Lee was infuriated by the proceedings, but could do nothing to change the situation.[16]

After his service in the Whiskey Rebellion, Lee's military and political roles shrank. In 1798, during the Quasi-War with France (which was fought entirely at sea), President John Adams asked Congress for authority to create an army in case the fight with the French expanded into a land war. Congress approved, and called forth Washington from his retirement at Mount Vernon to assume command. In selecting subordinate officers, Secretary of War James McHenry proposed that Lee be commissioned a major general in the provisional army, a temporary rank rather than a permanent commission in the regular army. Lee accepted, and as in their past service during the War for Independence, he and Washington conferred on several matters relating to the new military force. The war never materialized, however, and in 1799 Lee ran for a seat in the U. S. House of Representatives. Washington was pleased at Lee's election, describing it as "grateful to my feelings." He hoped that Lee could help sustain the Federalists against the growing power of the Democratic-Republicans, who had been strengthened by the unpopularity of President Adams.[17]

It was during his single term in Congress that Lee delivered the best known speech of his career. On December 14th, 1799, George Washington died at Mount Vernon and Congress selected Lee to give the eulogy. Some four thousand mourners, including President and Mrs. John Adams, Alexander Hamilton, and a host of other dignitaries were gathered at the German Lutheran Church in Philadelphia on December 26th when Lee strode to the pulpit to deliver his address, which included a description of Washington in terms that have never been forgotten: "first in war; first in peace; and first in the hearts of his countrymen." The eulogy was widely praised, printed, and circulated throughout the United States in the form of a pamphlet. The U. S. Senate officially described Lee's address as "eloquent and impressive," while the House of Representatives issued their own expression of gratitude to the Virginia congressman. Lee's funeral oration for Washington marked the high point of his public life after the Revolution.[18]

*****

Lee's Financial Misfortunes

Since the end of the Revolutionary War Lee had experienced financial problems that seemed to increase with each passing year. In 1783 he owed money to his friend and fellow soldier, Colonel Otho Holland Williams of Maryland, prompting Lee to assure Williams on December 15th that he would "try to furnish the cash though [Lee's] disappointments are complicated." By the following April Lee still had not paid, and Williams pressed him for the money, insisting that he needed the funds to repay a debt of his own. Lee claimed that he had entrusted the payment to a mutual acquaintance, who had apparently not delivered the cash, and promised that he had "almost enough in hand" to make the payment in twelve days. Evidently Lee made good on his promise, because in 1791 he and Williams remained friendly and Williams told Lee that he had named his newborn son "Henry Lee Williams" because Lee's leadership during the war "left on my mind indelible impressions of gratitude and affection."[19]

Lee also sold part of his first wife's Stratford Hall estate to raise money. Matilda Lee inherited the remaining share of the plantation upon her mother's death in 1789, and by that time Lee had sold about 2,600 acres of the 6,595 that had comprised the property at the time of his marriage to Matilda. Shortly before her death in 1790, Matilda Lee, perhaps aware of her husband's lack of financial acumen, signed a deed of trust granting Stratford Hall and other property she owned under the management of her cousins Ludwell Lee and Richard Bland Lee until her children reached adulthood. Her husband, however, was granted permission to continue residing at the estate. Lee's father took similar measures to protect his own property from his son when he drew up his will. While Lee's mother and younger brothers received the bulk of Lee Hall and other family property, Lee himself was bequeathed only a small piece of land near the Lee Hall plantation and some undeveloped acreage in Kentucky.[20]

Lee's financial problems were rooted in his unshakable belief that he could make a fortune in land speculation, a belief that was shared by many in the early days of our Republic. His many ventures included the purchase of a tract of land at the falls of the Potomac River, which he named Matildaville in honor of his first wife. The property remained undeveloped and thus attracted no buyers. The results were similar for Lee's purchases of land in Kentucky, Pennsylvania, North Carolina, and Georgia, as well as elsewhere in Virginia. In 1797 Lee formed a partnership with Robert Morris to purchase land in the vicinity of Washington, D. C., the new federal capital that was being constructed. The plan came to naught: Lee lost his $40,000 investment and Morris went to jail. Another spectacular failure occurred when Lee purchased 300,000 acres of land in Virginia and sold it to a group of investors. The purchasers surveyed the land and found that the tract encompassed only 134,000 acres. Lee had been cheated in his purchase, and the investors who bought the land ceased making payments to him when they discovered that they had been misled about the size of the property. Lee tried to cover his losses by borrowing from his relatives, and often failed to repay them.[21]

Lee's irresponsible financial dealings also involved his friend and former commander, George Washington. In 1795, after purchasing some property in Kentucky from Lee, the president was disturbed to learn that Lee had apparently sold the same parcel to someone else. "To suspect Genl. Lee of fraud in this transaction I cannot," Washington wrote, "and, as it is almost improbable that it should be the result of forgetfulness, I conceive that the two sales cannot be for the same land." Washington believed that Lee had simply made a mistake when he sold the property. The two friends apparently resolved the matter, since four months afterward Washington sold Lee his share in the Dismal Swamp Company at a discounted price. However, Lee failed to make the promised payments and Washington began to exert pressure to collect the debt:

> "The period for payment of the second Installment of your Bond is past, and the first Installment is only partially complied with. … It Cannot be more unpleasant for you to hear, than for me to remind you of these things, but it is necessary for me to do so, and to express a hope that some vigorous measures are in train to fulfill your engagement with me."[22]

By September 1798, Washington struggled to find a way to extract some form of payments from Lee, offering to accept land "almost any where, or any thing productive, or unproductive, at what it would fetch in the market; provided the title is indisputable." When Lee offered to compensate Washington with lots in the new capital city, the former president found that the town lots were only half the size of standard city lots, but that Lee was valuing them at a higher price than full-sized lots. Washington declined the offer and instead suggested that Lee pay his debt with land near Harper's Ferry, or in Loudoun County, Virginia. "I would accept it in payment rather than make difficulties, or be involved in disputes," Washington wrote in a placating tone. Despite making efforts to collect the debts owed to him by Lee, the former president never succeeded.[23]

Lee's financial difficulties shattered his reputation. To partially satisfy his creditors, Lee sold as much of the family land in Westmoreland County as he could claim title to. His father-in-law, Charles Carter, changed his will in 1803 to prevent Lee from inheriting any of his property; all would be bequeathed to Ann and her children. In 1805 Nathaniel Pendleton, a lawyer in Alexandria, offered a $250 reward for Lee's arrest. Lee owed Pendleton $25,000.[24]

Lee spent the next several years trying to avoid or hold off his numerous creditors. He asked President Madison in 1808 to appoint him to an informal diplomatic post in the Portuguese colony of Brazil. Madison declined, and Lee approached his remaining friends and tried to sell them land. Given the record of his past financial dealings, it is not surprising that he found no buyers. On April 24th, 1809, he was imprisoned in Westmoreland County for debt. He was later transferred to the Spotsylvania County Jail, but even in prison, his creditors continued to harass him.

Nevertheless, he found time while in confinement to write his memoirs of the Revolution. Lee hoped that the publication and sale of his two-volume book would provide him with some financial relief. It did not, and in 1810 after almost a year in prison, Lee reluctantly admitted that he was insolvent, a legal measure similar to declaring bankruptcy. The admission allowed him to be released from prison, but his remaining assets were handed over to government officials for distribution among his creditors. Given the tangle of Lee's financial affairs, the task proved nearly insoluble.[25]

Ann Carter Lee and her children moved to Alexandria shortly after Lee's release from prison. The family survived on the charity of Ann's relatives. Lee joined them but his presence among the Carters was not welcome. They believed that he had neglected his wife Ann and his children, while Lee in turn blamed all of his misfortunes not on his own financial ineptitude, but on Thomas Jefferson. Lee seemed to think that had it not been for Jefferson and the Democratic-Republican triumph over the Federalists, he would have enjoyed a more successful postwar career.

In his memoirs, Lee had criticized Jefferson's performance as a wartime governor of Virginia. He also asserted that the former president had used his authority as commander-in-chief to fill the army's officer corps with loyal Democratic-Republicans, politicizing the army at the expense of more capable officers, notably Lee himself.

When President Jefferson imposed an embargo in response to the British ship *Leopard* firing on the U.S. ship *Chesapeake*, Lee published the pamphlet *Cursory Sketch of the Motives and Proceedings of the Party Which Sways the Affairs of the Union* in the fall of 1809 which claimed that "Jefferson rules by exiling from the public councils of the state and nation truth, honor and intelligence...." These attitudes may have influenced Lee's subsequent decision to travel to Baltimore and fight for the Federalist cause there.[26]

*****

Confrontation with the Baltimore Mob

Lee had not been reelected to Congress in 1800 because he continued to be identifed as a staunch Federalist in the public mind. This made his return to politics nearly impossible, given that Virginia and its two most prominent living sons, Jefferson and Madison, embodied the new Democratic-Republican political ascendancy that began when Jefferson was elected president in 1800. Yet Lee adhered to his principles, an attribute that nearly cost him his life shortly after the outbreak of the War of 1812 in June of that year. Like most Federalists, Lee opposed the war, and in July 1812 he traveled to Baltimore, Maryland, to assist his friend Alexander Hanson, the publisher of a Federalist newspaper, the *Federal Republican*, in a city dominated by Democratic-Republicans. Hanson had denounced the war in print and his political opponents responded by destroying the newspaper's office. Hanson had been forced to flee Baltimore, but returned on July 26th with several Federalist friends.[27]

The next day Hanson and some other Federalists began handing out new copies of the *Federalist Republican* on the streets of Baltimore. A mob gathered and forced Hanson, Lee, and their allies to take refuge in a house. After dark the crowd stormed the building, and the Federalists inside fired on them. Three people were wounded, one of whom later died. Soon the militia arrived on the scene, and Lee and his colleagues agreed to surrender and be placed in safe custody in the jail. Lee, Hanson, and the other Federalists were taken there on the morning of July 28th, but that night the militia was dismissed. The mob then stormed the unguarded building, and in the ensuing melee Lee was struck on the head with a club, had his nose slashed by a knife, and was badly beaten.

James Lingan, a Revolutionary War veteran and general in the Maryland militia, was beaten to death by this mob, an outrage that produced a public backlash. George Washington Parke Custis, step grandson of George Washington, offered the eulogy to a gathering so large that it had to be taken outdoors from St. John's Church in Rockville, Maryland. (Lingan's body was reinterred in Arlington National Cemetery in 1908).

Lee escaped death only by lying entirely motionless as members of the mob probed the bodies that were strewn in the street. One rioter poured hot wax into Lee's eye to search for signs of life. After the assault, he was treated by a doctor, then taken to York, Pennsylvania, for refuge. He could barely speak, and suffered from impaired vision even after he returned to Alexandria, Virginia, where he had moved in 1810, his wife and children having relocated there earlier. When Lee had recovered sufficiently to travel, he left the United States for the West Indies in May 1813, ostensibly to recover his health, but probably also to avoid his persistent creditors.[28]

*****

Caribbean Odyssey and Death

After leaving the United States in May 1813, Lee lived briefly on a series of islands in the West Indies. He claimed to be seeking the ideal place to recover his health, but none of the islands seemed to suit him. Among the places he resided for various periods were Cuba, Haiti, the Windward Islands, Guadeloupe, and Barbados. Beginning in October 1813 and continuing until March 1814, while Lee was at Barbados, he opened a correspondence with Sir George Beckwith, a British official. Lee hoped that he could somehow serve as an unofficial mediator and broker a peace between the United States and Britain, but his efforts failed. He later sailed to the Bahamas, where he realized that his health was beginning to fail. In 1818, at the age of sixty-two, Henry Lee finally boarded a vessel bound for the United States. At Lee's request, the ship's captain put him ashore on Cumberland Island, Georgia, on March 10th. He had decided to go there because his former friend and commander, Nathanael Greene, owned a plantation on the island. Greene had died in 1786, but his daughter still owned the plantation and took the old soldier into their home. Lee's condition steadily deteriorated, and he died on March 25th, 1818. Henry Lee, having triumphed in one battle after another against the British army, had at last succumbed to the physical and emotional toll that resulted from his political defeats, financial troubles, injuries, and illness. He was buried in Georgia with full military honors. In 1913 his body was relocated to the Lee Chapel at Washington and Lee University in Lexington, Virginia, where he lies next to his famous son, Robert E. Lee, who had been president of that institution after the Civil War.[29]

*****

Henry Lee: A Retrospective

Henry Lee was the subject of controversy throughout much of his own lifetime, and has remained so up to the present day as historians continue to debate his military career and his often tumultuous life after the Revolutionary War. Some chroniclers of Lee's life have judged him unfavorably, although George Washington's step-grandson insisted that future generations would find Lee's name "inscribed" atop the list of "illustrious men who flourished in the age of Washington." Other writers, however, have built a catalog of criticisms. Twentieth-century historian Paul C. Nagel concluded that Lee was "arrogant, vain, imperious, ambitious to a fault, and painfully sensitive. He quarreled easily." Nagel added that Lee believed that military operations were most likely to succeed only when he was personally in command, apparently overlooking Lee's successful operations with Francis Marion, Andrew Pickens, Otho Holland Williams, Anthony Wayne and others. Lee biographer Charles

Royster rendered a similar verdict, characterizing Lee as driven by a "single-minded ambition that he was unable to fulfill," and that he "was neither a leading nor a typical figure in war or politics or enterprise."[30]

Such judgments underrate Lee's exceptional record of military success during the Revolutionary War, which some early writers did make known. For example, in a new edition of his father's memoirs which was edited by Robert E. Lee and published in 1869, the famous son proudly described the older Lee's service in the early years of the War with a veteran soldier's understanding of the rigors of wartime service

> "he was always placed near the enemy, intrusted with the command of outposts, the superintendence of scouts, and that kind of service that required coolness, address, and enterprise."

The son's understanding of these operations came from experience. He had personally performed legendary scouting missions during the Mexican War, and he had commanded the flamboyant young cavalryman Jeb Stuart during the Civil War.[31]

Throughout most of the war Henry had influential relatives in the Continental Congress. He valued his own ideas, offered them freely to the most senior commanders and defended them vigorously. It is not surprising that his fellow officers would take note of a brash young officer in his early twenties, who was dressed and mounted in fine array, and who did not hesitate to capitalize on his personal access to the commanders of the army. It may appear to some that he found it difficult to separate his desire for victory in the struggle against Great Britain from his personal thirst for recognition. In spite of these potential sources of contention, Lee was respected by his fellow Continental officers sufficiently to be selected after the War as one of Virginia's representatives to the founding national meeting of the Society of the Cincinnati.

In spite of some troublesome relationships in the Army, Lee's wartime service shows that he could and did cooperate effectively with many fellow officers, and that his cooperation produced achievements on the battlefield that played an important role in winning American independence.

Lee's relationship with George Washington indicates that he could be a dutiful subordinate, following orders, accepting advice, and learning from his commander. The two cooperated effectively throughout the time that Lee served in the northern theater, and Washington handled Lee with the ideal balance of control and latitude that enabled Lee to excel. When on occasion the general found it necessary to correct Lee for some mistake, Lee accepted the criticism and did not allow it to impair his relationship with the commander-in-chief. The fact that the two men were longtime friends undoubtedly influenced their interaction and gave Washington insights into Lee's personality that enabled him to use the ambitious young cavalryman in the most appropriate manner. While serving under Washington, Lee distinguished himself with his raids to supply the Continental Army at Valley Forge during the winter of 1777-1778, his valorous and successful stand against great odds at Spread Eagle Tavern, and his raid on Paulus Hook.

Washington, however, was not the only officer with whom Lee interacted effectively. Lee played a key role in Anthony Wayne's successful assault on Stony Point, and unlike several other officers involved in the operation, did not complain when Wayne failed to acknowledge his contribution in his official report. In addition, Lee willingly submitted to Francis Marion's authority in South Carolina, allowing the two officers to cooperate in the capture of several critical British outposts. Lee and Andrew Pickens likewise formed a highly successful team in their campaigns in Georgia and the Carolinas. In Lee's final military operation, the abortive attack on Johns Island, he did not challenge Nathanael Greene's decision to place Lt. Col. John Laurens in overall charge of the attack; instead, Lee graciously accepted the situation.

As these examples indicate, Lee was not constantly engaged in quarrels with fellow officers. On the contrary, he had no difficulty in cooperating with, or acting as a subordinate to, officers he deemed worthy of their positions. All of the officers who were on good terms with Lee: Washington, Greene, the Marquis de Lafayette, Wayne, Marion, Pickens, and John Laurens, were bold, enterprising, and extremely capable. These were hallmarks of Lee's own leadership and therefore he had no problem working with men who shared his attitude toward military leadership. The officers with whom he quarreled were those who quibbled over rank, sought to enhance their own reputations by criticizing the achievements of others, and in Lee's eyes lacked the true merit that qualified them for command. All of those elements were apparent among some of Lee's critics during his trial by court-martial for his actions at Paulus Hook.

Lee's relationship with Nathanael Greene was more complex, deteriorating over time from friendship and trust to anger and unhappiness as Lee's military service neared its end. Until the Battle of Eutaw Springs in September 1781, the two men were close, and Greene clearly respected and trusted Lee. After the battle, Lee complained that Greene failed to give him appropriate credit for his performance, an accusation that Greene denied. Yet the two men may not have really understood the true source of Lee's dissatisfaction. Lee was unquestionably distressed by Greene's battle report that accurately stated that the Legion cavalry had been "baffled in an attempt upon the right," but Greene had also mentioned Lee's personal performance on the battlefield favorably in his official report to Congress.[32]

Part of Lee's unhappiness after the Battle of Eutaw Springs may have been based less on receiving credit for what he and his command did during the battle than with being recognized for having proposed the strategy that led to the engagement. For weeks before the battle, Lee had coaxed and cajoled Greene into moving against the British army, pointing out the great opportunity that lay before the American commander, and finally convinced the general to undertake the operation. Greene's report did not credit Lee for originating the plan, and that, along with criticism from some of Lee's fellow officers about his actions on the field at Eutaw Springs, may have been the source of the Legion commander's frustration.

However, his performance at the battles of Guilford Courthouse and Eutaw Springs has been criticized by some writers. It is clear that Lee was superb at partisan warfare, which required him to act apart from the main army to provide a screening force, gather intelligence and strike the enemy at vulnerable points. His skills shone brightly when he engaged in these types of activities, but his performance in the two set-piece battles has been questioned.

At Guilford Courthouse, when he departed with his Legion for what he believed was his assigned position at the left of the third Continental line, the British cavalry attacked a contingent of Virginia riflemen that was left behind, and some later writers have faulted Lee for this, although he seems to have acted with hard military logic and good battlefield judgment. At Eutaw Springs, the Legion cavalry was not in position to make a decisive charge when Greene wanted it to attack, although Lee's personal performance on that field received the strongest praise from the American commander.

One astute observer realized that Lee became involved in these controversial situations because he had complete authorization to roam the battlefield and use his own judgment on where he would operate. This approach was unlike most of his fellow officers, particularly those in the infantry, who were typically assigned a spot in the line and expected to stand with their unit. Lt. Col. John Eager Howard, the outstanding Maryland officer who has been called "one of the finest regimental commanders in American history," told historian William Johnson in 1808 that Lee "was considered as priviledged to act as he thought proper." If, as Howard asserted, Washington and Greene had given Lee the latitude to act as he saw fit, neither those generals nor any other officer could complain if Lee acted with the discretion allowed him, even if his decisions sometimes drew him to what he thought was the decisive point, but which in fact took him away from places where he could have made a greater impact.[33]

When viewed in its entirety, and in appropriate context, Lee's military record emerges as among the best achieved by any officer of comparable rank during the Revolution. He earns additional merit for the care with which he equipped and led the soldiers of his Legion. No other American cavalry regiment or legion can match the accomplishments of Lee's Legion, and none were better at withstanding the fury of battle against their much-feared counterpart, Lt. Col. Banastre Tarleton's British Legion. Lee's success in neutralizing the British Legion's vaunted dragoons was a major factor in American success in the southern campaign.

On several occasions Lee demonstrated a volatile temperament that injured his reputation. His orders to behead an American deserter, to give no quarter to British Legion prisoners during a skirmish, and his threats to hang the commander of Fort Watson for making what Lee judged was an unnecessarily long resistance, indicate that Lee sometimes let his anger get the better of him. On the other hand, the hated loyalist officer Thomas Brown had unusual praise for his treatment by Lee after his capture in Augusta. "From Colonel Lee, who commanded the Continental Legion, a gentleman of the most honourable and liberal sentiments, and from his officers, the King's troops, experienced every security and attention....Colonel Lee and his officers exerted themselves in uncommon degree, and took every possible precaution to protect the prisoners from violence."[34]

That a young and aggressive Lee might have succumbed to combative instincts in some of these unfortunate incidents is very believable, however his treatment of Brown and others suggest that they were not the norm. Lee served almost continuously for more than five years, usually on the front lines, in near-constant contact with the enemy, therefore it is not surprising that the combination of danger, fatigue, privation, and the burden of command would occasionally lead to unfortunate outbursts. Every American commander, including Washington and Greene, sometimes showed their humanity by experiencing moments of anger and rage during the long and difficult war.

Lee's wartime achievements have also been belittled by some early historians who were at least partially motivated by political leanings which differed from Lee's. Thomas Jefferson, who had been Lee's political adversary for a generation, encouraged William Johnson, a Supreme Court Justice whom he had appointed, to write a history that would challenge Lee's memoir. Jefferson was delighted with Johnson's work, *Sketches of the Life and Correspondence of Nathanael Greene*, writing to Johnson that "Lee's fable you have put down" and noting that he was pleased to see "the Romance of Lee removed from the shelf of History to that of Fable."

Lee's memoir is a soldier's story, with front-line warriors as the heroes—men like Greene, Williams, Pickens, Marion, Kirkwood, and many others, including, of course, George Washington, men who wore the uniform and fought the fight with valor, skill and determination. Jefferson had no role in this main story line, and the part of Lee's memoir that particularly rankled him was Lee's criticism of his performance as Governor of Virginia during the war. He wanted to destroy Lee's credibility as a writer of history to preserve his own place in the Revolutionary story.[35]

In his effort to discredit Lee's description of the Battle of Eutaw Springs, Johnson cited Nathaniel Pendleton, an aide to Greene who had been commended for his performance in the battle, with the assertion that the narrative in Lee's memoir is inaccurate, an observation apparently not publicly stated until long after Lee's memoir had been published and after the cavalryman's death in 1818. Johnson was then delighted to present a source that he said would correct Lee's writing, stating that

> *"Fortunately, we have it in our power to quote the man who, we believe, never errs on the events which he describes. Colonel Otho Williams wrote a minute account of the occurrences of this battle, which our good fortune has thrown into our hands. And it has led to inquiries from Colonels Hampton, Polk, Howard, Watts and several others of the distinguished men of that affair, which have enabled us to submit the following account of it, with confidence, to our readers."*[36]

Johnson may not have known that Williams admired Lee's wartime service, and that the two men had developed an enduring friendship. Williams showed the depth of the relationship when he named a son Henry Lee Williams, "to perpetuate in my family the remembrance of that friendship which originated at a time when the test of merit could not be mistaken, when the exertions for liberty were most necessary, and when the arms of freemen were most effectual." Williams did not forget "the ardour, activity, and enterprise with which you (Lee) conducted the legion." Williams had died in 1794, his life tragically shortened by tuberculosis that he contracted while he was a prisoner of war after his capture at the Battle of Fort Washington in 1776; Lee had died in 1818. In their quest to have future histories contain a narrative more to their liking, Johnson and Jefferson ignored the mutual respect between two warriors who were no longer there to provide their first-hand remembrances, and who, in their youth, had shared the privations of life in the field, lived together in harm's way, and fought shoulder-to-shoulder against great odds to help win our country's independence. The bond of mutual respect between Williams and Lee was the type that only soldiers who have been in combat together can truly understand and appreciate.[37]

Lee had had a long and notable political career after the war as a Federalist congressman and Governor of Virginia who supported President Washington and vigorously supported having a stronger Federal goverment. So politically motivated writers scoured all available documents to find things to criticize in Lee's combat operations. Other writers seem to have found it difficult to separate the travails of his life after the war from his wartime record. He was also a land speculator who, after he had accumulated large losses, tried to correct the situation with foolish maneuvers that sometimes reeked of dishonesty. Family members were embarrassed by his situation, and initiated various legal maneuvers to protect their estates from his untrustworthy hand. He could not provide for his wife and family. However, he did provide instruction in ethics, literature, and financial dealings in letters that he wrote to his sons in the final years of his life. Maybe his most enduring legacy as a father is the asceticism and self-control that Robert E. Lee developed under the tutelage of his mother, based, at least in part, on his father as an example of what not to do.

Henry Lee's life began with great promise as a member of a respected and successful family of Viginians, early graduate of Princeton, and a war hero, but his later years brought defeat and tragedy. It is sometimes difficult in view of his financial problems to look back and see the young cavalry officer on whom Washington and Greene relied so heavily, who exercised independent command when he had barely entered his twenties, and who never shrank from battle even against great odds.

It appears that some writers may have considered the entire record and been affected by his late-in-life difficulties to discolor Lee's early military accomplishments. A twentieth century writer, presumably reviewing all available documents over two hundred years after the end of the war, concluded that success in military operations "appeared to depend on whether Harry and only Harry was in charge."

By contrast, Lee's comrade-in-arms, Otho Holland Williams, wrote a few short years after the war that "the readiness with which you aided all my endeavors and the soldierly sympathy, which, in the most critical exigencies, you felt and expressed for me, as the responsible officer, left on my mind indelible impressions of gratitude and affection."[38]

One writer who looked back respectfully on Harry Lee's military service was Robert E. Lee, his famous son who commanded the Confederate Army of Northern Virginia during the Civil War. After that war, he chose, after realizing he couldn't write his own, to spend many hours reviewing his father's life and military record, and issued a new edition of the older Lee's memoirs. Robert E. Lee was deeply proud of his father's contributions to the winning of American independence. Among the many accolades which Robert reproduced in the new version of the memoirs was a letter from George Washington to the President of Congress on October 11th, 1780.

"Major Lee has rendered such distinguished services, possesses so many talents for commanding a corps of this nature, and deserves so much credit for the perfection in which he has kept his corps as well as for the handsome exploits he has performed..." [39]

Throughout the war, George Washington struggled to find capable subordinates who could help him lead American forces to victory. In elevating Henry Lee to command of the Legion, he had found exactly the type of officer he sought, and Lee more than repaid the general's confidence with his critical contributions to winning American independence. Washington reiterated his great confidence in Lee when the Legion was ordered to the Southern Theater: "I believe it will be found very useful. The corps itself is an excellent one and the officer at the head of it has great resources of genius." [40]

The commander-in-chief himself served over eight years in this war, sharing camp life and combat operations with his men from the very outset until the final treaty of peace. He had a deep appreciation for those who served with him, and he had a soldier's innate respect for performance in combat. Washington also understood that the uncertainties of war sometimes result in abject failure. Having experienced a humbling defeat himself as a twenty-two-year-old commander at the surrender of Fort Necessity during the French and Indian War, he sustained his deserving officers through hard times. For example, when he continued to rely on the judgment of Nathanael Greene after his poor decisions at Fort Washington in 1776, Washington understood that the "fortunes of war" can have an unanticipated effect on the finest soldiers.

Henry Lee's performance during the Revolutionary War was not flawless, but he was in the saddle for over six long years, and much of that time was spent in the face of the enemy. He developed and commanded an elite unit, which followed him loyally through the toughest front-line trials, and which relentlessly served the demanding needs of Washington and Greene for rapid movement, intelligence gathering, and hard-hitting combat efficiency. The brash and well-educated young Virginian could exude strong self-confidence that could annoy some of his peers and older officers, but his effective partnerships with proven combat leaders such as Francis Marion, Andrew Pickens, and Otho Holland Williams dispel any notion that he was consumed by his own interests. He had driving ambition, but it was one that sought distinction for soldierly acts in the face of the enemy.

When George Washington was seeking a commander for the American Army during the Whiskey Rebellion, he wrote to Henry Lee that "I conceived few men were better qualified for such a command than you." This is the treasured testimony of one front-line soldier to another, and a lasting tribute to the Revolutionary War service of the bold young cavalryman who commanded Lee's Legion.[41]

1   Royster, *Light-Horse Harry Lee,* 57; Nagel, 163-164.
2   Royster, *Light-Horse Harry Lee,* 58; "Society of the Cincinnati," author unknown, *William and Mary Quarterly,* Vol. 9, No. 3 (Jan. 1901), 192-193;Edgar Erskine Hume, "Light-Horse Harry and His Fellow Members of the Cincinnati," William and Mary Quarterly, Second Series, Vol. 15, No. 3 (July 1935), 275.
3   Chernow, 497-498.
4   Hume, "Light-Horse Harry," 276; Journals of the Continental Congress, Feb. 1, 1786; Nagel, 136.
5   Hume, "Light-Horse Harry," 276; Royster, *Light-Horse Harry Lee,* 96-97, 99; Nagel, 169.
6   Nagel, 168.
7   Nagel, 165, 176; Royster, *Light-Horse Harry Lee,* 134; Hume, "Light-Horse Harry," 277; Lee to Washington, Apr. 29, 1783, in Jared Sparks, editor, *The Writings of George Washington,* Vol. 10 (Boston, MA: American Stationers' Co., 1837), 344 (quotation).
8   Washington to Lee, May 6, 1793, Washington Papers, LOC (quotations); Nagel, 175.
9   Royster, *Light-Horse Harry Lee,* 98 (quotation)
10 Gordon S. Wood, *Empire of Liberty: A History of the Early Republic, 1789-1815* (New York: Oxford University Press, 2009), 129-130; Lee, *Memoirs,* 44-45 (quotations).
11 Washington, "Opinion of the General Officers," Mar. 9, 1792, Washington Papers, UVA (quotations); Washington to Lee, June 30, 1792, Washington Papers, LOC (quotation); Wood, 130-131.
12 Wood, 134-136.
13 Wood, 136-137; Lee to Washington, Aug. 26, 1794, Washington Papers, LOC (quotation); Royster, *Light-Horse Harry Lee,* 130-131 (quotation).
14 Wood, 138; Royster, *Light-Horse Harry Lee,* 133 (quotation); Washington to Lee, Oct. 20, 1794, Washington Papers, LOC (quotation). For a more detailed examination of Lee's time in command, see Leland D. Baldwin, editor, "Orders Issued by General Henry Lee During the Campaign Against the Whiskey Insurrectionists," *Western Pennsylvania Historical Magazine,* Vol. 19, No. 2 (June 1936), 79-111.
15 Lee to Washington, Aug. 26, 1794 (quotation), Washington to Lee, Aug. 26, 1794, Washington Papers, LOC; Wood, 138 (quotation).
16 Nagel, 176.
17 Wood, 245; James McHenry to Washington, July 18, 1798; Journal of the Senate, July 18 and 19, 1798; Washington, Memorandum, Oct. 15, 1798; Washington to Bushrod Washington, May 5, 1799, Washington Papers, LOC (quotation).
18 Gerald E. Kahler, *The Long Farewell: Americans Mourn the Death of George Washington* (Charlottesville: University of Virginia Press, 2008), 32-34; Journal of the Senate, Dec. 27, 1799; Journal of the House of Representatives, Dec. 27, 1799.
19 Lee to Williams, Dec. 15, 1783 (quotation), Apr. 17, 1784 (quotation), Williams to Lee, Apr. 10, 1784, Jan. 30, 1792 (quotation), Otho Holland Williams Papers, Maryland Historical Society, Baltimore.
20 Nagel, 165, 167.
21 Nagel, 165-167; Royster, *Light-Horse Harry Lee,* 172-174.
22 Washington to George Lewis, July 27, 1795 (quotation), Washington to Dismal Swamp Company, Nov. 16, 1795, Washington to Lee, Jan. 25, 1798 (quotation), Washington Papers, LOC; Royster, *Light-Horse Harry Lee,* 177.
23 Washington to Lee, Sept. 29, 1798 (quotation), Nov. 4, 1798 (quotation), Washington Papers, LOC.
24 Nagel, 166 (quotation), 178, 179.
25 Royster, *Light-Horse Harry Lee,* 181-185; Nagel, 181.
26 Royster, *Light-Horse Harry Lee,* 195-196; Nagel, 181-182; Emory M. Thomas, *Robert E. Lee, A Biography, (New York: W. W. Norton, 1994).* 1 (quotation)
27 Nagel, 182; Royster, *Light-Horse Harry Lee,* 156-157 (quotation).
28 Royster, *Light-Horse Harry Lee,* 159-167; Nagel, 181, 182; James E. Peters, *Arlington National Cemetery; Shrine to America,* (Bethesday, MD: Woodbine House, 2008) 127, 128.
29 Royster, *Light-Horse Harry Lee,* 3-7, 247; Nagel, 182-184. For Lee's negotiations with Beckwith, see

"Major-General Henry Lee and Lieutenant-General Sir George Beckwith on Peace in 1813," *American Historical Review*, Vol. 32, No. 2 (Jan. 1927), 284-292; Nagel, 184.

30 Custis, 363 (quotation); Nagel, 162 (quotation); Royster, *Light-Horse Harry Lee*, 16 (quotation), 241 (quotation).

31 Lee, *Memoirs*, 16 (quotation).

32 Greene to Thomas McKean, President of the Continental Congress, September 11, 1781, in Conrad, editor, *Papers of Greene*, 9:332 (quotation).

33 Piecuch and Beakes, *Cool Deliberate Courage*, 4 (quotation); "Howard's Notes on Johnson," 1808, Henry Lee Papers, Library of Virginia (quotation).

34 Thomas Brown to David Ramsey, Dec. 25, 1786, in George White, editor *The Historical Collections of Georgia* (New York: Pudney & Russell, 1855), 618 (quotation).

35 Thomas Jefferson to William Johnson, October 22, 1822. Jefferson Papers. LOC (cited in Royster, *Light-Horse Harry Lee*, 218, 219), (quotations).

36 William Johnson, *Sketches of the Life and Correspondence of Nathanael Greene, Major General of the Armies of the United States in the War of the Revolution*, 2 vols. (Charleston, SC: A. E. Miller, 1822), 2:221.

37 Otho Holland Williams to Henry Lee, (c. December 1791 – February 1792), in Henry Lee, IV, *Remarks Historical and Critical on Johnson's Life of Greene*, 125, 126, cited in Royster, *Light-Horse Harry Lee*, 193 (quotations).

38 Nagel, 161 (quotation); Otho Holland Williams to Henry Lee, (c. December 1791 – February 1792), in Henry Lee, IV, *Remarks Historical and Critical on Johnson's Life of Greene*, 126, (quotation).

39 Lee, *Memoirs*, 29 (quotation).

40 Washington to John Mathews, Oct. 23, 1780, Washington Papers, LOC.

41 Washington to Lee, June 30, 1792, Washington Papers, LOC (quotation).

APPENDIX

THE LEES OF VIRGINIA

Henry "Light-Horse Harry" Lee was not the only member of his family, which had been prominent in Virginia for four generations, to become a champion of colonial liberty. His older cousin, Richard Henry Lee, had been publicly advocating for American rights in the Virginia legislature since 1765, when the British Parliament first attempted to impose direct taxes on its American colonies by passing the Stamp Act. The Lees' opposition to British policy marked a significant shift in the family's political principles, because the Lees had achieved their position at the pinnacle of Virginia society, at least indirectly, through the auspices of the royal government via the patronage of the colony's governors.[1]

The first Lee to settle in Virginia was Richard Lee, who arrived at Jamestown in 1639 or 1640. Born in Worcestershire, England, in 1618, Richard Lee was the son of John Lee, a cloth merchant, and Jane Hancock Lee, whose family pursued a similar occupation in the town of Twining. Despite his rather humble origins, Richard Lee managed to gain the attention of Sir Francis Wyatt. When King Charles I appointed Wyatt royal governor of Virginia in 1639, Wyatt brought Lee with him. Upon their arrival in the colony, Wyatt appointed Lee clerk of the quarter court.[2]

Shortly after settling at Jamestown, Lee improved his position by marrying Anne Constable, whose family had solid political connections in England. Therefore, although Governor Wyatt fell into disfavor with the king and was replaced as governor by Sir William Berkeley in 1642, Lee retained his office. Lee evidently impressed the new governor with his efficiency, since Berkeley appointed him to be attorney general of Virginia in 1643. Lee's continued rise to prominence was meteoric. By the time of his death in 1664 he had held elected office as a representative in the colony's House of Burgesses and the appointed offices of sheriff, secretary of state, militia colonel, and a member of the governor's executive council.[3]

Lee's financial fortune increased accordingly. He obtained land grants from the colonial government, and established a plantation north of the York River that was worked by nearly forty indentured servants. In addition to farming, Lee dabbled in trade with the neighboring Powhatan Indians and invested in a ship. The profits were used to acquire more indentured servants and slaves to expand his tobacco production. The Lees established their residence at Dividing Creek in Northumberland County, on the Chesapeake Bay, where their estate encompassed 1,900 acres. Lee acquired an additional 6,600 acres along the Potomac River, other land in Maryland, and even an estate in Stratford-Langton in England, near London. When he died on March 1st, 1664, the English property was sold according to his instructions; the proceeds and his 15,000 acres of American land, slaves, and livestock were divided among his widow and children.[4]

Richard and Anne Lee's second son, Richard, was pursuing his education in England at the time of his father's death and remained there, supported by his share from the sale of the Stratford-Langton estate. The studious Richard Lee II, who had been born in 1647 on the family plantation in Gloucester County, Virginia, made a strong impression on his English acquaintances. According to Richard Lee II's grandson, William, Richard "was so clever that some great men offered to promote him to the highest dignities in the [Anglican] Church if his Father would let him stay in England." However, after completing his studies Richard Lee II returned to Virginia to help manage the family properties.[5]

Richard Lee settled on the family's Paradise Plantation south of the Pianketank River in Gloucester County, the first land that his father had been granted in Virginia. While managing the operations of the property, he maintained his interest in academic study, accumulating a "celebrated" library, reading extensively, and often taking notes "in Greek, Hebrew, or Latin." He continued to lead a reclusive life until the death of his older brother John in 1673. With the role of family patriarch thus thrust upon him, Richard Lee moved to John's plantation at Machodoc, just inland from the Potomac River in Northumberland County. A year later he married Laetitia (Lettice) Corbin, whose father Henry owned a neighboring plantation. Then, following in his father's footsteps, he won election to the House of Burgesses. In 1676 he was appointed to the governor's council.[6]

Lee's appointment to the council came at an inauspicious time. His fellow councilor Nathaniel Bacon, recently arrived from England, used the poor state of Virginia's economy and the fear of Indian attack to assail Governor Berkeley's conciliatory Indian policy. Whipping poor Virginians into a frenzy of rage, Bacon assembled an armed force and slaughtered a number of peaceful Indians before turning on the governor. Lee, an outspoken supporter of Berkeley, was captured by Bacon's followers and held prisoner for almost two months at Middle Plantation (Williamsburg) while Bacon and his followers burned Jamestown and forced Berkeley and his allies to flee. Bacon, however, died in October 1676 and the rebellion collapsed. Although Berkeley was recalled to England and dismissed from office for failing to keep order, Lee retained his position on the council.[7]

Lee's political role expanded in the years after Bacon's Rebellion as he was appointed to additional offices, including justice of the peace, colonel of the Westmoreland County militia, and collector of revenue for Virginia's Potomac

River ports.[8]

When Parliament deposed King James II in 1688 and established a constitutional monarchy under King William III and Queen Mary, who was James II's daughter, Richard refused to swear allegiance to the new rulers. He evidently believed that royal authority was absolute and that Parliament had exceeded its constitutional authority by removing James from the throne. The English government responded to Lee's intransigence by dismissing him from the council and his collector's post, but restored him to both positions after he played a key role in quelling unrest in Virginia over payment of quitrents to the Fairfax family.[9]

At the end of the seventeenth century, Lee retired from public life, living quietly at Machodoc with Lettice. She died in 1706, and Lee remained at the plantation, engaged in his studies, until his death in 1714. Two years earlier, Virginia Governor Alexander Spotswood had praised Lee as "a gentleman of as fair [a] character as any in the country for his exact justice, honesty and … loyalty. In all the stations wherein he has served in this government, he has behaved himself with great integrity."[10]

During their marriage Richard and "Lettice" Lee had six children: five sons and a daughter. The youngest child, Henry, was born in 1691. Since inheritance laws of that era sought to preserve estates by favoring the older children, Henry received a relatively small legacy consisting of some land adjacent to the Machodoc plantation along with slaves and horses. He continued to live at the Machodoc house with his older brother, Thomas. The brothers enjoyed a close relationship, and they jointly invested in land along the upper Potomac River. In 1722 Henry married Mary Bland, daughter of another prominent Virginia family and related to two others, the Randolphs and Bennetts. The couple built their own home, Lee Hall, on Henry's property. Like his father and grandfather, Henry Lee became active in politics; "every local office was held by Henry at some point, except that of burgess." Henry also took over his father's duties as collector of revenue, which Governor Spotswood had first assigned to Thomas Lee, who later transferred the position to his younger brother.[11]

By the time of Henry Lee's death in 1747, Lee Hall had become one of the finest plantations in Virginia. Henry Lee specified in his will that his wife would own the house until her death, and Mary Bland Lee remained there as mistress of the plantation until 1764, whereupon in accordance with her husband's will their second son, Richard Lee, inherited the estate. At the time of Henry Lee's death his third son, Henry, Jr., was attending the College of William and Mary. He and his younger sister Laetitia, who like her grandmother was called Lettice, eventually left Lee Hall and established their own households.[12]

After graduating from college, Henry Lee, Jr., pursued a career as a lawyer in Westmoreland County on the Potomac River west of the Machodoc plantation. On December 1st, 1753, he married Lucy Grymes, "a famous beauty" whose parents, like Lee's, were members of Virginia's gentry. Lucy's mother, Frances Jenings Grymes, was the daughter of the royal governor, Edmund Jenings, and Frances Corbin, the sister of Laetitia Corbin Lee, Richard Lee II's first wife. Henry Lee, Jr., and Lucy chose in 1754 to settle on Corbin land that had passed to the Lees as part of Laetitia Corbin Lee's dowry, and that Henry Lee, Jr., had inherited from his father. The two-thousand-acre estate in Prince William County (west of the confluence of the Potomac and Occoquan rivers) became the site of Leesylvania, the couple's new plantation home on the Potomac. Lee's inheritance "also included twenty slaves" and "much livestock" to get the plantation operating. In addition, Lee had inherited almost 3,500 acres farther up the Potomac in Fairfax County.[13]

Henry and Lucy Grymes Lee constructed their new home on a "high, rocky point of land jutting out into the Potomac River" that they called "Freestone." The red brick house stood "two and a half stories high … with a huge chimney on either side. Two-story porches … were on the front and rear entrances. A succession of terraces descended" to the river. Despite its elegance, historian Ethel Armes observed that compared to the luxurious homes of other gentry planters, the Leesylvania house seemed to be no more than "a comfortable farm house."[14]

Characteristically, Henry Lee, Jr., became involved in local politics. He was elected to the House of Burgesses, where he served for some two decades, and was appointed colonel of the Prince William County militia and presiding justice of his court district. It was in these various capacities that Lee became acquainted with one of his neighbors, an ambitious young man who had not only once cast an eager eye on the beautiful and as yet unmarried Lucy Grymes, but also lived about twenty miles north of Leesylvania on land that had once belonged to the first Richard Lee. This neighbor, George Washington, soon became a good friend of Henry Lee, Jr., and would develop a close connection with his son, Henry Lee III, during the younger Lee's childhood that would grow into an effective military partnership during the Revolution.[15]

Just over two years after her marriage to Henry Lee, Jr., Lucy Grymes Lee bore their first child, Henry Lee III, on January 29th, 1756. After completing his military service in the Revolutionary War, Henry Lee III married Matilda Ludwell in 1782. The marriage produced three children, two of whom survived to adulthood. Three years after Matilda Lee's death in 1790, Henry Lee married again. He and his second wife, Ann Hill Carter, had five children, the most famous of whom was Robert E. Lee, born in 1807. Like his father, Robert E. Lee pursued a military career and served as a Confederate general in the Civil War, earning a reputation as the most brilliant and capable officer in that conflict.[16]

1   C. G. Lee, *Chronicle*, 136.
2   Nagel, 8-9.
3   Nagel, 9-10.
4   Nagel, 9, 12-16.
5   Nagel, 16, 21; Armes, 18 (quotation).
6   C. G. Lee, *Chronicle*, 21, 23; Nagel, 22; Armes, 18 (quotation).
7   Nagel, 24-25; C. G. Lee, *Chronicle*, 251-252.
8   Nagel, 26.
9   Nagel, 26. Quitrents were a relic of the feudal era, and were financial payments made to a landowner by tenants or to a land grantor by property owners in lieu of performing required personal services. The Fairfax family unsuccessfully attempted to revive this medieval practice by demanding quitrent payments from tenants on their property and from landowners who had acquired their holdings from the Fairfax family.
10 Nagel, 27, 29; Armes, 19 (quotation).
11 Nagel, 31-32, 34, 36, 40-41 (quotation); Armes, 39; C. G. Lee, *Chronicle*, 85.
12 Nagel, 46, 50.
13 Nagel, 158-159.
14 Armes, 226, 228.
15 Nagel, 13, 159.
16 Nagel, frontispiece, 164; Lee, *Memoirs*, 15.

BIBLIOGRAPHY

Primary Sources – Manuscripts

Alexander, William (Lord Stirling). Papers. New-York Historical Society, New York, NY.

Barnett, Thomas. Pension Application S8041, May 28, 1833. National Archives, Washington, DC (hereafter NA).

Boyd, Thomas. Pension Application S17286, Aug. 20, 1833. NA.

Burke, Thomas. Papers. North Carolina State Archives, Raleigh.

Clenney, William. Pension Application S32182, Nov. 16, 1839. NA.

Clinton, Sir Henry. Papers. William L. Clements Library, University of Michigan, Ann Arbor.

Cockerham, David. Pension Application S8240, Aug. 15, 1832. NA.

Eakin, Samuel. Pension Application S3317, Oct. 16, 1832. NA.

Efland, John. Pension Application S6814, Aug. 18, 1832. NA.

Falls, William. Pension Application S6834, Nov. 21, 1832. NA.

Findley, Samuel. Pension Application R14168, Nov. 19, 1836. NA.

Gaulden, William. Pension Application W7509, April 15, 1833. NA.

Geren, Solomon. Pension Application W80, Sept. 15, 1832, NA.

Graham, Joseph. Pension Application S6937, Oct. 30, 1832. NA.

Hackney, Joseph. Pension Application S6973, Sept. 19, 1832. NA.

Hall, Moses. Pension Application W10105, Nov. 7, 1835. NA.

Harris, Jonathan. Pension Application W4979, Aug. 16, 1833. NA.

Higdon, Philip. Pension Application S10839, Dec. 12, 1834. NA.

Journal of the U. S. House of Representatives. Library of Congress, Washington, DC.

Journal of the U. S. Senate. Library of Congress, Washington, DC.

Journals of the Continental Congress. Library of Congress, Washington, DC.

Lee Family. Papers. Virginia Historical Society, Richmond.

Lee, Henry. Letter, 22957. Library of Virginia, Richmond.

--------------. Papers. Library of Virginia, Richmond.

--------------. Papers. Virginia Historical Society, Richmond.

Lenoir, William. Pension Application S7137, May 1, 1833. NA.

Lofton, Thomas. Pension Application S17114, Dec. 10, 1832. NA.

Luckey, Robert. Pension Application W4368, Oct. 30, 1832. NA.

McConnell, Manuel. Pension Application S2773, Sept. 18, 1832. NA.

Miles, Thomas. Pension Application R7168, May 27, 1833. NA.

Moore, William. Pension Application S183, Aug. 20, 1820. NA.

Rocky Mount Collection. DuPont Library, Stratford Hall, Virginia.

Rutledge, William. Pension Application S4171, Sept. 25, 1832. NA.

Smith, Daniel. Pension Application S7550, Dec. 28, 1835. NA.

Vandiver, Matthew. Pension Application S9500, Feb. 22, 1833. NA.

Washington, George. Letters. Library of Virginia, Richmond.
------------. Papers. Library of Congress, Washington, DC.

------------. Papers. University of Virginia, Charlottesville.

Williams, Otho Holland. Papers. Maryland Historical Society, Baltimore.

Primary Sources – Published

Adams, John, et al. *Founding Families: Digital Editions of the Winthrops and the Adamses.* C. James Taylor, editor. Boston: Massachusetts Historical Society, 2007.

Baldwin, Leland D., editor, "Orders Issued by General Henry Lee During the Campaign Against the Whiskey Insurrectionists." *Western Pennsylvania Historical Magazine*, Vol. 19, No. 2 (June 1936), 79-111.

Bland, Theodorick. *The Bland Papers: Being a Selection from the Manuscripts of Colonel Theodorick Bland, Jr. of Prince George County, Virginia.* Charles Campbell, editor. Vol. 1. Petersburg, VA: Edmund & Julian C. Ruffin, 1840.

Clinton, Sir Henry. *The American Rebellion: Sir Henry Clinton's Narrative of His Campaigns, 1775-1782, with an Appendix of Original Documents.* William B. Willcox, editor. New Haven, CT: Yale University Press, 1954.

Commager, Henry Steele, and Richard B. Morris, editors. *The Spirit of Seventy-Six: The Story of the American Revolution as Told by Its Participants.* New York: Harper & Row, 1967.

Cornwallis, Charles, Earl. *The Cornwallis Papers: The Campaigns of 1780 and 1781 in the Southern Theatre of the American Revolutionary War.* Ed. Ian Saberton. 6 Vols. Uckfield, East Sussex, UK: Naval & Military Press, 2010.

Gibbes, Robert W., editor. *Documentary History of the American Revolution, consisting of Letters and Papers relating to the Contest for Liberty Chiefly in South Carolina*, Vol. 3. New York: Appleton, 1857.

Greene, Nathanael. *The Papers of General Nathanael Greene*. Richard K. Showman, Dennis M. Conrad, and Roger N. Parks, editors. 13 Vols. Chapel Hill: University of North Carolina Press, 1976-2005.

Hamilton, Alexander. *The Papers of Alexander Hamilton*, Vol. 2. Harold C. Syrett, editor. New York: Columbia University Press, 1961.

James, William Dobein. *A Sketch of the Life of Brig. Gen. Francis Marion and a History of his Brigade from Its Rise in June 1780 until Disbanded in December 1782*. Marietta, GA: Continental Book Co., 1948.

Journals of the Continental Congress. Worthington Chauncey Ford, editor. Vols. 2, 7, 10, 11, 14, 18, 22. Washington, DC: US Government Printing Office, 1905.

Journals of the House of Burgesses of Virginia, 1770-1772. John Kennedy Pendleton, editor. Vol. 12. Richmond: Virginia State Library, 1906.

Lamb, Roger. *An Original and Authentic Journal of Occurrences during the Late American War from Its Commencement to the Year 1783*. Dublin, Ireland: Wilkinson & Courtney, 1809.

Lee, Henry. "Henry Lee on the Southern Campaign." George F. Scheer, editor. *Virginia Magazine of History and Biography*, Vol. 51, No. 2 (Apr. 1943),141-150.

----------. Letter to George Washington, Aug. 22, 1779, http:// secondvirginia.wordpress.com/2010/08/19/battle-of-paulus-hook/. Accessed Jan. 16, 2012.

Lee, Henry. "Letters of General Henry Lee." *Virginia Magazine of History and Biography*, Vol. 6, No. 2 (Oct. 1898), 153-158.

----------. "Major-General Henry Lee and Lieutenant-General Sir George Beckwith on Peace in 1813." *American Historical Review*, Vol. 32, No. 2 (Jan. 1927), 284-292.

----------. *Memoirs of the War in the Southern Department of the United States*. Robert E. Lee, editor. New York: Da Capo Press, 1998.

Proceedings of a General Court Martial, held at Brunswick, in the State of New Jersey, By the Order of His Excellency Gen. Washington, Commander-in-Chief of the Army of the United States of America, for the Trial of Major-General Lee. New York: J. M. Bradstreet & Sons, 1864.

Tarleton, Banastre. *A History of the Campaigns of 1780 and 1781, in the Southern Provinces of North America.* London: T. Cadell, 1787.

Taylor, Thomas. "A Georgia Loyalist's Perspective on the American Revolution: The Letters of Dr. Thomas Taylor." Ed. Robert S. Davis, Jr. *Georgia Historical Quarterly*, Vol. 81, No. 1 (Spring 1997), 118-138.

Washington, George. *The Diaries of George Washington.* Donald Jackson and Dorothy Twohig, editors. Vols. 2 and 3. Charlottesville: University Press of Virginia, 1978. vol. 2, 1976.

----------. *The Writings of George Washington*, Vol. 10. Jared Sparks, editor. Boston, MA: American Stationers' Co., 1837.

White, George, editor. *The Historical Collections of Georgia.* New York: Pudney & Russell, 1854.

Secondary Sources – Articles

Hall, Wilbur C. "Sergeant Champe's Adventure," *William & Mary Quarterly*, Second Series, Vol. 18, No. 3 (July 1938), 322-342.

Hume, Edgar Erskine. "Light-Horse Harry and His Fellow Members of the Cincinnati." *William and Mary Quarterly*, Second Series, Vol. 15, No. 3 (July 1935), 271-281.

McGroarty, William Buckner. "Captain Cameron and Sergeant Champe," *William & Mary Quarterly*, Second Series, Vol. 19, No. 1 (Jan. 1939), 49-54.

----------. "Sergeant John Champe and Certain of His Contemporaries," *William & Mary Quarterly*, Second Series, Vol. 17, No. 2 (April 1937), 145-175.

Sherman, William Thomas, "Lee's Legion Remembered: Profiles of the 2d Partisan Corps as Taken from Alexander Garden's Anecdotes." http://archive.org/details/LeesLegionRemembered

Rauch, Steven J. "'A Judicious and Gallant Defense': The Second Siege at Augusta, Georgia, 22 May-5 June 1781." *Southern Campaigns of the American Revolution*, Vol. 3, Nos. 6-8, June-Aug., 2006, 32-50.

-----------. "Prelude to Augusta: The Capture of Fort Galphin, 21 May 1781." *Southern Campaigns of the American Revolution*, Vol. 3, No. 5, May 2006, 22-25.

"Society of the Cincinnati." *William and Mary Quarterly*, Vol. 9, No. 3 (Jan. 1901), 192-194.

Woodruff, Caldwell. "Capt. Ferdinand O'Neal of Lee's Legion." *William & Mary Quarterly*, Second Series, Vol. 23, No. 3 (July 1943), 328-330.

Secondary Sources – Books

Armes, Ethel. *Stratford Hall: The Great House of the Lees*. Richmond, VA: Garrett and Massie, 1936.

Babits, Lawrence E., and Joshua B. Howard. *Long, Obstinate, and Bloody: The Battle of Guilford Courthouse*. Chapel Hill: University of North Carolina Press, 2009.

Bakeless, John. *Turncoats, Traitors and Heroes*. Philadelphia, PA: J. B. Lippincott, 1959.

Bass, Robert D. *Swamp Fox: The Life and Campaigns of General Francis Marion*. Orangeburg, SC: Sandlapper Publishing, 1974.

Billias, George Athan, editor. *George Washington's Generals and Opponents: Their Exploits and Leadership*. 2 Vols. New York: Da Capo Press, 1994.

Black, Jeremy. *War for America: The Fight for Independence, 1775-1783*. Gloucestershire, UK: Wrens Park Publishing, 1998.

Borick, Carl P. *A Gallant Defense: The Siege of Charleston, 1780*. Columbia: University of South Carolina Press, 2003.

Boyd, Thomas. *Light-horse Harry Lee*. New York: Charles Scribner's Sons, 1931.

Bright, Jeffrey, and Stewart Dunaway. *Pyle's Defeat, The Most Comprehensive Guide: Case Closed*. Privately published, 2011.

Buchanan, John. *The Road to Guilford Courthouse: The American Revolution in the Carolinas*. New York: John Wiley & Sons, 1997.

Caruthers, Eli. *Interesting Revolutionary Incidents and Sketches of Character, Chiefly in the "Old North State," Second Series*. Philadelphia, PA: Hayes & Zell, 1856.

Cashin, Edward J. *The King's Ranger: Thomas Brown and the American Revolution on the Southern Frontier*. New York: Fordham University Press, 1999.

Cecere, Michael. *Wedded to My Sword: The Revolutionary War Service of Light Horse Harry Lee*. Westminster, MD: Heritage Books, 2012.

Chernow, Ron. *Washington: A Life*. New York: Penguin Press, 2010.

Custis, George Washington Parke. *Recollections and Private Memoirs of Washington, by his Adopted Son, George Washington Parke Custis. With Illustrations and Explanatory Notes by Benson J. Lossing*. Philadelphia, PA: J. W. Bradley, 1861.

Draper, Lyman C. *King's Mountain and Its Heroes: History of the Battle of King's Mountain, October 7th 1780, and the Events which Led to It*. Cincinnati, OH: Peter G. Thompson, 1881.

Edmonds, Thomas J. *The Tactical Retreat of General Nathanael Greene*. Privately published, 2006.

Farrier, George H. *Memorial of the Celebration of the Battle of Paulus Hook, August 19th, 1779*. Jersey City, NJ: M. Mullone, 1879.

Garden, Alexander. *Anecdotes of the Revolutionary War in America, with Sketches of Character of Persons the Most distinguished, in the Southern States, For Civil and Military Service* [First Series], A.E. Miller, Charleston, 1822.

Garden, Alexander. *Anecdotes of the American Revolution: Illustrative of the Talents and Virtues of the Heroes of the Revolution, Who Acted the Most Conspicuous Parts Therein.* [Second Series]. A.E. Miller, Charleston, 1828.

Gerson, Noel B. *Light-Horse Harry: A Biography of Washington's Great Cavalryman, Henry Lee.* Garden City, NY: Doubleday, 1966.

Gordon, John W. *South Carolina and the American Revolution: A Battlefield History.* Columbia: University of South Carolina Press, 2003.

Hartley, Cecil B. *Life of Major General Henry Lee.* New York: Derby & Jackson, 1859.

Hartmann, John W. *The American Partisan: Henry Lee and the Struggle for Independence, 1776-1780.* Shippensburg, PA: Burd Street Press, c. 2000.

Hayes, John T. *Massacre: Tarleton and Lee, 1780-1781.* Fort Lauderdale, FL: Saddlebag Press, 1997.

Heitman, Francis Bernard. *Historical Register of Officers of the Continental Army during the War of the Revolution, April, 1775, to December, 1783.* Washington, DC: W. H. Lowdermilk, 1893.

Higginbotham, Don. *The War of American Independence: Military Attitudes, Policies, and Practice, 1763-1789.* Boston, MA: Northeastern University Press, 1983.

Horry, Peter, and Mason L. Weems. *The Life of General Francis Marion.* Philadelphia, PA: Joseph Allen, 1852.

Hutchins, John Milton. *Light Horse Harry Lee Versus Bloody Ban at the Action at Spread Eagle Tavern, January 20, 1778.* Lakewood, CO: Avrooman-Apfelwald Press, 2007.

Johnson, William. *Sketches of the Life and Correspondence of Nathanael Greene, Major General of the Armies of the United States in the War of the Revolution,* 2 vols. Charleston, SC: A. E. Miller, 1822.

Kahler, Gerald E. *The Long Farewell: Americans Mourn the Death of George Washington*. Charlottesville: University of Virginia Press, 2008.

Lee, Cazenove Gardner, Jr. *Lee Chronicle: Studies of the Early Generations of the Lees of Virginia*. Dorothy Mills Parker, editor. New York: New York University Press, 1957.

Lee, Henry IV. *The Campaign of 1781 in the Carolinas; With Remarks Historical and Critical on Johnson's Life of Greene*. Philadelphia, E. Littell, 1824.

Leitch, Alexander. *A Princeton Companion*. Princeton, NJ: Princeton University Press, 1975.

Lengel, Edward G. *General George Washington: A Military Life*. New York: Random House, 2005.

Massey, Gregory D., and Jim Piecuch, editors. *General Nathanael Greene and the American Revolution in the South*. Columbia: University of South Carolina Press, 2012.

Nagel, Paul C. *The Lees of Virginia: Seven Generations of an American Family*. New York: Oxford University Press, 1990.

Pancake, John S. *This Destructive War: The British Campaign in the Carolinas, 1780-1782*. University: University of Alabama Press, 1985.

Piecuch, Jim. *The Battle of Camden: A Documentary History*. Charleston, SC: History Press, 2006.

----------. *The Blood Be Upon Your Head: Tarleton and the Myth of Buford's Massacre*. Lugoff, SC: Southern Campaigns of the American Revolution Press, 2010.

----------, editor. *Cavalry of the American Revolution*. Yardley, PA: Westholme Publishing, 2012.

------------, and John Beakes. *"Cool Deliberate Courage": John Eager Howard in the American Revolution*. Charleston, SC: The Nautical & Aviation Publishing Co., 2009.

Royster, Charles. *Light-Horse Harry Lee and the Legacy of the American Revolution*. Baton Rouge: Louisiana State University Press, 1981.

----------. *A Revolutionary People at War: The Continental Army and American Character, 1775-1783*. Chapel Hill: University of North Carolina Press, 1979.

Sherman, William Thomas. *Calendar and Record of the Revolutionary War in the South: 1780-1781* (2013, 8th edition) http://archive.org/details/ CalendarAndRecordOfTheRevolutionaryWarInTheSouth1780-1781

Symonds, Craig L. *A Battlefield Atlas of the American Revolution*. Charleston, SC: The Nautical & Aviation Publishing Co., 1986, Thirteenth printing 2011

Troxler, Carole Watterson. *Pyle's Defeat: Deception at the Racepath*. Graham, NC: Alamance County Historical Association, 2003.

Urwin, Gregory J. W. *The United States Cavalry: An Illustrated History, 1776-1944*. Norman: University of Oklahoma Press, 1983.

Willcox, William B. *Portrait of a General: Sir Henry Clinton in the War of Independence*. New York: Alfred A. Knopf, 1964.

Wood, Gordon S. *Empire of Liberty: A History of the Early Republic, 1789-1815*. New York: Oxford University Press, 2009.

Wright, Robert K., Jr. *The Continental Army*. Washington, DC: US Army Center of Military History, 2000.

Archeological Reports

Ferguson, Leland G. "Archeology at Scott's Lake: Exploratory Research, 1972, 1973." Columbia: South Carolina Institute of Archaeology and Anthropology, 1975.

Smith, Steven D., James B. Legg, Tamara S. Wilson, and Jonathan Leader. *"Obstinate and Strong": The History and Archaeology of the Siege of Fort Motte*. Columbia: South Carolina Institute of Archaeology and Anthropology, 2007.

INDEX